SOUTHERN IRISH PROTESTANTS

SOUTHERN IRISH PROTESTANTS

Histories, Lives & Literatures

IAN d'ALTON

EASTWOOD BOOKS

First published in this editied collection 2024 by Eastwood Books

Dublin, Ireland
www.eastwoodbooks.com
www.wordwellbooks.com

First edition

Eastwood Books is an imprint of the Wordwell Group

Eastwood Books
The Wordwell Group
Unit 9, 78 Furze Road
Sandyford
Dublin, Ireland

The Wordwell Group is a member of Publishing Ireland, the Irish Book Publishers' Association.

ISBN: 978-1-916742-50-5 (Paperback)
ISBN: 978-1-916742-63-5 (ePub)

British Library Cataloguing in Publication Data.
A catalogue record for this book is available from the National Library of Ireland and the British Library.

Copyediting by Emer Condit
Layout and design by Wordwell
Printed in Ireland by Sprint Books

Cover quotation: Butler Papers, TCD Ms 10304/399/1 (undated), reproduced by kind permission of the executors of the Hubert Butler estate and the Board of Trinity College, Dublin.

FOR

June
Andrew, Leanne and Alex
Philip and Claire

CONTENTS

ACKNOWLEDGEMENTS

The inspiration for this book came from two friends. Some time ago Professor Eugenio Biagini of Cambridge University suggested that I should try to bring together my writings on southern Irish Protestants. My former colleague and great friend Felix Larkin, then undertaking a similar enterprise, was encouraging and positive. Between the two of them they supplied enthusiasm and impetus and I am immensely grateful to both. Otherwise the training by my mentors—Oliver MacDonagh and Edward Norman—all those years ago kept my feet firmly on the ground (although not without the odd flight of fancy). The scholarship, style, nerve, verve and flair of my historian friends Tom Dunne and Ida Milne are ever to be aimed for, if not always achieved. Ida, my co-editor on our 2019 book of essays *Protestant **and** Irish*, particularly encouraged me—with many satisfying conversations—to explore my identity through the histories I've written. Joe Ruane has been an important influence on my thinking. Special thanks for special insights and assistance go to Fergal Browne, Peter Costello, Nicola Darwood, Anne Dolan, Terence Dooley, Roy Foster, Larry Geary, Peter Hanna, Susan Hood, Finola Kennedy, Virginia Kennerley, Trisha Oakley Kessler, Joe Lee, Vivian Valvano Lynch, Deirdre McMahon, Tim McMahon, Patrick Maume, Dermot Meleady, Miriam Moffitt, David Nolan, Eunan O'Halpin, Patricia Orr, Christopher Ridgway and Brendan Twomey. Felix's foreword is a mirror to my soul; this book is full of his perceptions. I also owe a special debt of gratitude to Alan Ford, who has been a forbearing and forensic commentator on my wilder and more improbable plans for this volume, and who has written a sparkling afterword. The archivists and librarians whose patience I've tried deserve a special commendation. I am grateful for the permission of various individuals, publishing houses and institutions to reproduce, in whole or in part, some of the essays and extracts from my essays, and each is acknowledged in an endnote. I am deeply appreciative of the work of and support from Ronan Colgan and his colleagues in Eastwood Books in getting this volume into print. They've done a great job.

Those closest to me have often had to put up with my abstracted moments when I've been immersed in a research project. This one has been no different. Much love to June, who has been in the front line and always supportive. My family—Andrew, Leanne, Alex, Philip and Claire—have tolerantly borne my enthusiasms. I really don't know what I would have done without their understanding. I lovingly dedicate this volume to them all.

ABBREVIATIONS

BC/SW: E. Bowen, *Bowen's Court* [1942] *& Seven Winters: Memories of a Dublin Childhood* [1943] (London: Virago, 1984)
BL: British Library
BMH: Bureau of Military History
CC: *Cork Constitution*
CE: *Cork Examiner*
CoIG: *Church of Ireland Gazette*
DIB: J. McGuire and J. Quinn (eds), *Dictionary of Irish Biography* (9 vols) (Cambridge: Cambridge University Press, 2009)
HC deb, HL deb: House of Commons/Lords debates, at Hansard.parliament.uk
IHS: *Irish Historical Studies*
IT: *Irish Times*
IUA: Irish Unionist Alliance
JCHAS: *Journal of the Cork Historical and Archaeological Society*
NAI: National Archives of Ireland
NLI: National Library of Ireland
PRONI: Public Record Office of Northern Ireland
RCB: Representative Church Body of the Church of Ireland
TCD: Trinity College, Dublin
TNA: The National Archives, United Kingdom
UCC: University College Cork

IAN D'ALTON: HISTORIAN OF 'A CONFIDENT MINORITY'

Felix M. Larkin

I knew of Ian d'Alton long before I knew Ian d'Alton. We were near-contemporaries as history students at our respective universities—Ian at University College Cork (BA, 1970), I at University College Dublin (BA, 1971)—and I first became aware of him at the annual conferences of the inter-varsity Irish History Students Association, where he was a star performer and acknowledged by the rest of us as perhaps the most promising historian of his generation. This view of him was confirmed by his success in winning the Royal Historical Society's Alexander Prize in 1972, followed by his sojourn at Peterhouse, Cambridge (1972–5), the Alma Mater of many eminent Irish historians, including Ian's great mentor in the field of history, Oliver MacDonagh.

Upon completion of his Ph.D in Cambridge, Ian joined the Irish Department of Finance, where I was already ensconced after an interlude of postgraduate study that was briefer and much less distinguished than Ian's. We quickly became friends as well as colleagues. Our friendship, based on a shared interest in history, was cemented by the fact that both of us spent the years 1977 to 1979 in the short-lived Department of Economic Planning and Development. Hived off from the Department of Finance, it was smaller and more collegiate than the austere Department of Finance of the mid-1970s. While we both returned to the Department of Finance at the end of 1979, neither of us would finish our careers there, though we remained within the public sector. In 1986 Ian departed to the Housing Finance Agency, where he was a treasury and funding manager and then Chief Executive Officer before retiring in 2012; I joined the National Treasury Management Agency in 1991, retiring early in 2009.

In 1980 Ian published his Cambridge doctoral dissertation as *Protestant Society and Politics in Cork, 1812–1844*. He asked me to read a set of the page proofs of the book for him, which I was happy to do. That was the beginning of an extraordinary collaboration. As we pursued our separate history interests in the intervening years—a welcome diversion, until we retired, from busy lives in the public service—we have read most of each other's work in draft and have commented on it, suggesting amendments, sometimes disagreeing, criticising when necessary. We respect one another's judgement—our friendship would not have survived otherwise—and I know that my work has been improved time and again by Ian's input. Ian has been kind enough to say the same about my input to his work. This collaboration continues and has been particularly fruitful since we retired from the public service and have more time for our respective history projects—which, incidentally, only rarely intersect.[1] That Ian has made good use of that time is evidenced by the essays in this volume.

These essays reflect the main focus of Ian's research and writing in history, which has been on southern Irish Protestants—his 'tribe', the word used in the introduction to *Protestant **and** Irish*, the collection of essays he edited with Ida Milne.[2] They have the rigour and discipline one expects from a well-trained historian, but one is always aware of an intensely personal angle. As Ian writes in the Introduction to this volume, his concern has been not merely 'to simply show "how it really was" for my peoplehood' but also 'to explain myself in terms of historical inquiry'. In *Seven Winters*, her memoir of her early childhood, Elizabeth Bowen writes about her parents as follows: 'Tradition was, it is true, to be felt behind them, and in indifferent matters conditioned their point of view. But in matters in which they felt deeply they arrived at conclusions that were their own.'[3] Ian observes southern Irish Protestants and their history from within the 'tribe', conscious of the tradition behind him but open to interrogating it and—like Bowen's parents—arriving at his own conclusions.

Ian has indeed argued that it is a distinctive southern Irish Protestant trait to need to explain one's self 'in terms of family and class background'—in other words, in terms of history.[4] On the other hand, the need to approach the past with a questioning—even sceptical—mind is a distinctive trait of the historian. Ian explains this well in an essay first published in 1990 and reproduced in this volume:

> History, as a script of the past, can be said to derive from folk memory, literature—and the work of historians themselves. Therefore, if he is to offer anything, the historian has to challenge the versions of previous historians, to test their theories, to measure the adequacy of their sources, and to make a critique of their conclusions. This is the historian's craft. It is why 'revisionism' is an essential precondition for a vibrant and useful historiography. Yet it is surprising how little understood this fundamental principle is.[5]

Applying this fundamental principle to the history of one's own 'tribe', as Ian has done, is a perilous adventure. Joseph O'Neill, in a passage from his *Blood-dark Track: A Family History* that Ian has sometimes quoted, notes that 'families and nations have self-serving editions of their past'.[6] Communities, too, have such 'self-serving editions of their past', and the southern Irish Protestant 'tribe' is no exception. Ian's work in elucidating the story of the southern Irish Protestant past—ranging widely over history, culture and literature—requires us to modify our perspective on that story. It is, inescapably, the story of the decline of a once-dominant minority who eventually found themselves beached on the wrong side of a revolution. However, instead of seeing the glass as half-empty, Ian suggests that the glass has been half-full. It is a bold claim, and one that Ian rejoices in—but many of his 'tribe', including other scholars, do not accept it.

Ian's approach is based on the realisation that, while the trauma of 'descendancy' was very real for southern Irish Protestants, things could have been a lot worse, as they were much worse for other minorities in Europe. There was no ethnic cleansing here comparable to that in Armenia and the Balkans in the twentieth century, and no repetition of 1641 or Scullabogue. His view is that 'Southern Irish Protestantism, considering its "dominant minority" status and political proclivities, got off lightly', and that for the most part the independent Irish state post-1922 'wrapped its Protestant citizens in cotton wool'.[7] In turn, southern Irish Protestantism did not withhold its loyalty from the Irish state, even after the declaration of the republic in 1949 and our departure from the Commonwealth. Ian considers 1949 to have been an important milestone in the assimilation of southern Irish Protestants into mainstream Irish society. He explains:

> Departure from the Commonwealth—unnecessary in the eyes of many—was not easily borne [by southern Irish Protestants]. Some sort of umbilical cord had been snapped. But it opened the potential, for the first time since independence, of a truly common patriotism to emerge, the Enlightenment concept of a *res publica*, facilitated by a generational change from those who had experienced the 1922 settlement; and by the opposition, the Catholic world, itself entering a prolonged period of disorientation.[8]

Thus, by 1963, Bishop Arthur Butler of the Church of Ireland could describe his community—Ian's 'tribe'—as 'a confident minority' in the modern Ireland then emerging under the gentle prodding of Seán Lemass and T.K. Whitaker.[9] No less significant in this process of modernisation was the impact of Pope John XXIII and the liberalising impulses of the Second Vatican Council. Southern Irish Protestants were now able, in Ian's memorable phrase, 'to establish an autonomous equilibrium with the contemporary'.[10] Within that equilibrium, the gulf—always there—between southern Irish Protestants and their northern brethren widened. It is significant that Ian is at pains to emphasise in the Introduction to this volume that he is '*not* a northern Protestant—there *are* differences ...'. The excesses of that species are an embarrassment to southern Irish Protestants, as are the excesses of northern Catholics to the majority population south of the border.

The 'descendancy' trope was, of course, only ever really valid for the landed gentry within the southern Irish Protestant 'tribe', and they were already in terminal decline before Irish independence. The experience of urban southern Irish Protestants, particularly those of the professional middle class, was different—less dystopian. Ian is a scion of that urban, professional middle class; he belongs to the world of Elizabeth Bowen's *Seven Winters*, set in Dublin where her father practised law, rather than to the world of Bowen's Court, her ancestral Big House in County Cork. This undoubtedly influences his rejection of the self-image of southern Irish Protestants as a 'tribe' under siege. As he points out in the Introduction, 'the steady stream of memoir, of ghosts often written of by ghost-writers, were mostly moaning whinges about lost houses and the iniquities of Free State and republic' and were of no relevance to his suburban existence. Moreover, born in 1950, he was the beneficiary of another generational shift: he belongs to a generation of southern Irish Protestants born after Ireland had left the Commonwealth who did not have to redefine their identity as their co-religionists had to do in 1922 and again in 1949. He may be a southern Protestant, but he is indisputably Irish and determined to be recognised as such and to play his part in the Irish polity—which he did with aplomb as a public servant. Curiously, his particular knowledge of the history of Protestant society in Cork will have given him a model for public service by the minority in how unionists had accommodated themselves to nationalist domination of Cork municipal politics long before 1922; they continued to make their presence felt.

Ian is fond of quoting these lines of doggerel by a County Clare unionist published in 1907:

> I am only a poor West Briton
> And not of the Irish best;
> But I love the land of Erin
> As much as all the rest.[11]

This captures both the southern Irish Protestants' sense of Irishness and their doubts about whether there would be a place for them in the new Ireland which was already emerging in 1907—an Ireland that was on a path that would lead to the Free State and, ultimately, to the republic. Similar concerns may arise again—and maybe sooner than most of us think—if reunification becomes a real possibility on this island. History does not provide unambiguous roadmaps for the future; history does not repeat itself. Nevertheless, in the event of reunification, the history of southern Irish Protestantism as elucidated by Ian d'Alton—the glass half-full rather than half-empty—may provide some comfort to northern unionists as they 'search for place in independent Ireland', to borrow the subtitle of *Protestant **and** Irish*. If so, then hope and history would truly rhyme.

PROTESTANT *AND* IRISH: SEEKING IDENTITY THROUGH HISTORY, BIOGRAPHY AND LITERATURE

Ian d'Alton

This book is a reflection of—and on—my own personal journey of discovery through the medium of history. I am a 'southern Irish Protestant'. In these three words—somewhere, somehow—lies my own sense of identity.[1] In truth, it tells more of what I'm *not* than what I am. I'm *not* a northern Protestant—there *are* differences between the northern and southern varieties, to put it mildly! By a not-so-subtle signalling I'm *not* English/British either, which apparently still sometimes needs to be said in the context of 'Protestant'. I'm *not* a Roman Catholic. That's a lot of 'nots' to be dealing with in a small life. It's clumsy too, and seems a tad overcomplicated. As I write in a 1990 essay reproduced in this volume, 'The term "southern Irish Protestant" encompasses an animal with geographical, crypto-cultural and religious characteristics which are peculiarly difficult to express within a coherent unity'. Most of my fellow-citizens are quite simply 'Irish'. It would never occur to them to describe themselves as 'southern Irish Catholics'. But as Edna Longley remarked in 1989, if Catholics are born Irish, Protestants have to 'work their passage to Irishness'—that is, if they want to. Today this self-identification has a somewhat quaint ring to it, a retrospective feel, an odour of mustiness. Modern Ireland is moving to another beat. Future historians of Irish ethno-religious groups in the twenty-first century are much more likely to be examining Poles rather than Presbyterians, Muslims rather than Methodists, queer society rather than Quakers. Identities are now much more fluid, often interpreted and expressed in terms of gender, sexuality, cultural affinity, even diet and lifestyle choices. In other words, the hell of an imposed and hereditary identity has been superseded by, well, a different sort of hell—one of one's own choosing from a marketplace where there's a maelstrom of identikits on offer. Me, I'm more or less stuck with what I grew up with. I'm comfortable with that, by and large.

A fundamental journey towards understanding identity is what this book attempts to illuminate. In some respects it takes its inspiration from southern unionist historian R.B. McDowell's reminiscences in his 1997 book *Crisis and Decline: The Fate of the Southern Unionists.* McDowell was fastidious in placing his memories *after* the history.[2] I'm more upfront, since this book should be understood and read as capturing some of the themes and subjects that have exercised me on my personal odyssey. Tom Dunne's *Rebellions* and Hubert Butler's *Escape from the Anthill* have been other inspirations. The volume comprises unpublished essays and also reworked published pieces. Most deal with the period from 1820 to about the 1960s. While I have referenced scholarship which subsequently appeared, these essays are of their time, and should be read as such. As an 'ecological' historian, I tend towards recycling and so there is some unavoidable repetition, which I've tried to minimise without compromising the integrity and completeness of each piece.

These essays, illuminating my development as a historian, cover six broad themes. The first looks at Protestant culture and Protestant lives. The second examines questions of historical process and cultural appropriation. The third interrogates southern Protestantism through literary luminaries—Elizabeth Bowen, Molly Keane, Lennox Robinson, William Trevor, Iris Murdoch. Through narratives of war, rebellion and conciliation, the fourth theme looks at how conflict and attempts at resolution shaped the southern Protestant identity. That shades into a fifth, the existential changes in the aftermath of the 1921–2 'settlement'. Finally, I interrogate the place of religious disputation in forming the Irish Protestant world-view.

The southern Protestant condition—or at least a noisy part of it—is mediated through these pieces. Some offer glimpses of what might have been had Protestants enthusiastically joined the national pilgrimage. Some show sturdiness, resilience and flexibility. Some are cautionary tales of frustration and failure. Some carry the dying of the light. I like to think that some of them are fun—the desiccated remains of the gentry contain more than their fair share of the odd, the eccentric and the just plain mad. Irresistible!

The place of the literary in my own journey through history is a foundational part of how and why I write. Long ago in University College Cork, Oliver MacDonagh introduced me to a world that I never really thought played a part in serious history-writing. I had read Maria Edgeworth, Charles Lever, Anthony Trollope, George Birmingham and Somerville & Ross before MacDonagh's revelation—but as stories, as entertaining invention. Yet history-writing is a creative endeavour, too: it has to be a work every bit as imaginative as novel, play and poem. MacDonagh opened a world in which fiction, drama and poetry—along with the lives of their writers—can often illuminate dark corners that light from the purely historical torch fails to reach. But he was always scrupulous about sounding a health warning. If the boundaries between history and literature are blurred and fuzzy there is the risk of contamination. One problem concerns the nature of historical writing itself—'the historical text as literary artefact'.[3] I see little wrong in a historian treating his or her work as a 'literary artefact'; Elizabeth Bowen's 'Notes on writing a novel' have much applicability to the historian who wants to engage a reader's attention.[4] The second problem centres on the uses to which the historian may put literary sources. As 'contemporary' writing, do Bowen's *The Last September* and Somerville & Ross's fiction carry an authenticity of history that maybe cannot be said of a 'historical' novel like Iris Murdoch's 1965 book about 1916, *The Red and the Green*, or William Trevor's *The Story of Lucy Gault*? Elizabeth Bowen was in little doubt: 'we must not shy at the fact that we cull the past from fiction rather than history'.[5] For her, fiction has the power to both create and re-create a historical past. My approach has been to excavate *her* historicity and, vicariously, her imagination, as well as that of others treated here who sprang from the southern Irish Protestant tradition, using their lives and literatures to reflect their sense of being—and, ultimately, my own.

***

It is often claimed that Protestants are inordinately interested in their family's and community's history and lineage. That was not my experience. You might think that the interior lives we led should have encouraged introspection and self-examination, yet after the traumas of the independence period some southern Irish Protestants exhibited an almost aggressive amnesia and wilful unwillingness to want to know about their community's history at all. *Un*history was safer than its opposite. In my case, I was woefully ignorant of my antecedents. As far as I was concerned, we were suburban south Dublin middle-class Protestants, and seemingly always had been. But in the mid-1960s I was given some interesting and somewhat disturbing documents. I learnt that in April 1929 a package had arrived at the premises of the Imperial Bank of Persia, Teheran. 'Via Russia', the envelope rather exotically says, and it was addressed to an employee of the bank. That employee, William d'Alton, was an ancestor. Doubtless with some anticipation he awaited the d'Alton family history, researched and written by a professional firm of London genealogists. The covering letter indicates that the funds earmarked for the research were now exhausted and Mussett & Co. had completed the project within the allowed budget.

Somewhat to my surprise, I found that the d'Alton side of the family apparently had a landed back story. In immaculate copperplate, Mussett's genealogy chronicled the story of a settler family in County Clare, Ireland, from sometime in the early eighteenth century—unexceptional minor gentry in a Protestant world, with the usual clutch of magistracies and militia commissions. It was one of relative prosperity and landholding, marrying within the Protestant ascendancy. We had a couple of biggish plain houses, much like Elizabeth Bowen's Bowen's Court, written about in this book. But the agricultural depression after the Napoleonic wars did for the d'Altons economically, the decline being exacerbated by a tragic alcoholism. Repairs were attempted by marriage into money via the daughter of a well-to-do Limerick merchant in the 1830s. She was Catholic and the d'Alton family turned. The lands eventually sold, the family moved to Dublin, where they became middle-class professionals—lawyers, doctors, bankers (oh, and one bookmaker). They acquired the affected *faux*-aristo surname, with its small 'd', apostrophe and capital 'A', an endless source of annoyance in a digital age. They remained loyal. As 'Castle Catholics' they still mixed with urban Protestants, and so it was perhaps not entirely unexpected that my paternal grandfather—a bank manager—married back into the Church of Ireland in 1918. Subsequently this branch of the family—in characteristic defiance of the *Ne Temere* decree—was baptised as Anglican, reverting to its southern Protestant roots. And that's why through nothing more than an accident of birth I am a 'southern Irish Protestant'.

Class mattered—and still matters—in Ireland. Until about the latter half of the twentieth century, there existed an important difference between Protestant and Catholic class structures. For Catholics the structure more or less stopped at the middle class. There was a compact upper middle cohort, but the middle class and lower middle class did not like them very much or trust them politically (and still less the surviving Catholic landed class).[6] For Protestants—more precisely my Anglicans—it existed all the way up, from a small working and agricultural labouring class, through farmers and urban professionals to the remnants of a vociferous and socially significant 'Big House' class. It even went further to the wider British landed class and then to the pinnacle, the Crown—an essay about Cork landlord A.H. Smith Barry illustrates that trans-island nature of the landed élite. That gave a different class dynamic to the two communities. And that is reflected, if I am honest, in the balance of enquiry in this book. The élites often have a 'voice' that is rarely heard from the working and middle classes.

But at least I can use my own 'voice' to articulate middle-class suburban professional Protestantism in the mid-twentieth century. From quite an early age I was aware that 'we' were different, or made to feel different, in the land of our birth. Where I grew up—in 1950s Dalkey, a salubrious seaside suburb in south County Dublin—Anglican church, rectory and primary school were all located together within a 'gated' environment. That alone gave us a sense of Otherness, a sort of metaphor, perhaps, for our self-contained transparent bubble floating in a sea of Catholicism—seeing it but not really able, or willing, to touch it. That sense of difference was reinforced by the rather exotic sport of my father and grandfather—yachting, with its connotations of loyalism, imperial identity and class consciousness. In the ordinary course of events, I'd probably have gone to Trinity College, joined a 'Kingstown' yacht club too and got a safe job in Dublin. But in 1962 my father's work took us to Cork, and the suburb of Douglas. For a while I might as well have been in Timbuctoo. The city seemed an alien place, and so *small.* The Cork accent was impenetrable. I had just started secondary school at the Methodist-sponsored Wesley College in Dublin when we were uprooted. A fraction of Wesley's size, my new school, Cork Grammar, had only 120 pupils, but it was a vital resource for a tiny community and it was successful. An essay in this volume includes a discussion on how an early headmaster equipped middle-class Cork Protestants for late nineteenth- and early twentieth-century competitive Ireland. That may be history, but it is also me.

Well into the twentieth century, Cork Protestants hardly had to move out beyond the stockade—born in the Victoria Hospital; learning to 'Be Prepared' in one of its six Cork Scout troops; equipped by Cork Grammar, High or Rochelle Schools for employment by the Bank of Ireland and Ulster Bank, Lester's chemists, Johnson & Perrott's motor establishment, insurance and milling companies, teaching, or as a Protestant lady's companion; reading the *Cork Constitution* and the *Irish Times*; socialising amongst the five masonic lodges in the city and eight in the county; singing with the choir of St Fin Barre's cathedral; kept off the demon drink by the 'Catch-my-pal' Total Abstinence Union and the Irish Temperance League; playing rugby with the Cork Constitution club, hockey with the Church of Ireland club, cycling with the Incorporated Church of Ireland Cork Young Men's Association, tennis with Muskerry lawn tennis club; rowing with Shandon boat club or sailing with the Royal Cork Yacht Club; looked after, if hard times fell, by the Protestant Orphan Society, the rescue home for Protestant Girls and St Fin Barre's Hostel for indigent men; spending old age in the Home for Protestant Incurables; buried by Cross's, undertakers. Even with a small Church of Ireland population of some 11,500 in 1971 we still had a sense of separateness supported by a denominational social and economic structure.

Douglas was an affluent middle-class suburb, a Dalkey in miniature. Its imposing 1875 Victorian Church of Ireland seemed actually somewhat bigger than Dalkey's. Although we weren't great church-goers, tribalism always talked; my mother and I became stalwarts of the church dramatic society and we helped out at fêtes and parish events.

The warmer waters of the ecumenical 1960s were already thawing the sectarian iceberg. Youth was starting to query the harsh proscriptions of *Ne Temere* and Catholic canon law. Never anything like as intense as its northern analogue, southern Protestantism nevertheless was fed by some streams of religious disputation. Three essays here look at an apocalyptic vision of what Irish church disestablishment would unleash, how anti-Catholicism was used to create a Protestant 'moral' citizenship in the new state, and a denominational theological dispute over a Catholic dogma in 1950. Yet at a certain level a shared, if narrow, bridge of Victorian culture spanned the sectarian divide, as evidenced in a piece on how the clerics—Catholic and Protestant—operated within that last all-island representative assembly, the 1917–18 Irish Convention.

Whatever about my own family history, at the end of the 1960s I found it difficult to find out about my tribe's antecedents and why I was what I was. Michael Viney's 1965 newspaper articles in the *Irish Times* about southern Protestants ('The Five Per Cent') had examined the contemporary scene, but not until Patrick Buckland's 1972 academic study of high southern Protestant politics in the period 1885–1922 (*Irish Unionism 1*) and Jack White's *Minority Report* in 1975 was there any coherent, detailed chronicling of this hidden, almost disappeared, people. Then the floodgates gradually began to open. By now there's a plethora of historical, cultural, economic and sociological exegeses of the southern Protestant 'condition'.

The Irish aristocracy's and gentry's (they disliked the term 'Anglo-Irish') foibles, houses, lives, loyalties, literature and loves feature heavily in this book. Their resources and education facilitated an outpouring of self- and group explanation which was at the last deeply subversive and wholly unrepresentative of the general southern Irish Protestant. The steady stream of memoir, of ghosts often written of by ghost-writers, were mostly moaning whinges about lost houses and the iniquities of Free State and republic, all bubble-wrapped in a suffocating snobbery. They had about as much relevance to my suburban existence as the proverbial fish has to the proverbial bicycle, but they provide fodder for some rattling good stories in this book. It has to be said that the notion of Irish loyalism is best exhibited in the Irish gentry, since it is generally uncontaminated by other loyalties.

War and rebellion shaped the Protestant experience in the twentieth century to an extent that it no longer does. Three essays here examine why the gentry went to war in 1914, and how Dublin and Cork Protestants faced the 1916 Rising; even then, there seemed already to be a sense of *fin de siècle* framing the minority's world-view. That did not necessarily mean giving up, submitting to the blindfold and the last cigarette. The ability to get on 'as best we can', as A.H. Smith Barry of Cork put it in 1913, is a much-underestimated characteristic of southern Protestants, evidenced in the essays about Smith Barry and other Cork Protestant characters over the long nineteenth century.

I have often attempted to put a framework on or structure over the southern Protestant story—to theorise it, if you like. One essay looks at it as an exemplar of how historical process works; another rather cheekily interprets the southern Protestant situation as akin to a form of Purgatory, a Catholic doctrine rejected by Protestants. Like the notion of Purgatory as a state of neither here nor there, it often felt as if we had been shunted into a sort of siding and then forgotten. That points up an important point about southern Protestantism—its relative unimportance to the Catholic 95 per cent of the population. Sustained and endemic overt sectarianism in the independent Irish state is hard to locate, maybe because it was quite difficult to find enough Protestants to be sectarian *against*. If we were out of sight, we were out of mind too. When de Valera offered his best wishes to newly independent India in 1947, invoking the blessings of not just God but also Our Lady, it probably never occurred to him that, while the deity could be a common point of reference for Irish citizens, the Virgin Mary certainly was not. As late as 1961, the Irish Vocational Teachers' Association caused serious offence to its Protestant members by consecrating itself to 'Our Lady'. Likewise, in the year I was born, 1950, a twopence-halfpenny stamp issued by the new republic must have caused my parents and their friends, many of whom had volunteered to fight against Nazi Germany, some unease. It carried all the symbols of 'National Catholicism': commemorating the Holy Year, featuring St Patrick and his insignia, and bearing the inscription 'Poblacht na h-Éireann'—'Republic of Ireland'. Were we Protestants thus in the tuppenny-ha'penny league? Perhaps. But ultimately we could take it or leave it—or just buy five halfpenny stamps.

There was a paradox in all this under-the-radar stuff. If we occasionally peered out from our ghettos and stockades, we exotic creatures were quite often pounced upon and deferred to (to our faces, at any rate). I was once asked by a very senior civil servant in the Department of Finance, quite seriously, if there was a Protestant 'take' on the then-recent budget. More times than I felt comfortable with (mainly because of guilt), I had to bear the entirely unreasonable burden of my community's being characterised as perhaps more honest and dependable than others, shall we say. It wasn't always easy to live up to these wholly imaginary standards. The problem with pedestals is that everyone can see you, and it's far too easy to fall off.

In 1970 I completed an arts degree at University College Cork. Nothing much beckoned from the outside world, so I decided to do an MA in modern Irish history. Why history? Well, in 1961 Edward Hallett Carr posed the question, 'What is history?' In my quest for identity I went one step further—what was history *for*? I was looking for a means whereby I might make some sense of why I was what I was—that is to say, the 'nation' that I was within and from which I had sprung. 'History' to me at the time was the channel through which we can come to some understanding of the world in which we find ourselves. It provides us, individually and collectively, with context, coherence and identity. *History* is important and unique because we *are* the past: we are the sum of all the events that have happened to, and in, the world. That was seductive.

If I was to excavate southern Irish Protestantism I needed to have cognisance of the 'Protestant' part, but not just as a tribal and secular label. My meeting with June (who later became my wife) introduced me to a closer engagement with the spiritual world of the Church of Ireland. Her father was a Church of Ireland rector and I began to get a better insight into the belief structure that was the inward and invisible grace illuminating the outward and visible world of family and community. This led me to think that historians and the Church had more in common than might appear at first glance. There is a sense in which both can approach their subject-matter—the nature and purpose of existence, what happened in the past—from the standpoint of *sub specie aeternitatis*, the perspective of the eternal. The Church claims to know our final, final end, so it gives it to us from start to finish. In the words of Jeremiah in the Old Testament, 'For I know the plans I have for you, says the Lord, plans for welfare and not for evil, to give you a future and a hope'[7]—God as a sort of back-to-the-future good-news historian, I suppose. And when historians study a topic they also know what came next, which permits them for that period at least the equivalent of a divinely inspired omniscience. They are little gods—not able to change history, but at least to know its end. That notion attracted me in the context of determining how I could assess my own sense of being. I could not predict my own course, but by the study of the history of the community from which I was cloned I could, perhaps, answer some of the questions that I found myself—unlike my Catholic fellow-citizens—having to ask.

Southern Irish Protestantism, as do all religious belief systems, likes to think that it is the repository of, and belief in, immutable and unchanging truths. In this reading, history is its handmaid with a duty to help mankind towards a proper moral path. The modern western historical mind has pretty comprehensively rejected this way of seeing history as a polemical vehicle for the ethical and moral. The cure for the disease, though, has been to expect historians to be a species of history cyborg, an artificial intelligence—semi-automatic researchers and writers, little more than the processors of, in German historian von Ranke's words, *wie es eigentlich gewesen*, 'simply to show how it really was'. This is the historian as detached detective, the excavation of the truth being the only guiding principle. The historian as *ethicist* has little purchase in a world that sees us as big girls and boys, able to cope with tussles between professional and confessional inclinations. The ancillary notion that completely morally neutered historians are of little use—and often crushingly dull—is not often on the radar either.

There is considerable power in western notions of objectivity, the idea that there is a discrete set of knowable and excavatable facts that are independent, as it were, of the excavator—in other words, the truth. The flaw lies, I think, in seeing it as absolute. But it can never be, at least not on this side of the grave. Faced with the possibility, then, that truth in this existence may indeed be contingent, the historian's task—to order, edit, sift and judge—is justified, the aim being to get as close to the absolute truth as possible. But by the same token this contingency gives historians grace to construct, conceptualise and argue a pathway, if you like, along which they can lead us. As John Buchan wrote in 1929:

> The past, if it is to satisfy intelligent minds, must be presented as a sequence of effects and causes.[8]

Inherent in that is an implicit acceptance not of the following of a *particular* path but of the *idea* of a path. Of what stone would that pathway be built? I thought that I could find it in our human nature as moral and ethical beings. To accept the *idea* of moral purpose in history is not necessarily antipathetical to the ideal of truth but quite simply a recognition that history is mediated by historians. Can we creatures of flesh and blood, corks bobbing on an ocean of virtues and vices, the products of particular times and inclinations, of beliefs and prejudices, sublimate our humanity with all its flecks and flaws to a vision of history that is 'simply to show how it really was'?

I wanted more than to simply show 'how it really was' for my peoplehood. I needed to explain myself in terms of historical enquiry, and that required analysis within the bounds of a proper historical method and framework. Thus in 1970 I began work on 'Southern Irish Unionism: a history of Cork City and County Unionists, 1885–1914'. That was the first of many pieces and papers over half a century on aspects of southern unionism and Protestantism, culminating in a collection of essays by historians in 2019 co-edited with Ida Milne, *Protestant* ***and*** *Irish: the Minority's Search for Place in Independent Ireland.*

I never did become a professional academic historian. It wasn't for lack of trying. In 1972 I was awarded the Royal Historical Society's Alexander Prize for a distillation of my MA thesis. That essay reads somewhat awkwardly now, like a newborn foal staggering around on shaky legs that are too long for it. I was, I think, one of the youngest recipients of the Prize since its inception in 1896. Virtually all previous winners went on to academic careers, some spectacularly so: Henry Phillips, John Neale, Richard Southern, S.T. Bindoff, G.W. Barrow, George Rudé, Maurice Keen. This serendipitous and unexpected event triggered offers of Ph.D studentships from Oxbridge colleges. On Oliver MacDonagh's recommendation, off I went to Peterhouse in Cambridge—high Tory, very

Anglican and determinedly single-sex, and the destination of many Irish budding historians. Peterhouse was an extraordinary place in the early 1970s. It was a hotbed of the new radical right, dedicated to ripping up the post-war social contract. Here were to be found the assiduous intellectual builders of what became Thatcherism, including historian Maurice Cowling, Church of England cleric Edward Norman and young, enthusiastic foot-soldiers like Michael Portillo. We shall meet Edward Norman again. According to my old friend Tom Dunne, later a history professor at UCC (who went up to Peterhouse at the same time), I was 'trailing clouds of glory' after the Alexander Prize.[9] It didn't feel that way. Although the architecture of University College Cork was much closer to Oxbridge than red-brick, Cambridge's spires were intimidating and somehow not dreaming at all—much busier than I had expected. But I made a set of lifelong friendships that had eluded me in UCC.

I rapidly succumbed to the émigré's disease of feeling more 'Irish' than 'southern' or 'Protestant'. That affected my historical trajectory. I had thought that I had had enough of scrabbling around in the nether reaches of regional Irish history, so before I arrived in Cambridge I had settled on studying early twentieth-century Labour municipal politics in the north-east of England (yes, really!). Anything but southern Irish Protestantism. The then-doyen of labour and trade union historians, Henry Pelling, interviewed me as my potential supervisor. After a small sherry or two and a long conversation, he looked at me over his glasses and murmured, 'Mr d'Alton, I don't think your heart is really in this, is it?' He was wise. It wasn't. In an alien land the siren pull of Ireland had become amplified and intensified. Cambridge's Board of Graduate Studies was a little dubious but I ended up studying … Cork Protestantism again, this time under the aforementioned Edward Norman, author of a then-recent highly controversial book on Irish history (the *Sunday Independent* said that parts read 'like a "Black-and-Tan" handout').[10] It seemed an unlikely mix, but Norman was an excellent and forensic supervisor. He came to my wedding in Dunmanway in 1975, observing with relish my 'Cork Protestants' in their native habitat. I completed the Ph.D more or less on time. It resulted in a book, *Protestant Society and Politics in Cork, 1812–1844*.[11]

I had been offered a post in the Irish Department of Finance in my second Cambridge year, with a deferral until my three-year scholarship was completed. Then as now, academic jobs were in short supply. So, unlike many of my contemporaries, I had an actual permanent and pensionable job in the offing, albeit in the bureaucracy and not the academy. I took it and the rest is, as one might say, *not* history; I finished my public sector career as CEO of an Irish financial State-sponsored body. I applied for some academic jobs in those early years but, apart from any other flaws they might have divined, I suspect that weary interviewers soon sussed out that I was probably a one-trick pony. Perhaps they could sense that I had an ulterior motive in my quest to be a historian. They were right—and they were wrong. I have enjoyed the historical method and found its prescriptions and disciplines useful in my career. I have engaged with and relished the idea of argument for its own sake. I love the 'writing' bit. Through the generosity of friends in the academy and outside it, I've been a Visiting Fellow at another Cambridge college, Sidney Sussex; I've lectured to students in Dublin, Cambridge and Limerick and given lots of papers to academic conferences in Britain, Ireland and the USA. Some of these are in this volume. I have occasionally been allowed out on day-release to write of other histories, ranging through such as medievalist British historian T.F. Tout, early twentieth-century French art medals, the abolition of capital punishment in Britain, press history and Irish-American investment in the early Free State, but I have always returned willingly to the open prison that for me is southern Irish Protestantism.

And one of the cells in that open prison is labelled 'history-through-literature'. I had already fallen in love with Elizabeth Bowen's writings when I finally met her one summer's afternoon in Kinsale. I had wangled an invitation to a tea party at Fairyfield, the County Cork holiday home of her friends Stephen and Lady Ursula Vernon. Elizabeth was holding court. I was 21 and completely tongue-tied. We had no important or, indeed, memorable conversation. Two years later she was dead. She haunts me still. I often felt that Bowen had been on much the same quest as I was—her religious beliefs were much like mine, the offcuts of the ethnic and cultural rather than the purely devotional. I would have agreed with her sentiment that 'To be a Roman Catholic myself would be as unthinkable as ever'. I'm not sure, though, that she carried that through to an interrogation of her 'Protestantness'; her Anglicanism was axiomatic and automatic. Nevertheless, I admired her ability to stand back, to look quizzically and critically at ourselves, to mark our journeys through the high roads and back roads of our history, and to paint difficult landscapes of identity and belonging. She did it dazzlingly. Essays here examine her place in Ireland through comparisons with how other writers from the Irish Protestant tradition have looked at theirs, and of course her iconic 'lost' house, Bowen's Court. As a writer she remains my exemplar.

***

Edward Norman wrote in his *History*: 'In Ireland time occasionally softens the memory; more often, alas, it does not'.[12] I'm not sure about the 'alas'. If my memories haven't softened it is because I value them. This book opens a window onto my own exploration of what I am and the historical genealogy which underpins that, but as a scholarly endeavour it stands on its own feet. If it marks my journey of identity, *contra* John Buchan these essays need not be read sequentially. Throw open the book and see where the pages fall. It weaves together history and literature, imagination and reality, lives lived well and not so well, and what a sense of place and attachment means to this little peoplehood on a small island

and to which I am privileged to belong. It may be presumptuous and utopian to offer the southern Protestant journey as possibly, in the fullness of time, one for consideration by my northern co-religionists and unionist friends. They're welcome to the template. But at the last this book is about the sheer joy of writing, the challenge of concept and argument and the pleasure in excavating the past. If readers get half the enjoyment out of reading the essays that I've experienced writing them then I'll rest satisfied.

I

PROTESTANT CULTURE AND PROTESTANT LIVES

1

CORK CITY'S PROTESTANT CULTURE IN THE EIGHTEENTH CENTURY[1]

For Irish Anglicans at the beginning of the eighteenth century, the great question—exemplified in Bishop Wetenhall of Cork's pamphlet *Case of the Irish Protestants* (1691)—was the reconciliation of their passivity towards James (being in fear of their lives and property) with a subsequent adjuring to the Williamite succession.[2] One hundred or so years later the context had changed and Irish Protestants had to reconcile themselves to a different reality: how to come to terms with the rise of Catholic economic, and then political, power. A vignette from January 1827 catches the pragmatism that Protestants had acquired during the eighteenth century. In that month, Jeremiah Murphy, a prosperous Cork Catholic merchant, holds an entertainment at his substantial suburban residence, Hyde Park. Amongst the guests are not only several Catholic dignitaries, including the bishop of Cork, but also members of the exclusively Protestant city corporation and other tories.[3]

Dublin, the first city of the kingdom, had outside intrigue and government activity as an overlay to its metropolitan concerns. Cork, however, could afford to be more introspective and provincial—to indulge in what David Dickson aptly terms 'second city syndrome'. Despite its increasing economic significance as an 'Atlantic city port', its politics remained local, its concerns selfish.[4] If, in 1690, Cork was described as 'a neat, wealthy and populous city', it did not appeal to all: it was 'an ambitious but ugly metropolis'[5] and, writing in 1736 to Swift, the Earl of Orrery excoriated 'the natural dulness of the place' where 'the butchers are as greasy, the Quakers as formal, and the Presbyterians as holy and full of the Lord as ever'. A year later, Alexander the Coppersmith described the Christian 'Stiles' in the city as Episcopacy, Quakerism, Anabaptism, Huguenotism, Popery … and Hypocrisy.[6]

At the beginning of the eighteenth century Cork Protestants were rapidly leaving a settler past behind them. Their outlook had been shaped by the Jacobite and Williamite episodes.[7] What is most significant about them—now living in a recognisably English town[8]—is that their ascendancy was already undergoing a process of considerable dilution. Two interrelated developments were responsible: the rapid growth of the city and the rise of a Catholic middle class. The population of the city was estimated as 17,000 in 1706. It had reached about 41,000 by mid-century and over 57,000 by 1796, despite the recurrence of famines and plagues (and the occasional riot) in the intervening years. By 1834 it was about 95,000.[9] While the numbers of Catholics and Protestants cannot accurately be estimated before the first fairly reliable early nineteenth-century censuses, it seems that the 'English' population was dominant in the city-centre parishes (two to one in St Peter) by 1659.[10] Thereafter, Protestants—despite increasing in absolute numbers from about 13,000 in 1736 to 17,000 by 1834—were proportionately in decline. In the former year, they were estimated to account for 33 per cent of the city's population; by the latter, the proportion had halved to about 18 per cent. An increase in absolute Protestant numbers in a century—31 per cent—was impressive but dwarfed by the 185 per cent increase in the Catholic population.[11]

At the same time the growth of Catholic economic power further weakened the city's 'Protestantness'. Cork in the 1700s was above all mercantile. A rich hinterland of pasture encouraged an export trade of cattle and cattle products, together with other manufactures produced locally, such as textiles. Its fine, secure harbour led naturally to a significant foreign provisions trade. In particular, it became pre-eminent during the century in the export of butter.[12] Perhaps because a significant part of that trade appears to have been in Catholic hands quite quickly (about 23 per cent by number of merchants, and 12 per cent by value by the early nineteenth century), Protestant pragmatism saw Catholics admitted to the Committee of Merchants in 1769 to ensure that quality standards were maintained.[13]

In the lower trades Catholics are found in a two to one majority by the 1730s and four to one by 1800, whereas they had only 20 per cent of the foreign trade business in 1758, a proportion that rose to little more than 35 per cent even by the 1820s.[14] Protestant hegemony is in those professions—the law, banking—that others could not enter easily. Nevertheless, from a standing start in 1700, by the beginning of the nineteenth century nearly half the barristers and physicians in Cork were Catholics.[15] Of course, a sectarian economic headcount must not be construed as a zero-sum game. If Catholics were entering the professions and the trades, it was largely because the city was growing and with it the market for goods and services. Especially from the 1770s onward, the port became the most significant for provisioning the king's armies and navy on the way to North America.[16]

Within the Protestant merchant nexus there was an unusually high turnover of families in both Dublin and Cork. The reasons for this are not clear, but it seems that, when money had been made, merchants tended to head for the social uplands, aspiring towards gentry and rentier status. There were also other outlets for Anglican sons in the armed forces and the Church, which may have drained off potential recruits to the merchant classes. These openings were denied to Dissenters. With more intense intermarriage patterns, it is perhaps not surprising to find longer merchant pedigrees within Dissenter and, indeed, Catholic families. While merchant families waxed and waned, there seems to have been little movement from Protestants in the lesser trades to the merchant classes generally.[17]

With regard to relationships between Catholics and Protestants, historians argue that rhetoric and reality often diverged. The rhetoric is that of Protestant divines railing against the doctrines of Catholicism and politicians warning of its political dangers. The reality was that this was not always carried over into relations between individuals, and the interaction of Protestants and Catholics was more complex than the legalities of the penal laws would suggest. There is evidence of growing religious tolerance on the ground from the 1760s onward.[18] Social geography also must be taken into account. Cork was transformed in the eighteenth century by suburbanisation in the north and south-east and reclamation of the river marshlands to the east and west of the old walled city, the filling of channels that—perhaps sadly—ended Cork's role as a 'Venice of the North'.[19]

It could be held that Cork was several 'cities' in this period: relationships within Protestantism and between it and Catholicism may have been influenced by the 'city' in which one perceived oneself primarily to have lived and moved. The administrative city was the Corporation's area of control, originally walled but extended as development progressed. The political city was the parliamentary borough—quite extensive, including huge rural and semi-rural tracts. The ecclesiastical city was considered to be the Church of Ireland's parishes of St Fin Barre, Holy Trinity, St Peter, St Paul, St Nicholas, St Mary Shandon and St Anne Shandon—a mix of suburban and rural. The social city was defined by the new, fashionable and salubrious suburbs in the north-west and south-east.

The Protestant and Dissenter population taken together can be analysed in a number of ways. The greatest concentration was found in the city-centre island parishes of St Peter, St Paul and Holy Trinity, with densities of more than six to ten times those in the other parishes. In terms of comparative numbers, Holy Trinity and St Peter were nearly one-third non-Catholic, and they stand out from the rest in that regard. There was a close correlation between the proportion of Protestants and the valuation of a parish, with Holy Trinity, St Paul and St Peter evincing the greatest wealth.

Within Anglicanism the relative position of parishes was a little more complicated. Suburbanisation in the eighteenth century started to change the social and economic mix. By the 1780s the professional classes and larger merchants were moving their residences out of the city centre and are found proportionately more in the relatively low-valuation parishes of St Anne Shandon and St Nicholas. Another measure of relative wealth is the cost of church pews. On this basis, one observer has divided parishes into two tiers: tier one contained Holy Trinity, St Fin Barre and St Anne Shandon, and tier two St Paul, St Peter, St Nicholas and St Mary Shandon. The centre, in other words, was no longer holding, and the richer Protestants were beginning to migrate to parishes in which they were a more visible minority. Was this the result of a greater feeling of security?

It is tempting to speculate whether this changing social and economic mix might have led to differing political stances between the Anglicans in the city centre and those in the outlying parishes.[20] The admixture of Protestant and Catholic, particularly amongst the poorer classes, is evidenced by such as Thomas Newenham's street-by-street census of 1807 for the parishes south of the river and the 138 small schools which children of all denominations attended in 1826. This highlights another point about Cork Protestantism: it had a complete class structure through to the late nineteenth century. Today, when the only substantial 'working-class'

Protestantism in the island is found in one city, Belfast, we need to be reminded that both Cork and Dublin had substantial numbers of artisan Protestants, evidenced by craft guilds in Dublin and charities in Cork devoted specifically to aid for working-class Protestant apprentices.[21] Proportionately more of these artisans lived in the north city parishes of St Anne Shandon and St Mary Shandon. As late as 1845 the Anglican rector of one of these was writing angrily to Sir Robert Peel about the plight of his parishioners, 'hundreds of them in the greatest distress'. Father Mathew's famous temperance movement was pre-dated by that of Revd Nicholas Dunscombe's in relation to his Protestant parishioners.[22]

At the other end of the social hierarchy, the aristocracy and landed gentry were well represented politically as well as economically in city life. Peers such as the Earls of Shannon, Cork & Orrery and Donoughmore and (sometimes former merchants and recently elevated) gentry such as the Longfields, Smith Barrys and Newenhams owned substantial lands within the liberties and thus had considerable political influence within the constituency.[23]

What of Dissenters? The congregations of (Ana)Baptists, Quakers, Presbyterians and later Methodists (1752) were relatively small and, while accounting for perhaps as much as one third of all non-Catholics in the 1670s, had rapidly declined in numbers and proportion by the early eighteenth century.[24] Prominent in city trade, the modesty of their places of worship at this time reflected their small numbers (for instance, about 200 Quakers in 1700) and a desire to remain unobtrusive. Nevertheless, in terms of income some Dissenting ministers 'were edging towards the "quality"'. In 1834 accounting for only about 1 per cent of the city population (but 7 per cent of the total non-Catholic population, and with nearly one third concentrated in one city-centre parish, Holy Trinity), Dissenters had achieved by that date a disproportionate influence in the city's cultural and intellectual life.[25] The relationship with Anglicans seems to have been complex, ranging from religious hostility to an acceptance on both sides that, ultimately, in the face of Popery they were on the same side.[26] As an example of this double-think, Cork Corporation was charging Quakers 'toleration money' in the 1690s while at the same time resolving to borrow from them when needed. Again, by 1756 Dissenters were allowed to accept and hold commissions in the local militia, thus placing them clearly on the same civil side as the Anglican establishment.[27]

Wealth seems to have stirred feelings of envy and rage: Bishop Wetenhall in 1699 ranted against 'the Quakers eager pursuit of wealth, and their effectual, wily and secret ways of getting it'. By contrast, in 1706 the Corporation was prepared to act on a complaint from the city's Presbyterians of a nuisance near their place of worship, explaining their action on the basis of 'This Board not being willing any annoyance or inconvenience should be put upon any persons in the service of God Almighty'. Tensions with Methodists arose, however, during the episcopate of Jemmett Browne (1745–72), when what was described as a 'mini-pogrom' was conducted against them by one Alderman Millerd, a relation of the bishop. The imposition of tithes and vestry-cess on Dissenters also fuelled anger in the early 1800s and pushed many towards radicalism.[28] Worth a particular mention are families of Huguenot origin. Numbering about 300 in the mid-century, and with their ministers ordained as Anglicans by the 1740s, they were prominent in civic politics, where at least five mayors bore Huguenot names between 1690 and 1800.[29]

***

Cork Protestant culture can be viewed through a number of prisms, including the guilds (twenty-four of them, of which six were formed during the century); freemasonry; the Volunteer movement from 1776 onwards; and parliamentary representation. It should be noted that, while the gentry tried to control the city's politics, usually at least one of the two members contrived to be a representative of the Protestant mercantile interest.[30] Here I examine Cork Protestantism through the two principal institutions with which it was most closely identified locally: the city Corporation and the Church of Ireland, particularly in its physical manifestations.

> If ever Mammon reigned in a country, it is in this. Every thing is measured by money, and the idea of consideration not derived from money, or the means of making it, is unintelligible.

This is a quote from *The Freeholder*, a radical newspaper, in 1827.[31] It is perhaps a fitting text within which the 'unreformed' Corporation—the city's civil administration, and an integral part of the Protestant Ascendancy—can be interrogated. The Corporation may not entirely have justified one hostile description of it as 'a set of low vulgar city jobbers'[32] but it might not have been too far off the mark. The Corporation benefited enormously from revenues which grew with the city over the eighteenth century. Income increased from £900 in 1715 to about £1,200 by 1732, reaching £7,000 per annum by 1820. It was used to fund a lavish municipal edifice.[33] Between one half and one third of the funds went on salaries and various *ex gratia* payments. The mayoralty was the great prize, with total emoluments in the early nineteenth century of about £2,000. The salary alone was worth £200 per annum in 1702–5. By 1721 it had reached £365, and by the early 1800s about £1,200. Next in dignity to the mayor, the two sheriffs were paid £50 per annum up to 1787, and thereafter a piece of plate worth about £100. Each Alderman of the Ward received about £180 per annum from court fines and fees. There were many other offices, including the Town Clerk (with £600 in the late eighteenth century) and a host of minor posts—butter weighmasters, bridewell-keepers, sword-bearer and the calculator of the assize of bread.[34]

How was control developed and maintained in the Corporation? Under various charters dating from Henry III to Charles I, the sovereign power in electing its officers had lain with the freemen. In 1721, however, the Corporation approved two by-laws which, taken together, were to concentrate power in the hands of a small clique. In effect, the nomination to the mayoralty was confined to those who had served as sheriff, and the nomination to sheriff was likewise restricted to nominees of the great officers of the Corporation. This put enormous power in the hands of the sheriffs, who also had substantial patronage in any case, having many offices and the city Grand Jury (which disposed of about £20,000 per annum at the end of the eighteenth century) in their gift.

The institutional bodies that governed the Corporation were the Court of D'Oyer Hundred (the entire body of freemen) and the Common Council (the great officers with other ex-sheriffs, to a total of twenty-four). The freemen were (apart from a very few grants especial) exclusively Protestant. They numbered about 2,500—surprisingly large when compared to those of Dublin at the same time (about 3,000–3,500). A freeman had to be the eldest son of a freeman or apprenticed for seven years to a freeman. Freedom acquired by marriage had long since died out. Reflecting the colonial origins of the community, in the eighteenth century it was still possible to claim the freedom by virtue of being a 'Protestant settler', but this right was dormant by 1800 and an attempt to enforce it in 1831 was faced down by the Corporation.[35] The body of freemen was by no means homogeneous. Residents in the city accounted for about 1,000; county out voters, mainly the middle gentry of the liberties, numbered about the same; and there were about 500 who were resident outside County Cork and who had generally been granted the freedom because of their status or position, such as lords lieutenant (for instance the Duke of Rutland), prominent politicians and judges (William Pitt the Elder, Lord Eldon) and military commanders (the Duke of Wellington).[36]

The Common Council had abrogated to itself the right of admitting freemen. The freemen chose the Common Council. Thus a closed circle was established, similar to the governance of Dublin from the late fifteenth century.[37] Moreover, just in case this did not achieve the desired level of control, a further, inner group had formed, known as the 'Friendly Club'. The Club's origins lay in the 1760s, when a group of Protestant merchant families felt that Lord Shannon, a large landowner within the city, had too much influence over the selection of mayor and resolved to do something about it. 'The effort was successful', the commissioners appointed to enquire into Irish corporations in 1833 laconically noted, 'but the members of the club, having discovered their power, continued it for other purposes, and its organisation has been ever since maintained so effectually, that the members of it, by acting together in the Court of D'Oyer Hundred, possess all the power in corporate affairs'.[38] The Club's strength was that it operated informally. Its ultimate object was to elect the sheriffs, thus recognising their centrality to the Corporation.[39] The Club had evolved a system of control that was devastatingly effective, requiring only that its nominees were supported by all members. In this it exhibited all the ruthlessness and discipline of the modern political party.

It is perhaps not surprising to find that the onion can be peeled further: the Club itself was dominated by a tightly bound clique. From an examination of mayoral, shrievalty and common speaker lists for the period it becomes clear that a small group of families were at the centre of the Corporation's web.[40] Not constant, as fortunes were made and dispersed, by the late eighteenth century a recognisably stable group had emerged—principally the families of Newsom, Lane, Allen, Besnard, Perrier, Gibbings, Bagnall, Leycester and some others, often originally Huguenots.

In many cases these were closely connected through intermarriage as well as business dealings.[41]

Patronage and profit must be set within the prevailing cultural mores of eighteenth-century Ireland; nevertheless, it is tempting to characterise the Corporation as little more than an extensive system of outdoor relief for certain Protestant families in Cork. Even though it may have seen itself as the linchpin of the city's Protestant establishment, pragmatism broke through; when it suited them, Corporation Protestants were quite willing to admit the right sort of Catholic into the system. By the end of the century, for instance, some 70, most prominent merchants, had been made freemen.[42]

***

If Mammon—in the form of the Corporation—was essential to the maintenance of Protestants' economic hegemony during the century, then God—through the medium of the Anglican Church—was what set them apart, moved them, formed their contemporary spiritual culture. This essay has not space to examine what Raymond Gillespie has described as 'the structure of belief of individuals'; we look rather at the 'outward and visible signs'.[43] The late seventeenth-century Irish Church may have seemed venal, corrupt and complacent, but scholars now recognise that there were numerous attempts to clean it up in the early eighteenth.[44] Absenteeism, laziness and nepotism were countered by busy bishops, improving clergymen, movements for the bettering of civil and godly manners, and societies for furthering the spread of the Gospel—and, principally, by education, evidenced by the rash of charity schools set up in the city between 1716 and 1728.[45] Progress was slow, however; by 1834 there was still non-residency amongst senior city clergy (one third of the vicars/rectors of the city parishes) and a substantial disparity in their provision with a noticeable bias—in the richer parishes the clerics had less parishioners with whom to deal.[46]

In the eighteenth century staking out territory was the imperative, especially after the unsettled period from 1641 to 1690 in which Protestants were visibly put on the back foot. The seventeenth century had seen Cork city as a 'contested space, with Catholic and Protestant groupings vying for superiority and recognition within the landscape'.[47] In the eighteenth century Protestants largely prevailed in this space, the most obvious manifestation of this being the building and rebuilding of Anglican churches. The most significant were Christ Church (Holy Trinity), between the Grand Parade and South Main Street, in which the Corporation assembled and worshipped, and St Peter, on North Main Street, the fashionable church for the upper classes. These were the churches in which the Jacobite governor of Cork, Lord Clare, ordered that all city Protestants, including Bishop Wetenhall, be confined in 1690.[48]

Largely owing to wartime upheavals, the Anglican churches were in a poor state of repair at the end of the seventeenth century.[49] In 1693 St Peter had been rebuilt, and it was also planned to reconstruct St Mary Shandon in the northern suburbs to cater for the growing Protestant population in that area. The insecurities of the century had left their mark, however, and made local Protestants cautious; ultimately the church was built closer to the centre of the city.[50]

Some observers see the wave of church-building and renovation in the early eighteenth century as having as much to do with demonstrating the economic and social superiority of Protestant over Catholic as with providing the built environment within which a better spiritual life could flourish.[51] It is noteworthy that even as late as 1800 Protestants and Dissenters had thirteen places of worship in Cork city, compared to nine Catholic churches. At national level, the Board of First Fruits was established in 1712 to ensure that Protestants had adequate places of worship. The Board provided funding, through parliamentary grant, for church-building right through to its abolition in 1834. In 1719 a Coal Act levied a tax of one shilling on every ton of coal and culm which passed into the city. This was to last for seven years, but was renewed again in 1726 as the costs of building and renewal mounted.[52]

The spate of Anglican church renewal in Cork city during the century (though not unique—Dublin had a similar outburst) is impressive.[53] It includes the rebuilding of Christ Church in 1720, and St Nicholas to serve the southern liberties in the same year; a new church of St Anne Shandon, with its now-famous steeple, in 1722; another new church, St Paul, in the city centre in 1723; and the reconstruction of the city's cathedral, St Fin Barre, in 1735 (opened for worship in 1738 and for the exclusive use of the upper tier of local Protestants, since it cost £10 per annum to lease a large pew, and £6 for a small one). None of these projects was cheap—for instance, the new Christ Church cost £5,328 despite being poorly constructed—yet the churches, including the cathedral, were largely built in utilitarian styles and with a keen eye to cost.[54] Architecturally, they did not particularly enthuse contemporary—or, indeed, later—observers: Gibson described Christ Church as 'now plain externally, as a barn, with the exception of a cut stone front', and the best that the antiquarian Charles Smith could say of it was that 'The body of this church is capable of containing three thousand people with good pews and galleries, and is all built of hewn stone'.[55] Cork's church architecture in the eighteenth century exhibited little of the dazzle of Dublin, yet the city saw in the period the construction of a number of substantial civic buildings, including the Custom House (1724), Corn Market (1740), Mansion House (1767) and stone bridges over the River Lee in 1712, 1713 and 1789.[56]

The State may have provided funds for church-building, but it is evident that the impetus came from local interests. It was not accidental that the activity in Cork to 1735 coincided with the energetic and reforming episcopacy of Peter Browne, sometime provost of Trinity College, Dublin, and bishop of Cork from 1709 to 1735.[57] Again, while resources came from taxes and imposts, a significant part of the funding was raised from local and voluntary contributions. In 1726 it was claimed that the parishioners of the two new churches of St Mary Shandon and St Paul raised £1,079, or about 30 per cent of the cost of building the churches.[58] The period of vigorous construction ended in 1738, but there were some modifications and embellishments made to the city's churches later in the century, notably the addition of a tower of bells to the cathedral in 1772. The last significant building project took place between 1783 and 1788, with the demolition and reconstruction of one of the city's oldest churches, St Peter. Despite a reputed cost of about £5,000, it too was generally considered to be small and unprepossessing in appearance.[59]

***

For Cork Protestants, the eighteenth century ended as had the seventeenth, with wars, rebellions and insecurity. The city was a vigorous centre of the Volunteer movement, the Court of D'Oyer Hundred at one time granting 300 guineas for the raising of a corps. The Cork Boyne Society, formed in 1776 to provide mutual assistance and to protect peace and prosperity, restricted its membership to the upper echelons of city Protestant society—no 'apprentice, menial servant, papist, or any person married to a papist' was to be admitted. Other city corps which had their origins in the local militias of the 1720s and 1730s were the True Blues (one of the oldest societies in Ireland, formed in 1745 and reconstituted as a Volunteer corps in 1778), Aughrim (1777) and Culloden (1778) societies.[60] Protestant Cork, victualling army and navy, was perhaps too busy making money out of the American and French wars to involve itself as heavily in the patriot game as Dublin and Belfast.[61]

Protestant culture in eighteenth-century Cork may not have sparkled with intellect, but it was not without its coffee-houses, convivial societies (the Water Club, the Cold Bone Club, the Atlantic Club), its Free Debating Society (founded in 1772), theatres, music gallery and 'French airs'. Its first newspaper was established in 1715, and English broadsheets were plentiful by 1748.[62] Lord Orrery's 'dulness' should not necessarily be taken as the leitmotif for the city's life of the mind during these years. Nevertheless, it is not until the early 1800s that a remarked-upon artistic flowering is found.[63] And yet ... if there was complacency and 'dulness', might this have been an effect of State-imposed Ascendancy in the 1700s? Perhaps Protestant imagination and energy needed to be unlocked by the vigorous challenges that began to shake and shape an increasingly post-Ascendancy society in the succeeding century.

2

KEEPING FAITH: AN EVOCATION OF THE CORK PROTESTANT CHARACTER, 1820–1920[1]

As early as 1837, a defeated Tory election candidate in Cork complained that 'it is almost useless for any *Protestant* of conservative principles to hope for success'.[2] By 1843 the high sheriff of Cork was in no doubt. Protestant morale in the city was low:

> the party here attached to the British connection have not the same confidence in themselves which they formerly had.'[3]

From the 1880s there is no shortage of the analysis of decline by insiders and outsiders in the intellectual periodicals—*New Ireland Review*, *Nineteenth Century*, *Contemporary Review*, *Blackwood's Magazine*, *Fortnightly Review*. By the beginning of the twentieth century the angst was in full flood, typified by the self-deprecatory and bewildered doggerel of a 1907 County Clare unionist:[4]

> Sweet land, farewell; sweet land, farewell;
> Where loyal and leal no more may dwell.
> For over the seas and far away
> The poor West Briton must sadly stray.
> He is out of fashion and out of date,
> And the deeds of old are forgotten of late.
> He brings no votes and he counts no more,
> And little is thought of the days of yore.
> And rare as the dodo, as all may see,
> A loyal West Briton full soon will be.

On the face of it, one might be tempted by these sentiments to view a unilinear descent from the early nineteenth century by southern Irish Protestants into what has been described as their modern-day 'acceptance of the need to live quietly and passively in their dying culture'.[5] Their history, however, is more complex than that: so complex, indeed, that another observer, son of the first, writing of the late 1970s, can reach a diametrically opposite conclusion and suggest that 'the prospects for Protestant survival seem much brighter than at any time since 1922'.[6]

The elements that went to make Cork Protestant society in the last century of the Union can perhaps be best illustrated through the lives of those who were amongst its most influential members. This chapter uses short biographies to illuminate important themes within, and influences on, Cork Protestantism and its political, social and economic structure over the period. Cork, with its strong regional identity, is particularly well suited for a study designed to evoke a close-knit community through its local leadership.

The major thread that runs right through the period and impinges on all facets of life is the tension between town and country. In its urban manifestation Protestantism often offered an inventiveness, freshness and vitality that could put the tired 'tea-and-cakes' unionism of the landed classes to shame. Perhaps this was because, rather than in spite of, the occasional indifference and frequent hostility of country to town Protestantism. A minor Cork landlord writing to W.H. Lecky in 1895 could not really say why, but he knew in his bones that 'we of the country have a standing grievance against the towns—they are ruining the country'.[7] Perhaps it was because, in Oliver MacDonagh's striking phrase, 'the cash economy was slowly advancing into the countryside',[8] followed in its wake by urban and suburban *petite bourgeoisie*. This was socially unsettling to the gentry and their attitudes did not change much over the century. The blackballing of the city merchants' attempts to join the Cork County Club in the 1830s was mirrored in the prohibition in the early 1900s on anyone 'in trade', whether Catholic or Protestant, joining the local tennis club in the tiny west Cork village of Timoleague, and in the establishment of the Munster Model Yacht Club in 1872 for those not socially elevated enough to be members of A.H. Smith Barry's Royal Cork Yacht Club.[9]

By 1881 Cork Protestantism was as much an urban as a rural phenomenon. Of the 45,000 Protestants in the city and county, nearly half could be classed as town-dwellers.[10] Moreover, land as a business was in trouble. In particular, unwise family settlements (as in the case of the Earls of Kingston), the Famine of 1845–7 and Gladstone's first attempts to settle the land question had left the gentry crippled by the twin diseases of over-mortgage and insecurity. In general, in the period of relatively buoyant agricultural prices between 1850 and 1875 landlords neither took immediate cash advantage by maximising rentals nor set a store of value for the future by investing in improvements.[11]

All this was by way of sharp contrast to urban Protestantism. The landlords who should have capitalised industrial and commercial concerns could not and did not. In 1899 eight railway, two steamship and four town gas companies based in Cork city boasted of a small number of landed gentry on their boards, but of the fifty-seven or so other major commercial enterprises in the city only two had landed representatives amongst their directors.[12] Capital realised by the resident gentry from inheritances or from the sale of land was usually invested in British gilt-edged stock or sound Irish securities.[13] By the end of the century urban and landed Protestants were heading in economically different directions. On the one hand the economic interests of the urban classes had perforce to lie with Ireland; on the other the centre of economic gravity of the dispossessed gentry, especially after the 1903 and 1909 Land Acts, increasingly lay elsewhere. It is hardly surprising that this led to a clear divergence of political attitudes, actions and aspirations as well. The two final biographical pieces in this chapter, covering secondary education and local politics, demonstrate this development.

Just as Cork Protestantism was not socially united, neither was it politically monolithic. A streak of liberalism and political dissent, admittedly never very wide or deep, runs from F.B. Beamish and the anti-Corporation men of the 1830s to Revd R. Anderson and the Protestant Home Rulers of the 1880s. Its significance lies not in itself particularly but rather in the contrast it offers to the actions and attitudes of the vast majority of Protestants. Their super-sensitivity to a fully realised minority position explains in large measure the almost violent reaction to those whom they saw as political renegades. They may have been, in the words of a contemporary, 'socially proud' because of possessing 'all the landed property of the country',[14] but the sense of being a minority pervaded and shaped their political activities, especially after the 1880s. Ostensibly political organisations like the Primrose League were really social buttresses for an isolated community. This also meant that the political influence of women like Lady Mary Aldworth and the Countess of Bandon was probably correspondingly more powerful than that of their nationalist counterparts. But if from as early as the 1840s Cork Protestants began to feel a wall behind their backs, this did not mean submitting to the blindfold and the last request. Men like Sir John Scott and Revd Ralph

Harvey all fought back in their different ways, and all with a measure of success.

It is perhaps fitting that the lives outlined here begin with the 3rd Earl of Kingston and Gerard Callaghan. Both bridge the eighteenth and nineteenth centuries. Kingston, straight out of the pages of Jonah Barrington's *Personal Sketches of his Own Time*, based his politics on the certainties of the earlier century, as his sad decline, financial and mental, sprang from the upheavals of the later. Callaghan's was new money, trying to buy respectability and the power which wealth inevitably had. They were political opponents yet each wielded power and used it in similar fashions. To each, dynastic interest and patronage considerations were paramount, and to excess. They used the rhetoric of the same cause—Catholic Emancipation—to further obsessive personal ambition. A convert from Catholicism, Callaghan whipped up anti-Catholic sectarian politics in the 1820s, though quite prepared to switch his alliances for personal ends. On the opposite side, Kingston was a self-confessed 'advocate for Emancipation, [not] from liberality but from necessity'.[15]

THE DECAY OF ARISTOCRATIC POWER: GEORGE KING, 3RD EARL OF KINGSTON, 1771–1839

The Kingstons were great landowners; their estates, centred on the town of Mitchelstown, amounted to nearly 75,000 acres in Cork and Limerick, with a nominal rental of about £40,000 per annum.[16] The first and second earls died within two years of each other, leaving combined debts of £90,000 and a £28,000 annual charge on the estates. This crushing burden was to be further added to by the third earl, George, who was born in 1771 and succeeded to the title in 1799. 'He was a tall, strongly-built man of handsome and commanding appearance and of an imperious temper', wrote one observer.[17] In Elizabeth Bowen's words, he had 'entered on life young'.[18] While still in his teens he had witnessed the killing of his sister's lover by his father, as she attempted to elope. In 1798, as a young militia officer, he was captured by rebels during the insurrection and narrowly escaped with his life. Until his mother's death in 1823 George had to be content to have the use of a pretty if isolated house at Glandore in west Cork.[19] This was not too burdensome. He had become an intimate of the Prince Regent and tended to spend a significant proportion of his time in London.[20] But George's father had not just kept him out of the Mitchelstown residence; he denied him control over the estate's revenues as well, so long as his mother remained alive.[21]

Perhaps he had prescience of his son's potential profligacy. As a descendant has rather ruefully put it, 'the year 1823 ushered in an era of folly and disaster which led finally to the ruin of the great Mitchelstown inheritance of the Kings'.[22] As soon as George got his hands on the money (or, more accurately, on a security for vast borrowings), he set about building a seat to match his pretensions. Travellers Mr and Mrs Hall may not have been overly impressed by what they described as a 'modern castellated mansion' but they were in the minority. Designed by the Pain brothers, it was a neo-Gothic fancy of immense proportions, consciously modelled on Windsor Castle. Everything about it was on a gargantuan scale. The cost was enormous, variously estimated at between £100,000 and £220,000. It was erected in two years with the employment of hundreds of workmen.[23] The castle was run lavishly even for the dissolute aristocracy of the south of Ireland. There were parties, balls, vast quantities of plate, liveried footmen, large chandeliers and great chefs—one was young Claridge, later of London hotel fame.[24]

George King careered on as if there were no tomorrow, which in a sense for him there was not. The debts continued to pile up. His son's literary equivalent to Mitchelstown Castle was an esoteric work on Mexican history published at a cost of some £32,000 to the estate.[25] Tocqueville said that by the 1830s the earl 'found himself burdened with

£400,000 of debts without hope of ever being able to pay them off'.[26] Eventually Kingston broke down under, it is said, the financial strain. He was declared publicly insane in 1833, his affairs were put in the hands of the Court of Chancery and he died in London in 1839.[27] While the proximate cause of George King's mental breakdown may have been his impossible financial affairs, Elizabeth Bowen might have divined the real reason:

> he epitomises that rule by force of sheer fantasy that had, in great or small ways, become for his class the only possible one. From the big lord to the small country gentleman we were, about this time, being edged back upon a tract of clouds and obsessions that could each, from its nature, only be solitary. The sense of dislocation was everywhere. Property was still there, but power was going. It was democracy, facing him in his gallery, that sent Big George mad.[28]

The Earl of Kingston saw himself as an amalgam of the feudal baron and the great Irish chieftain; he was popularly known as 'the Chief of the Galtees' in Cork in the early 1820s.[29] He hankered after the title of White Knight borne by his mother's Geraldine ancestors and regularly badgered Robert Peel for its royal recognition.[30] On receiving a final refusal from Peel in 1823, he imperiously claimed that 'I shall be satisfied with a recognition of the people and that nothing can deprive me of—I am proud of the title and of the affection the … people bear to it'.[31]

Lord Kingston also ran county politics like a great feudal lord. The Kings' political philosophy was openly dynastic. They controlled almost 10 per cent of the County Cork freeholder votes before reform in 1832, and they 'would never give their interest to any but a good Protestant'.[32] To the great political families in Cork—Bernards, Boyles, Cavendishes, Hares, Hedges, Longfields, Hydes, Smith Barrys—power was all about patronage.[33] The essentially transactional and unprincipled nature of this policy significantly retarded the development of a specifically Protestant political consciousness in Cork. Paradoxically, while Catholic Emancipation and parliamentary reform meant a quantum leap forward for political Catholicism, it also had the same effect on political Protestantism. This was particularly evident in the small parliamentary boroughs of Bandon, Mallow, Kinsale and Youghal, where a new aggressive sectarian Protestantism was freed from the lordly arrangements of the great landed proprietors.[34]

DEVELOPING URBAN SECTARIAN POLITICS: GERARD CALLAGHAN, 1796–1833

One of Kingston's fiercest opponents in Cork city was Gerard Callaghan. Gerard was the third son of Daniel Callaghan, a Catholic merchant who had ridden to prosperity on the back of the Cork victuals trade during the wars in America and with France. The family owned city land as well as the largest distillery. Gerard's background was thus similar to many of the men who later supported O'Connell. He was educated in England. In 1811 he was described as 'a slight young man, rather elegant in his appearance, affected in his manners, and anglicised in his accent'.[35] He became a Protestant convert and with family money procured a seat in parliament for Dundalk, remaining as MP for two years until 1820.

Callaghan can lay claim to the creation of an urban Protestant political consciousness in Cork in the 1820s. What he first had to overcome were the grandee dynasties that had controlled city politics, on and off, since the 1750s. These great landed families—the houses of Cork, Kingston, Donoughmore, Colthurst, Warren, Longfield, Hare *et al.*—used the city as a convenient political battleground for their own inter-family warfare. The poor Protestant freemen in the city and the Catholic forty-shilling freeholders in the liberties were equally expendable cannon-fodder.

The aristocrats and leading landed families patronised the city in every sense in the 1820s. They were often gratuitously offensive to the inhabitants, as when in 1828 they resolved to set up a 'County Club' with membership restricted to 'gentlemen of the county only'. When some prominent city merchants had to be admitted in order to maintain the financial viability of the venture, a large number of these 'gentlemen of the county' resigned *en bloc*.[36] Gerard was one who felt such social slights keenly, precisely because he was excluded from the social set. This, however, in no way diminished his own pretensions; in fact it was a matter of local comment that, at a dinner he hosted in 1826 for the assize judges, all the dishes were named in French.[37]

Breaking the political stranglehold of the grandees required allies, and Callaghan was not averse to using the combined power of Catholic and Protestant merchants to achieve this end. He had already foreshadowed this in 1820 when he stated that 'neither in the Irish parliament, nor the imperial parliament since the Union, were the commercial and manufacturing interests of Ireland represented'. As president of the city's Committee of Merchants in 1815–16 he also acted as a lobbyist on behalf of all the merchant classes.[38] Callaghan tried to mobilise this Catholic support in 1820, when he stood for election against the sitting MP, Sir Nicholas Colthurst, and the Hon. C.H. Hutchinson (of the Donoughmore family).[39] The attempt failed, however, and from then on it was an increasingly sectarian Callaghan who (with his brother Daniel) spent an estimated £30,000 on contests in Cork city between 1820 and 1830.[40]

With Catholic Emancipation and the rural agitation of the 1820s, the tenor of the times encouraged a sectarianisation of society at all levels. By the time of a city by-election in 1826, Callaghan's claims to the representation had been accepted by a significant proportion of those lesser landed gentry who possessed votes as freemen and by influential elements in the city Corporation.[41] The Brunswick Club movement (a sort of semi-detached Orangeism) between 1826 and 1829 further pushed the Corporation men and Protestant middle classes into Callaghan's camp.[42] In 1829 the Club helped Callaghan to achieve his ambition. After an expensive and keenly fought contest, he was elected MP at a city by-election, but his moment of triumph was short-lived. The occupational hazard of running a campaign on money rather than morals asserted itself and he was unseated on petition.[43] If the aristocratic faction thought that it had routed the upstart it was quickly disabused of the notion. Callaghan promptly had his brother Daniel (a Catholic) nominated as the candidate of the Brunswick ultra-Protestant faction. The grandees, backed by the political Catholics, had as theirs a prominent landowner, William Newenham. When architect Sir Thomas Deane (a leading member of the Corporation) wrote that 'he was most awkwardly placed between family connection, friendship and Protestantism' he was only expressing a degree of confusion felt by many.[44] The issue was that 'Cork shall never be made a borough', and the aristocrats were narrowly, but decisively, beaten.[45]

Gerard Callaghan was successful in creating a sectarian polity by loosening a lower-middle-class urban Protestantism from the shackles of a patronage-dominated aristocracy and gentry. By 1830 the bulk of the grandees had been tamed. No longer was there talk of 'the scandalous coalition of the nobles, forcing into the heart of the city, county speculations'.[46] By then the *Cork Constitution* newspaper, the mouthpiece of Cork Protestantism, would 'not think it altogether just to proscribe the youth of proud and distinguished families from representing places which would call themselves independent'.[47]

THE DIFFICULT PATH OF A PROTESTANT LIBERAL: FRANCIS BERNARD BEAMISH, 1806–68

The 1830s may have witnessed the growth of a sectarian cleavage in Irish politics but there were those who still crossed the line or affected not to recognise its existence. If, as one observer stated, 'fragmented localism'[48] was the dominant political and social reality of Ireland in the nineteenth century, then the career of Francis Bernard Beamish, MP for Cork City from 1837 to 1841 and from 1853 to 1865, is comprehensible. The Beamishes had become one of the great mercantile families of Cork. Originally minor gentry from around the west Cork town of Bandon in 1792, William Beamish had with William Crawford entered into a partnership with Messrs Allen and Barrett and founded a major brewery. One of Cork's principal firms, it employed 350 men by the 1860s. Well managed in its early years, it was fortunate in the fecundity of one of its founding families. Of William Beamish's eleven sons, no fewer than five became partners on his death.[49]

Francis was the eighth son. His eminence in city life was entirely predictable. He was a magistrate and a deputy lieutenant and was elected a freeman in 1827. After municipal reform, he became mayor of Cork in 1843 and high sheriff in 1852. That marked his political outlook. 'A moderate liberal and supporter of Lord Palmerston' was the description given of him by a descendant.[50] He was a little more than that, however. Beamish was one of the few Protestants openly to support O'Connell in the 1820s and 1830s. He was prominent as one of the 'Friends of Civil and Religious Liberty', a pro-Catholic Emancipation group in Cork in 1829, and there is little doubt that he felt that Catholic political aspirations should have been largely satisfied by the grant of Emancipation and the reform of municipal government.[51] An enthusiast for repeal of the Union he was certainly not. The radical O'Connellites admitted as much at the election of 1837 when Beamish was chosen as a candidate.

He would be expected to attend parliament only on the municipal and tithe questions.[52]

Beamish had few public political skills: 'a bad speaker, he was not able to aid the cause much but he always attended [meetings] and did his best'.[53] 'His best' was largely given to the effects of national measures on his local world. If repeal was never a real political concern, the imposition of stamp duties (April 1830) was, as were the coal tax (March 1832) and the tithe question (January 1834).[54] Above all, it was in Beamish's attitude to the unreformed Cork Corporation that his political, economic and social views came together. The Corporation was an edifice of seemingly sectarian privilege founded in fact on a base of economic monopoly and financial corruption. Throughout the 1820s and 1830s Beamish was amongst those Protestant liberals who consistently criticised it.[55]

By the 1830s, however, the liberal Protestants were starting out on a lonely and dangerous journey. The pustule of sectarian politics was irritated on the one hand by evangelical Protestantism and rural agitation and on the other by the increasing influence of the Catholic priesthood at local political level.[56] This at once created a permanent minority/majority axis and led inevitably to the charge that the liberal Protestants were either dupes or decoys.

It is rather piquant that Gerard Callaghan had tried to use the Catholic city plutocracy as precisely similar bait in his struggle with the Protestant aristocracy in the 1820s. The O'Connellite party in Cork was much more successful in its mirror-image operations throughout the 1830s and 1840s. Mainstream Protestant opinion was well aware of the dangers posed by liberal and pro-repeal Protestants. 'Let every Conservative elector be … on his guard against the canvass of Mr Beamish', warned the conservative *Cork Constitution* newspaper at the 1837 city election.[57] Beamish's vote-pulling power was revealed at the first elections for the reformed

Cork Corporation in 1841, when in the most Tory ward he easily topped the poll.[58]

THE SOCIAL DIMENSION OF CORK UNIONISM: LADY MARY ALDWORTH, 1840–1920

The organic interaction between the social and political sides of the mid- and late nineteenth-century Cork Protestantism is epitomised by Mary Catherine Henrietta Bernard, first daughter of Francis, 3rd Earl of Bandon. Like most of the Cork gentry, she married within her own local set. Her husband, Richard Aldworth, owned about 8,700 acres in counties Cork and Limerick, producing a gross rental of some £2,600 in 1882. In common with many of her class and sex, Mary Aldworth led a busy and varied life. She was involved in local politics (as a Poor Law guardian), amateur theatricals and the promotion of agricultural education,[59] and all this while managing the domestic intricacies of a Big House. Elizabeth Bowen has perhaps best caught the extent to which these houses and their ancillary activities dominated the lives of those who loved them and lived in them. For instance, in the late 1890s Edith Somerville inherited her family home at Castle Townshend, Co. Cork. She set about reorganising the garden, renovating the house, running the demesne farm, introducing Friesian cattle, buying, training and selling horses in America, designing and supervising the building of a cottage, caring for Violet Martin after her riding accident, becoming Master of Foxhounds of the West Carbery hunt and writing hundreds of letters to her brother Cameron.[60]

Given the relative isolation of the Big Houses and the sectarian axis of Irish politics, it behoved southern unionists to find an organisational form that would best marry the social and political necessities of the age. They found it in the Primrose League. Throughout the late nineteenth century, unionist imperial ideology was the counter to Irish nationalism. The League facilitated a celebration of the imperial dream, and with its habitations (as branches were styled), knights and dames of several grades, it appealed strongly to a caste becoming more and more obsessed with the minutiae of its own social gradations.

The growth of the Primrose League was phenomenal. In 1885 there were 11,000 members in the United Kingdom. Five years later membership had almost reached one million. Of equal significance was the growth in women members. In 1885 they accounted for one in six, by 1890 over one in two.[61] In Cork the League took root in 1884. By 1891 it had over 4,000 nominal members, and the branch had to split into four—Bandon and west Cork; Mitchelstown, Fermoy and Castlelyons; Kinsale; and St Patrick's (Cork City and environs). Lady Mary Aldworth was nominated ruling councillor (convenor) of the Mitchelstown habitation, while her sister-in-law, the Countess of Bandon, performed a similar function in Bandon. Lady Mary was an accomplished and fluent speaker, much in demand at Primrose League gatherings.[62]

How the Primrose League worked within practical politics is best demonstrated during the 1893 Home Rule crisis. Under the leadership of Lady Bandon, the League in Cork constituted itself as the 'Cork Loyal Women's Committee' with its own offices, responsible for the collection of unionist newspapers and the raising of funds.[63] Channelled into political modes, the relatively strong sense of caste amongst the landed classes might have been a bulwark for southern Irish Protestantism. But in Cork, as elsewhere, organisations like the Primrose League always had an inbuilt propensity to degenerate into 'tea-and-cakes' toryism.[64] Often politics offered little more than an excuse for social intercourse. Not only the weather might explain why a purely political meeting of the League in Cork city in January 1891 (at the height of the Parnellite agitation) attracted about sixty people,[65] while ten times that number turned up at a League garden party in the hot August of that year.

That August meeting of St Patrick's Habitation was held in the grounds of Sir George Colthurst's (landlord, railway investor, cricketer, *ci-devant* liberal unionist) Blarney Castle.[66] The event was well organised; in the social sphere, if not in the economic or political, the gentry could be relied on to put on a good show. The open-sesame to the proceedings was a perforated ticket, one part of which carried the holder over the Cork–Muskerry railway line, another admitted to the grounds and the third entitled them to refreshments. The ladies outnumbered the gentlemen ten to one, we are told. There was a band, dancing, stalls, sideshows and the minimum of political speeches. The conclusion from this example of social unionism is that within the Cork landed Protestant community the unionism was the veneer and the socialising the underlying necessity.

PROTESTANT HOME RULE IN CORK: REVD R. ANDERSON, 1849–90

While the grip of sectarianism on politics tightened perceptibly from the 1850s, it did not squeeze out all non-conformist political thinking. Nevertheless, as the careers of Revd Robert Anderson and his friends show, difficult as it was to ride different political and denominational tigers in the 1830s, it was practically impossible by the 1880s. Anderson's was a conventional clerical career. Following curacies in various west Cork parishes from 1870, he was appointed to the living of Drinagh, Dunmanway, in 1875, an area with a relatively numerous population of Protestant farmers.[67] Anderson was unexceptional in every way except in one regard: he was a convinced and public advocate for Home Rule. He had arrived in Cork at a time when political and economic sensitivities had been greatly heightened by land agitation, widening of the franchise, the coherence of Parnellism and the imminence of a general election.

There was a sense of apocalypse, then, when it was announced that a branch of the Protestant Home Rule Association (hereafter PHRA) had been set up in the city. The initial reaction of the unionist establishment was to ignore the phenomenon, but when the *Irish Times* reported a Protestant meeting in Cork in November 1885 at which 'a series of resolutions ... containing pronouncements on Home Rule, and other planks on the national platform' had been discussed, the local unionists had to take notice.[68]

A week after the *Irish Times* report, the 'New Departure'—so styled sarcastically by the *Cork Constitution*—had been flushed out of the city's political undergrowth. The movement published a statement of aims on 19 November 1885.[69] Its position on Home Rule was markedly moderate:

> While we shall endeavour to uphold the integrity and unity of the Empire, we see no reason why the legitimate demand of the Irish people for the management of purely Irish affairs in their own country should not be conceded ...

They also favoured a reasonable settlement of the land question, encouragement of trade on protectionist lines and reform of local government. In these latter issues they were not far removed from the positions occupied by moderate unionists like Horace Plunkett at a national level and Sir George Colthurst at a local level. What really set Cork unionists ablaze, however, was the PRHA's perceived 'abject surrender'[70] to majority feeling on Home Rule:

> We deprecate the proposal to contest every seat at the coming election, regarding opposition of this character as calculated to intensify and increase the feelings of irritation which unhappily exist ...

This 'cringing' rather than their support for Home Rule *per se* unleashed a storm of vituperation about the Protestant Home Rulers' heads. The *Cork Constitution* tried ridicule: 'during the summer holidays, and when excursion tickets are available at a cheap rate, it is not surprising that the members of the "Irish P.H.R.A." should pay a visit to Dublin', while an anonymous letter-writer in the same paper showed how inconceivable a separation of political and religious feeling could be by posing the question of whether R.A. Atkins, one of the movement's leaders, was 'really a Protestant at all'.[71]

As a concerted political movement, the Protestant 'New Departure' in Cork was neither influential nor long-lasting, but its demoralising and destabilising defections from the unionist cause were keenly felt. Its period of greatest public activity was between the general elections of 1885 and 1886. Local meetings were held; delegations, despite the ribbing of the unionists, were sent to PHRA gatherings in Dublin; resolutions in favour of Home Rule were moved by its adherents in Cork Corporation; and members filled one of Parnell's nomination papers at the 1886 election.[72]

What were the movement's characteristics? First, despite the innuendoes of the *Cork Constitution*, it was 'respectable'—that is to say, it was composed largely of men of property and commercial standing. Of the leaders, Henry Dale, J.C. Leslie and B.J. Alcock were prosperous merchants; R.H. Rutter and G.J. Roche were wine merchants, Richard Martin a hotel proprietor, Revd R. Anderson and Revd M. Kerr clerics (the latter a Presbyterian), and R.A. Atkins a newspaper proprietor, company secretary, insurance agent and landowner.[73] Secondly, the movement was youthful: the vast majority of members were under forty. Thirdly, while economically conservative, it had been spawned from an unlikely source, the Church of Ireland Young Men's Association, whose radical credentials included a debate in 1891 as to whether the Unionist or Parnellite candidate should be supported at a by-election, and which in 1893 discussed the women's franchise.[74] Fourthly, it was overwhelmingly Anglican in the character of its membership. Finally, it espoused a wholly materialistic and imperial view of nationalism, seeing Home Rule purely as the means to an end of poverty, disorder and disunity. Any transcendental aspect to Irish nationalism seems to have passed the 'New Departure' by. The difficulties of Gerard Callaghan in being accepted into the tory gentry camp in the early years of the century were mirrored by the uneasy relationship between the Protestant Home Rulers and nationalists. As Alderman John O'Brien of Cork claimed in 1886, 'we don't seek the support of the "New Departure" gentlemen: we only seek honest support'.[75]

The fate of Anderson typifies the even more virulent reaction of Cork Protestantism to any hint of public political apostasy. Anderson was in an exposed position. His parishioners, a vindictive lot, taking a leaf out of their nationalist neighbours' books, boycotted him. A charge that he rashly made against the landlord combination, the Cork Defence Union, of circulating defamatory literature about him had to be publicly retracted. Reduced to near-destitution, he was forced to rely for bodily support on the proceeds of public lectures given on nationalism.[76] He died of lung cancer in 1890, leaving a penniless young family. It remained for the nationalist *Cork Examiner* to set up a fund for their relief.[77] The unionists' violent response to Anderson may have been because, of all things, he was a clergyman of the recently disestablished Church of Ireland. Worst of all, however, he saw nationalism in terms of something more than a balance sheet.[78] This, above everything, made him incomprehensible to most unionists and, ultimately, more subversive.

THE ADAPTABILITY OF URBAN UNIONISM: SIR JOHN SCOTT, 1849–1931

In his own way, John Harley Scott was as radical as Anderson in a period of vital transition and transformation for Cork Protestants. Son of an architect, he rapidly rose to commercial eminence to become chairman of a major shipping company, trustee of Cork Savings Bank and president of the Chamber of Commerce. In public life he was a justice of the peace and sometime high sheriff and lord mayor of Cork.[79] His particular political genius lay in exploiting the fault lines of local nationalist politics in the city, broadening and deepening the fissures wherever he found them. On at least three occasions between 1890 and 1918—during the Parnellite split in the early 1890s, at the time of the first local government elections in 1899 and during the O'Brienite phase of the early 1900s—he worked to ensure that Cork unionists would play a pivotal role in local politics.

The gladiatorial circus was provided by Cork Corporation. The results of the 1885 general election—in which southern loyalist and unionist candidates were comprehensively defeated—meant that if southern unionism wanted 'place' in the polity it would have to concentrate on local rather than parliamentary electoral politics. At local level the combination of a substantial property franchise with concentrations of Protestant voters in small areas meant that the 'Protestant vote' could be of significance if marshalled and motivated. Just how significant was clearly shown in Cork, where with 15 per cent of the population the unionists in the 1880s and 1890s were able to control up to one third of the seats on the city Corporation.

The first reaction of many Cork unionists to the Parnellite split was unfortunately (for the local Parnellites) ill-thought-out and counter-productive. Just as Parnell, a landlord, could not entirely reject his own class, so Protestants could not equally spurn his claims on their indulgence.[80] Besides, here was a golden opportunity to engage in a little priest-baiting, with the unexpected bonus for once of a substantial portion of the Catholic population onside. The nationalists, then, should be left to tear themselves to pieces, and an ideal chance occurred when the death of Parnell in 1891 created a parliamentary vacancy in one of the two Cork city seats. The advice of Chief Secretary of Ireland Arthur Balfour and the Dublin Castle administration was to stand aside from nationalist infighting.[81] The local unionists could have created mayhem through tactical voting, but the gentry, largely dormant in city politics since Gerard Callaghan's time, sprang into life and ambushed a surprised city unionism. They imposed an Orange landlord, D.P. Sarsfield, as unionist candidate; the liberal unionists, the Methodists and even the Church of Ireland Young Men's Association revolted; and the anti-Parnellites were encouraged to vote in numbers greater than otherwise might have been the case. Even if Scott had stood (and city unionists, when they realised what the die-hards were up to, attempted to draft him in to limit the damage), little would have been achieved.[82]

Parallel to head-on confrontation, a new (and ultimately more productive) tack was tried. Between 1891 and 1895 the unionists moved forward politically by means of a tacit alliance with the Parnellite forces, increasing loyalist representation substantially on the city Corporation. The Parnellites, however, were unwilling, at the last, to allow the unionists to have the prize they so badly wanted: the mayoralty. They threw the bone of high sheriff to Scott in 1892, which netted him a knighthood. But no more than that. By 1895 unionist patience was exhausted. Not without much agonising, the majority of unionist councillors decided to switch their support to the anti-Parnellites. As part of the deal, Scott was elected mayor for 1896. Not all anti-Parnellites could swallow such bitter medicine. The nationalist *Cork Examiner* was outraged. 'Our counsels have been disregarded', it thundered, 'and we have for the ensuing year, as a consequence, a Unionist Mayor and a Unionist Sheriff to speak for the Catholic and National city of Cork.'[83]

The Parnellite split revived Cork unionism. Scott converted the moribund parliamentary registration society into a vehicle unashamedly more modest in its aspirations: the winning of municipal seats. A 'Unionist Hundred', elected by city rate-payers only, was set up, with eleven representatives from each of eight municipal wards, and twelve for the city liberties. Scott ensured his control by the election of his father-in-law as president of the new body.[84] The price of such political activism was, however, a sometimes dangerous visibility, often exacerbated by sectarian tensions just below the surface in other forums.[85] Cork unionism reacted in two ways in the 1910s to reduce this visibility. When William O'Brien made a pitch for Protestant participation in his All-for-Ireland League, Cork Protestants supported him in the secrecy of the ballot-box. No longer was there talk of unionist parliamentary candidates. Lord Castletown might rail against such closet O'Brienites as 'a nice lot of cowards', but the lessons of the Parnellite period had been well learnt and Cork unionists now knew how to use their electoral muscle to maximum advantage. The strategy thus adopted worked. It is doubtful whether O'Brien and Healy would have been elected as MPs for Cork city in either 1910 election if the Protestant vote (numbering about 1,500) had not almost solidly plumped for them.

The second unionist response was to imitate the chameleon. By 1911 a unionist party by that name had all but ceased to exist within municipal politics. This did not mean that Cork unionists had opted out. Quite the converse—they were still well represented in local government, but now under the banners of 'independents', 'commercial candidates' or tangential supporters of the All-for-Ireland League. It is significant that this represents integration rather than assimilation well before the end of the Union.[86]

PROTESTANTS IN THE NEW CENTURY: REVD RALPH HARVEY, 1851–1925

Sir John Scott encapsulated the political resilience and adaptability of a generation of Cork Protestants that had had its formative years in the immediate post-Famine era, at a time when Irish Protestantism was visibly on the defensive. So in his turn was Ralph Harvey one of those who were instrumental in equipping the generation that would have to face new competitive pressures from a rising Catholic middle class.

Protestant economic power in Cork city may have still been formidable in the 1880s but its relative position had been considerably eroded over the previous half-century. Two significant processes had taken place within Cork city Protestantism between 1833 and 1881: the denominational balance within many of the more prestigious and lucrative occupations had almost been reversed,[87] and within Protestantism itself there was a substantial change in class balance. In 1881 two thirds of Protestant males could have been described as being in skilled occupations. The 'hundreds' of Protestant inhabitants 'in greatest distress' graphically described by a city parish rector in 1845 were no longer much in evidence.[88] Increasingly, city Protestants were being forced to slug it out with their Catholic neighbours on a rapidly levelling playing-field. Lacking the network of large Protestant-controlled firms which in Dublin acted as an employment reserve, Cork Protestants needed to be equipped to compete on home—and foreign—territory. This was principally to be delivered through an aggressive and relevant education system.[89]

It is in education that a further clear distinction between landed and city/small-town Protestants was evident. From at least the early nineteenth century the landed classes, especially those with decent incomes, were educationally abandoning Ireland. In 1833 the thoughts of Captain Otho Travers, a recruiting officer for the East India Company in Cork, 'were greatly occupied in fixing upon some English school for my boys the advantages of which I see more clearly every day'. Lionel Fleming's grandfather had been educated at Kilkenny College, but his father had been sent to school in England. Likewise, Henry Cole Bowen's sons went to Midleton College in the 1780s, but their sons were given an English education. An examination of Bateman's *The Great Landowners of Great*

Britain and Ireland reveals that a majority of the indigenous Cork landlords listed therein (most of whom underwent their formal education before 1850) attended English schools and the universities of Oxford and Cambridge.[90]

For those who could not afford or who did not care for an English secondary education there existed prior to the 1870s a plethora of small schools in Cork—for example, Bishop Crowe's school at Cloyne, Midleton College, Fermoy College, Bandon Grammar School and St Edmund's College, Dunmanway, whose 'situation is unrivalled for healthiness and beauty of scenery, and, being completely in the country, is removed from the vices and temptations incident to towns and villages'.[91] Most of these schools provided at best an indifferent education. The situation was somewhat better in Cork city, where schools such as Dr Porter's and Mr Hamblin's, and Mr Knapp's Academy, had high standards and good reputations. Girls were excellently served by the Rochelle Seminary (founded 1829) and the High School and Kindergarten (founded 1876).[92]

Amongst the founders of the latter was William Goulding, Conservative MP for Cork city between 1876 and 1880, who, with Thomas Osborne, a city merchant, and the Anglican archdeacon of Cork, was instrumental in establishing a new city school for boys in December 1881. The resurgence of Home Rule sentiment had not blunted Osborne's desire to see an 'Irish' education for Cork Protestant boys:

> The school was simply set on foot … with the object of inducing persons who had been sending their children to England, to educate them at home.

He suggested that

> It is a great pity that Irish parents who labour at home and expect their sons will live in the country for weal or woe, will not see how desirable it

> is to keep up the connection during the time of their education with the people amongst whom they are to live subsequently ... they did not want to make Englishmen of their boys. There was much to admire in the Irish character and they wanted to maintain it.[93]

It was not enough, however, to sit back and let the pupils drift in, which is what the school's management seems to have done. While the school was itself a product of the revolutionary change effected in Irish secondary education by the 1878 Intermediate Education Act, the highly competitive atmosphere engendered by the Act meant that schools had to be promoted and well run. In its first flush Cork Grammar School attracted forty-nine pupils; this number then proceeded to drop every year from 1884 to 1887. Under the incompetent headmasterships of Edmund Arblaster (1881–4) and John Berry (1884–7) the school neared collapse. Results—on which a successful use of the 1878 Act was predicated—could not be achieved without numbers. Numbers could not be kept up without results. Drastic action was needed to ensure that the school would have a future. Salvation, as it turned out, appeared in the unlikely form of Revd Ralph Harvey.[94]

Harvey was a bluff, tough Yorkshireman who had come to the school as a junior assistant master in 1883. Educated at the universities of Leeds and London, he was a classicist and historian. Ordained an Anglican priest in 1893, he followed a church career in tandem with his headmastership, which he held until 1908. In that year he resigned and accepted nomination to the north Cork parish of Charleville, where he remained until his death in 1925.[95]

Stephen Farrington—later Cork city borough engineer and one of Harvey's star pupils—was singularly unimpressed. Harvey was tall and broad, with a square-cut rust-red beard. That beard would have done justice to a South Sea pirate and, according to Farrington, should have been accompanied by a sunburnt, cutlass-carved physiognomy. Instead,

Harvey sported a pink and white 'Dresden china complexion', giving him an alien and rather terrifying appearance, especially to small boys. Farrington maintained that Harvey instituted a reign of terror which was immoral, 'having no relation to conduct', and unpredictable, 'having no relation to cause and effect'. Farrington admitted that this might have been no bad thing: '… thriving communities are known to have lived on volcanoes'.[96]

Whatever about Harvey's general demeanour, there is little doubt that he created a successful school as measured by his own (and many others') lights. He concentrated on five areas of activity: the achievement of examination successes within the Intermediate system; a bias towards the Royal University rather than Trinity College, Dublin; an emphasis on applied science and practical entrance to the civil service and mercantile careers; an improvement in the physical premises of the school; and a further cementing of Anglican influence over management and teaching.

The Church of Ireland's extension of control over Cork Grammar School mirrored what was happening on the Catholic side of secondary education.[97] In 1889 the City of Cork Church School Board was established to manage Anglican primary schools. The Grammar School was brought within the Board's sphere in March 1890 under the provisions of the 1885 Educational Endowments (Ireland) Act.[98] This was just one of the local instances of the increasingly vertical denominational control of education that the 1878 Act did nothing to hinder, despite provisions designed to avoid such a danger.[99]

The school's infrastructure was never to Harvey's satisfaction. Despite his alleged toughness, he saw no educational merit in imposing Dickensian physical conditions upon his boys. Management, however, took a somewhat different view, and dissension over premises was to be the proximate cause of Harvey's resignation. From the first the school was located in a cramped and unsuitable inner-city location. It took Harvey nine years to obtain a modest extension to the premises, and it was a further six before substantial alterations were completed. 'Personally', said Harvey in 1901, 'this fact of improved premises is more satisfactory to me than all our long list of successes.'[100] By 1908 increased numbers were again putting considerable pressure on resources. At that stage Harvey felt that only new school buildings would fit the bill. But the bill—in this case £20,000 (an enormous sum)—was too high to pay.[101] The failure of a scheme to raise funds for a new school bitterly disappointed Harvey, who saw the institution condemned for the foreseeable future to an overcrowded and inadequate existence. He resigned as headmaster shortly afterwards.

Harvey's principal educational achievements were to equip his pupils with serviceable academic qualifications, involve the school more with Queen's College, Cork, and use the Intermediate system to maximum financial advantage. In these limited aims he was successful. Given the small size of the school, it provided for a surprisingly wide range of careers and further education. Pupils were prepared for a plethora of universities, English and Irish. Entrance examinations for the home and colonial civil services, the armed forces, the Royal Colleges of Surgeons and of Science, the banks and accountancy were also taken. Pitman courses in typing and bookkeeping were taught, as were 'city and guild' vocational and technical subjects. Less frequently, entrance scholarships for other schools—principally English public schools—were competed for.

The bias towards the Royal University rather than Trinity College, Dublin, appears to have had the support of a surprising number of parents. Twice as many pupils took the examinations of Queen's College Cork as attended TCD during Harvey's headmastership, and in 1896 it was said that more pupils from the Grammar School passed into the Royal University than from any other Protestant school in the south of Ireland. This, in turn, was reflected in the high percentage—25 per cent—of Protestant students at Queen's College Cork by the turn of the century. The bias against TCD seems to have troubled some of the more conservative Church of Ireland elements, though. This cut little ice with Harvey; 'Ireland was not the richest country in the world', he brusquely asserted, 'and the fees of Trinity College compared unfavourably with the RUI'.

In general, Harvey was a staunchly unfashionable proponent of Pearse's 'murder machine'. Under his control, the Intermediate examinations became the very *ne plus ultra*, the touchstone, of the Grammar School. Its resources were single-mindedly focused on the examinations, so that in 1898, 1900 and 1901 it was adjudged to be, respectively, the third, fourth and sixth most successful Protestant school in Ireland. Nothing could be further from Harvey's attitude than that of his predecessor, who in 1886 had declared that 'the preparation for this examination [the Intermediate] was so arranged as not to interfere with the regular work of the school'. Early into Harvey's headmastership the Intermediate *was* the 'work of the school', so much so that external examiners were dispensed with in 1893 and internal school examinations after 1898.[102]

This heavy emphasis on the Intermediate examinations made many members of the governing body uneasy. The bishop of Cork timidly suggested in 1907 that, for pupils, 'The real object [of education] was that their characters might be formed, and that they might learn to be earnest, faithful, true and diligent'.[103] Harvey clearly felt this to be nonsense. He always maintained that the Intermediate system was sound in principle, if somewhat capricious in practice.[104] He denied that the system led to cramming, though it is not surprising to find that the Intermediate inspectors uncovered clear evidence of it.[105] To the last, Harvey asserted that the Intermediate system was vital to the school's continued existence: 'if he [Harvey] did not produce examination results quickly there would be no school—nothing left but the four walls … Except for the Intermediate system of payment of results the Cork Grammar School would not live six months.'[106]

'A SCRIBBLE IN THE MARGIN OF HISTORY'?[107]

Pattern and process are the staple of the historian. At a distant glance, the final century of 'political' Protestantism seems to offer a surfeit of coherence in this regard. Analysts have duly risen to a tempting bait. The conventional wisdom persists in setting southern Irish Protestantism in a tragic mode almost before the ink was dry upon the Act of Union. That is largely due to the almost irresistible urge to concentrate on the landed gentry as its true (often its only) representative, but even as applied to the landed classes the inevitability of tragedy has been overblown.[108] Hindsight, literary artifice and the need for personal explanation led writers like Elizabeth Bowen and Lionel Fleming to see in the gentry the introverted integrity of a lost cause. Most of the time, however, the bulk of that class simply had a 'cyclically static' view of itself. Right through to 1920, if something untoward happened they had been there before: 1919 was a rerun of 1798; land war in the 1880s echoed the 1820s rural agitation; relative political quiescence in the early 1900s mirrored the post-Famine years. Granted, a secular trend established itself during the century, as power and privileges were gradually eroded in the face of advancing democracy. But, as Theo Hoppen writes,

> What is in the end remarkable about the landed gentry of nineteenth-century Ireland is not the fact that its power outside Ulster fell into ruins during the 1870s and 1880s, but that, by a generally acute maximisation of advantages, it was able to retain a strong voice in political and electoral affairs for as long as it did.[109]

Yet from an insular perspective placed into a wider context it is not really remarkable at all. The integration of even the most *haut* of the Irish aristocracy into the life of the people around them was greater than that of their counterparts in much of continental Europe. The

Catholic bourgeoisie may have been few in numbers; the landed classes may have been intensely suspicious of the towns; but there was a sufficient, if narrow, bridge of shared Victorian culture joining the two. And while the gentry's power in parliament, local justice and local government waned over the nineteenth century, their prestige remained largely intact. Conor Cruise O'Brien's 'Indian summer'[110] is perhaps appropriate as a metaphor for those who pioneered motoring, flying, photography, typewriters and telephones. At the end of the century the gentry were still setting the style, even if that style was brittle and often vacuous.

There was a kind of constancy about the Irish unionist Protestant landed classes through the century. What changed was the world outside. By 1920 'Ireland' as a political entity no longer existed; the Union was all but dead; their landed base had gone. All that most of them were left with were their Big Houses as a sort of social fig-leaf, out of scale and out of time with their surroundings—and, of course, their Protestantism. Much more intriguing in the century from 1820 to 1920 are the Protestant urban and suburban classes and the minor clergy, the political dissenters, represented by Callaghan, Beamish, Scott and Anderson—the people of Shaw, Hyde and Yeats. Somerville & Ross may have accused the town of being 'full of second-hand thinking'[111] but the fact is that even in their most vibrant novel, *The Real Charlotte*, town and city, though remote and threatening, are the ultimate arbiters of life outside them.

Furthermore, it is clear that the town's perception of place in the community was anything but 'cyclically static'. Free trade in religion (after 1829), in municipal government, in the post-Northcote/Trevelyan imperial and home civil services, left Cork urban Protestants with a fight on their hands. As a result, they had to become better equipped to meet the challenges of the day. Often prosaic, their tendency to go with the flow may have been their saving grace. Beamish's commercial interests gelled with his liberal leanings. Callaghan's dynastic ambitions grafted themselves onto a sectarian and anti-aristocratic root. Scott pragmatically exploited cracks in the nationalist façade. It is perhaps a measure of the relative strengths of survival of urban and landed Cork Protestantism that while Lord Kingston's fantastical imagination has left no permanent mark on the landscape, Ralph Harvey's pedagogic utilitarianism has a living and lively descendant.[112]

3

IMAGE AND REALITY IN THE LIVES OF THE NINETEENTH-CENTURY GENTRY OF EAST CORK AND WEST WATERFORD[1]

INTRODUCTION

Historians are always looking for angles. One is that in all individuals and communities there are creative three-way tensions between how they are, how they see themselves and how they are seen by others. These tensions provide the bearings for establishing senses of self- and group identity, coherence and otherness. The French psychoanalyst Jacques Lacan has argued that our most cherished beliefs about ourselves are fictions. The purpose of this essay is not to try and demolish the well-proven scholarly analyses of the gentry but rather to look critically at some of the perceptions, the fictions about them (and by them), by counterpointing aspects of their existence against the image that they presented to the world and to themselves.

THE AREA

The physical space covered in this analysis is the broadest possible definition of the Munster Blackwater River catchment, a sort of triangular area with its corners at Mitchelstown, Dungarvan and Cloyne. Dervla Murphy has lyrically described this land: 'Everything is congenial: every curve of the hills and valleys, every bend of the rivers and streams, every distinctive seasonal scent of fields and woods'.[2] This is the former East Riding of Cork[3] and in Waterford 'the prosperous Coshmore & Coshbride barony, with its planned landlord economy and estate towns of Lismore, Tallow and Cappoquin',[4] as well as the somewhat less rich Decies-within-Drum. These lands were owned and inhabited by Smith Barrys, Burke Roches, Penrose-Fitzgeralds, Brodricks, Kings, Longfields, Usshers, Ponsonbys, Gardes and Ryes; Cavendishes, Villiers Stuarts, Musgraves, Nugents, Keanes, Chearnleys, Fuges; Sherlocks and Powers; Bagges and Bowles. This is, these are, the gentry. Generically they have been—if anything—over-analysed. Four studies in particular provide source, inspiration and illustration for this essay. Mark Bence-Jones's *Twilight of the Ascendancy*, published in 1987, is a baroque chronicle of eccentricity. W.J. McCormack's *Ascendancy and Tradition in Anglo-Irish Literary History from 1789 to 1939* sets the juices flowing and the mind racing. Jacqueline Genet's edited volume *The Big House in Ireland—Reality and Representation* is rather short on reality (46 pages) and long on representation (246 pages) but nonetheless thought-provoking for all that. Perhaps most significant are works by or co-edited by Terence Dooley, of which his 2001 book *The Decline of the Big House in Ireland* is a most serious, sober analytical work, grounded on much detailed research.

THE ECONOMIC REALITY

It suited agitators to represent the landed gentry as a monolithic bloc, rapacious and ruthless, overwhelmingly Protestant and often significantly absent, in mind as well as body. The acceptance of such was vital to a larger political purpose—and, indeed, it was hugely successful. Not only Irish-America but also significant swathes of liberal England bought it. And in it were large elements of truth. But it skated over three important aspects of the nature of landholding in Ireland. First, the landed economy was somewhat more than Cromwellian land-grabbers. There were significant institutional outliers—corporate estates held by such as the London guilds, the Church of Ireland, TCD, the railway companies and, at a local level, Waterford Corporation, the College of Physicians and the trustees of Waterford College.[5] Secondly, the nineteenth century saw a new class of investor in land—in it for the money, unencumbered by paternal notions of duty and responsibility. Thirdly, while the largest estates were substantially Protestant-owned,[6] there was a sub-class of Catholic landowners but of mainly small estates—the 1861 census of occupations by religion throws up the intriguing statistic that fully 40 per cent of landed proprietors in Ireland were Catholic but held only about 20 per cent of the acreage.[7]

Again, Protestant tenantry in southern Ireland is a little thin on the ground, but it existed. Furthermore, Cork and Waterford landowners as a whole weren't particularly prosperous. Very few would have satisfied Richard Griffith's 1844 definition of a great landowner: 'A gentleman with from 6,000 to 10,000 acres of good arable land'. Bateman's 1883 definition was those with over 3,000 acres and £3,000 valuation; twelve landowners in this area of Waterford fell into that category. Unwise family settlements and the Famine, followed in smart order by the Encumbered Estates Court, picked off many gentry families by mid-century. Rapaciousness and ruthlessness were the consequences of inefficiency and incompetence, not the reverse—summed up in the landlords' failure to keep rents in line with rising prosperity in the 1850s and 1860s and thus experiencing all the heavier a fallout in the 1870s when times got bad again.[8] At one end of the spectrum was such as Lord Midleton, whose incompetent agent Thomas Poole allowed arrears of £70,000 to accumulate between 1806 and 1838.[9] At the other was such as Arthur Hugh Smith Barry of Fota, who substantially improved his Cork and Tipperary estates between 1870 and 1890.[10]

FRAGMENTATION AND COMPLEXITY

Mapping the gentry's houses and estates in this area, there are two concentrations: one in a relatively narrow line from Midleton to Youghal, the other in the Blackwater and Bride river valleys.[11] The distribution of these houses is largely coincident with land quality and socio-economic comforts—for instance, sparse in the mountainous northern parts of the area and in the Drum Hills. Under the microscope, landed society appears much fragmented and its interrelationships quite complex.[12] The coastal area of west Waterford demonstrates in microcosm that complexity. Here are some seventeen Big (or Biggish) Houses,[13] but many do not represent the principal residences of landed estates. Why they do not show up as such is that a significant number were held on lease from larger estates such as Villiers Stuart, Fuge and Paul. It can get even more entangled: for instance, Clashanahy on the coast east of Youghal was a house held on lease in 1851 from the de Decies estate by Sir Richard Musgrave, himself a large landowner to the north. Glenwilliam, just south of the modern N25 road, was leased by Richard Fuge to a Catholic cleric, while the same Fuge himself was leasing a house, Glencorran, from the Villiers Stuart estate. All of this shows that care must be taken in defining economic and social relationships within and between the gentry families.

This introduces an important observation: the extent of change and mobility within the gentry classes over the nineteenth century. Landed society over time was not static and monolithic. Within a long secular decline—in 1884 Waterford had eighty-one county families, by 1918 fifty-three—we find significant 'churn' in the families that made up county society. For example, in west Waterford, of recognised county families in the 1850s, only a little over one third of these appear to have still been there in 1918—eleven families out of thirty-four identified in the period 1837–1919 stayed the course. What one might expect is true: the bigger landlords—Devonshire, Villiers Stuart, Keane, Musgrave, Bagge, Chearnley and Smyth—had the best survival rate.[14]

THE BIG HOUSE

If landed families are more ephemeral than they appeared to be, where, then, can we find the essence of gentryness? Seeking a sturdy reality, a potent image, it must surely be the Big House. It is encapsulated in Molly Keane's fictional *Aragon*—Villiers Stuart's Dromana with a dash of Devonshire's Lismore Castle:

> Aragon stood high above a tidal river. So high and so near that there was only a narrow kind of garden between house and water. It was almost a hanging garden: as Spanish as the strange name Aragon ... Beauty so correct and satisfactory since then there has never been; nor so much dignity with so little heaviness ... It was the quietest, most solemn garden. The parliaments of rooks in the woods below, only an echo here, a ring for the circle of the quiet.[15]

Over the course of the nineteenth century the house grows ever more important, as the gentry withdraw from time to place in a troubled search for identity. As a social élite, by and large they relished the exclusivity and otherness that it represented. The houses played their part as the outward and visible material sign of social and economic standing. Big Houses might be big, but they could be, and were, trumped by *Great* Houses. Kings and Keanes were on different levels: the latter's Cappoquin House is 'Big', but it is not the Kings' Mitchelstown Castle. Similarly, the Chearnleys' very fine Salterbridge does not really measure up to the grandeur of nearby Lismore Castle.[16]

If the house was a significant marker of identity, it was not always a wanted one. Yeats's 'passion and precision' came with a price. Prisoners of their futures, the gentry's relationship with their houses was not universally benign. Like damp in a wall, that uneasiness seeps out from the literary. The heroine of Lennox Robinson's 1926 play *The Big House* may have fiercely claimed her Big House as her life, her faith, her country,[17] but the owner, her father, had other ideas: all he and his wife now want to do is to abandon Ballydonal and move to Brighton.[18] Likewise, the wreck of the Major in Jennifer Johnston's novel *The Gates* could only rail against *his* Big House—'I hate it. I've always hated it.'[19] Some souls were immune to destruction, or just joyous. When her house was burnt, Beatrice, Lady Glenavy exhibited a startling sense of release:

> I went round to the garden at the back of the house and stood in the wind and the rain in an ecstasy of relief—no one had been shot or burnt. As I watched the flames in the bedroom windows I had a most wonderful moment feeling that everything that I owned was being destroyed. No more possessions—I experienced an extraordinary sense of freedom.[20]

If the Big Houses did not live forever, another popular misconception is to associate their ends almost exclusively with the Irish revolutionary period. Like the families who lived in them, however, there's a continuous 'wash out' through the nineteenth century, for all sorts of reasons.

As an extreme instance, Cappagh House, in Decies-within-Drum, no longer exists: it indeed *was* washed away by an apolitical sea. Accidental immolation in particular was a constant threat. The NUI Galway landed estates database records seventy-six Big House fires in Munster and Connacht—most accidental, it seems—from the late eighteenth to the mid-twentieth century; two prominent examples were D'Loughtane in Waterford, and Lota, just west of Cork city.[21] And it is noticeable that fire as image is tailor-made for the fiction of the Anglo-Irish Big House and the resolution of plot, from Somerville & Ross's *The Big House of Inver* through Elizabeth Bowen's *The Last September* to J.G. Farrell's *Troubles*. The destruction of the house led to 'the readiness with which many Protestant writers have embraced, or at least acquiesced in, the imagery and language of extinction'.[22]

SOCIAL LIFE

How did the gentry see themselves? Lineage and place in society jostled for attention. Such a world involved a great deal of class- and gender-consciousness, in which 'family trees were meticulously composed'[23] and in which 'grandeur has become snobbery, fanaticism has dwindled to eccentricity'.[24] It really mattered whether one was a deputy lieutenant, Poor Law guardian, grand juror or magistrate. These Lilliputian gradations were significant to insiders and were often the cause of much social friction in this tiny world.

But what about the business side of gentry life, namely responsibility for overseeing the earning power of the estate? Sooner or later the bills arising from maintaining a luxurious lifestyle had to be paid, and doubtless landlords lost sleep over how they and their heirs were going to make ends meet, with a shrinking and uncertain rental and onerous settlements. If many landowners were incompetent and uninterested, nevertheless a goodly number took their stewardship of the property as 'life custodians' seriously and went over the books every year with their agents and accountants, keeping an eye on rent receipts and debt burdens. And the women played their part in managing servants and the domestic economy. An example in west Cork was Edith Somerville, who did both. Careful management was especially necessary after the post-1879 depression and outbreak of the land agitation in order to ensure that creditors could be kept at bay.

As a class, the gentry may have been collapsing into an increasingly interior life as the end of the century approached, a variant of 'drug-dull fatalism',[25] but there were still some institutions and activities which provided external purpose. The Church of Ireland after disestablishment is a case in point. The gentry took to its new governance, national and parochial, with some enthusiasm—for instance, of the ten lay members of the standing committee of the diocesan synod of Cork, Cloyne and Ross which first met on 23 November 1869, at least eight were of the gentry class.[26] This might be characterised as the Church of Ireland's own 'Home Rule' moment, with its general synod and legislative structures aping the imperial parliament at Westminster. It has been suggested that Isaac Butt's Home Government Association, the forerunner of Parnell's Home Rule movement, was built on and peopled by those who had begun to appreciate expanded political horizons through their involvement with the new church situation.

In the same vein was politics. In Waterford county from 1830 to 1867 Tories and Liberals carved up the parliamentary representation between them, helped by the fact that the county returned two MPs to Westminster. Three great landowners dominated: the Tory Beresfords (the Marquesses of Waterford) in the east, and the Whig–Liberal Duke of Devonshire and Villiers Stuart family in the west. Satellite moons—Talbots, Musgraves, Carews, Nugents, Barrons, Keanes and the like—circulated around these great bodies. Actual written election compromises appear to have existed in the majority of elections from 1830 to 1866. In 1867 the pact came to an acrimonious end,[27] just on the cusp of a reinvigorated Home Rule movement. Quick off the mark as always(!), it took nearly ten years for the gentry interest to recognise the danger when at a by-election in 1877 the Marquess of Waterford formally joined with the Duke of Devonshire in promoting a joint Liberal candidate against the Home Rule nominee, but by then it was too late. (It didn't help that at the by-election that candidate was a London carpet-bagger, a Mr Lehmann, with a name unmercifully ripe for puns.)

Politics as a mishmash of spectator sport and social existence emerges in the Primrose League, founded in memory of Disraeli, which came to Ireland in 1884. Early on, women had their own organisation within the League. The first Ladies' Grand Council, based in London, had no less than two Waterford grandees on it: Lady Charles Beresford and the Dowager Marchioness of Waterford. While this was 'tea-and-cakes' unionism, it had its serious side too. Primrose League 'dames' were out in force to support evictions on the east Cork Ponsonby estate in April 1890.[28] Ultimately the League bolstered morale and enabled the gentry, in compensation for their diminishing role in Ireland, to reinvent themselves as part of a larger Imperial project.

Morale was important, but practical politics was still a serious business. Two elections, both in County Cork, deserve mention. The first is in 1867, when a young Arthur Hugh Smith Barry, later notorious as the scourge of the Plan of Campaign and New Tipperary in the late 1880s and early 1890s, was elected unopposed at a by-election. In view of his later political allegiance, it is perhaps surprising to learn that he stood as a Gladstonian Liberal, in favour of Irish Church disestablishment, denominational education and an extension of the franchise 'as will include all that is really intelligent amongst the working classes'.

The other contest is that for the new division of Cork East in 1885. The recently formed unionist umbrella body, the Irish Loyal and

Patriotic Union, decided, very unwisely as it turned out, to contest fifty-two seats in southern Ireland at the general election. Post-Ballot Act, it was wholly humiliated in fifty, explicitly demonstrating the numerical weakness of southern unionism.[29] The Union's candidate for Cork East was Henry Villiers Stuart. He had been an MP, briefly, in 1873–4, for Waterford County and, while not endorsed by Butt's Home Government Association, was in favour of 'an extension of the principle of self-government within the limits compatible with the integrity of the Empire'.[30] He did not stand in 1876 but was returned in 1880 for the county, as a Liberal with a vague tinge of Home Rule. By 1885, while the Land League's excesses had somewhat diluted his national leanings, his candidature was, to put it mildly, slightly off-standard for the ILPU. Billed as the 'Loyalist and Labour candidate', his main plank, with tenant purchase, was as an advocate for the rights of agricultural labourers—a somewhat curious position for a major landlord in west Waterford with over 30,000 acres.[31] A landlord–labour alliance against the grasping gombeen men and tenant farmers, while seeming rather bizarre, perhaps reflected Villiers Stuart's own unlikely life—described in the *Dictionary of Irish Biography* as MP, clergyman and Egyptologist[32]—and death: he drowned in a freak boating accident on the Blackwater in 1895.

THE NARRATIVE

Villiers Stuart's championing of agricultural labourers offers a glimpse of moral purpose. Here was a reason for being, a place in the narrative—indeed, a narrative in itself. We see it in the activities of the 'Ladies Bountiful' of the Big House, too. Some gentry wives and daughters, such as the Countess of Desart, the Gore-Booth ladies and some of Plunkett's and Æ's [George Russell's] female friends who answered Sir Horace Plunkett's call to duty in his *Noblesse Oblige* (1908), gave charitable help to poor widows and ragged children while promoting cottage industries on the estate.

Was it mere duty, though, that informed the gentry's attitude towards local government reform in 1899? Their control of local administration had abruptly ended with the abolition of the grand juries. It seemed impossible that any ex-grand juror would have had any chance in the first local government elections. It seemed implausible that the Conservative minister Gerald Balfour's call for 'the natural leaders of the people' to stand in the first local government elections would be heeded.[33] Yet in County Cork nine divisions were contested by gentry unionist candidates. With a Protestant electorate of little more than 10 per cent, their average vote was 17 per cent, with four exceeding 25 per cent, despite considerable nationalist and priestly opposition. Unionists did even better in urban and rural district council elections. And though unionists won no seats in Cork and only three in Waterford, it was not a bad result. It is notable, though, that it was obtained by considerable evasiveness about Home Rule and a relentless focus on contemporary practical and material issues—land purchase, old-age pensions, free libraries, village hospitals, a Catholic university and the like.[34]

It raises the intriguing possibility of what might have been if the gentry *had* grasped the Home Rule nettle. One commentator, even if ironically, in 1890 looked for purpose: 'The landlords … could remain in the country for the discharge of other and more useful functions, national and municipal, than they have ever performed as the "English Garrison".' That commentator was Michael Davitt.[35] Writing in the *Fortnightly Review* as late as 1908, Sydney Brookes optimistically and unrealistically suggested that 'As an alien caste, they have conspicuously failed; as a native aristocracy it is still possible for them to succeed'.[36]

Thus, despite everything, elements of engagement and empathy are not entirely absent. There is no gainsaying the gulf, of course; apart from an alienating sectarian chasm, the gentry, as magistrates, were always sitting in judgement on the people. But it is well to remember that the greatest hatreds often derive from, and feed on, Freud's 'narcissism of small differences'.[37] There are more unspoken commonalities than perhaps is generally recognised. If many landlords saw their tenants as dim, feckless, devious wastrels, this was almost exactly reciprocated.

Who now reads Terence McGrath? His entry in the *Dictionary of Irish Biography* describes him as a 'clear, vigorous, observant and humorous writer'.[38] 'Terence McGrath' was the pseudonym of Sir Henry Blake, sometime resident magistrate in Tuam and later governor of Hong Kong. He published a book entitled *Pictures from Ireland* in 1880, and from 1907 lived near Youghal. Blake is worth reading, if only once. Drawing on his experiences as a magistrate and with obviously a considerable command of the economic *minutiae* of Irish life at the time, in *Pictures from Ireland* he quizzically observes such stereotypes as 'A land jobber', 'The tenant's friend', 'An absentee's agent', 'A dispensary doctor' and 'A "gombeen" man'. One essay, 'A landlord of the old school', is probably closest to how Blake thought the gentry saw themselves at the start of the Home Rule agitation. 'To the Irish landlord the year 1879 will present itself in time,' he wrote presciently, 'as one of the saddest in his history. In 1848 when famine decimated the people, the bonds of sympathy still existed between them and their landlords ... the tenants have themselves cut the cord of sympathy with the landlords, and turned upon them with a savage vituperation as undeserved as it was unexpected.'

In what he called the 'imperialism of the peasant class',[39] Marx identified a mechanism by which peer and peasant could claim common interests. While this might have worked in revolutionary France, it didn't resonate in Ireland. A lethal combination of 'shopkeeperate' and sacerdotalism stood between them. The gentry were intensely suspicious of the towns and downright hostile towards the priests. Blake reflects this in his portrait of the landlord as having 'With the inherited instincts of his class ... a firm belief in the moral inferiority of the Roman Catholic people … The parish priest is considered by the landlord … in his secret heart as a dangerous viper to whom all the troubles of the country can be traced.'[40] The paradox remains, of course. Independent Ireland—in Tory Arthur Balfour's self-satisfied phrase, the 'Ireland that *we* made'[41]—was indeed landed, devout and conservative, but not in the sense that would have tolerated the likes of Smith Barry and Villiers Stuart as its leaders.

Three nineteenth-century novels loosely associated with Cork and Waterford lend credence to Roy Foster's contention that 'nationalist and unionist Ireland confronted each other … from positions of monolithic security; competition was unnecessary'.[42] One is Anthony Trollope's *Castle Richmond*, published in 1860 and set recognisably just west of Mallow. It has its moments as a rather poignant Famine novel, but for our purposes its interest lies in its emphasis, which is a cat's cradle of gentry love-stories. It speaks to a self-contained, selfish and self-important world where even information is sectarianised—Trollope writing in this instance trivia about yet another broken Ascendancy engagement, and of the rector's spouse '… jealous that a Roman Catholic priest should have heard such completely Protestant news before the Protestant parson and his wife'.[43]

By the end of the century popular fiction was ploughing a different furrow. The newly educated Catholic classes were uninterested in 'Protestant news'; they wanted stories about their own. *Ballybeg Junction*, a comic piece written by Waterford-born author Edmund Downey in 1895, recreates a town, possibly based on Dungarvan, in which virtually all the characters, in direct opposition to Trollope, are of the Celtic genre. In *Ballybeg Junction* there's not a horsewhipping, choleric, port-crippled member of the gentry to be seen. Interestingly, any aliens are represented by *English* intruders. If Lionel Fleming could suggest that in west Cork before the Great War 'Nothing counted for about three miles on any side of us, because there were no Protestants until then',[44] here is Downey's Catholic counterblast, in which the Irish gentry had in turn already been written out of the script some forty years before Elizabeth Bowen could lament that 'in the life of the new Ireland ... the lives of my own people become a little thing'.[45] Similar is Julia M. Crottie's 1901 novella *Neighbours*. Subtitled *Annals of a Dull Town*, it is reputed to be modelled on Lismore but, if it was, few analogues of nearby Devonshires, Chearnleys, Musgraves or Keanes soil its pages either. Maybe they weren't dull enough.

CONCLUSION

Whatever the reason why Irish landed society collapsed, it was not from a shortage of examination, analysis and prescription. Leaving aside the obvious polemics from implacable enemies convinced that the gentry were beyond redemption, there are dozens of quite thoughtful and forensic dissections of its defects and its strengths from friends and sceptical sympathisers in the periodical journals, pamphlets and newspapers of the later nineteenth century. And that is not to mention a veritable tsunami of self-analysis and breast-beating from its own, such as Lords Castletown, De Vesci and Dunraven, Sir Horace Plunkett and, indeed, Sir Henry Blake. There were lots of excuses, yet none of them worked. Fitting perfectly into Sidney Webb's 'inevitability of gradualness', landlordism and its associated society crumbled in slow motion from 1880 to 1910. But why? Perhaps we are forced back to the cultural to seek the real reason, for it is surely Elizabeth Bowen's *Death of the Heart*. Maybe the disintegration is better explained by Dostoevsky than by Dooley. Not enough dreams and too much hope, to turn a quote from modern songwriter Bruce Hornsby on its head. Image gradually displaces reality; all we are left with is Molly Keane's 'only an echo here ...'.[46] The gentry burn out, are burnt out and, like smoke in the air, can then be just blown away.

4

PURPOSE AND THE IRISH LANDED GENTRY: THE LIFE OF ARTHUR HUGH SMITH BARRY, 1843–1925[1]

What were the Irish landed gentry *for*? Goldwin Smith, writing in the *Contemporary Review* in 1885, suggested that 'Landlordism, it is to be feared, however beneficent and picturesque in theory, is practically a failure. Where there is no obligation to work, pleasure in most of us gets the better of duty.'[2] Much later, Shane Leslie was in no doubt: 'Country life was entirely organised to give nobility and gentry … a good time'.[3] In this reading, the women had children, parties, visits and gossip—'comings-and-goings, entertainments, marriages'.[4] The men had horses, foxes, guns, cards—and women.[5] To take one very prosaic example, drinking to excess was something that both the gentry and their tenantry could understand. Writing of Fota, Co. Cork, in the early nineteenth century, Lady Charlotte Smith Barry described 'the great quantity of wine that was consumed there, the big decanter which holds nine bottles … being refilled many times, the door having previously been locked and the key thrown out of the window'.[6]

John Banville's subversive Big House novel *Birchwood* contains the observation that 'We imagine that we remember things as they were, while in fact all we carry into the future are fragments which reconstruct a wholly illusory past'.[7] That has application as to how landlordism has been historicised. Perry Curtis explored the nature of the demonising of Irish landlords since the Famine, focusing on the land war and the depiction of evictions. Drawing on the National Folklore Collection, his conclusion was that the stereotype, shaped by the Famine but constructed in sharp detail in the 1870s and 1880s, long outlasted the reality.[8] In modern times the distortion has been no less, often fostered through the literary by their own kind, with partial and attractive writing. This has largely trumped the actuality, despite a string of more sober studies from the nineteenth century onward. It was not from a shortage of contemporary examination and prescription—now largely forgotten and unread—that landlordism, as a purposeful system, collapsed.[9]

It is too easy to see the Irish gentry as caricatures from *Vanity Fair*. This is a contemporary satirical take from 'The Twilight of the Ascendancy' by the Scottish poet George MacBeth:

Good afternoon. So good
Of you to have come. Here we all are.
... This is Edwina, my wife's
Lady's maid, she's
Percolating coffee, in a colander. Will you
Have some?

... This is the drawing-room and this
Is the room
For folding newspapers. Mind the drip.

That's Edgar, paring his nails. A cousin, yes.

… Who is this, darling? Ah yes, this
Is Roger Longrod, who
Does the drains. Thank you, Roger,
There's no need to shake hands.

… Anyway, there you have it. Lorimer Hall
In all its glory. I look
Forward to your book, especially the photographs
Of the dove-cotes and the footmen's loo.

… Do come again, when you've time
And the energy. We'll do the cow-byres, too. [10]

One of the few Irish landlords who could never be accused of conforming to the stereotype was Arthur Hugh Smith Barry. As late as 1910, *Vanity Fair* was caricaturing him as a typical Irish landowner, one of its 'Men of the Day' series.[11] Bucking the perceived trend, he held on for a long time, but he was exceptional. In his day he was significant.[12] Lord Midleton's verdict in the 1930s was that 'Smith-Barry … had a *cachet* which no one else could aspire to', and that he was 'the one resident Southern landlord of capacity who commanded general confidence'.[13] Born before the Famine, he died three years after the foundation of the Irish Free State a wealthy man, about €30 million in today's money. His gross estate was proved at £492,277, his personal estate at £295,487, but that in the Irish Free State was only £46,800.[14]

Smith Barry was one of an influential group of United Kingdom landed proprietors with property in England as well as Ireland. This structure of what we might call 'transnational' landholding was not uncommon. In Smith Barry's case, he could be classed as more Hiberno-English than Anglo-Irish; his estates consisted of 13,000 acres in Cork,

8,600 in Tipperary, 3,000 in Cheshire and 2,000 in Huntingdonshire, with 79 acres in Cork city and 6,200 in County Louth. He had a town-house in London—20 Hill Street, Berkeley Square, Mayfair, which may have come through the second Lord De Tabley, who married Smith Barry's mother in 1871 (his father died in 1856)—and, more exotically, a winter residence on the Mediterranean in Algeria.[15] In the 1870s the valuation of the Irish lands amounted to some £32,000, the English estates to £9,200. On Smith Barry's death the Irish properties, which were entailed, passed to his brother and then to his nephew, Robert Raymond Smith Barry. Somewhat mysteriously, perhaps, given Arthur Hugh's activities during the land war and his very public unionism, the house survived the 1919–23 period unscathed. In 1936 the Cork estate of Fota Island that had been substantially improved by Smith Barry and his father[16] was acquired by Arthur Hugh's daughter, Dorothy Bell, who sold Marbury Hall, the Cheshire residence (now demolished). On her death in 1975, Fota ceased to be lived in; it is now the property of the Irish Heritage Trust. As we will see, for Smith Barry the English lands provided a parliamentary power base, but his political and economic interests remained almost exclusively Irish-oriented.

Arthur Hugh was born on 17 January 1843 at Leamington, Warwickshire, the elder son of James Hugh Smith Barry and Elizabeth Jacson.[17] In 1915 he wrote that 'My mother was a delicate woman and I apparently a poor and weakly specimen; friends I am told used to say "poor Mrs. Smith Barry, she is not likely to live long and as for that wretched baby she will never be able to rear it".'[18] Succeeding to the estates in 1856 while still a minor, he was educated at Eton and between 1863 and 1865 at Christ Church, Oxford, where he did not proceed to a degree. While he seemingly had a full social and sporting life there—he was president of the notorious Bullingdon Club[19]—the impression given is that he was not particularly clubbable and he is a curious absence from the memoirs of many of his contemporaries. For instance, his brother-in-law Lord Dunraven mentions him only in passing.[20] Like his father a keen yachtsman, he was Admiral of the Royal Cork Yacht Club from 1890 to 1925 and a member of the Royal Yacht Squadron.[21] Cricket was a passion, too—he was a member of the MCC. Smith Barry was a strongly built man who used his physique to be a hard-hitting batsman; usually in the middle order, he was also a capable reserve wicket-keeper. He was not in the XI at either Eton or Oxford but soon became much in demand for a variety of club sides on either side of the Irish Sea.[22]

His first marriage was in 1868 to Lady Mary Frances Wyndham-Quin, third daughter of the 3rd Earl of Dunraven and Mountearl. 'They are South of Ireland people', he wrote to his English solicitor, 'so you see I am going to become more closely connected … with the country.'[23] As a child he travelled a great deal in France and Italy, partly for his mother's health and partly because money was tight after the Famine and went further on the Continent. The love of travel continued and he was abroad a great deal between 1874 and 1886.[24] The house in Algiers was bought largely for the benefit of his wife's health. It was

> an old Moorish Villa at Mustapha Superieure which belonged to the family of an old Mufti who had owned it for generations: it had never had a European to spoil its character which had been the case with nearly all the Moorish villas around Algiers. It was a most picturesque old building full of old columns and tiles and some very fine plaster work, although a most fascinating place with vines and outer courts and a quaint old Moorish garden.[25]

They spent each winter there from 1877 until Lady Mary's death in 1884. They had a son, who died in infancy, and a daughter. Smith Barry's second marriage in 1889 was to Elizabeth Post, widow of Arthur Post, an American of wealthy family[26] and daughter of General James Wadsworth (died 1864), commander of the military district of Washington during the American Civil War and a rich landowner.[27] It is probable that she brought considerable money to the marriage from both her father and her first husband.[28]

Smith Barry was sometime a member of the Irish Loyal and Patriotic Union, the Primrose League and the parliamentary consultative committee of the Irish Unionist Alliance, in which he was prominent until 1913 when, in Lord Midleton's phrase, he 'had run his course'.[29] He was a vice-president of the Irish Landowners' Convention. He was at the apex of Cork county life, being a deputy lieutenant and a justice of the peace, high sheriff in 1886, an occasional member of the Grand Jury and a Poor Law guardian. After he ceased to be an MP for Cork County in 1874, he nevertheless continued to take an active political role at local level and was to be found in attendance at numerous political meetings up to 1912.

In his English incarnation he was a magistrate for Huntingdonshire and Cheshire and high sheriff for Cheshire in 1883. Appointed a privy counsellor for Ireland in 1896, he was elevated to the peerage in 1902 as Baron Barrymore of Barrymore in the County of Cork.[30] In the 1918–22 period he stood against the die-hards of the Southern Unionist Committee, which had broken with the Irish Unionist Alliance.[31] Eventually he came to support Lord Midleton's accommodative Anti-Partition League. He died on 22 February 1925 at his London residence.[32] His remains were cremated at Golders Green cemetery, London; the altar cross in Christ Church of Ireland, Rushbrooke, Co. Cork, stands in his memory. The title died with him.

Thus far this is the conventional, measured, planned life trajectory of many of the Irish landed gentry in the period, but Smith Barry was 'a clear cut above the average class of Irish landlord'.[33] He came to embody the family's motto, 'Boutez en avant' (loosely translated as 'Push forward'), which was boldly emblazoned prominently, almost as an advertising slogan, at the main gates to Fota. This became evident early on. As the head of one of the great families of Cork, it was expected that he would follow a political career. An opportunity presented itself in 1867 at a by-election for the county. Arthur Hugh's family antecedents and university education would have ineluctably pointed him towards the Conservatives[34] and it was rumoured that he had been invited to stand.[35] If so, he declined; even before the Ballot Act Cork conservatism offered little prospect of electoral success. It was an astute move, although it might have been more the result of careerism in the absence of paternally influenced conservatism. Standing thus as an 'Independent Irish gentleman', he was criticised for the anodyne nature of his election address. As one observer said, it 'will justify any course he may adopt'.[36] Smith Barry was excoriated as being 'yesterday the first of the Tories; today he was the last of the Liberals'.[37] Other Liberal candidates withdrew, leaving Smith Barry unopposed[38] as a supporter of Gladstone and of modest measures of franchise, church and land reform.[39] Crucially, it was a relatively calm period in the conflicts over land. Politics reflected this quiescence. 'It is many years since there has been in the County a contested election that excited less interest or enlisted less enthusiasm', was the *Cork Constitution* newspaper's verdict on the somnambulant election.[40]

The 1868 election in Cork was again an internecine Liberal affair. Smith Barry won, in a three-cornered contest. He had voted (but not spoken) in the previous parliament for Gladstone's resolutions in relation to the Irish Church, and he was more positive this time in his declared support for disestablishment and denominational education. Along with McCarthy Downing, another large landowner in the county, he prevailed over a cousin of the Earl of Cork. During the 1868 parliament he had an 'anonymous and unspectacular performance',[41] dutifully voting for the Irish Church Bill and for Gladstone's 1870 Land Act.[42] In 1906 he described the period from 1867 to 1874 as one in which he was 'young, guileless, and simple'.[43] In truth it seemed that, despite his long years in parliament, the act of getting into the House of Commons was not much to his liking; the enormous constituency of Cork County—'which had to be visited and canvassed from North to South and East to West, stopping at all sorts of horrible inns and calling upon and drinking with every sort of squire and parish priest'—was hugely expensive (costing him nearly £7,000 in 1868) and time-consuming (the canvass took six weeks).[44]

No-one was neutral about Smith Barry. To his opponents he was variously 'a pernicious little noodle of a Cork landlord', a 'vainglorious little bashaw', 'the galloping snob of Rotten Row', an 'aggressive busybody',[45] a 'man of lofty incomprehension' and 'a virulent partisan'—these last three by Catholic Archbishop Thomas Croke.[46] William O'Brien characterised him at this time as 'the most dreaded man in Ireland'.[47] To an admirer like Lord Midleton he was possessed of 'characteristic courage and foresight', with 'claims on the confidence of the South which I could never hope to achieve'.[48] In 1887 the *Cork Constitution* newspaper lauded 'the great services that he is acknowledged to have rendered to the loyal inhabitants of this City and Province'.[49]

Whatever about his character, probably all could agree that he was an assiduous man of business. What seems to have brought this talent into focus was his coming into the management of the substantial Smith Barry inheritances in 1868. From here on, it is landed economics that engage his attention;[50] and it is not as the relatively liberal Dr Jekyll—supporter of church disestablishment and franchise extension—that he is remembered, but rather as the arch-tory Mr Hyde of the Plan of Campaign and wrecker of William O'Brien's 'New Tipperary' town. Once in control of his estates, he commenced in both England and Ireland a process of tightening up on tenancies and ridding the properties of lax legal and financial practices. On the Tipperary town estates the absenteeism of the landlord had resulted in a loss of control over tenancies and thus a loss of income. Together with a new land agent, he cracked down on his tenants, particularly middlemen.[51] He learnt his stuff, evidenced by the rather tedious detail often given in his parliamentary speeches.[52] Money was his main mover, and he had a considerable grasp of the financial world.[53] He was an original nominee of Shawe-Taylor to the land conference in 1902 that resulted in the 1903 Land Act, but declined.[54] A political opponent in Cork, D.D. Sheehan, claimed that Smith Barry was purely obstructive when it came to land reform, although Smith Barry felt that the 1903 Act which started the final transfer of the ownership of the land from landlord to tenant 'will, I believe, if given time, work satisfactorily and carry out the policy of the Government to a very large extent'.[55] Right up to 1917 the question of evicted tenants—both generally and on his own estates—was a particular bugbear.[56] As late as that year Smith Barry was frustrating the attempts of Tipperary Urban District Council to acquire his land for housing.[57] And while he held to a consistent point of view—that a contract was a contract and that 'It is a dangerous thing to point out to Irish tenants that there is a means of escaping from the payment of their obligations'[58]—he acquiesced in the passage of a private parliamentary Act in 1905 that restored to their leases some of the town tenants that had had them cancelled in the 'New Tipperary' imbroglio.[59]

His parliamentary career subsequent to 1886, when he became Conservative and Unionist MP for South Huntingdonshire, sponsored by the Earl of Sandwich, was as undistinguished as his former one as a Liberal. He was only fourth on the list of preferred candidates in 1886, as Lord Sandwich detailed (in front of Smith Barry) at a Borough of Huntingdon Conservative Association Tea and Smoking Concert in April 1886.[60] Holding forty meetings he won, but not by much: he had a majority of 161 over his Gladstonian opponent, Thomas Coote, a coal merchant. His 1886 election address was tailored to his constituency—land reform in the English context, opposition to the disestablishment of the Church of England (a bit of an Aunt Sally) and local government reform. His margin in 1892 was even slimmer at twenty-two votes, but he was returned with a larger majority in 1895.[61] While consulted by Gerald Balfour about the 1898 Irish Local Government Bill,[62] he was never apparently considered for political office, despite the high regard in which he was held by Gerald's brother Arthur.[63] As early as 1896 he was being talked of for a peerage but in the event did not receive it until 1902.[64] In a typically mischievous commendation, nationalist MP Tim Healy in 1888 suggested that he should be appointed as under-secretary in Dublin Castle: 'He saw sitting opposite one of the largest landowners in the South of Ireland, the hon. Gentleman the Member for Huntingdonshire (Mr. Smith Barry), a Gentleman who had never had any difference with his tenants, and a Gentleman against whom no personal accusations had been made'.[65] But the suspicion must have been that he was a one-trick pony. From Smith Barry's perspective, of course, that was exactly the point: concentrate on what you can do, and do it well.

An examination of his activity in parliament between 1886 and 1900 demonstrates that his interests lay almost exclusively in the Irish land issue. His first recorded speech was in 1887, on the matter of the Plan of Campaign; his last as an MP was on the subject of Irish illiterate voters. Of his 150 or so interventions in both the Commons and the Lords, all but seven related to Irish affairs; the overwhelming majority of these were concerned with land purchase, the Plan of Campaign, evicted tenants' rights and so on.[66] Only one directly concerned his constituency.[67] Otherwise he had an undistinguished parliamentary career, serving on a couple of minor select committees (Foynes Harbour and the Fishguard and Rosslare Railways and Harbours Bill) and asking questions on vaccinations in Hong Kong, on fertilisers and feeding stuffs and on rates and tolls of canal companies.[68] His only English political office was as a vice-chairman of the National Union of Conservative Associations, a titular role.

He was one of three Anglo-Irish MPs from Cork who sat for English constituencies in the late nineteenth and early twentieth centuries; the others were (Sir) Robert Penrose-Fitzgerald (Cambridge city, 1885–1906) and (Sir) J. Pretyman-Newman (Enfield, 1910–18; Finchley, 1918–23). Insofar as it was useful, these provided parliamentary representation for those Anglo-Irish landlords and southern Protestants who had lost it after the extension of the franchise in 1884 and the abolition of the small boroughs. As the *Cork Constitution* newspaper put it, 'Although Mr Smith Barry has not been elected for an Irish division we have no doubt that the many thousands in the county and city of Cork, who have no direct exponent of their views in parliament, will feel that in him and Mr R.U. Penrose-Fitzgerald they have fast and firm friends, who know of their wants and who will not be unwilling to advocate their interests'.[69] Indeed, it must have seemed to their somewhat bewildered English constituents that these 'Anglo-Irish' MPs were more Irish than Anglo.[70] There was often palpable impatience with their over-emphasis on Ireland,[71] not to say unfamiliarity with their persons—at an 1892 unionist demonstration in Smith Barry's honour in Cheshire, despite Smith Barry being careful to emphasise his 'Cheshire blood' the local newspaper reported that he 'was not generally recognised by the audience'.[72]

Smith Barry's second parliamentary coming coincided with his involvement in two well-known particular episodes in the Irish land wars of the later nineteenth century. These demonstrate his single-mindedness and efficiency—qualities in short supply amongst the Irish landlord classes. The first was in relation to combating boycotting. The Property Defence Association established in 1880 was already in that arena. The PDA's strongest branch was in Cork, but the organisation was not particularly effective; the result was the foundation of the Cork Defence Union in September 1885.[73] Denigrated as 'The Royal Cattle-Lifting and Outrage Manufacturing Association' by nationalist W.J. Lane,[74] the CDU was a well-oiled machine. It had a paid secretary, established a London office and a robust and reticent financial structure designed to outwit nationalist lawyers. This efficiency bore all the hallmarks of Smith Barry. A parallel organisation, the Irish Defence Union, headed by Lord Bandon and highly approved of by the Irish chief secretary, was based in London for lobbying and fund-raising purposes.[75] By the end of October 1885 local branches of the CDU were in process of being set up at Tallow in County Waterford and in Kilmallock, Charleville, Queenstown and Passage West in County Cork.[76]

Providing flying columns of labourers and machinery for boycotted persons,[77] opposing the renewal of licences for boycott-supporting publicans, hiring blacksmiths, labourers and carpenters and organising stores and outlets for produce,[78] the CDU's success lay in avoiding direct involvement in rent disputes, evictions and forced sales. As Smith Barry wrote to *The Times*:

> It [the CDU] is not in any respect an organisation for the purpose of enforcing the payment of rents, or for the especial defence of land-owning interests. The system of boycotting and intimidation affects the liberty of not only landowners, but also merchants, farmers, shopkeepers, artisans and even labourers ... The aim of the C.D.U. is to afford such persons an organised assistance, so that they may carry on their occupations.[79]

Or so it claimed, although at its inaugural meeting a resolution resisting any decrease in judicial rents was passed, and there is evidence of the secretary taking an active part in at least one eviction.[80] It could not help but be political: for instance, in May 1886 its committee passed a resolution against Home Rule.[81] The Cork Defence Union continued in existence into the new century, but its critical work had been completed by 1890 with the gradual collapse of the Plan of Campaign. The most high-profile entanglement with the forces of tenantism involved the nationalist-led South of Ireland Cattle-Dealers' Association in the winter of 1885–6. The CDU took on and forced a draw with the Association when the cattle-dealers, assisted by coal porters, refused to send their stock to England on the City of Cork Steam Packet Company along with the cattle of boycotted persons.[82]

Smith Barry is best remembered for his involvement in one of the most significant disputes in the land war.[83] The Ponsonby estate at Youghal, some 10,000 acres, was the first on which the Plan of Campaign was adopted, in November 1886, and Charles Talbot-Ponsonby himself was an example of how apparent bloody-mindedness and avarice were the consequences of bad luck, inefficiency and incompetence, not the reverse.[84] Earlier than often noted, by 1887 Chief Secretary Arthur Balfour was already bemoaning Ponsonby's weakness and the rumours that he was about to negotiate a settlement with the tenants through Canon Keller, the parish priest of Youghal.[85] In a letter to Edward King-Harman, Balfour dangled the bait of government assistance if the landlords could assist Ponsonby. His *cri de coeur* was that 'It drives me to despair to see the game so ill-played by the landlords; who will not apparently energetically combine together for any other purpose than to abuse the Government', and 'contemptible as I think the Irish Landlords are for not having had the spirit to combine [with] each other I should be very glad in those cases where the Plan of Campaign has been started without the Shadow of an excuse, to go out of my way to aid the Landlord in his struggle'.[86] King-Harman agreed—'The folly and apathy of the class has been simply heart-breaking'—but he drew Balfour's attention to Smith Barry, who confirmed Balfour's concern about the effect of an unwise settlement on the land economy.[87] Smith Barry had form in this area: in 1885 he had called on landlords to combine just as the nationalists did, and in December 1886 he established the County of Cork Landowners' Association. By then he was already taking a detailed interest in Ponsonby's woes; he was bankrolling the Youghal landlord from an early stage.[88]

Balfour had found a soul as stern as his own. In early 1889 matters came to a head with the rejection by Ponsonby of a deal brokered between his former agent and Canon Keller which if it had been accepted would have precipitated a serious depreciation in land values in southern Ireland. Balfour, like Smith Barry, saw this as a 'social revolution' that had to be countered.[89] In a coup instigated by Balfour[90] and backed behind the scenes by Smith Barry, a dozen or so of the wealthiest landlords in Britain joined in a scheme to purchase the estate—'it is by combination that the tenants have been successful; and, in my opinion, it is only by combination that they can be adequately met'.[91] The syndicate consisted of the Dukes of Norfolk (a Catholic), Devonshire and Westminster; Lords Fitzwilliam, Ardilaun and Derby; Walter Morrison; and Smith Barry. Each put up £10,000. Balfour was hopeful that the Duke of Bedford and Lords De Vesci and Pembroke would join. Lord Revelstoke (a Baring, of the banking family) pledged £5,000.[92] In all this Keller and the nationalists seriously underestimated Smith Barry's resolve and competence. Some lengths were gone to in order to keep the financing details under wraps; William O'Brien later claimed that a prosecution against him was abandoned because Smith Barry would have been called to give evidence at which those might have emerged.[93] Smith Barry's trusted agent Horace Townsend was brought in to manage the estate. 'Compromise was outside the syndicate's terms of reference';[94] an offer from the syndicate having been rejected, all the tenants were cleared from the estate by October 1890 and the Plan finally collapsed in February 1892.[95]

Smith Barry's victory was further underlined by events on his Tipperary estate, which had been the scene of a rent strike in sympathy with the Ponsonby tenants (although it appears that Smith Barry had had some runs-in previously with his tenants).[96] With 'words of pitiless hauteur', he gave ten minutes to a deputation of Tipperary tenants, headed by their parish priest, Canon Cahill, who had travelled to London to remonstrate about the Ponsonby situation.[97] Following the Ponsonby débâcle, O'Brien had encouraged tenants to set up a town—'New Tipperary'—to try and outflank the landlord economically.[98] Despite the spin put on it by O'Brien, it failed disastrously at a cost of £40,000.[99] Later, an unrepentant Smith Barry recognised his own significance in seeing off the Plan of Campaign:

> Certainly he had done all he could to avoid evictions on his own estates when it was at all possible to avoid them; but when it was necessary for the sword to be drawn he had of course felt bound to carry the matter through, and he owned he had been responsible for a good many evictions that had taken place in other parts of the country.[100]

Here is demonstrated a strong sense of moral certainty. At the apogee of the land war in 1890 he had looked into his own heart and had not found any doubt:

> For my part I have done what I believe to be my duty, not merely as an Irish landlord, but as an Irishman who loves his country … whatever may be the result to myself, I shall continue in the course I have chosen, because I feel in my conscience that I have done what is right.[101]

This may have emerged from character:

> a very strong personality … quite fearless; indeed of remarkable courage both physical and moral, an excellent conversationalist, with a command of language … for though shrewd, with much cleverness and appreciation of mental qualities … not profound … somewhat prejudiced … did not suffer fools gladly … rather merciless … criticisms could bite … heart was warm … friendship to be trusted … wit rather than humour … restless and loved travelling.

So far as one can judge, this about sums up Arthur Hugh, but it is actually a description of his mother.[102] He was single-minded, stubborn, unimaginative—in the phrase of Cork nationalist MP J.C. Flynn, one of the 'unteachable landlords'.[103] That was precisely his strength. Land was a moral as well as an economic anchor. He saw himself as a good landlord; indeed, generally, so did even the likes of his bitter opponents. William O'Brien—while condemning him for his leadership of the Ponsonby 'eviction syndicate'—wrote from the hindsight of 1920 that he was 'unimpeachable in the management of his own private property'.[104] Even Canon Keller acquiesced in that judgement.[105] And family and its continuity expressed through landownership are crucial to understanding the likes of Smith Barry. The irony, of course, is that he was himself a 'tenant for life' under the terms of his father's will.[106] This coincidence of circumstance did not apparently engender any feelings of empathy with his own tenants. It also raises questions about his proclaimed connectivity with Ireland. Like many landlords, he did not invest any of his considerable personal wealth in Irish land or securities,[107] yet he did not take advantage of getting cash and a bonus free of the entail from the 1903 Land Act. The barony of 1902 was consciously a re-creation of a former peerage of the (Irish) Barry family; his English estates would have furnished an appropriate title had he so wished. He toyed with the idea of standing for the Irish Senate. And he held on to his lands to the bitter end—they were eventually compulsorily acquired under Saorstát Éireann's 1923 Land Act.[108]

Smith Barry's was an instinctive unionism. From 1886, when he spoke at meetings in Liverpool and Chester organised by the Irish Unionist Alliance's predecessor, the Irish Loyal and Patriotic Union,[109] and as chairman and vice-president of the Alliance in the early 1900s, he held firm against anything but the most modest form of Irish local self-government. Like many of his class, he was incapable of seeing Irish nationalism in transcendental terms, categorising it merely as the vehicle for the people to acquire a greater, but what he felt would be an illusory, prosperity.[110] The organic connection between land, religion and nationalism, and how each fed off and reinforced the other, seemed beyond his comprehension—in 1886 he said that 'he did not see why the land question should be mixed up with the Home Rule question',[111] and he seemed genuinely to believe that.

His attitude to the union was conditioned by landed and economic imperatives, not the other way round. If money was an issue, he could be found—on the fringes at least—in the camp of the critical. He attended the first meeting on the question of the over-taxation of Ireland held in Ireland in Cork on 12 December 1896 and convened by his friend Lord Bandon. Yet, unlike Lord Castletown, Anglican Bishop Meade, Sir George Colthurst or the unionist lord mayor Sir John Scott, Smith Barry did not speak, and later stated in a letter to the press that he was 'present merely as a spectator'. Subsequently he seems to have absented himself from the landlord convention on 28 January 1897, where many unionists denounced the burden of excessive taxation. This seems uncharacteristic, but at that stage he may not have wished to jeopardise the chances of a peerage by openly supporting reform.

Along with others such as Lords Dunraven and Castletown, he was prepared to offer some support to William O'Brien's All-for-Ireland League.[112] This may have been tactical: when one of the O'Brienites, Moreton Frewen, wanted to resign as MP in 1911, Barrymore was reported as saying that 'we in Cork no longer interest ourselves in O'Brien and his Party and … we shall take no trouble to register our people and without our support O'Brien has no future'.[113] In 1909, with the peerage safely under his belt, he even shared a platform with O'Brien—each had serious concerns about the Liberal government's forthcoming Land Act.[114] In 1914 he joined with O'Brien and Lord Dunraven in a recruiting campaign.[115] Two years earlier, with Home Rule much closer, his recognition of the political realities had seen a softening of tone. At a meeting of the unionists of Munster on 20 April 1912 to protest against the third Home Rule Bill, it was painfully obvious how these now-isolated remnants of the gentry class tiptoed around the religious and ethnic issue—as Barrymore put it, 'They did not speak there in the same loud and plain tones that their friends in Ulster did'. Even the type of language being utilised by northern and southern Protestants was on a markedly divergent course by 1912. Couched in quasi-religious terminology, the verbal imagery of the North was of the unstoppable collective will, with phrases such as 'intensely earnest in their advocacy of a righteous cause', 'determined not to be deprived of their Imperial birthright' and so on.[116] The southern discourse was that of 'soft power', if it was speaking of any power at all. At the Munster meeting—perhaps reflecting Barrymore's utilitarian stance—virtually all the local speakers concentrated on the damage to the country's finances and economy that they felt the Bill would inflict. This line was continued in a speech to the Irish Landowners' Convention in Dublin in 1913, when Barrymore, it was reported, excoriated Home Rule, but principally because a Home Rule parliament's first port of call for tax would be the land.[117]

Barrymore's penultimate speech in parliament in 1913 was on the Home Rule Bill, at last recognising the inevitability of its passage. 'We have done all that we can', he said. 'We in the South cannot say we will not have Home Rule, because we are in a considerable minority, and if Home Rule is forced upon us we shall have to bow under it and get on as best we can.' But he ended on a note of hope: 'I myself am not so much afraid of Protestants as such being trampled upon in the South as are many of my friends in Ireland'.[118] It should be noted, though, that while in the aftermath of his comprehensive victory in the Plan of Campaign in 1891 he had leased out his principal English residence, he took back the lease on the death of the lessee in 1914, coinciding with the passage of the Home Rule Act. It was a typical Barrymore insurance policy.[119] Ultimately, he was always an unreconstructed unionist.

Barrymore saw a place for the landlord even after the dispossession of the 1903 Land Act. In 1907 he set out in a typical tone of utilitarian superiority the purpose of the gentry in the new dispensation:

> And, I venture to submit, it would be a very great misfortune to the country generally, because I do not suppose that anybody wants to drive out of the country landlords who are living in the country, who are spending their money there, who are working at their farms, and so forth, because those farms are probably the best cultivated farms in their neighbourhood; they set a good example to their neighbours, they probably employ a good deal more labour than an ordinary tenant-farmer does, the cottages and buildings are generally in very good order; and I think it would be a very great misfortune to the country if men of that kind—and there are a great many of them—ceased to exist.[120]

But managing his land in Ireland was not entirely the same as managing it in England. In his pseudo-autobiographical novel *My Tower in Desmond*, S.R. Lysaght encapsulated the differences in attitude between the English and Irish landed classes. Writing of an English gentry house, he remarked that 'every detail of the place spoke of something that had to be paid for, instead of, as with us, something that had to be made to pay'.[121] This was perhaps a revealing exposition of the two somewhat opaque cultural worlds which Smith Barry had to straddle.

Competent management, though, was not enough. By the early 1900s it was far too late for this to produce any significant dividend—economic, cultural or political. The point about the Irish landed gentry, as William O'Brien said as early as 1887, was that it had missed its opportunity to become relevant.[122] In 1908 Sir Horace Plunkett was realistic: 'we have failed … so to identify ourselves with the national life as to establish our influence upon the only sure foundation—popular goodwill'.[123] More telling, perhaps, was his recognition that defining 'national life' was the prerogative of the other side. Nevertheless, some of the gentry themselves seemed to think that they still held societal place; in 1915 Barrymore wrote about arriving at his own 'Tower in Desmond':

> It was during the summer of 1847 [he was four years old] that I paid my first visit to Fota: my mother and I ... arrived in the boat from Bristol to Cork; my father met us with a six oared gig at Passage and we landed at the Tower [the point at Fota where guests could arrive by sea] and we were dragged by the labourers up to the house, fifty five years later the grandsons of these men dragged my wife and daughter and myself upon the same journey when King Edward had conferred a peerage upon me at his coronation.[124]

Here was the belief in an unchanging sense of deference over half a century. It perhaps points up a certain lack of reality—apparently he could not envision that perhaps the grandsons of 1902 were almost certainly actors. It suited their Edwardian self-interest to dissemble; it did not mean that they believed in what they did. In that, Barrymore's tale was an illusion, a delusion.

Landlords and their associated society crumbled in slow motion from 1880 to 1920. In effect, landlord*ism* was finished off by its inutility and economic redundancy; land*lords* became irrelevant because of their politics, their religion and their cultural distance. At the last, once land had been exchanged for land bonds, perhaps the Irish landed gentry (though not, it must be said, Arthur Hugh Smith Barry) were left with no real purpose other than Goldwin Smith's 'pleasure'.

II

EXPLAINING THE SOUTHERN IRISH PROTESTANT

5

SOUTHERN IRISH PROTESTANTISM: A PERSPECTIVE ON HISTORICAL PROCESS[1]

I

Over sixty years ago Oliver MacDonagh enunciated a precept for historians that to this writer represents a yardstick against which the competence of a historian in his craft can still be well measured:[2]

> the more highly articulate, the more firmly established, an historical concept, the more are historians conscious of its inadequacy ... Willy-nilly, every corner of the subject is inhabited by concepts, and the less the historian is aware of their presence in his mind ... the more powerful are they likely to be ... in leading him astray.

If 'concept' is the static mode, 'process' is the dynamic by which historians interpret and analyse historical phenomena. The object of a historian's interest is often selected—consciously or subconsciously—by the perceived strength of the processes upon which it is deemed to rest, yet imposing them on any given set of historical events is not always as easy or as virtuous or as self-evidently useful as it may at first glance appear. With MacDonagh's maxim in mind, then, this essay sets out some general reflections on historical process, its significance and how it is perceived, using the historical phenomenon known as 'southern Irish Protestantism' as illustration and exemplar.

> Every historian must have a thesis, some principle of illumination to guide him, and the value of his work will largely depend upon the sanity and profundity of that thesis.[3]

Self-evident, perhaps, but its essence is that any definition of such thesis, or 'historical process', is ultimately subjective. For this writer it is the means by which a series of interconnected actions or changes, consequent upon one another in time, can be demonstrated to have a coherent and logical pattern. It is important to note that process can be defined as exogenous or endogenous—that is to say, process is created directly and externally by an observer or internally by the very strength of the historical substructure itself.

Process of the first kind is generally more likely to be imposed on broad overviews of history where the data being analysed are often widely separated in time and space. A parallel in the scientific sphere is perhaps the application of mathematical formulae to the movement of galaxies within the universe. In both these cases, the historical and the mathematical, an imputation of process and pattern is as much a leap of informed imagination, of an essentially artistic endeavour, as the application of near-certainties. Process of the second kind is best demonstrated by the specialist study, the examination of small stretches of time and space: the differential calculus of history. Process as an understood matrix often fits more tightly over such studies. The interconnections between data are more easily comprehended by the mind's eye, and the internal buttresses to the structure are therefore often all the stronger.

The fashions of the age also impinge to some lesser or greater degree on the perception of historical process. It may be a commonplace to say that historians are no less indifferent to the contemporary cultural mores than are painters, philosophers, scientists or politicians. Nor, indeed, should they be. Integrity, though, demands that any such influences should be declared, made transparent. As historians find that as the processes they are trying to uncover become complex and intertwined, as the distances between event signposts become greater, they are forced back on leaping, chamois-like, from concept to concept. If their intellectual footing is sure and the bedrock of their source material secure, they will succeed. If not, they may be tempted to use the current socio-political perceptions of the age as a bridge and perhaps their own moral stances as a handrail. Historical analyses of such type, from Carlyle to Churchill, when carried to extremes may be eloquent and entertaining, and may even by such virtue acquire a status independent of their intrinsic historical worth, but they are little more than a polemical wolf in a historical sheep's clothing. Their constructions may be superior, their motives frequently ulterior.

There is, of course, a balance to be considered. 'Letting the facts speak for themselves' is the antithesis of process. In its own extreme, it is no more than an anarchy. It need hardly be said that historians can never possess perfect knowledge about any subject, no matter how small-scale or circumscribed. They have to sift, to edit, to extrapolate: they have to judge. It is the relative extent to which they impose that judgement that is of concern. This does not mean that they should let an inevitability of gradualness sweep them along on a gentle wave of predestined certainties. If they do, their historical writing loses its capacity to surprise, and its passion—and passion, if sometimes painful, is uplifting and educative. A completely neutered historian is of little use to anyone.

Besides political polemic and intellectual fashion, literary form also acts as an obfuscator to a determination of historical process and the perception of its validity. A debate is still in progress about the proper relationship, if any, between history and literature.[4] The arguments cover two interrelated problems. The first concerns the nature of historical writing itself: 'the historical text as literary artefact'.[5] In the pre-Romantic words of Thomas Arnold in 1842, 'the mere language of the historian'[6] must be of concern to the reader. The writers of history must be aware that the historical aspects of any writing will often suffer under the burden of literary intent and construction, and that literature, being art, is naturally freer of the conventional boundaries of verifiable fact and opinion which are the stuff of the workaday historian. Yet history that is engrained into the artifice of literature often lifts itself above almost unforgivable structures of process and image. Truly, the form of the medium becomes the message, and the imposition of process itself becomes a process of literary challenge. 'For all that fair is, is by nature good' is always an insidious danger to be recognised, even if it cannot be avoided.

The second question centres on the uses to which the historian may put literary (or, at least, non-evidential) sources. This is a large matter which cannot be dealt with in detail here. Suffice it to make the point that, while 'the imaginative writer can be read as a fellow-historian who shares the commitment to putting some pattern on the chaos of human experiences, and to presenting that pattern in a meaningful and persuasive manner', it is also 'hard for the novelist to disengage himself from problems generic to his calling, and more narrowly, peculiar to himself ... the change over from invention to analysis is not easily made'.[7] And, as seen below, the filtration of historical process through literary form creates its own limitations.

The successful validation of any given historical process is dependent on the satisfaction of certain criteria. The historical phenomena under examination must be sequential in time; must be closely integrated within a contiguous space–time continuum; must be internally consistent; and, most importantly, must be consistent within a larger whole. The significance of these last two cannot really be overestimated. Demonstrating, for instance, that the 1878 Irish Intermediate Education Act was flawed in its internal consequences for the Irish education system must be reconciled convincingly with the extraordinary increase in academic and literary achievement in the country beyond the 1890s.[8]

II

Within a broad framework of Irish history, it is proper to ask whether 'southern Irish Protestantism' is perceived to be a coherent and important phenomenon. The answer must be a somewhat qualified 'yes': a 1989 survey of Irish history, for instance, while displaying an extensive awareness of the place of religion, lists two references to 'sodomy' in its index but none to 'southern Protestantism'.[9] There is a substantial literature on aspects of the Protestant community in Ireland, ranging from P. Buckland's *Irish Unionism 1* (1972), through J. White's *Minority Report* (1975) and D.H. Akenson's *Small Differences* (1988) to modern works by Heather Crawford, Robin Bury, Deirdre Nuttall and David Jameson. J.C. Beckett's *The Anglo-Irish Tradition* (1976) was perhaps the best attempt at a comprehensive overview, but it was marred by a polemical tone. A balanced synthesis which embraces the cultural and psychological as well as the social, political and economic is still awaited. Meanwhile, what we have are partial glimpses, tantalising insights, elements of processes not yet fully articulated.

I think that the apparent lacuna is explicable. The term 'southern Irish Protestant' encompasses an animal with geographical, crypto-cultural and religious characteristics that are peculiarly difficult to express within a coherent unity. This difficulty is compounded by another. Southern Protestantism's political importance, except to itself, was ephemeral. It had little separate political identity per se for at least twenty years before the end of the Union, and none after. It is currently seen primarily in cultural terms as the rejected womb of deviant nationalists, and politically in terms of its see-saw self-important/self-debasement-like role in the period from the Devolution débâcle in 1904–5 to the Irish Convention of 1917–18 and the supplicant visit of Archbishop Bernard to Michael Collins in May 1922. This latter vision is both shaming and potent, evoking contempt rather than pathos at Bernard's asking 'to be informed if they were to be permitted to live in Ireland or if it was desired that they should leave the country'.[10] And so any historical coherence which southern Protestantism was deemed to have possessed tends to be projected backwards and forwards from this period. This has given it a sort of glaciated preservation, inimical indeed to the idea of process, and needing an intellectual blowlamp to unfreeze it.

This treatment (or, rather, non-treatment) begs the question: do southern Irish Protestants offer a legitimate, self-defined group upon which the analysis of process can properly be placed? After all, the definition of the group is itself an articulation of the process of choice. But with that caution in mind, I think it does. It is now generally accepted that in nineteenth-century Ireland, as well as purely spiritual beliefs, one's Protestantism or Catholicism determined one's fundamental social, cultural, political, economic and social attitudes. Religion was 'that fixed point of Irish identity', 'that confessional divide that remained the structural reality of Irish politics'.[11] Neither is the geographical delimitation arbitrary nor inconsequent: north and south quickly determine their differences early in the nineteenth century. With the first religious censuses in the 1830s, a special sense of physical minority amongst Protestants in the areas outside Ulster and Dublin rapidly and pervasively establishes itself.[12] North–south tensions within Irish Protestantism arose long before their apotheosis in the Buckingham Palace conference and the Irish Convention. For example, the initial meetings to formulate a constitution for the newly disestablished Church of Ireland reveal a geographical and ecclesiological divide already well-worn and well understood.[13]

A spatial framework is easier to define than a temporal. 'There is no road without an end', proclaimed Oliver MacDonagh;[14] the problem with southern Irish Protestantism is that the road is still under construction, its route not generally agreed upon. But whatever about the end-point, a clear starting-point can be readily justified. The Act of Union cannot be gainsaid as a major turning-point, the fulcrum about which Irish historical passions and contemporary politics revolved (revolves?), 'the thing to be for or against, the simple reason for everything'.[15] The selection of the end-point, though, is a major determinant of the outcome of process. Historians should possess an internal image of where the process is leading to, even though they may be extremely professional in disguising the fact. The historiographical problem is that the end-point selects the historical perspective, and ultimately the process described is determined by start and finish. As Roy Foster expresses it, 'this runs the risk of reading the story backwards—over the shoulder, in a sense'.[16] That this is no academic shibboleth is shown below. There must be some explanation why expert observers, examining broadly the same evidence, differ so strongly about southern Protestantism's present and future, which are derived from its past. To take two extremes: Jim Beckett saw present-day southern Protestants 'dwindling, in all appearance, towards a painless extinction', while Desmond Bowen asserted that 'the prospects for Protestant survival seem much brighter than at any time since 1922'.[17]

What follows, then, is a personal perspective on how historical process in relation to southern Irish Protestantism has been observed and analysed by certain influential historians of Ireland in the period to 1990. Modern historical and literary theorists tend, I am told, to cluster around two basic schools of thought on what history is, or should be. The 'narrative' school sees historians as consciously submitting to the inevitable organic interaction between their subject-matter and its expression. The 'scientific' school persists in its search for a structure of 'language' and 'expression' that would allow history to mirror reality.[18] Without denying or superseding the generic validity of this classification of argument, I should like to exemplarise and highlight some of the general points made concerning historical process as well as shed some light on the treatment by historians of a specific Irish historical question by identifying three broad schema of process: 'universal framework', 'grand tragedy' and 'linear reactivism'. Where individual historians are categorised this reflects my own interpretation. I apologise in advance to any who might feel misrepresented: I can only claim good faith. And the point must be made that neither individual historians nor their writings can be neatly and exclusively pigeon-holed.

'Linear reactivism' broadly reflects the narrative school. It is perhaps best defined by what it is not—a sort of historical paper-chase in which the finishing line is who did what, and how and to whom. From the historian handling this process is required a highly developed sense of almost agricultural continuity—the logical ordering of carts and horses, chickens and eggs. Culture, and religion in particular, seems acutely sensitive to reactive changes in the historical temperature. Let us take one example. Desmond Bowen, in his *The Protestant Crusade in Ireland* (1979), posits a period of intense religious activity amongst Protestants started by the Anglican archbishop of Dublin in 1822, with his launch of a 'second reformation'. This is in many ways a reaction to a season of unrelieved pressures on the 'Protestant' cause, ranging from Catholic Emancipation through the tithe wars and the dismantling of the municipal corporations to the ultimate disaster (for Protestants as well as Catholics) of the Famine. Bowen sees, in turn, an ultramontane victory as the direct result of the 'second reformation', and, by a leap of pure imagination, the present-day 'acceptance by Protestants of the need for them to live quietly and passively in their dying culture'.[19]

If the process is applied to the generation beyond 1870, however, a different view of southern Protestantism begins to emerge—somewhat less timid, more aggressive. In the economic sphere it is observed in the relatively robust landlord reaction to the land war from 1879; in the political sphere it seems, on the surface, to lead to Buckland's and Beckett's era of 'confidence'. But in truth morale amongst the unionists was shattered long before 1914, and a much more convincing case can be made for seeing a process of 'confident opposition'[20] in the considerable Protestant input to the cultural revival between 1890 and 1916. D.G. Boyce applies a reactivist process insofar as he perceives Yeats, Hyde *et al.* turning to culture as essentially a reaction to being forced political eunuchs. In the Ireland of the 1890s that was the only course open to them if (as Terry Eagleton contends) they felt that their rightful place was at the head of the nation. They had, in effect, to create a nation, or at least a definition of nationality, that would reconcile their need to express their Irishness with 'their true position as leaders rather than men'. These 'rogue sons of the Ascendancy' were, it has been suggested, well aware of what they were about: emphatically, they were not 'innocently' opening 'a Pandora's Box'.[21]

Boyce suggests that this attempt at a cultural putsch failed because of an internal paradox: 'the very self-consciousness that Yeats and Hyde sought to provoke only heightened and increased the existing sectarian and political divisions in Ireland ... Irish society was too divided on sectarian lines to enable any Protestant, however talented or committed, to enter the experience of the other side'.[22] And Yeats and his friends were having a similar effect on Protestants, moving cultural Irishness away from an indifferent acceptability to them in the 1880s and 1890s. This assertion of the primordial nature of the sectarian divide casts the Protestant culturalists as refugees making their way to the boundaries of the divide, carrying their pre-Christian Celticism on their backs, only to find themselves turned back at the frontier, with the added indignity of suffering the wholesale confiscation of their intellectual and artistic baggage, which is bowdlerised and vulgarised out of all recognition. The reactive process repeats itself. Yeats, in particular, trudges back to the relatively barren wastes of southern Protestantism and takes up with the remnants of the ex-unionists, only because, 'as a confirmed outsider, he knew a minority when he saw one'. And through the medium of the *Irish Statesman*, George Russell, Yeats, Plunkett and other like minds fight a rearguard action through the 1920s against 'the concept of society that would prevail, the criteria of liberty … that alone would be acceptable … defined by Catholic and nationalist values'.[23]

From the 1930s to the 1960s the reactive process ceases to have any real meaning, simply because the Protestants, in the main, refused to react—not so much Edna Longley's 'elaborate quadrille' as William Trevor's seedy 'ballroom of romance' in which one partner voluntarily remained a wallflower.[24] A sort of paradoxical confusion was working itself out, grounded in southern Protestants' increasing sense of numerical minority. From the early 1800s they were coming to terms with this perception. On one level they were (with a few exceptions in the Dublin and Ulster border areas), and knew they were, in a permanent minority. The psychological compensation for this was a retreat into their own sectarian voluntarist groups—the Bible societies, the Orange Order, Freemasonry, the Protestant Operative Associations, the Primrose League and so on.[25] 'Nationalist and Unionist Ireland confronted each other, politically speaking, from positions of monolithic security; competition was unnecessary.'[26] On another level, however, southern Protestants were still part of a larger United Kingdom majority; they were, to that extent, not strangers in their own country. But the cascading effect of the land war, Parnellism and, above all, the cultural revival created a tangible notion of the separateness of Ireland, an Ireland that looked on them 'as illegitimate children of an irregular union between Hibernia and John Bull'[27] and inexplicably demanded their inclusion within and exclusion from the nation at one and the same time. This was the real reason for their 'identity crisis'. Bad verse from a County Clare unionist in 1907 captures the bewilderment:[28]

I am only a poor West Briton
And not of the Irish best;
But I love the land of Erin
As much as all the rest.
As much as all the noisy,
The rampant, roaring tribe,
Who scoff at our glorious Empire
And cavil, and carp, and jibe.

If a point has to be determined at which southern Protestants in their hearts recognised the disintegration of the United Kingdom as a politico-cultural unity, it was in 1885, marked by the foundation of the Irish Loyal and Patriotic Union. A replacement, though, was at hand for the UK level, which has, perhaps, obscured the significance of this fundamental change. From at least the 1880s, 'our glorious Empire' was the natural focus for many southern Protestants, offering an escape, physical and metaphysical, from a suffocating and inward-looking Ireland. Independence hardly disturbed southern Protestants from the acquired faculty of living on two levels, although the levels themselves may have altered in character. There was nothing new in this. As exemplified by the history of Cork city Protestants from the 1890s, they were already conscious of their minority status, careful of openly antagonising their Catholic/nationalist neighbours, and ultimately pragmatic in their treatment of the British connection.[29] Yet 'if southern Protestant spokesmen had indeed been at pains since 1922 to stress their happiness with the non-discriminatory nature of the Free State', this sometimes was only a thin veneer. Beneath the surface 'private opinion still hankered after the old days'.[30] This echo of a 'Sinn Féin' philosophy allowed southern Protestants after 1922 to defend what, before, had been the indefensible—their economic position, their social superiority and, above all, their educational advantages. The successful defence of these primary interests required that Protestants should neither provoke nor be provoked. This is how they moved to the 1970s accommodation with such relative success, and why, as an instance, Yeats's incendiary and provocative 'we *against whom you have done this thing* [my italics] are no petty people' in 1925 was greeted with such horror on the Protestant side.[31]

The scope of the 'grand tragedians' could hardly be further removed from a scenario of realistic reactivism. Their process of 'grand tragedy' is Russian in its gloomy pessimism. It is intense, predeterministic, emotional, inevitable: the introverted integrity of a lost cause—Protestants (and Catholics) 'caught inextricably in the web of their tragic history'.[32] It is perhaps fitting that one of the most influential modern initiators of this school of process was not a historian. Elizabeth Bowen's *Bowen's Court* is a historically subversive book, in the sense that its greatest effect is subliminal. Here, indeed, is a 'meaningful and persuasive' pattern; yet buried beneath a carefully sculpted piece of historical literature is an 'autobiography', a polemic of personal explanation in which the individual, the family, the ancestral home become almost of one substance, in both time and space. The emotional balance sheet is cumulative, not brought to account in each generation, and the emotional capital at the end is correspondingly and misleadingly large.

'Grand tragedy' as process is always unstable. It requires in the Irish context the literary artifice of an Elizabeth Bowen, a William Trevor, a Jennifer Johnston to sustain it. It also needs characters that are somehow larger than life. In the context of southern Irish Protestantism it is a process tailor-made to fit around the landed classes. This works, as

Mark Bence-Jones has shown.[33] The trouble is that others have quite deliberately attempted to apply the process to the generality of southern Protestants, and here it begins to break down. Even if the landed classes 'may be regarded as spokesmen for the whole body of the Anglo-Irish', they were increasingly out of touch with the wider constituency which they professed to represent.[34] To take an example: as early as 1881 over half of the Protestant community in County Cork was effectively urban and suburban. Its principal concerns, political and economic, were correspondingly different from (and sometimes inimical to) the gentry's. Cork city Protestantism from the 1880s to the 1920s exhibits freshness, vitality and innovation: above all, a willingness to adapt.[35] On the other hand, landed society in the nineteenth century had become brittle and vacuous: 'it could exist in detail—comings-and-goings, entertainments, marriages—but the main healthy abstract was gone'.[36] It is much less true to ascribe this 'death of the heart' to urban Protestantism of the same vintage.

'Grand tragedy' lends itself to the graphic image to make its point. It is no coincidence, moreover, that its dominant metaphor—dusk, twilight—springs from the natural rather than the man-made world. The use of twilight as an image, in the remote sense, may have developed from the identification, in romantic imagery, of the land with light and shade, a notion itself derived from nineteenth-century English romanticism. The image of twilight has, if anything, become more pervasive. Jack White used it in passing in 1975. F.S.L. Lyons aimed it at a predominantly academic audience in 1983. Mark Bence-Jones has it in the title of his popular work published in 1987. Perhaps in an interpretation unintended by its protagonists, 'twilight' *is* an appropriate metaphor—but simply as transition from one state to another, not necessarily as a slide towards darkness.

An image used more potently is that of the Protestant community as garrison. Best sustained by Beckett, it suits the process of 'grand tragedy':

> They [the Irish Protestants] had no power to come to terms on their own behalf; but they lived in constant fear that terms would be arranged behind their backs; that a vital out-work might suddenly be surrendered; and even that, sooner or later, the whole fortress would be abandoned and they themselves left to their fate.[37]

The garrison, of course, is not just metaphor: it was reality. Any red-blooded northern Protestant would have the image of Londonderry in 1689 before him. And it is therefore predominantly an image comprehensible largely to northerners. It is surely no coincidence that Bandon, which fulfilled the garrison role and actually became a significant refuge for Protestants fleeing from violent rural agitation in the early 1820s, was the most Orange of southern towns.[38]

We can presume that Elizabeth Bowen must have read Somerville & Ross. If so, a key is offered to how the process of 'grand tragedy' may be validated. Like *Bowen's Court*, *The Real Charlotte* (1894) and *The Big House of Inver* (1925) work because, ultimately, they deal with timeless human traits: greed, hubris, lust, envy, self-sacrifice. There may be specifics of time and place helping the process of inevitable tragedy on its way—Elizabeth Bowen's personalising of the Big House, especially in *The Last September*, where those who fire it are its 'executioners', is a prime example—but the essence of the process is universal, innate and endogenous. The rot, if rot it is, sets in from within.[39]

On the other hand, those 'tragedians' who see the predicament of southern Irish Protestants as unique and specific, not universal, soon run into difficulties. A significant symptom is that there is little real agreement on where the process either starts or finishes. Bence-Jones sees the decline starting in the 1870s and not yet ended. Lyons put the starting-point variously at 1865 and 1903. Beckett maintained that decline began soon after the Union, while Jack White chose the period between Queen Victoria's

Diamond Jubilee in 1897 and 1914, when Protestants 'began to feel and show a lack of confidence in their own identity', with the Great War as the final *coup de grâce*.[40] Patrick Buckland's *Irish Unionism 1* typifies the problems of attributing the tragic process to the specific. He postulated a clear downward-spiralling process to southern unionism (note—not to the landed classes alone) from 'confident opposition' in the 1880s to 'the end' in 1922. But as has been pointed out by Ronan Fanning, Buckland was 'a victim of his own methodology'.[41] In other words, in the 'failure' of southern Protestantism was incubated its very success. If it had tried to maintain a too-distinct political identity its economic and social integration with the new state might have been considerably more painful than it actually was. It should be remembered that those who really could not bear the change of regime had left by the end of the 1920s; those who remained were freed from an albatross of history. 'Acquiescence seemed the only course open to them; and they adjusted themselves to the new conditions more quickly and with less difficulty than might have been expected.' This is J.C. Beckett on the Anglo-Irish, but although he is writing here about the Protestant anti-unionists after 1801, it is significant that the comment is just as appropriate to the position of the post-1921 Protestants.[42] If they could resurface, regroup, readapt after 1801, 1829, 1841 and 1869, why not after 1921?

The 'frameworkers', who comprise my third categorisation, go some way towards answering that question. Process as 'framework' falls into the structuralist school of history. It can be defined as a conceptual matrix which, if placed over any specific event or series of events, explains them within the context of the matrix's own logic. The problem with 'framework' is thus its potential for circularity, though it need not be. The sole criterion of any framework's success is its universal validity. And as the most developed frameworks tend to be in the possession of individual historians, an analysis on that basis is appropriate.

K.T. Hoppen offers 'patterns of change and continuity' in which the predominant are those of continuity. He explicitly rejects linear reactivism, especially that of the 'Whig view of history'. Hoppen's framework is one of 'fragmented localism' as 'normalcy' in Irish political and social life; only during relatively brief episodes like the land war and the revolutionary period of 1918–21 was this state transcended. Hoppen here is applying to nineteenth-century Irish history a sociological concept developed for the twentieth.[43] This is an implicit rejection of Buckland's point that 'Irish society had ceased to be localised' by the beginning of the twentieth century. Hoppen suggests a much closer integration of Protestant and Catholic life, especially in the towns, than has generally been hitherto accepted. The polity is seen as small-scale, mutually parasitic: Protestants and Catholics represent 'two sides of the same coin'.[44] Once again the acid test is where is southern Protestantism now? If one accepts Kurt Bowen's and Jack White's view of an increasingly integrated, largely urbanised society, then the localist framework offers a clear path towards it. (Incidentally, it is somewhat confirmed in the negative. In Northern Ireland the 'normalcy' of politics is not localism, and the results, in terms of an integrated society, are plain to see.)

Hoppen's framework is spatially determined; a behavioural framework of the collective psyche is on a different plane. Roy Foster (1988) and Donald Akenson (1988) have both articulated a reductive, syllogistic species of framework. Akenson in particular brings a keen iconoclasm to the question of the primary divide in Irish society. And it is interesting to note that, while he cannot find much to differentiate them, he comes to the conclusion, as most historians have, that the divide is ultimately one of Protestants and Catholics. His framework is the self-contained nature of the Protestant and Catholic cultures:

> ... systems of conceptualization and attitude that have explained with remarkable efficiency to the Irish Catholic and Irish Protestant how the world operates and what the right thing to do is in any given situation.

To each side, the opposition was 'simply "the others", whose world lay alongside ours but never touched'.[45]

Such a process represents an ordered, mutually exclusive *weltgeschichte*, the antithesis of Lyons's cultural anarchy. Protestants and Catholics adopt 'a psychological syllogism that ... covers all the possibilities: in politics and nationality it allows both sides to be religiously exclusive, while at the same time pretending not to be'. Foster has similarly identified the phenomenon: 'an Irish habit of historical-political argument ... the effort to negate an opposing case by claiming that an event (1641, 1691, 1798, 1801) should not have happened, was thus in a sense illegitimate and could therefore be discounted'. Akenson's process is self-sustaining, once it has been kick-started. As one side learned that the other was acting in a wrong (i.e. 'profane') manner, that side's worldview was somehow confirmed. That was comforting. This led to another contradictory attitude in the political sphere: contests, in the sense of winning, in the end did not matter, and often to the minority near-victories uplifted morale more than did near-defeats. Akenson also manages to mould the 'localist' framework into his own by, first, downgrading localism's significance relative to the conceptual differences between Protestants and Catholics, and secondly by emphasising their ability to co-operate on 'small matters' by the very strengths of their respective belief systems.[46]

Oliver MacDonagh's cross-dimensional framework is scrupulously defined within, and confined to, the landed classes. He interprets the processes of the gentry's history in the nineteenth century through the opaque glass of literature, which he sees as having its own evidential integrity. The gentry, according to MacDonagh, withdraw from 'time' to 'place' over the century, with 'place' increasingly seen in sectarian terms. This is an echo of Lionel Fleming, writing about his childhood before the Great War: 'Nothing counted for about three miles on any side of us, because there were no Protestants until then'.[47] In the same way, Elizabeth Bowen's universality sees the Big Houses as islands or ships at sea.[48]

MacDonagh's thesis that 'the physical precincts were now central to identity', though grounded in many ways in the novels of Maria Edgeworth, William Carleton and especially Somerville & Ross, is corroborated by the political world of Hoppen's localism. Functionally, like the Cheshire Cat, the gentry appear to fade away from the mid-nineteenth century. Like the Cat's grin, however, they are still there, but already in another dimension. Here, in the introverted Lilliputian worlds of *The Irish R.M.* and *The Real Charlotte*, the landed classes weave Bence-Jones's social filigree and indulge amongst themselves in a variant of Freud's 'narcissism of small differences'.[49]

III

History, as a script of the past, can be said to derive from folk memory, literature—and the work of historians themselves. Therefore, if they are to offer anything, the historians have to challenge the versions of previous historians, to test their theories, to measure the adequacy of their sources and to make a critique of their conclusions. This is the historian's craft. It is why 'revisionism' is an essential precondition for a vibrant and useful historiography. Yet it is often surprising how little understood this fundamental principle is. An extraordinary claim was made in 1983 that 'the time has now come when the role of the Anglo-Irish is a question which needs no further attention as such'[50]—a parochial iteration of the 'end of history' concept so favoured by commentators after the collapse of communism in Europe after 1989. Not for that historian Oliver MacDonagh's dictum set out at the head of this essay. If proof be needed, however, of the unwisdom of asserting that the last word has been written, since 1983 numerous major works have appeared offering new interpretations of and fresh insights into the Anglo-Irish specifically and southern Irish Protestantism generally.[51] There is at least one reason why it is certain that 'further attention' will indeed continue to be paid to this topic: I cannot find any consensus in identifying historical processes that will comprehensively explain the course of Irish Protestantism over the period from 1801 to the 1980s. There is yet work to be done, though whether, by definition, it can come from Irish historians of Ireland is a moot point. These historians themselves locate the primal divide in Irish life as the sectarian, but they cannot claim to be *sui generis*. They themselves form part of the very processes they purport to articulate. Is it a coincidence that those who have treated of southern Protestantism extensively (including this writer, it must be said) come mainly from that Protestant tradition?

Whether we like it or not, we stitch ourselves into the very process of explanation.

I inferred at the beginning of this essay that historians must be aware of the effect of contemporary mores upon their work. The process operates, of course, in two directions. Politicians often argue a contemporary case by reference to the perceived past. Would the Franco-British reaction to Suez in 1956 have been the same if it could not have been 'justified' by reference to the failure of appeasement and the image of Munich? In Ireland, political memory is a mighty oak: that is to say, the living generation carries within it concentric rings of historical remembrance, each built upon the other. Past and present achieve a conflation into an immediacy almost independent of time. This has an important consequence for historians. It puts them in a potentially powerful position, in theory, to influence contemporary political development.

I say 'in theory' for it seems not to have been realised in practice. This is perhaps best illustrated by the outcome of the New Ireland Forum—that attempt in 1983–4, initiated by Dr Garrett FitzGerald, to achieve a consensus amongst all-island nationalist politicians on the 'problem' of Northern Ireland. In the modern Irish context, the Forum offered a moment at which the interface between history and contemporary politics might have been most significant: a point at which processes relevant to the Forum's deliberations, and identified by historians, might have figured in its conclusions. Yet nothing of the sort happened. The dog did not bark in the night: there was no dog. Three decades peculiarly rich in the research and interpretation of Irish history seem to have passed the politicians completely by.

Why? If there is one thread running (as we have seen) through recent Irish historiography, it is the significance of the sectarian divide within Irish society. Historians may differ on its effects; most recognise its structural primacy. The Forum Report—the nearest we possess to an 'official' history of modern Ireland—wilfully denies either its historical importance or, indeed, its conceptual validity, thus, by default, and with excruciating exquisiteness, throwing the epitome of *petits bourgeois* politicians into the arms of the small Marxist school of Irish history. Maybe those same politicians cannot be blamed if the historians did not turn up on the night. Of the 317 written submissions to the Forum, only two were from professional historians; of the thirty-five individuals who were invited to present orally, again only two were historians.[52] As a result, there was little exploration of a central and crucial issue in the current debate about Northern Ireland: the processes by which southern Irish Protestantism had reached its current status in the Republic (and the lessons which might be learned therefrom). There was no real examination of the Protestant–Catholic problem in Northern Ireland within its wider, all-Ireland and historical contexts. Perhaps the historians were uninterested. Perhaps they were arrogant enough to assume the self-evident nature of their conclusions. Perhaps they simply did not want to become involved. In Ireland, making a historical point can often be misconstrued; and process, ultimately, has often been a delicate phial of nitro-glycerine, lethal if mishandled.[53]

6

THE BORROWERS: SOUTHERN IRISH PROTESTANT WRITERS, CULTURAL APPROPRIATION … AND PURGATORY[1]

In the summer of 1928, poet Louis MacNeice suggested to writer John Hilton that he should write a 'Baedeker's Guide to Purgatory'.[2] It was a nice conceit—MacNeice, a son of the Irish rectory,[3] clothing a Catholic dogma in the livery of a Prussian Protestant. Protestants do not 'do' purgatory. That attractive Catholic idea of achieving sinless perfection by being tormented in some limited purgatorial way stands against the stern Protestant belief in sanctification by grace alone. Nevertheless, cultural appropriation in modern Ireland is a phenomenon well-recognised by scholars, from Declan Kiberd's 'Protholics and Cathestants' to Roy Foster's 'How the Catholics became Protestants'. So is there utility in treating religious dogma as cultural rather than theological and thus 'borrowable'? I think there is. Here, then, *my* conceit is to subject the southern Irish Protestant condition after independence to its own 'Baedeker's Guide to Purgatory', using the purgatorial elements of, first, seeking cleansing from defilement; second, bearing the burden of 'not good enough for heaven'; and, third, coping with an existence in the 'intermediate state'. I do this principally through the prism of some selected Protestant writings in the poem, the play and especially the novel.[4]

'The Romish Doctrine concerning Purgatory ... is a fond thing, vainly invented, and grounded upon no warranty of Scripture, but rather repugnant to the Word of God' is the firm Anglican rejection in the 1562 Articles of Religion. The doctrine has remained largely a nullity in Protestant consciousness; in extinguishing its imaginary flames 'we need not go far to fetch water', as the seventeenth-century Archbishop Ussher put it.[5] It is no coincidence that the same Article of Religion also proscribes indulgences and pardons. If souls could have their time in purgatory reduced or even eliminated, this implied that God could be manipulated.

In the modern period of adversarial religious tension between the 1920s and 1960s, purgatory—though a sideshow when compared to, for instance, the Anglican reaction to the declaration of the Assumption as a Catholic Article of Faith in 1950—came in for some handbagging.[6] Protestant theology has not, however, universally rejected the idea of a purgatorial state. The creeds of St Athanasius and the Apostles imply that the final entry into heaven or hell will not happen until the day of judgement, but they are silent as to where the soul resides between death and that day.[7] This leaves open the prospect of some sort of 'rest and refreshment and of closer union with Christ preliminary to the Resurrection',[8] in which imperfect individuals still need to be perfected so that they may enter the presence of God.

PURGATORY AS A PLACE OF CLEANSING

It may seem like a sort of celestial car-wash, a place where souls are douched, dried and polished, emerging spotless of sin. But sin and its taxonomy is a complicated place for the Protestant. C.S. Lewis's image of the voluntary purge, sitting in a dentist's chair saying 'I need to go through this', is excruciating, reflected in William Trevor's novel *The Story of Lucy Gault*,[9] in which personal transgression is conflated with communal burden—that of being merely Protestant, one that seemed incapable, by definition, of being remitted or mitigated or amenable to any expectation of purification. In the novel Everard and Heloise, Lucy's parents, are determined to abandon their Big House before it is burnt—but little Lucy flees and is lost, presumed dead. They go anyway and are placed by Trevor—with an echo of Diarmuid and Dervorgilla in Yeats's *The Dreaming of the Bones*[10]—in the realm of the lifeless. 'We are playing at being dead', says Everard Gault to his wife, and much later on he remarks to the found Lucy as they visit a Protestant graveyard, 'We are among our own people'.[11] Trevor inverts the sequence of sin, guilt, atonement; Everard and Heloise pay in advance by a wish-fulfilment to be burnt out for their as-yet-unknown sin against Lucy. But Trevor cannot sell them a Protestant indulgence and the Gaults are condemned to leave the house without being cleansed. Not for them Vera Kreilkamp's 'subversive sense of necessary completion'[12] in the 'hospitable furnace' of Elizabeth Bowen's burnt Danielstown in her novel *The Last September*, or in Lennox Robinson's smoking ruin of Ballydonal in his 1926 play *The Big House*.[13]

If there were to be a purgative, though, how would it be effected? It's a bit more than a dentist's drill. The fate of Danielstown and Ballydonal offers an obvious path: fire, which is the predominant cleansing agent in the Catholic image of purgatory.[14] It is also tailor-made for the fiction of the Anglo-Irish Big House and the resolution of plot, from Somerville

& Ross's *The Big House of Inver* through Bowen, Robinson and Molly Keane to J.G. Farrell's *Troubles*. And not just in the tinder-dry period around independence. It is often said that accidental fire was as destructive to these houses over the two centuries of their ascendancy—but how accidental was it?

> Was it chance or choice which brought her
> To the big house on the hill? …
>
> Each morning she'd light the only fire in the house—
> that is until I set the whole place ablaze
> with ninety-nine parts carelessness
> to one part malice aforethought.[15]

The Irish revolutionary period between 1919 and 1923 focuses the intensity of the blaze. And from the inside, from the writers who chronicle these historical burnings, the sense is one almost of longing for the cleansing fires. Even nature is complicit: in *The Last September*, 'Behind the trees, pressing in from the open and empty country like an invasion, the orange bright sky crept and smouldered'.[16] Sometimes the symbolism of guilt, atonement and sacrifice is remote and unfathomable. In Robinson's play, 'Is that why we're to be burnt?' is the English-born Mrs Alcock's cry of incomprehension at Ballydonal's destruction as reprisal for a Civil War execution far away in Dublin.[17] Kate, Mrs Alcock's feisty daughter, understands, though. From such a death comes the declaration of a new beginning, a resurrection, a reincarnation:[18] 'I believe in Ballydonal, it's my life, it's my faith, it's my country'. Likewise, Molly Keane's Aragon 'was to endure, purged by fire and rain and sun and frosts, of its evil and its ghosts, good and bad',[19] until it too could be rebuilt by a younger and refreshed generation.

It is tempting to characterise these conflagrations as a Lewisian reluctant, but necessary, purgatory. Robinson's, Bowen's and Trevor's characters offer little psychological resistance to the arsonists. And yet … even then the ultimate consuming seems insufficient to allow the desired release of the soul into the transcendental. In *Killycregs in Twilight*, a 1937 quasi-sequel to *The Big House*, Robinson, with the awful 1920s and 1930s behind him, identified the folly and impracticality of rebuilding:

> I wish we'd been burned out in the Troubles … I wouldn't have behaved like that fool-girl in the play, *The Big House*. I would never have rebuilt Killycregs. I'd have thanked God to be quit of it.[20]

Historian Oliver MacDonagh maintained that for the Anglo-Irish 'the physical precincts were … central to identity'.[21] Nevertheless, as Robinson's sour aside demonstrates, it was not always a wanted identity. If David Thomson saw life in Woodbrook as 'entire, complete in itself and concentrated',[22] the wreck of the Major in Jennifer Johnston's novel *The Gates* could only rail against *his* Big House: 'I hate it. I've always hated it.'[23] St Leger Alcock in Robinson's play is equally rejectionist: 'I'm just damned glad it's all over and there's no reason to make an effort any more'. And with a baleful watchfulness these houses police their inhabitants[24] as Elizabeth Bowen's Danielstown in *The Last September* does—'looking longest after them, like an eye, a window glittered'.[25] Iris Murdoch's Rathblane, in her '1916' novel *The Red and the Green*, has a 'formidable sinister stillness',[26] and in *The Unicorn* Gaze Castle lives up to its name with its 'staring windows'.[27]

A PLACE FOR 'THOSE NOT GOOD ENOUGH FOR HEAVEN'

If, in the 1955 words of an evangelical Dublin rector, purgatory was for the 'in-between ones' who are 'not good enough for heaven, not bad enough for hell', this surely resonated with the self-perception of the Protestant condition after 1922.[28] And the trope is a significant one in Protestant novels, plays and poems, as well as in journals like the *Irish Times*, the *Church of Ireland Gazette*, the *Irish Statesman* and the *Bell.*

A spate of nostalgic, often drippingly acerbic, unsettled Protestant memoir and chronicle appeared from the 1920s onwards from such as Tom Henn, Joan De Vere, Bindon Blood, Monk Gibbon, Frances Moffett and Annabel Davis-Goff. This was a dreary architecture of the soul, an almost zombie literature. It is Robert Tobin's 'imagery and language of extinction' and Elizabeth Grubgeld's 'sense of continuity and dissolution, influence and irrelevance, identity and nothingness'.[29] All are more or less saying the same thing: 'we are outsiders, aren't we just!' Here, in the introverted miniature worlds of *The Irish RM* and *The Real Charlotte*, most are preoccupied with lineage, economic hardship, a vanished utopian childhood and, above all, a degenerative view of history.[30] Its tone is elegiac, and it wallows in a rancid soup of grand tragedy, psychosis, regret and self-doubt, registering close to ten on the Dostoyevsky misery scale.

It is also theatre within theatre: St Leger Alcock, the owner of Ballydonal in Robinson's *Big House*, 'felt for so many years like a bad actor cast for a part far too heroic for his talents'.[31] If they were actors, though, this meant that reality could be dodged, and a dreamy unreality—or, more darkly in Louis MacNeice's formulation, 'drug-dull fatalism'[32]—is a constant in the literature from Somerville & Ross to Jennifer Johnston. Iris Murdoch in *The Unicorn*—set in a fantasy Gothic Ireland—has an ear for this stagey, repetitive *ennui*. 'Days seemed of immense length and their simple pattern already seemed … monstrous, as if the monotony were inherent and not cumulative.'[33] This was indeed the purgatory of a perpetual Protestant afternoon tea.

Their sense of unworthiness was intimately bound up with whether they felt that they belonged to the *patria*, or not. Literally and psychologically that *patria* had formerly belonged to them, but not now. Doubt is all over the writings. The houses don't escape—for instance, in Murdoch's *The Unicorn*, Gaze Castle is 'belonging yet not belonging'[34] to the landscape of which it is part. Sometimes their inhabitants didn't know whether *they* belonged or not, their status that of the Danbys in Elizabeth Bowen's *A World of Love*—'uncertain, never secure, never defined'.[35]

The French proto-fascist Catholic nationalist Charles Maurras once tried to argue that Protestants do not belong anywhere, because they are faithful not to the land and its dead but to abstract ideas. That is challenged in the empathetic words of Somerville & Ross, and why they should not be considered rootless:

> The very wind that blows softly over brown acres of bog carries perfumes and sounds that England does not know: the women digging the potato-land are talking of things that England does not understand. The question that remains is whether England will ever understand.[36]

George Russell's poem 'On Behalf of Some Irishmen not Followers of Tradition' expresses a striking sense of why the 'alien tradition' matters:

> They call us aliens, we are told,
> Because our wayward visions stray
> From that dim banner they unfold,
> The dreams of worn-out yesterday …[37]

So does John Hewitt—a northern Protestant, but no less relevant for that—in his complex poem 'Once Alien Here':[38]

> Once alien here my fathers built their house,
> claimed, drained, and gave the land the shapes of use,
> and for their urgent labour grudged no more
> than shuffled pennies from the hoarded store
> of well rubbed words that had left their overtones
> in the ripe England of the mounded downs …

Hewitt asserts that he is 'as native in my thought as any here'. But, as Russell intimates, Irish Protestants belong to 'an idea' because they are not allowed to belong to a nation. They have none but fellow souls in a conditional purgatory, trapped in a friendless and alien culture. Some did get out. Louis MacNeice thought 'of the North of Ireland as prison and the South as a land of escape'[39] but, fleeing from a literal and grim Ulster religiosity where hell-fire was a stronger image than purgatory, his poetry needed to be rooted in pleasure. That ultimately the warm, sensuous mouth of 'ripe England' gave him, not the censorious pursed lips of 1920s Ireland, north *or* south.

MacNeice, Beckett and others physically left. Was there any other way out? To seek sanctification by entering the nationalist heaven was the route adopted by some. But even ardent republicans like the Methodist Alice Milligan found the going tough in a milieu that had more than a touch of zealous 'National Catholicism' about it. As George Boyce has written, 'Irish society was too divided on sectarian lines to enable any Protestant, however talented or committed, to enter into the experience of the other side'.[40] In truth, perhaps many would have been happy to avoid calling Lionel Fleming's 'Head or Harp' at all, hoping that by some serendipitous chance the coin could always land on the edge. That was close to impossible, of course. But for most Protestants after independence in 1922 the new Irish Free State had about it an unacceptable whiff of pietistic Catholicism, irritating to their delicate nostrils. What to do? It existed, and that fact, however unpalatable, had to be dealt with.

One significant southern Irish Protestant characteristic was often to pretend an awareness of only that within its comprehension or on its wavelength. Elizabeth Bowen's training was a campaign of 'not noticing' her father's bouts of mental illness, and 'not noticing' is something that Irish Protestants are very good at. The corollary of this is that even Catholic spaces could thus be Protestantised. Andrew Chase-White in Murdoch's *The Red and the Green* feels that his family 'occupied or pervaded Ireland, managing to inhabit most of its corners'.[41] And even if there are no Protestants conveniently available, the Catholic space is often completely voided anyway. Lionel Fleming wrote of his Cork rural childhood before the Great War: 'Nothing counted for about three miles on any side of us, because there were no Protestants until then',[42] echoed in Joseph Hone's 'High on the hill behind two white gates, we were a world and a law unto ourselves'.[43]

THE INTERMEDIATE STATE

Building on this facility, Protestants in the 1920s reacted by literally creating an 'intermediate state' of their own—we might call it the 'Protestant Free State'. This was not an uncongenial purgatory. Taking as text Lennox Robinson's Kate Alcock, with her subversive and challenging 'Ireland is not more theirs than ours ... we've spent so much time sympathetically seeing theirs that we've lost sight of our own',[44] and 'expert at keeping themselves warm in cold houses',[45] it was a place in which they saw an Ireland they wanted to see, interpreting symbols and substances in a way concordant with their sense of identity. In this reading, the Free State was a constitutional monarchy. Royalists could still see the king's cyphers on postboxes while blanking out the Saorstát Éireann monograms. Likewise, the Free State passport might have had a sixpenny consular stamp in Irish but it was His Britannic Majesty who requested that the bearer pass freely. Protestant ladies insisted on curtseying to Governor-general Tim Healy. Language was used as a sort of coded freemasonry in which Dún Laoghaire was still Kingstown, Cobh Queenstown and Port Laoise Maryborough.

That parallel Protestant Ireland was bolstered by economic privilege and social exclusivity. With their own hospitals, schools, doctors, lawyers, large firms and farms, a university and churches, social and sporting organisations, Protestants could live a Protestant life and die a Protestant death without much troubling the other side. Which suited the other side, too. Whether through ignorance or design, Catholic transcendental nationalism found it difficult to comprehend an Irishness that involved notions of cultural Britishness but a strong spatial identity with their particular bit of the island. And it also encompassed political aloofness but active economic engagement; a sense of moral individualism but a tribal religiosity; and a utilitarian approach to patriotism. The historian Lecky had put it thus: 'I have never looked upon Home Rule as a question between Protestant and Catholic. It is a question between honesty and dishonesty, between loyalty and treason, between individual freedom and organised tyranny and outrage.'[46] What is memorable about Austin Clarke's poem on the 1949 funeral of Douglas Hyde, a former president of Ireland and a member of the Church of Ireland, is how he captures a rare moment of Catholic unease with that parallel Protestant universe:[47]

At the last bench
Two Catholics, the French
Ambassador and I, knelt down.
The vergers waited. Outside

> The hush of Dublin town,
> Professors of cap and gown,
> Costello, his Cabinet,
> In government cars, hiding
> Around the corner, ready
> Tall hat in hand, dreading
> *Our Father* in English. Better
> Not hear that 'which' for 'who'
> And risk eternal doom.

What emerged in the Ireland of the 1920s to the 1960s was an elaborately choreographed dance in Trevor's 'ballroom of romance'. Protestants went out of their way to avoid overclaiming the national space. When they did, as did Yeats in his 1925 Senate speech on divorce, 'We, against whom you have done this thing, *are* no petty people'—hijacking, with one provocative present tense, the sensitive Catholic ownership of 'now'—the reaction was furious from both appalled Protestants and contemptuous Catholics. Another Protestant exodus was not in the interests of either side.

Protestants avoided potential incendiary conflict by shifting their claim on Irishness away from the political and onto the religious and the moral. In 1932, on the occasion of celebrating the 1,500th anniversary of the arrival of St Patrick in Ireland, the Church of Ireland thought it could get away with a declamation of its Patrician historicity and catholicity as she 'enters upon the sixteenth century of her history'. The Anglican archbishop of Dublin was even moved to claim that the Church of Ireland was 'the most Irish thing there is in Ireland'. But it was a very particular kind of Irishness he was claiming, standing for abstract values of economic rectitude, a conservative social outlook, internationalism and moral purity. This was the painting of a *patria* in which Protestants could feel they had a legitimate place, by leapfrogging history backwards over the inconveniences of the Norman invasion, the Plantations, the Reformation and the Penal Laws.

In terms of the purgatorial, of course, southern Protestants had little idea whether this intermediate Protestant state, once they had passed through it, prefigured heaven or hell. That particular point of passage was in 1948 on the declaration of the Irish Republic. For nationalists it may have finally settled an issue of domestic politics that had festered since 1922, but it was no less significant for southern Protestants too, freeing them from an albatross of history, of having had to live with sometimes contradictory loyalties. But if they eventually came to accept a 'Republic', it was one with an extremely small 'r'—one of the Enlightenment, seeking to unite Catholic, Protestant and Dissenter in the acceptable form of another, as yet unknown, 'intermediate state'.

***

In his 1934 poem *Valediction* Louis MacNeice wrote:[48]

> The land will remain as it was,
> But no abiding content can grow out of these minds
> Fuddled with blood, always caught by blinds …

Purgatory, too, like Ireland, may be a constant; but if it exists—like Ireland—its constancy must surely be moderated by the inconstancies of the consanguine souls that populate it.

7

PROJECTING IRISH PROTESTANT SOFT POWER THROUGH ANTI-CATHOLICISM IN THE EARLY TWENTIETH CENTURY[1]

I

At the back of the now-defunct Hibernian Bible Society's shop in Dublin's Dawson Street was a section with polemical Protestant pamphlets and books. Colloquially known as the 'Hate Counter', the anti-Catholicism displayed there was so virulent that it was said that even the staff steered Catholic priests in the shop seeking to 'know thine enemy' away from it.[2] The 'Hate Counter' did not survive into the last quarter of the twentieth century. A politer public ecumenism replaced robust theological and canonical challenge with the cultural 'Protestantisation' (and increasing secularisation) of Irish Catholicism;[3] and Protestantism found itself—possibly somewhat to its surprise—with an enemy not much interested in fighting back, as Catholicism wrestled with its own demons. Anti-Catholicism for Protestants in the southern state more or less lost its purchase and they had to find alternative ways of signifying their Otherness.

In the first half of the twentieth century things were somewhat different. Protestantism in the island faced a seemingly existential threat. Northern Protestants reacted by creating a political unit that would guarantee their hard power and, they hoped, would throw a protective ring around their religion. They could also, with the confidence of numbers, loudly articulate a strongly polemical anti-papalism and anti-Catholicism that was often crude, vulgar and violent.[4] That option was not open to the scattered minority in the territory that would become the Irish Free State in 1922. Hard power had vanished well before independence; Protestants clung to the coat-tails of the British administration, basking in a rather tattered and faded glory as the 'Establishment'. In many respects, regime change merely exposed the nakedness of the minority's already politically powerless position. But if now politically neutered, no longer part of a wider United Kingdom majority, was there some substitute drug, some moral methadone that might wean them off Britishism and allow them to imagine place in the new Ireland? I suggest that a conception of 'soft power' performed that function. 'Soft power' as originally formulated by Joseph Nye[5] has traditionally been applied to State action and interaction but it has a utility that is transferable to other worlds—those of the community and the individual. The Irish revolution started by Catholic Emancipation and which got into full swing with the disestablishment of the Church of Ireland in 1871 saw the Protestant position having to move towards 'soft power' if it was to retain any influence in the new Ireland. Here it is argued that anti-Catholicism was the agency through which a vision of 'soft power' was articulated. The focus here is on how southern Protestants used it, in a context in which, in Edward Norman's phrase about the nineteenth century but still relevant to the twentieth, 'educated Protestants regarded Catholicism as inimical to the proper conduct of civil affairs and national prosperity alike'.[6]

II

What did anti-Catholicism actually mean in early twentieth-century Ireland? That wasn't always obvious: there is often a sense of building with Lego bricks that didn't quite click. Was it a perpetual retelling of the morality play that was the Reformation? An animus against the institutional Roman Church? A specifically Irish Protestant class bias against a *petit bourgeois* largely rural priesthood that seemed to revel in its ability to make its flock jump? Against papal authority? Against the irritating—to Protestants—conflation of Irish nationalism and Catholicism? Against the Catholic Church as populist trimmers—'When Rome cannot check a thing, she sanctions it'?[7] Against Mariology? Did it become an *ad hominem* and *ad feminem* aversion to Roman Catholics as individuals and communities seen as supine and subservient slaves to a sacerdotal tyranny? Ambiguities abounded. John Gregg, the alpha and omega of the Church of Ireland in the first half of the twentieth century, archbishop of Dublin from 1920 to 1938, archbishop of Armagh and primate from 1939 to 1959, was a stern and consistent anti-Romanist when it came to doctrine. Yet, according to his daughter, Gregg had 'great admiration for a magnificent institution, for the devotion of so many of its sons and daughters, for the firmness of its discipline and for the unity of its teaching'.[8] Indeed, he was not averse to a bit of Roman authoritarianism himself; for instance, in 1950, on the occasion of the promulgation of the Catholic dogma of the Assumption, he forbade his clergy from commenting and issued a rare pastoral letter more akin to a papal bull than anything else.[9]

In 1909 Gregg had established his credentials with a series of sermons on *The Primitive Faith and Roman Catholic Developments*, which remained in print for over half a century and doubtless graced the Hate Counter. It was a critical hodgepodge of the institutional Catholic Church and its doctrines and ceremonies. The first two sermons dealt with the papacy, particularly its claims to supremacy and infallibility. The third was an excoriation of 'The cult of the BVM'. Condemnation of distasteful monetary transactions was in a sermon on 'Indulgences', and dubious theology in one on 'The invocation of saints'. Gregg's final sermon was what he described as 'Our own position', and that was principally concerned with what Anglicanism was *not*—uniformity 'by stifling individual freedom of thought', 'mechanical observances', 'obedience at the expense of truth' and so on.[10] Pre-Churchillian 'blood, sweat and tears' was captured in 'We have nothing to offer you by way of purgatory to frighten you, or indulgences to smooth your path'. Even before the end of the Union it reflected a trope of standing against the odds and of presenting a moral path if the political road had a 'Do not enter' sign on it—which it did after 1922, when Protestants in the Free State found themselves beached on the wrong side of a revolution, their unionism redundant and its political expression neither possible nor prudent. Loyalism degenerated into a nostalgic royalism and a ghettoised existence in a pale and parallel entity—what we might call the 'Protestant Free State'.

Having said that, they could still exercise a form of 'hard power' in the economic sphere. Money talked, as it always does, even if in muted Protestant tones. Protestants in the southern state comprised only 7 per cent of the population in 1926 but punched well above their demographic weight. 'Protestant' generally meant 'prosperous'. As one illustration, of seventy-eight motor cars in Limerick city in 1913–14, over fifty were owned by Protestants.[11] At the Irish Free State's founding, they comprised around between a fifth and a half of professional males. Protestants owned nearly one third of the larger farms;[12] on the other hand, they comprised less than 3 per cent of agricultural labourers.[13] Likewise in the commercial world: of the managerial classes in 1926, over 15 per cent were Protestant, with a heavy over-representation in important industries such as railways, brewing and distilling, textiles and construction.[14]

Most of their customers were Catholic, and anti-Catholicism had to operate within, and be cognisant of, these temporal realities. Thus it had to confine itself largely to the 'Hate Counter' or go underground—a matter in private between consenting adults. Patrick Campbell, writer and humorist, was unflinching in the portrayal of his parents' sense of difference from the Catholic majority. In their public lives in Dublin the Campbells were worldly, well educated and embedded in Irish life. His mother, Beatrice Elvery, was a renowned artist, his father the administrative head of an important ministry in the new Irish government. Yet, as Patrick recalled, 'I came from a Protestant home wherein Catholicism, and all its words and works, was the subject of constant derision':

> Bad Irish art was dismissed by my mother with the inevitable, 'But what else would you expect from the tenement Catholic mind?' My father, only half in jest, used to deliver great rolling denunciations based upon, 'The bottomless squalor of Roman Catholic superstition—' and conclude with a string of Hail Mary's in the genteel accents of a Dublin Civil Servant.[15]

That was mirrored in a very different Protestant environment; Frances Moffett, who grew up in a strict Dissenter household in the west of Ireland in the early twentieth century, described how sectarianism was passed through children's rhymes. Where it came from wasn't obvious: she wrote that despite 'considerable religious tolerance in my parents … in some insidious way, we soon learnt almost to despise Roman Catholics'.[16] But to despise Catholics didn't necessarily mean enthusiasm for conversion: 'We should resist the temptation to make proselytes', warned Canon George Chamberlain in 1932.[17] Anyway, southern Protestants were too busy repelling Catholic marriage marauders to have the energy to carry the fight into enemy territory. Not for them the heroine in Lennox Robinson's 1926 play *The Big House* who challenges her local rector 'to make room for parsons who believe in their religion enough to fight for souls with every weapon that God has put into their hands'.[18] The ginger-group evangelism of such as the trouble-making Irish Church Missions added as much edge to intra-Protestant tensions as to problematical Protestant–Catholic relations. Proselytism would break the new rules of keeping the head down. And even where it was attempted it tried to go with the grain. Methodism—which embarked on a new enthusiasm for evangelism and renewal following partition—adapted to southern Irish circumstances with 'an open-minded attitude to the new Ireland and a determination to identify with it'.[19] Colportage—the visiting of homes to distribute and sell the Scriptures and devotional books—was a particular feature. Bicycles were the chariots of this anti-Roman invasion, belief its armour and devotional literature its weaponry.

Anti-Protestantism was the other side of the coin. While the vast mass of Catholics probably gave little thought to Protestants, a shrill and dismissive minority in such as the *Catholic Bulletin* newspaper saw Freemasons and Free Staters under every bed. This perplexed many Protestants, especially—as Gregg acknowledged—the 'many thoroughly indifferent and merely nominal' ones that existed.[20] If they didn't register, why were they pilloried? Was it just as an irritation for being the Protestant pebble disturbing the placid calm of the Catholic pond—the 'uneasiness caused by our simple presence', as one cleric put it?[21] And Catholic authorities could be as dismissive and as downright rude about Protestantism in public as the Campbells about Catholicism in private. In December 1931 Cardinal MacRory refuted the right of the Church of Ireland 'to pose as the heirs of St Patrick, and of the early Irish Church'.[22] As late as 1950, Alfred O'Rahilly wrote disparagingly of 'the prelates of this little man-made Church' who 'could only be regarded by their flock as convenient officials under the constitution of 1870'.[23] Some on wilder shores went so far as to deny any legitimacy to Protestantism: J.P. Ryan of *Maria Duce*, a lay Catholic organisation, described 'all non-Catholic sects' as 'false and evil, irrevocably so', and recommended their proscription.[24]

But even if there was a steady suboceanic Atlantic Drift of sectarian feeling, open provocation on both sides was relatively rare. Why? The Irish Free State, not perfect, reflected many of the mores with which a conservative and relatively prosperous Protestantism was at ease. Methodists welcomed 'the puritanical trend in family law and the discipline of the press'.[25] An exchange of correspondence in the *Irish Times* in early 1950 relating to an excoriation of the 'liberal ethic' by a Catholic priest had much of the running taken up by liberal Catholics rather than Protestants, and the *Church of Ireland Gazette* in 1951 was on the same side as the Catholic hierarchy when the newspaper condemned a 'Mother-and-Child' health scheme as 'communist interference in the family'.[26] So, with their property, livelihoods and lives well protected, left to manage their own firms and farms, schools, hospitals and a university, secure in a cat's cradle of social and sporting organisations, broadly content with a conservative ethic, happy to converse with themselves through the letters pages of the *Irish Times* and the *Church of Ireland Gazette*, what could an overt anti-Catholicism contribute to their position, and how could it be expressed in a manner that would not result in disaster?

III

Perhaps in those circumstances a more interesting question is why they would want to. Contained in their DNA was leadership and a certain élitism that could not easily be foresworn. In 1933 the dean of Ross suggested of the Church of Ireland that 'her sons and daughters have taken part in everything that concerns the welfare of the country, and their only wish has been that a larger share should come into their hands'.[27]

Many thought that they could run Ireland better. In 1920 the novelist Edith Somerville's fictional landlord Dan Palliser wonders about his fellow rural district councillors: 'How, with materials such as these, was he, or anyone else, to build Jerusalem in Ireland's green and pleasant land?'[28] In 1921 the *Church of Ireland Gazette* was somewhat miffed that a Protestant offer to participate in the new government was ignored,[29] although in October 1922 W.T. Cosgrave held a meeting with Lord Desart in which Cosgrave indicated an outward willingness to listen to suggestions on such topics as land purchase, double taxation and the safeguarding of TCD.[30]

So, how was frustrated leadership to be exercised? The obvious route was to ascribe Ireland's ills to something that could not be laid at the feet of the minority—and that, of course, was *Romanism*. Duty and patriotism demanded that Protestants should attempt to rescue Ireland from Roman Catholicism's alleged moral and ethical failings. It might seem perverse to suggest that this move was easier to make in an independent Ireland than in a United Kingdom but, no longer carrying the burden of history and politics, southern Protestants gained the freedom to be free. No longer having to follow a *table d'hôte* unionism with all its attendant baggage, they could choose from a much richer, wider and deeper *à la carte* menu. Indeed, they could even cook up their own confections of citizenship. Southern Protestants rather valued—as Methodist minister Fred Rea put it in 1937—a convenient distance from 'identification with the ruling power'.[31] That was unlike in Northern Ireland, where 'In its relations with the Government of Northern Ireland the Church of Ireland had stepped easily into the position a state church would have occupied'.[32]

IV

That distance allowed southern Protestants to be 'hurlers on the ditch', as the Irish expression goes, enabling them to commentate on soft-power notions of ethical and moral superiority that were resistant to, and stood above, the crudities of the democratic numbers game and governmental politics. This is where they thought they could have heft. Underpinning these notions was a mind-set that saw the Reformation as just that, the winnowing-out of corruption in doctrine and institution, of reversion to the 'primitive faith' idea of Catholicism. If the Church of Ireland was the lineal descendant of St Patrick's 'primitive faith', then it was the genuine article—'the most Irish thing there is in Ireland', as Archbishop Gregg asserted in 1932. Protestants, by virtue of these intellectual gymnastics, were the true patriots, and thus anti-Roman Catholicism was legitimised on both religious and national grounds.

Unlike Gregg's provocative 1909 sermons, a more sophisticated and careful Protestantism in the new Ireland learnt to say the same thing in 'dog-whistle' fashion, this time couched in a subtle comparative with Catholics and Catholicism, characterising Protestants as *Hiberniores Hibernis ipsis*, as better citizens, morally purer, with a higher sense of duty. Everything was brought into the mix, from Girl Guides (good) to gambling (bad).[33] Protestantism represented itself as a distribution centre for moral backbone and ethical direction for the new *civitas.* Tempered in the flames of adversity, as Gregg put it in 1909,

> to be a Protestant is to have a harder battle to fight, a more exacting duty to fulfil, than Roman Catholics have. More rests with yourself; you have nobody to drive you; you must be your own taskmaster.[34]

In 1932 he set the tone, averring that 'the life of the citizen … provides a sphere in which moral qualities are needed if public life is to hold together'. According to him, Anglicans should 'serve the highest interests of the nation, and ... uplift its standards of character and conduct'.[35] His novelist daughter went further, putting venomous words into the mouth of a fictional Protestant heroine quarrelling with a fiery Catholic republican in the 1930s: 'you need people like us to keep you sane'.[36]

Some conceived morality in terms of setting an example—not so much anti-Catholicism as pro-Protestantism. The vision of the bishop of Limerick in 1944 was of Protestantism as precept: 'To set our own house in order, to live hopefully in it in neighbourly fashion, to express a method of living valuable to the State'.[37] Others saw it as underpinning participatory citizenship in social service, such as at the Church of Ireland's 1932 commemoration of the 1,500th anniversary of the arrival of St Patrick, when Revd R.M. Gwynn urged Protestants to get involved in bodies outside their own denominations, emphasising the importance of personal work, the prophetic and propagandist nature of the Church and the necessity to act rather than talk—an indirect reference, really, to the stereotype of the Catholic Irish as blatherers rather than busy bees.[38]

Carving out a distinctive place in the moral marketplace wasn't always easy in an era when most Catholics and Protestants—publicly, at any rate—were equally condemnatory of the deadly sins. One way in which anti-Catholicism could be used was in attitudes towards Sunday observance; Sabbatarianism was distinctly Protestant, with an added advantage in keeping Protestants away from the cultural contamination of the Irish games of hurling and football, usually played on Sunday. Another useful differentiation was gambling.[39] The purpose of the state, according to the rector of St Catherine's Dublin, was, like Sparta, to make its citizens good.[40] Gambling wasn't good. Particular animus was directed against 'the degradation of the Sweepstakes',[41] a government-enabled monopoly lottery that provided funds for hospitals while considerably enriching its pious Catholic owners. Its perceived unproductiveness and the creation of a class of 'undeserving rich' were excoriated by Anglican clerics. In

1932 Revd Bolton Waller encouraged Protestants 'as Irish citizens' to be 'prepared to speak out plainly and clearly against things evil'.[42] Gregg had a similar viewpoint: he 'could never forgive the Jesuitical doctrine that "it is right to do evil that good may come"'.[43]

It seems that the southern Protestant projection of 'soft power' through the moral and ethical was almost entirely about themselves in the context of community self-regard, wanting and needing to be *seen* as offering a different path. Despite the rhetoric, actually achieving anything would have greatly surprised most Protestants. Whether anyone outside their community would take up their prescriptions was in a sense neither here nor there. 'There' was a place they had been, and many still hankered after. 'Here' was where they found themselves, and they had to make the best of it. Broadly, they did.

III

LITERARY LUMINARIES

8

'DEVOTED LADIES': INTERROGATING NOVELISTS ELIZABETH BOWEN AND MOLLY KEANE[1]

If, as the poet Thomas McCarthy has claimed, the Anglo-Irish are 'born for remembrance',[2] this has surfaced not only in the formal memoir but also in the virtual reality of the novel, the play and the short story. Here is cast a coldish eye on two women writers who in differing ways hold a mirror to the society of which they were ineluctably part. From Lady Morgan through Maria Edgeworth, Somerville & Ross, Susanne Day and Dorothea Conyers to Barbara Fitzgerald and Jennifer Johnston, there is a rich, imaginative and distinctive feminine Anglo-Irish literature. Elizabeth Bowen and Molly Keane—born some five but dying more than twenty years apart—are close to being its last representatives. If Keane's daughter, Sally Phipps, feels that comparison between the two '… is inevitable, but a bit of a cul-de-sac …',[3] this writer wouldn't agree, seeing them as complementary in style, outlook and quality rather than anything else.

Elizabeth Dorothea Cole Bowen, who lived from 1899 to 1973, was the only child of Henry Bowen and his first wife, Florence Colley. Henry, a Dublin barrister, suffered from intermittent mental illness, which resulted in Elizabeth and her mother living from 1905 with relatives in Kent. 'I only thought I thought she was lovely because I loved her', wrote Bowen in her 1942 autobiographical fragment *Seven Winters*.[4] But Florence died young and Elizabeth was raised in England by aunts. Later she mused that 'Possibly, it was England made me a novelist',[5] and she wrote often of the plight of the orphaned, dislocated child.

Elizabeth was educated by governesses and at day-schools. Downe House boarding-school near Orpington, Kent, which she attended between 1914 and 1917, was a place where, as she said, 'personality came out in patches, like damp through a wall'.[6] Here she 'learnt to define happiness as a kind of inner irrational exaltation'.[7] School writings show her mannered style there from the first. Bowen entered the London County Council School of Art in 1918, but she only stayed for two terms. She ended her formal education by subsequently studying journalism, which served her well in her later literary life.

Molly Keane was, in her words, a 'great chum' of Elizabeth Bowen's, but their lives followed very different paths. Born Mary Nesta Skrine in 1904 at Ballymore Eustace, Co. Kildare, her mother was a poet who, as 'Moira O'Neill', wrote *Songs of the Glens of Antrim* and published two novels, *The Elf Errant* and *An Easter Vacation*.[8] Molly's Latin temperament clashed with her mother's Ulster Victorianism and her childhood was not particularly happy. Troubled mother–daughter relationships infuse her fiction, from the novels *Full House* and *The Rising Tide* in the '30s to *Good Behaviour* and *Loving and Giving* in the '80s. 'I have no education,' she claimed. 'I could never learn my grammar—it was always the same to me as arithmetic.' Supervised at home by a succession of governesses, she spent some time at the French School, Bray, Co. Wicklow, where, homesick and disliked by prim girls, she escaped by writing.[9]

Bowen started her literary career in 1923 with a volume of short stories, *Encounters*. That year she married Alan Charles Cameron, assistant secretary for education in Northampton. The marriage is as impenetrable as that of Iris Murdoch and John Bayley. Following Cameron's appointment as Oxford's secretary for education, a decade there from 1925 saw the publication of three volumes of short stories and four novels. Of these, *The Last September* is perhaps the most significant. It paints a picture of the Irish gentry in 1920 in muscular, but terminal, decline. Behind the façade of set-piece dinners, tennis parties and army camp dances, all know that the end is approaching. These characters, with their conflicting desires and divided loyalties, are heading for unavoidable disaster, and this is clear from the outset. As a critic has written,

> What makes *The Last September* so vividly poignant is that it never turns a judgmental eye on either side of its many small skirmishes, whether it's a nation fighting for independence from a ruler reluctant to cede control or a girl struggling to free herself from a paternalistic society that has served her people well for centuries. Instead, it merely presents its complicated world as a given, and lets us follow its inhabitants as they try to navigate clear paths for themselves through moral uncertainties.[10]

The book was brought to film in 1998, with a screenplay by John Banville.

If money was not quite as important to Bowen in her early years, it was certainly so to Keane, although it could be held that the necessity to supplement a meagre dress allowance and feed an expensive hunting habit hardly qualified her as the epitome of the starving artist. Since it was her view that a woman who wrote had no chance with men—'I would have been banned from every respectable house in County Carlow'—she determined upon a *nom-de-plume*. She finally settled on the gender-neutral 'M.J. Farrell', apparently the name of a public house spotted, characteristically, on return from a day's hunting. As such she wrote eleven novels between 1926 and 1951. The first, *The Knight of*

Cheerful Countenance, a frivolous romance, was published, appropriately enough, by Mills & Boon.

Bowen would never have been published by Mills & Boon, yet she also is often dismissed in a faintly patronising way as intelligent but not intellectual. Angus Wilson's comment is typical:

> For all her years spent … among Oxford academics she remained always an upper-class woman of hardy, firm intelligence; she was never the slave of the brilliant academic world as Virginia Woolf, a greater genius, too often was.[11]

Nevertheless, she apparently moved easily in Oxford circles. New friends amongst the university's intelligentsia in the '20s included Isaiah Berlin, David Cecil and Cyril Connolly. And Bowen set some store by her serious work. Her prefaces and her 'Notes on writing a novel', she said, 'were not journalism, and I stand by them … for which I would wish survival'.[12]

Both Bowen and Keane were striking women. Keane possessed the stereotypical classic mannerisms and features of the Irish gentry, together with an attractive face, brown eyes and a cut-glass accent, allied with a formal social behaviour. A bust by John Coll is in Waterford County Library. Bowen, though rather waspishly described by Virginia Woolf as 'a very honourable horse faced, upper class hard constricted mind', attracted admirers of both sexes. 'Hers was a handsome face, handsome rather than beautiful, with its bold nose, high cheekbones and tall forehead', remarked May Sarton, one of Elizabeth's female pursuers.[13] Atmospheric portraits of Bowen include a painting by Patrick Hennessy in Cork's Crawford Gallery and an Angus McBean photograph in the National Portrait Gallery, London. An attractive stammer, sometimes bothersome, dated from her mother's death. Charming but occasionally snobbish, in later years she came rather to like American glitz and easy manners. She dropped people ruthlessly, however, and her behaviour could be casual, unpredictable and somewhat disconcerting. When once asked by David Cecil to a family dinner, she is said to have replied: 'David, I think you know by now that I want to see you either alone or at a large party'. Few got close, but those few tended to be of high quality. 'Whom one sleeps with is always rather important', ambiguously declaimed Bowen in another context.[14] At Oxford she had an affair with the critic Humphry House.[15] Lovers and good friends slid one into the other. Seán Ó Faoláin was one such, of whom she had initially enquired of a friend: 'Is he nice? He might possibly be quite dim.'[16]

Keane had no such pretensions. Her upbringing was classic *fin-de-siècle*, with horses and dead animals sometimes seeming more important than children and the living. This was reflected in the early novels. Of this phase of her writing, *Mad Puppetstown* is perhaps the most enduring. A happy childhood, a counterpoint to Keane's own, tragically ending in war, is wistfully captured and lyrically described in bright-cut phraseology: 'the very house looked languorous. It seemed to open the pores of its stones to the day ... A slippery thread of a path spun its way across the field to an unseen gateway, where, under the trees, the air trembled, laden blue in the heat.'[17] Of the other novels, *Devoted Ladies*, published in 1934, is the most notable. It was daring for its day, appearing only six years after Radclyffe Hall's lesbian novel *Well of Loneliness* was banned for obscenity. Its satirical subject-matter—the attempted prising apart of a pair of lesbians by a man—both has a modern feel and is somewhat quaintly dated. And certain academics have been unable to resist the temptation to claim both Keane and Bowen as feminist and lesbian writers.

In the 1930s Bowen thrived in Oxford, New York, Italy and, increasingly, London, where she moved in 1935 when Cameron joined the BBC. Two of her finest novels—*The House in Paris* in 1935 and *The Death of the Heart* in 1938—date from this period. The latter is a forensic examination of upper-middle-class values, with its 'bitter kernel'[18] grounded in the end of her affair with Marxist intellectual Goronwy Rees. It deals with the way that society and individuals function only by deception. This was reflected in the indirectness of her prose. Physical action tended to be minimal, with plot often complex and difficult to follow.

Both, we might say, had children. Molly Keane had two daughters, Virginia and Sally. Bowen's 'child', on the other hand—like most children, troublesome and expensive but also an object of pride, love and refuge—was Bowen's Court, near Doneraile, Co. Cork, the house she had inherited from her father on his death in 1930. Elizabeth often established identity by conflating person and place, leading her to represent the latter (especially houses) as living entities. In *The Last September* the rebels who destroyed the Big House were its 'executioners';[19] in *The House in Paris* she wrote of 'sending vibrations up the spine of the house';[20] and in *The Death of the Heart* even the furniture has life. In *The Heat of the Day*, Holme Dene, the house of the spy, Robert Kelway, is 'a house made for surveillance, a man-eating house'.[21] Her own house was similarly characterised; writing of its demolition in 1960, she was glad that Bowen's Court 'had a clean end. It never lived to be a ruin.'[22]

Place encourages the lyrical in both writers. Here, from her second (1928) novel, *Young Entry*, is Molly on the Irish morning:

> On they jogged, by blackberry-filled hedges and twisting bye-roads. The sky lightened slowly to disclose the witching sadness of the Irish countryside. They rode by little tumbled houses—lonely on the edges of dull, purple bogs; here, was a burnt fox covert … there, a haunting, wet little wood, where the old twisting birch stems were like crooked, silver spells and the tang of purple loosestrife rose on the smoke of the morning.[23]

Bowen can be sparer, but no less evocative. This, from her last novel, is her depiction of Eva Trout's house, 'Larkins':

> Larkins was set in plum orchards, of which acres extended on three sides. The house was itself built of plum-coloured brick. Square, two-storeyed, five sash windows in front (three above, two below) with a door in the middle, it was not unlike a house in a child's drawing. Its gaze was forthright.[24]

And Larkins was not unlike, in Virginia Woolf's phrase, the 'great stone box', the house personalised by Elizabeth in her important social and family history, *Bowen's Court*. 'A Bowen, in the first place, made Bowen's Court', she wrote. 'Since then … Bowen's Court has made all the succeeding Bowens.'[25] Written at the height of the Second World War between 1939 and 1941, *Bowen's Court* is family chronicle with a literary sense—superb story and subversive history. The story is of individual Bowens in each generation, the family, the ancestral home, piling up into one unreal reality. The subversion, as in *The Last September*, is in her portrayal of Anglo-Irish life as a predetermined grand tragedy. Unlike Keane, however, Bowen lived and worked in two separate worlds: a cosmopolitan literary England and a decaying, brittle, often shallow Anglo-Ireland. Each had an impact on the other, but her Irish life had a pervasive influence on her perspective. Bowen wrote on England as an outsider. This 'death of the heart' of her caste infused her work and informed the attenuation and malaise of many of her characters.

For both, love and its expression was central to their lives and their writing. For Elizabeth it was an essential part of her religious belief; it is said that she could not imagine a God who would not accept love as the reason for human departure from any strictly laid-down code. This formula stood her in good stead during all the years with Cameron, a man of ambiguous sexuality. The Second World War loosened the accepted rules of morality further, but Elizabeth was always of 'good behaviour'. She felt that the war was 'the most interesting period of my life', and she is certainly one of the finest evokers of the Blitz. Her short piece 'London, 1940', with its chilling, one-line paragraph ending—'We have no feeling to spare'[26]—will tell you all you need to know of a time which few of us could ever imagine experiencing. She, at least, had some 'feeling to spare': in 1941 the hothouse live-for-the-day atmosphere of London encouraged an intense relationship with urbane Canadian diplomat Charles Ritchie. Though later married, he continued to be an intimate friend right up to her death. The attachment to Bowen, he wrote early on in 1942, 'will bind me as long as I live';[27] and nearly a year after she had died he confessed to his diary that

> I need to know again from her that I was her life. I would give anything I have to give to talk to her again, just for an hour. If she ever thought that she loved me more than I did her, she is revenged.[28]

The novel *The Heat of the Day*, published in 1948 and dedicated to Ritchie, was based on their affair.

For Molly, love seemed to have begun and ended with her perfect man—a gentleman farmer, 'Bobbie' Keane, nephew of Senator Sir John Keane. Molly's characteristic description of a passionate and intimate relationship from its start in 1933 was that 'in those days it wasn't done—but of course it was done'. They married in 1938. Keane was Molly's ideal—a beautiful rider, witty, intelligent. He encouraged her to take writing seriously. She was devastated when following relatively routine surgery he died in 1946.[29]

Bowen's marriage, on the other hand, could hardly have been described as anything but bizarre. Perhaps, as she said in 1935, marriage 'appeared an achievement or way of making one's mark, also … it would be difficult to settle to anything else until this was done'.[30] The marriage provided domestic stability as counterpoint to her frenetic literary and social life. Thus life with Alan Cameron—a decorated war hero and an intelligent administrator with a deliberate line in boring stories—was internally rationalised while at the same time remaining an enigma to her friends. Bowen, it must be said, was discreet about her affairs and Cameron seemingly tolerated them.

For both writers, the necessity to make money was a constant backdrop to their writing lives. In Keane's case it was the spur to a remarkable literary renaissance in her late seventies. The lasting grief occasioned by Bobbie's death had been reflected in her virtual cessation of writing from the late 1940s until the 1970s, but she returned spectacularly to the literary scene at the age of 77 with the novel *Good Behaviour*. Written when, as she said, she was 'too old to ride to hounds, too poor to pay a gardener, but possessed of a rattling good idea',[31] it was completed in 1978. The manuscript, though, was rejected by Collins, which had been her publishers. Actor Dame Peggy Ashcroft, a friend, persuaded her to persevere and it was published in 1981 by Andre Deutsch to critical acclaim, being short-listed for the Booker Prize in that year. It's a black Protestant comedy, offsetting pathos and glittering success against a vision of the gentry *milieu* as one of solitude, poverty, hopelessness and futility—but always of good behaviour. It was successfully adapted for television by Hugh Leonard in 1983.

In Polly Devlin's perceptive phrase, Keane 'observed and preserved … the sounding of the tocsins and the minutiae of the last days of the Irish Raj',[32] but her writings, especially in their later phase, are not just stories of a vanished culture. There is a contemporary-feeling satire that strikes a chord with a generation of readers too young to have a familiarity with the Anglo-Irish universe within which she moved. There was a more than a soupçon of acid, though; not particularly disguising the origins of many of her characters, she doubtless created the odd thought of lucrative libel actions in south of Ireland Big House drawing rooms. Her last novel, *Loving and Giving*, published in 1988, mirrors Bowen's *Eva Trout* (1968) with its shocking, violent end. Once again the themes are the Irish gentry's conflation of place with person and its obsession with stifling any acknowledgement of the untoward.

Fuelled by the necessity to make a living from *her* craft, Bowen's prodigious output in the late '40s and early '50s consisted largely of workaday pieces—articles, broadcasts, criticisms, introductions, prefaces, reviews and travelogues. Her eighty or so short stories—described as 'brilliant' by Angus Wilson—were of more even quality than her novels. She does shorter better. The subjects were diverse, ranging through wartime London, children, hotels—and ghosts; spectacularly, a long evening glove comes alive in her 1965 short story *Hand in Glove* and commits murder.

Cameron, ill and alcoholic for a long time, died in 1952. The last of the typical Bowenesque novels, and also her final wholly Irish-centred fiction, *A World of Love*, was published in 1955. Its 'darkened mirror'—her own phrase—reflected Bowen's preoccupations at the time about money, a shabby Irish house and a shabbier heroine. She had stayed on in Bowen's Court, stacking up financial problems as a generous hostess of the 'Big House'. Attempts to keep it in the family failing, it was eventually sold to a local farmer. Bowen thought that it would be lived in again, with children, but it was not to be. It was demolished in 1960.

Bowen's attitude to political Ireland always seemed ambivalent. If her observation-point as a writer was, in Hermione Lee's phrase, as the 'spy inside the gates', this was mirrored in her wartime role as a provider of intelligence for the British Ministry of Information. Moving between London and Bowen's Court, she conveyed Irish opinion to the Ministry; Colonial Secretary Lord Cranborne found her reports 'sensible and well-balanced'.[33] This episode in particular has led hostile observers to brand her as little more than a traitor. She was nothing of the sort, of course.[34] As for many southern Irish Protestants in the half-century or so after independence, it would not have seemed strange to Bowen, in what she said were 'the perpetual transits' across the Irish Sea between Anglo and Irish, to maintain a dual loyalty without any particular sense of strain. The demolition of the house, though, rather than its sale, seems to have hardened her heart. In 1963, in the second edition of *Bowen's Court*, the best she could say about the Treaty was that 'I believe in its promise'.[35] Just before her death, she surprised Hubert Butler by vehemently exclaiming that 'I hate Ireland', though Butler felt that it was her illness talking.[36]

Both Bowen and Keane tried their hand at writing for the stage, Keane being conspicuously more successful. Bowen's single unpublished play, *Castle Anna* (1948), was notable only for Richard Burton's debut. Keane's were Cowardesque, with fine characterisation and pointed wit. Many were produced by John Gielgud. *Spring Meeting* (1938), *Guardian Angel* (1944) and *Treasure Hunt* (1949) were mildly fashionable for their time, while *Ducks and Drakes* (1941) and *Dazzling Prospect* (1961) were not, the latter—in a post-John Osborne world—being particularly out of place. The dreadful reception afforded to *Dazzling Prospect* was one of the subsidiary reasons why Keane was reluctant to take up the pen for years afterwards.

The later life of both writers is a contrast in stability. Keane returned to Ireland in 1952 on completion of her daughters' education, moving to a small but beautifully positioned clifftop house in Ardmore, Co. Waterford. In later years she achieved a recognition that was not given to her earlier. She was elected a founding member of Aosdána (an arts academy under the aegis of the Irish Arts Council) in 1981, which provided a small, but valuable, stipend. In April 1996 she died at home following a fall and lies in the churchyard of St Paul's Church of Ireland, Ardmore.

Bowen led an itinerant existence after the sale of Bowen's Court in 1959. Eventually in 1965 she settled in Hythe, Kent, close to her childhood home. An establishment figure, in 1948 she had been appointed CBE and subsequently lectured for the British Council abroad. She was—if a curious choice—a conscientious member of the Royal Commission on Capital Punishment, which was influential in leading to the eventual abolition of hanging in the UK. She lectured on the art of the novel in her many visits to American universities as writer-in-residence after the war. Two further books—*The Little Girls* in 1964 and *Eva Trout; or, Changing Scenes* in 1969—saw greater physicality and action. *Eva Trout* was short-listed for the Booker Prize and awarded the James Tait Black Memorial Prize in 1970. Elizabeth had been a heavy smoker all her life and she was diagnosed with lung cancer in 1972. With Ritchie present, she died in February 1973. She is buried, with Cameron, in St Colman's, Farahy churchyard, Co. Cork, beside the site of Bowen's Court.

Of the two, Bowen has to be considered the greater writer. She has seen a renaissance in recent years. Influenced by James, Proust and Woolf, she has a secure place in the canon of literature in English, a significant bridge between the Bloomsbury set and later writers like Iris Murdoch, Anthony Powell and Muriel Spark, and with echoes of the American novelist Edith Wharton. She may have wanted to establish herself as an English, even a European, novelist, but one of her best novels—'which of all my books', she said, 'is nearest my heart'[37]—will always be *The Last September*, her most overtly Irish, and she knew it. In it, her ear is perfect, her sense of place confident, her tone elegiac. There is little of the angst expressed by a character in Lennox Robinson's play *The Big House*, set in 1921–3: 'we were ashamed of everything, ashamed of our birth, ashamed of our good education, ashamed of our religion, ashamed that we dined in the evenings, and that we dressed for dinner …'.[38] There may have been relative poverty at Bowen's Court—in an eerie echo of Robinson, Virginia Woolf in 1934 described the Camerons as 'keeping up a ramshackle kind of state, dressing for dinner and so on'[39]—but there was never shame.

If Bowen is a novelist who in the ultimate writes of the generic human condition, Keane represents a different image, chronicling a specific Irish gentry world. In a fit of self-parody in her 1934 book *Devoted Ladies*, she describes herself as

> some hysterical Irish novelist, writing her seventy thousand words through which the cry of hounds reverberates continuously, where Masters of Hounds are handsome and eligible men and desirable young women override hounds continually, seeing brilliant hunts on incredible three-year-olds; and all—after even the hardest day—are capable of strong emotion at night.[40]

She even has a character in the book describe her own 1928 novel *Young Entry* as 'full of the lowing of hounds and everyone stuffing themselves with buttermilk scones dripping with butter'.[41] Her fiction is contrarian in a way that Bowen's is not. Molly considered herself an iconoclast in both her view of Ireland and her personal life—'a great old breaker-awayer', as she described herself in an interview in *The New Yorker*.[42]

There is a subtle difference of atmosphere between the two writers. It is not easy to pin down, but perhaps best analogised by seeing Bowen's work as Art Nouveau in character and construction—organic, flowing, inconclusive. Keane, on the other hand, is more Art Deco—geometric, angular, decorative and mysteriously functional. Both are, in somewhat different senses, the literary children of Edith Somerville and Violet Martin. With Keane, the genealogy is perhaps more obvious, her surrealism and her Big House settings reflecting the *Irish RM* stories. The substantial literary line for both writers, though, runs from Somerville & Ross's best and most serious books, *The Real Charlotte* and *The Big House of Inver*. Keane's blackish humours and sharp characterisation, and Bowen's treatment of the timeless traits of desire, greed, hubris, ennui, are all founded in these earlier works.

We can do no better than quote two critics' verdicts: Mary Gordon in the *New York Times* sums up Keane's early novels as 'brilliant evocations of a world that strained to combine, to its peril, the old way of life that centred on hunting and the foreign modern influences of cocktails, homosexuality, adultery and inappropriate fur coats',[43] while Hermione Lee says that Bowen demands attention not just because of her literary lineage (Jane Austen, Henry James, the Anglo-Irish and French novelists) but more so because of her 'formal mastery of an idiosyncratic style, her sense of place, for her brilliance as a short-story writer, for her creation of troubled, complicated, modern characters'.[44] Her obsessions, too, lend sharp focus to her stories—betrayal, the supernatural, war life, the perceptions of children—and, above all, the dislocation and dispossession of an entire society.

Today, anyone who undertakes a pilgrimage to Farahy churchyard will now only sense ghosts. Elizabeth Bowen's grave crouches for shelter against a westering wall. Close by, the wind shakes the barley where once stood the 'great stone box' of Bowen's Court. Nothing is left. Can the Anglo-Irish way of life, then, be characterised, at the last, as no more than an illusion? Perhaps. But if the rot had long set in from within, if there was little left but an empty shell, we are indebted to these 'devoted ladies' whose literary craft has, in effect, placed a preservation order upon it. A new, a higher, reality has been created.

9

'NO MORE AUTUMNS': THE ANGLO-IRISH AND THE DEATH OF THE HOUSE, 1919–23[1]

At the very end of Elizabeth Bowen's 1929 novel *The Last September* a character remarks about Danielstown, the Big House at the story's centre, 'Every autumn, it strikes me that this place looks really its best'.[2] But, in Bowen's words, there would be 'no more autumns' for Danielstown: it was burnt down in the Irish War of Independence. Bowen characterises the house's destroyers as its 'executioners'. Death's finality is used in a very particular way by Elizabeth Bowen. In those novels and short stories that treat of her people—the minor Anglo-Irish gentry of southern Ireland—she utilises a process of transference, anthropomorphising the Big House. She puts literary flesh on stone bones. This is more than a literary device; it speaks to Carl Jung's theories of the persona and our use of archetypes—mental frameworks to interpret and explain the world around us. One of those archetypes is the humanised house. When the house faced death or died, the effect was to strip away permanence, to drop its inhabitants into an unknowing void leading to dislocation, angst and misery and an overwhelming sense of loss. This essay evokes the Big

House as a permanent member of the family. It opens a window onto why the revolutionary period between 1920 and 1923 was so traumatic for the gentry and why in many respects the narrative of Big House death can be seen through the human stages of grief—denial, anger, bargaining, depression and acceptance.

'Revolutionary' has two meanings. If the gentry's life revolved around the Big House, that sense of revolution mirrored the gentry's world-view as cyclical rather than linear—echoing Yeats, 'the soul of man lived many lives'.[3] Already dying by 1920 as its socio-economic position became ever more precarious,[4] the house was still more than Vera Kreilcamp's 'receptacle of illusion, a richly evocative symbol of its occupants' encapsulation in the past'.[5] As has been pointed out, 'as the Big House died as a social actuality, it was reborn in Irish literature'.[6] And the novelist, the playwright and especially the poet are best placed to bring the house alive:

The house rang, in cuckoo-clamour;
He sang all evening; a blacksmith
Beating our worries to better shape.
With the power of Spring he spelled out
That the frail hold on the old house
Would nevertheless be strong enough …

… The double cuckoo, caroling
Somewhere in curtain trees disclosing view;
Plays orchestra to perfection;
Lawn, haven and point. The house solidly
Attends; weather-slated, fanlighted,
Wrapped in a gentle Georgian dream.[7]

The conventional interpretation of the Big House is as a canvas, a set—in Molly Keane's words, 'a backdrop to romance'; '… a symbol of unity, a stage setting for an image of cohesion';[8] a 'representative if miniature theatre', as Elizabeth wrote of her own Bowen's Court.[9] Here, in the introverted Lilliputian worlds of Somerville & Ross's *The Irish RM*, *The Big House of Inver* and *The Real Charlotte*, the landed classes try to keep boredom at bay.

Many of the Anglo-Irish had a passionate attachment to their Big Houses; particular examples are Lady Gregory's devotion to Coole, Edith Somerville's embrace of Drishane and Elizabeth Bowen's desperate quest to keep Bowen's Court going in her straitened '50s. Oliver MacDonagh explains this by emphasising how 'the physical precincts were ... central to identity'[10] as over the course of the nineteenth century the gentry withdrew from time to place. They increasingly 'turned to geography in the attempt at patriotization'.[11]

The gentry saw themselves, measured themselves, through the prism of their houses.[12] It mattered to the Earl of Kingston that King George IV didn't turn up to his lavish and costly castle at Mitchelstown.[13] It mattered to the Earl of Listowel that the Prince of Wales visited *his* house, Convamore, in 1885.[14] Both were burnt in the early 1920s. Convamore was the first to go, in 1921. There may have been no obvious human casualties (apart from Mrs Wrixon-Becher's false teeth)[15] but that misses an essential point. The Scottish satirical poet George MacBeth catches it:[16]

> Yes, I'm sorry
> For those bricks and mortar, crashing joists
> And ancient floorboards. Houses don't have feelings,
> Do they? Lucky for us that they don't.

The literature is saturated with the sense that the Big House *was* endowed with feelings. As an almost sentient organism, it is often, in Gearóid Cronin's phrase, 'the real central character of the story'.[17] The subtitle of Lennox Robinson's 1926 play *The Big House* is 'Four scenes in its life'.[18] Robinson, through his observer, Revd Brown, was 'extraordinarily interested in watching this house and the fight it's making'. One of his characters, Despard, asks, 'What the dickens is it fighting for?' Robinson's answer? 'Its life.'[19] This is about as elemental as it can get. Like humankind, natural decline and decay could ultimately be accepted, but death by violence was of a different order.[20] The resonance with the just-finished Great War—'they shall grow not old, as we that are left grow old'—is obvious. As if to underline the effect of a violent end, as Gemma Clark perceptively points out, the houses in *The Last September* are given human names—*Daniel*stown, Mount *Isabel*, Castle *Trent*.[21] So is Robinson's Bally*donal*.

That's not accidental. Bowen's central characters are often her houses, and they exemplify how such houses are placed in the gentry's narrative. The house could exhibit several distinct personalities—ancestor, parent, guardian, child. A venerable aged relative, it moulds people through sheer longevity.[22] Then again, the Big Houses are 'essentially female structures that embody the principles of order, security, and stability and create meaningful space for birth, nourishment, sleep and death'.[23] Novelist Molly Keane's Aragon 'was a very female house both within and without and wore the more exquisite moments of the year with a wonderful grandeur and quietness … there was a calm and kindness about its lines'.[24] These are mothers, and when a mother is lost, as Bowen's was to cancer when Elizabeth was thirteen, then the houses—'pavilions of love'[25]—perhaps attain an even deeper significance.[26]

And yet Phyllis Lassner's suggestion that Bowen's 'portraits of empty but claustrophobic houses challenge our stereotypical associations of family homes with a nurturing and beneficent female essence'[27] may not be too wide of the mark either. In Lassner's reading, Bowen's houses were actually more like austere, desiccated, touchy maiden aunts than broad-bosomed, matronly smiling mothers. So, if the house is something other than maternal for Bowen, then is it a protector or defender, perhaps? And indeed Elizabeth, unlike her own coping with her father's mental illnesses by a campaign of 'not noticing', has Danielstown, like a stern and competent custodian, in charge, noticing everything—'the vast façade of the house stared coldly over its mounting lawns'.[28] The primacy of this protectorate is established, where 'the mansion piled itself up in silence' over the visitors' voices.[29] Two of its occupants drive out, and the house watches: 'looking longest after them, like an eye, a window glittered'.[30] The real-life south-west-facing Bowen's Court had lots of glittering windows.

The anthropomorphic house can be what its inhabitants want it, or need it, to be. It may have held much more significance for Elizabeth than just as ancestor, nurturer or protector. Bowen's marriage was childless. Yet the *house* Bowen's Court can be seen either as the mother she lost—'I was the child of the house from which Danielstown derives', she wrote in 1942[31]—or, more empathetically, as the child she never had—wayward, expensive, exasperating, but also loved and loving, a point of hope, a place of refuge.[32] In turn, the *book Bowen's Court* was *its* offspring, so to speak, and a grandchild to Bowen's imagination. Thus the loss of a burnt house is not just that of stones and mortar, or paintings and silver.[33] In the last sentences of *The Last September*, the door of burning Danielstown may have 'stood open hospitably upon a furnace'[34] but its owners, the Naylors, were seeing much, much more than red-hot stones. This was truly a funeral pyre for all the generations of a lost family.

The extent to which the house was seen as having its own dynamic, separate from the family who inhabited it, is an intriguing question. Bowen wrote of the house 'living under its own spell'.[35] It often asserts the right to be welcoming on its own account: Bowen, in her short story 'The Back Drawing-Room', remarks that people's gates and doorposts have expressions, and that those expressions are often of what she calls 'Irish hospitality'.[36] Sometimes, indeed, the house is a mysterious stranger and has an almost sinister force. In Robinson's Ballydonal, the house ensures that, through the agency of a drunken butler, its titular owner, St Leger Alcock, hasn't been down to his wine cellar for six months.[37]

That was a dark and interior side: the house with its 'intense, centripetal life' could be suffocating and often hostile to its inhabitants; relationships were not universally benign.[38] The heroine of Robinson's play, Kate Alcock, may have fiercely claimed her Big House as her life, her faith, her country—'we think Ballydonal *is* life, our life'[39]—but the owner, her father, had a darker perspective, one of depression. One smoking ruin slumped in the midst of another, he recognises that his house was moribund long before it was burnt down: 'I'm just damned glad it's all over and there's no reason to make an effort any more'. That's depression. Ballydonal may have attracted Kate back from London but it repels her English-born mother, who never took to 'this white elephant of a house', a revulsion hidden for many years from her family.[40] In truth, the senior Alcocks are quite ambivalent about the house. For St Leger Alcock and his wife, abandonment is a function of economic necessity; it is then easier for them to leave.[41] William Trevor in *The Story of Lucy Gault* uses much the same trope but more savagely and less metaphorically. Bowen, faced with selling her house, had a similar dilemma, and answered it in much the same way. Why might this have been? Here is bargaining, maybe. There were reasons enough to let go. The house was a black hole into which financial and emotional capital vanished, often for little return.

Yeats wrote in his drama *Purgatory*[42]

> But he killed the house; to kill a house
> Where great men grew up, married, died,
> I here declare a capital offence.

Why were these houses killed? It seems a simple question to answer. The debate is almost invariably couched in terms of the observable, the apparent real: the necessities of military strategy, of sectarian conflict, of the stubborn re-emergence of historical grudges over land, of personal scores settled and so on. Specifics can be identified—the targeting of Anglo-Irish senators' houses by anti-Treaty forces is a particularly obvious example.[43] While Bowen's Danielstown is a victim of the 'proper' conflict—that of independence—Ballydonal's killing is reprisal for a Civil War execution far away in Dublin, and unfathomable for all that, like being run over by a bicycle rather than a Bentley. 'Is that why we're to be burnt!' is the Hampshire-born Mrs Alcock's futile cry of incomprehension.[44]

Maybe beneath the surface there lurked something deeper and darker in the executioners' subconsciousnesses—'a symbolic purging of the historic enemy'.[45] That enemy has been placed in the present by reference to a distant past and thus a legitimate target, as exemplified in Michael Hartnett's poem 'A Visit to Castletown House':[46]

> I went into the calmer, gentler hall
> in the wineglassed, chattering interval:
> there was the smell of rose and woodsmoke there.
> I stepped into the gentler evening air
> And saw black figures dancing on the lawn.
> *Eviction, Droit de Seigneur, Broken Bones,*
> And heard the crack of ligaments being torn
> And smelled the clinging blood upon the stones.

Maurice Farley's poem 'Stately Home' carries the same sentiments:[47]

> We follow guides through rooms and galleries,
> Stare at ancestors' portraits in the hall,
> Remembering how long ago they took
> Our weeping daughters from their wedding feasts,
> Chattels to be used and given back,

> Droit de seigneur.
> To-day their heir must bolt connecting doors,
> And wait in patience till closing hour
> Restores his house, made stale by breath of crowds,
> And cigarette butts ground into the floor,
> Something we have used and given back,
> Droit de seigneur.

The house here is both innocent and guilty but ultimately a co-conspirator, always on the same side as its inhabitants. It is just as alien and as intrusive as those who occupy it. In this the executioners concur with the gentry. Elizabeth Fingall's house had 'windows staring across the country like blind eyes … looking out across the country which they possessed but never owned'.[48] By 1920 Hartnett's depiction of eighteenth-century arrogance had been superseded by a sad realisation of being frightened rather than frightening:

> The house seemed to be pressing down low in apprehension, hiding its face … It seemed to gather its trees close in fright and amazement at the wide, light, lovely unloving country, the unwilling bosom whereon it was set.[49]

'Formidable, reasonable, stately, the Big House spoke in a strange accent; it did not speak to the Gaelic heart.'[50] When it could, though, it was still powerful; it is said that when raiders arrived to torch Lord Waterford's Curraghamore they fled when the flitting moon shone suddenly on the gilded cross on a coat of arms over the door.[51] Maybe the rebels had to work hard to overpower the Big House; thoughtful IRA leader Ernie O'Malley recounted carrying out manoeuvres in demesne lands to rid his volunteers of 'their inherent respect for their owners'.[52]

And sometimes what is not there is as significant as what is. With regard to the burning of Ballybritt Castle in County Offaly in 1923, a local newspaper noted that 'it was difficult to assign any reason' for its firing. In the same county, the reasoning for those who destroyed Otway Toler's Durrow Abbey was a rather vague 'to burn imperialism out of the country'.[53] Fota in Cork emerged inexplicably unscathed despite being the home of Lord Barrymore, frustrater of the Plan of Campaign and leading light of southern Irish unionism.[54]

The colours of the imagery in *The Last September* are orange and red and russet and yellow and rust-brown—all autumnal shades but also those of fire, *the* symbolic purgative, as well as accessible.[55] Fire was to the Big House as kryptonite to Superman. Accidental burning was a constant threat:[56] seventy-six Big House fires are recorded in Munster and Connacht, for instance, from the late eighteenth to the mid-twentieth century.[57] By opening the house 'to the Irish sky', in J.G. Farrell's formulation,[58] fire enabled the landscape to reclaim what was its own, through the agency of those other fundamental elements of water, wind and earth.[59] The ritual of destruction often required the occupants to watch the funeral pyre. In June 1921 Lord and Lady Bandon had to witness the burning of Castle Bernard; the feisty elderly countess defiantly sang *God Save the King* in her nightdress on the lawn as the castle behind her burned. In Molly Keane's novel *Two Days in Aragon*, Sylvia Fox is unluckier: tied to a laurel tree, she has to *face* the house as it is consumed by fire 'so that she might watch her own soul burning'.[60]

Thus, while at the last some houses await Bowen's 'executioners', most cowered in the countryside thankfully unnoticed, lucky to survive, living on, dying in their beds.[61] It is reckoned that around 300 or so were destroyed deliberately between early 1920 and mid-1923, representing some 20–25 per cent of the total.[62] The further up the social scale the greater was the proportionate destruction, though; 45 per cent of peers' residences in Munster and 22 per cent in Leinster were destroyed in the revolutionary period.[63] The process continued after independence, as the gentry increasingly became unlanded. Rising labour costs, economic inutility and the local taxation policies of the Free State government and its successors were probably responsible for far more deroofing than the incendiaries ever were.[64] Of those that were fired some were rebuilt, but not many. Often they had to slum it with down-market and brash newcomers, replete with damp courses and central heating. In Bowen's backyard in north Cork, the Evanses of Carker abandoned the Big House in the 1950s and built a bungalow in front of it. Yet the house *was* restored in the early 2000s.[65] Castle Bernard was never rebuilt, though: a later Earl of Bandon constructed a bungalow close to it, too.

Kate Alcock's ambition for the destroyed Ballydonal—'We'll build it up again'[66]—was a pretty hopeless folly. This was denial. In the post-independence world, many of the Big Houses accepted their fate, purging their apostasy and guilt and seeking salvation by 'submitting to Rome' in the shape of the Catholic religious orders who purchased them for use as convents of nuns or houses for priests and brothers. Many others simply died of old age, such as Pallastown, near Kinsale, home of the Heard family, knocked down in the 1960s after significant deterioration.[67] Some had near-miraculous resurrections. Lord Mayo rebuilt Palmerstown House in County Kildare in the 1920s. Sometimes new money moved in, rescuing such as Castle Hyde and Ballynatray House, both on the Blackwater.[68]

If the Big Houses always sheltered their quota of ghosts, the revolutionary burnings turned many of the houses themselves into nothing *but* ghosts, like Kilbarran in Bowen's story 'The Back Drawing-Room'.[69] Bowen's Court turned into a sort of ghost, too. It was demolished by a new owner in 1960 after Elizabeth was forced to sell.[70] Ozymandias-like, only a few stones are left today. And yet … Bowen's Court points the way as to how the gentry might have come to the acceptance of the losses in the revolutionary period. It was not necessarily as a ghost but rather as a preservation of memory in what Elizabeth called the 'livingness' of these houses. In an afterword to the book *Bowen's Court*, three years after its demolition, she wrote that 'when I think of Bowen's Court, there it is … it is part of the character of Bowen's Court to be, in its silent way, very much alive'.[71] And, indeed, there it still is—it remained on the maps of north Cork for many years after it had been razed; it exists in the book *Bowen's Court*; and, in an imaginative sense, continues to be brought to life again every last September at a commemorative Anglican evensong in the little Bowen church at Farahy. Whether as reality, ruin or reimagination, the gentry can have taken some small comfort in that the Big House has proved surprisingly difficult to kill.

10

BOWEN'S COURT AS 'AN AESTHETIC OF LIVING': A LOST MANSION'S SIGNIFICANCE IN THE IMAGINING OF THE IRISH GENTRY[1]

Hermione Lee's 1981 literary biography of Elizabeth Bowen has two entries in its index for 'Bowen's Court'—one in plain typeface, one in italics.[2] This encapsulates how this building has come to be seen. The house had its own existence as a sturdy reality in the landscape—that's the plain typeface entry. But it also possesses an italic, imaginative, historical and literary significance as Elizabeth's eponymous biography of the house and its inhabitants, originally published in 1942. This essay contrasts the ordinariness of this lost mansion with its place in the literature and the imaginative history of Anglo-Ireland.

Bowen's Court *the house* gets more mentions than it deserves in the literature of the Big House in Ireland—not because of its innate architectural merit or its grand history, or the political and economic importance of its inhabitants, but rather because historians like Terence Dooley[3] probably find, like this writer, that they are seduced by the descriptive power and style wielded by Elizabeth in the book *Bowen's Court*. 'A Bowen, in the first place, made Bowen's Court', she wrote. 'Since then, with an alarming sureness, Bowen's Court has made all the succeeding Bowens.'[4] Photographs of the house—which are relatively few anyway—are almost redundant. With an artist's eye, Bowen places the house in its geographic setting: a limestone area of south-west Ireland, a land of middling fertility, lots of rivers and streams, few lakes, framed by, to the north, the imposing Galtee Mountains and Ballyhoura Hills. The countryside about seemed to have 'an inherent emptiness of its own'.[5] In *Bowen's Court* Elizabeth contrasted 'the intense centripetal life' of these Anglo-Irish houses with the 'plastic emptiness' of the country around it.[6] A corollary of this emptiness, though, was isolation—'"*you* are a long way from everywhere!"', her visitors often said.[7] And yet she can also write that 'The country is not as empty as it seems', and goes on to describe how she saw the indigenous (that is, Catholic) population suddenly appearing in the countryside, especially on Sundays and festivals.[8] This is not as contradictory as it sounds. One important characteristic of the Anglo-Irish was an ability to filter out those not of their class or religion, exemplified by Bowen's 'Sometimes for days together a family may not happen to leave its own demesne'.[9] They sought—they found—their own. And the gates of Bowen's Court were set as far up the road as possible to the then-fashionable spa town of Mallow.[10]

It has to be said that the house itself had little stylistic or architectural merit.[11] Building commenced in or around 1765 by Henry Cole Bowen and was completed some ten years later at the confident high-water mark of the eighteenth century's Protestant Ascendancy in Ireland.[12] Elizabeth's description is atmospheric and three-dimensional:[13]

> Bowen's Court … is a high bare Italianate building. It was intended to form a complete square, but the north-east corner is missing. Indoors, the plan is simple; the rooms are large, lofty and few. The house stands three stories high, with, below, a basement sunk in an area. Outside the front door a terrace, supported on an unseen arch, bridges the area: from this terrace the steps descend to the gravel sweep. The house is built of limestone from a nearby quarry; the south front and long west side are faced with cut stone—the mouldings and corners are marble-sharp …
>
> The great bare block—not a creeper touches it—is broken regularly by windows; in the south façade there are twenty … in the west side eighteen, in the shorter east side six, in the north back six … When the sun is low, in the early mornings or evenings, the house seems, from the outside, to be riddled with light.
>
> Indoors, the rooms with these big windows not only reflect the changes of weather but seem to contain the weather itself … on winter mornings … the plaster and marble indoors, even the white woodwork, looks also frosty and hard. When rain moves in vague grey curtains across the country … grey quivers steadily on the indoor air, giving the rooms … the resigned look of being exposed to rain.
>
> Bowen's Court is severely classical and, outside and inside, is very bare … There has been no attempt to break any space up … This is Bowen's Court as the past has left it—an isolated, partly unfinished house, grandly conceived and plainly and strongly built.

Inheriting the house on the death of her father in 1930, the England-based Bowen and her husband Alan Cameron stayed there sporadically until he retired in 1952, when they returned, as they thought, to live there for a long time. But Alan died that year. Elizabeth remained on, stacking up financial problems as a generous hostess, trying to keep the money coming in by frantic writing. Something had to give: the house had to go. Attempts to keep it in the family failing, it was eventually sold to a local farmer at the end of 1959.[14] Bowen thought that it would be lived in again, with children, but that did not happen. It is not quite clear why the house had to be torn down. It may have been a decision based on hard-headed considerations of money. Yet there are those who would see in that action a final reckoning in the wars over land that had bedevilled Ireland for centuries—ironic, perhaps, since Bowen's Court had survived the Troubles of the early 1920s, unlike its neighbours Ballywalter, Convamore and Rockmills, all destroyed in a single night, and the Bowens seem to have been regarded as decent landlords.[15] Elizabeth put a brave face on this disaster; she professed to be glad that her house had 'had a clean end. It never was a ruin.'[16] According to her lover Charles Ritchie, she was not afraid to revisit the site in later years.[17]

That's the house. It is safe to say that, without its Elizabethan serenade, Bowen's Court would have merited little more than a line in any catalogue of Irish lost mansions. As it has turned out, the book *Bowen's Court* has attracted a great deal of attention, principally from cultural and literary scholars. Contradicting the house's physical modesty, it has come to stand for those who see in the Anglo-Irish world of the twentieth century a particular trope—one of an inevitability of sadness and loss, with a soupçon of just dessert thrown in. Colin Reid has a striking phrase about the Protestant nationalist Stephen Gwynn, that he was 'dominated by … pursuit of an imagined Ireland'.[18] One way in which that 'imagined Ireland' could be created, a cultural identity declared and defined, was through the literary. And there's a lot of it. Bowen once described one of her novels as 'fiction with the texture of history'; in many respects, *Bowen's Court* is history with the feel of fiction.[19]

After Irish independence in 1922, words were really the only weapons at the disposal of the Anglo-Irish. Drawing, then, on Bowen's non-fictive pieces on the Big House—*Bowen's Court*, of course, but also her distilled essay 'The Big House' published in the Irish magazine *The Bell* in 1940[20]—this discussion is broadened to encompass the Big House as an imaginative power in telling the southern Anglo-Irish story. That story is one of isolation, too much roominess, exclusivity, but also refuge and utility. For a wider comprehension, reference also needs to be made to Bowen's 'Irish' novels, *The Last September*, published in 1929, and 1955's *A World of Love*.[21]

The Last September is a story of the final days of a County Cork Big House, Danielstown, and its inhabitants in 1920. As the country around rises in rebelliousness, these characters with their conflicting desires and divided loyalties are heading for unavoidable disaster, and they all know it. At the end, the Big House burns as its owners watch. Bowen's ear is perfect, her sense of place confident, her tone elegiac in this novel.[22] *A World of Love* was, in her phrase, a 'darkened mirror' and reflected her preoccupations after Cameron's death about money, a decrepit Irish house and a tired heroine. She was at a low ebb when writing it, and it shows. Here is a smallish Big House—Montefort—that stands as a metaphor for the 'Descendancy'[23] that many Anglo-Irish felt they had become after the Second World War. The house's decrepitude is a mirror to its inhabitants' condition, and it has become almost a ghost in the landscape which it once dominated. 'Montefort? Pity that place has gone' is the remark made by a neighbour who should have known better, and a casual visitor says 'No idea there was anyone living here'.[24] To all intents and purposes this miniature mansion is *already* lost. As are its inhabitants.

The central metaphors with which the Big Houses are most often associated are internalised: 'a place of isolation, exclusion and enclosure', but also 'a symbol of unity, a stage setting for an image of cohesion'.[25] In its destruction, whether by murder or euthanasia, the house appears to symbolise the death-throes of a class in Ireland. But there's perhaps a little more. The Big House is a set, a backdrop, a screen against or upon which the everyday tiny dramas of Anglo-Irish life could be portrayed and projected, a 'representative if miniature theatre', as Elizabeth wrote of Bowen's Court.[26] In fiction, for roundness, the setting had to carry an aura not just of space but also of time. Lennox Robinson's stage directions for his 1926 play *The Big House* capture this—'the effect of all being a comfortable room containing the vestigia of generations'—and gels with Bowen's 'pellucid silence' of Danielstown, 'distilled from a hundred and fifty years of conversation'.[27]

The Anglo-Irish may be inescapably tied to the landscape—and this emerges in Bowen's fiction, from *The Last September* and *A World of Love* through a plethora of short stories such as 'Summer Night' and 'The Happy Autumn Fields', but it is so often a relationship of murderous love. In an essay on Bowen's interaction with this terrain of north Cork,[28] Eibhear Walshe points out that there are considerable contradictions between how Bowen represented landscape in the book *Bowen's Court* and in her fiction. In *Bowen's Court* the landscape is not threatening; by contrast, in the fiction it *is* hostile, a proxy, perhaps, for those people the Protestant Irish gentry could not, or would not, see.

Bowen's use of chiaroscuro, of shadow and light, in *The Last September* reflects that sense of partially glimpsed menace that was a constant companion to the gentry in the 1920–2 period. It also creates a dimensional feel which is critical to the book. She is not trammelled by geography, but even if she was, her 'Big House' has to have a 'Big Garden' too; as in *Bowen's Court*, she lavishes attention on it.[29] From its very first pages, Danielstown's demesne land is an integral part of *The Last September*.[30] In all this, space is central to Bowen, whether it be sufficient, insufficient or over-abundant, or just ordinary—Danielstown is characterised by cooking smells that pervade the house, giving it a sense of smallness, even of the commonplace.[31]

In Bowen's fiction, villas are often painted, in a literary sense, by numbers, so that the reader can achieve an appropriate visualisation.[32] And it must be remembered that Bowen spent most of her life in city houses and suburban villas, not Big Houses. In a truly domestic sense, Bowen's

Court was not that central to her life. At the end she retreated to the Kent coast, where she and her mother had also gone many years before when her father's mental illness had become too great to bear. Reflecting that, Bowen suggested in her essay 'The Big House' that 'The paradox of these big houses is that often they are not big at all—that is, when compared to Irish great houses'.[33] In the world of her fiction, what is striking is the notion of the Big House, no matter what its physical size—from the large Danielstown in *The Last September* to the smaller Montefort in *A World of Love*—as being unable to accommodate emotionally all who seek shelter in it. Elizabeth's contention is that 'Life works to dispossess the dead, to dislodge and oust them. Their places fill themselves up; later people come in; all the room is wanted.'[34]

At the last these houses are represented as being as much the victims of war and its collateral damage as their inhabitants. Like people, they have glorious ends, or cower in the countryside, thankfully unnoticed, lucky to survive, living on, dying in their beds. Bowen's Court survived. Danielstown is the unlucky one, but brave in its own way. 'Behind the trees, pressing in from the open and empty country like an invasion, the orange bright sky crept and smouldered', as the house awaited its fate.[35] And here is a clue to what the Big House really means to Bowen. While comprehending the house as stage set or background is a necessary condition for understanding how the Anglo-Irish lived, and saw, their lives, it is that 'the house is the real central character of the story'.[36] This anthropomorphic sense runs through Bowen's other writings: in *The House in Paris* she wrote of 'sending vibrations up the spine of the house'; in *The Heat of the Day*, Holme Dene, house of the spy, Robert Kelway, is 'a house made for surveillance, a man-eating house'. And if the house is a character, then in Bowen characters can be houses. Mirroring the description of the English soldier Gerald Lesworth's character in *The Last September* as 'rare and square—four-square—occurring like houses in a landscape, unrelated and positive', in her last novel, *Eva Trout*, the house,

Larkins, has human character; it, too, is soldierly, four-square—'its gaze was forthright'.[37]

The anthropomorphic house may have held much more for Elizabeth. She remained childless, yet the house Bowen's Court can be seen either as the mother she lost when only 13 or, more empathetically, as the child she never had—wayward, expensive, exasperating, but also loved and loving, a refuge, a point of hope; the house, as she says, 'was made happy by the presence of our relations'.[38] This family chronicle with a literary sense, described as 'an act of pietas' by Roy Foster and as an act of 'imaginative family elegy and empathy' by Neil Corcoran, is a superb story but also a subversive history.[39] The story is of individual Bowens—the family, the ancestral home—becoming almost of one substance in time and place. The subversion lies in the misleading perception that history and emotional capital pile up—in Elizabeth's words, 'With the end of each generation, the lives that submerged here were absorbed again. With each death, the air of the place had thickened: it had been added to.'[40] The gentry might be no more than holograms in a solid landscape, but this version of Protestant history had—or appears to have—an attractive and believable reality for those who wish to believe. *Bowen's Court* has a central place in that believability.

In one sense, while the fiction doesn't mirror what the historians and anthropological sociologists have established, it carries its own validity. The detachment and introversion of Danielstown's and Montefort's worlds are in tune with the generality but not the particularity of historical reality. Danielstown burns; it is tempting—and the novel encourages us so to do—to characterise its destruction and, by extension, the historical burnings, as a sort of *suttee*, the Anglo-Irish flinging themselves on the funeral pyre. And with immolation may come resurrection; renewal through fire is age-old imagery in many cultures, but in the case of the Irish Big House it rarely happened. Instead, its owners suffered merciful release from the house as tyrannous invalid aunt forever banging on the bedroom floor for attention; the spoilt, demanding child gobbling up resources; the complacent sleepy sentry in a hostile territory. By and large an unimaginative race, in reality the Anglo-Irish bore their dispossession stolidly. The gentry in 1922 had been here before. They could be there again, or so it seemed. Echoing Yeats, history was cyclical; 'the soul of man lived many lives'.[41] Cultural stasis is the balance between remembering the future and imagining the past. This transcendental level is perhaps reflected in the fiction: the Big House renews its life by drawing in the spirits of the dead, as from the nearly ghost republican who brushes past the heroine Lois in the garden of Danielstown.

In contrast to this sense of the Anglo-Irish as alien and unwanted, Bowen's Court—the template for Danielstown[42]—escaped the turbulent 1919–23 period almost unscathed. Elizabeth's description of her father's funeral—an Anglican service held in the open air at Farahy church so that Roman Catholics could attend, which they did in their hundreds—is particularly poignant.[43] Nevertheless, while outwardly the gentry's *raison d'être* might have appeared in reasonable order at the beginning of the twentieth century, it was increasingly disengaged: an engine running, but in neutral. If that disengagement—socially, culturally, economically, as much voluntary as involuntary—had begun long before Irish independence in 1922, it was because, in Elizabeth's words about the gentry's life as early as the 1830s, 'It could exist in detail—comings-and-goings, entertainments, marriages—but the main healthy abstract was gone'.[44]

Where Bowen's fiction and non-fiction dovetail is in an avoidance of the Big House's workaday economic and social role by giving it a life and a characterisation almost independent of those who inhabited it. Bowen, whose writing is indirect and oblique, creates not just one but several distinct personae for Danielstown in *The Last September*. This grows organically from her childhood, and is somewhat in antithesis to it. In Bowen's fiction the Big House is often as mysterious as a stranger, a romantic Gothic behemoth. In Virginia Woolf's appalled phrase about Bowen's Court, this 'great stone box'[45] represents the magical *deus ex machina* which, as in the later novels of Iris Murdoch, enables the plot to be justified and resolved.[46] And Bowen engenders a faint sense of menace and furtiveness in the house's attitude towards its human inhabitants.

If the essence of its personalisation by Bowen lies in her need to see the Big House as elemental life-force, it is obvious that many, their economic justification largely gone by the early 1900s, were already dying. It has been argued[47] that Bowen—influenced by notions of usefulness and economic autonomy prevalent in 1930s Ireland—represents the gentry as a professional class, thus seeing its decline as, in essence, the consequence of a changing economic world rather than as the victims of 'an overemotional economy that binds Bowen's class to the land of Ireland'.[48] Ultimately, there is a certain lack of sentimentality for, an absence of loyalty to, the Big House, exemplified by the Naylors' abandonment of Danielstown in *The Last September* and by the senior Alcocks in Robinson's *Big House*. Bowen was faced, in real life, with the same dilemma, and answered it in much the same way. This reading goes some way towards validating her utilitarian vision in the 1940 essay 'The Big House':

> From the point of view of the outside Irish world, does the big house justify its existence? I believe it could do so as never before.[49]

In *Bowen's Court* Elizabeth stoutly maintained that the gentry 'are tougher than they appear'.[50] That this was allied to the sturdiness of their houses was evident. It did not necessarily conflict with her sighing conclusion that 'In the life of … the new Ireland … the lives of my own people become a little thing'.[51] In a parallel Protestant-gentry world, largely self-contained and inward-looking, littleness might not matter. But where utopianism breaks in is in her justification for the Big House's continued relevance. Is the House to be a source of capital? Or a focus for agricultural efficiency and innovation? Or a tourist trap? No;

in her phrase, it is to be 'sociable'. This seems to be code for no more than a place where the two primal kinds of Irish—Roman Catholic and Protestant—can meet, talk and resolve. In this, it *is* an unrealistic sentimentality, and falls far short of a vision for a sustainable future.

Yet it might be legitimately held that the sustainable future was as likely to be socio-cultural as anything else. In this interpretation, *Bowen's Court* is just one more reinforcement of an Irish literary redoubt that runs from Charles Lever to William Trevor. In this it has become a cliché, a distorting lens, the stuff of coffee-table books, a deliberate representation of the introverted integrity of a cause lost a long time ago.[52] The fiction of Anglo-Irish nostalgia has possessed a life outliving its subject-matter, just as *Bowen's Court* has outlived the house. Saddled with their genealogy, hostages to their futures, the gentry struggled with the often contradictory centrifugal and centripetal force of their houses.

> The door, that shadowy door
> Closes. And the mind is closed.
> A disembodied eye
> Roves through the big house …[53]

They had built their own open prisons.

11

ELIZABETH BOWEN ILLUMINES THE *IRISH* MURDOCH[1]

INTRODUCTION

Captain Macmorris, the stage-Irishman in Shakespeare's *Henry V*, is full of choleric existential angst:

> Of my nation! What ish my nation? Ish a villain, and a bastard, and a knave, and a rascal. What ish my nation? Who talks of my nation?[2]

Six hundred years on, the Irish continue to navel-gaze about identity and nationality and often to be as touchy as Macmorris about it. Philosopher and novelist Iris Murdoch (1919–99)—Shakespearian in sympathy,[3] Irish in proclaimed identity—was a case in point. What, indeed, 'ish' her nation? In her biographer Peter Conradi's words, Murdoch had 'a lifetime's investment in Irishness'.[4] She has the imprimatur of the Royal Irish Academy's *Dictionary of Irish Biography*: 'Born in Ireland with careers outside Ireland'.[5] So that's that, then; Iris as Irish is established, and now we can all go home. But this tells us nothing. Her own description, 'Of Anglo-Irish parentage',[6] which appeared on dust-jackets from 1961, is curious—not just because it may be gilding the social lily somewhat but also because it emphasises origin as tribe rather than place. It raises a question. If Murdoch had a professed Irishness, what was it?

CRITICS

Critics have explored Murdoch's identity from early on. In 1975 Donna Gerstenberger, in a series entitled 'Irish Writers', identified 'an explicit persistent consciousness of Ireland as a force in Murdoch's fictional world'.[7] In 2001 Conradi addressed it comprehensively in *Iris Murdoch: A Life* and concluded that her sense of Irishness was 'a source of reassurance, a reference point, a credential, somewhere to start out from and return to'.[8] In 2008 Frances White argued that in terms of national identity Murdoch was neither 'here nor there',[9] and suggested that Murdoch was rejected by Ireland. She was dismissed by Irish literary scholar Norman Jeffares in 1982[10] and she doesn't even merit a mention in Declan Kiberd's 1995 magisterial proclamation of the canon of Irish literature.[11] Yet she was always recognised by the literary 'Protestant' establishment, signified by honorary degrees from Trinity College Dublin and Queen's University Belfast. Belatedly, the Irish state offered a validation with the issue of a commemorative postage stamp on the centenary of her birth in 2019. There is now a blue plaque at her birthplace in Dublin's Blessington Street.

RATIONALE

Maybe this is the clue. Irishness has often been seen as a 'holistic axiom'. At base, it was (and still is, to a large extent) set within religious boundaries, Protestant and Catholic—especially so in the literary sphere. Murdoch was well aware of this primacy. In her Irish Gothic novel *The Unicorn*, almost the first question asked of the English Marian Taylor when she arrives at Gaze Castle is 'What is your religion, child?'[12] That enquiry stands proxy for a larger one about identity. Both are perhaps delusional, though no less real to their adherents for all that. Marian gives the wrong answer—none—and is set firmly outside the Pale. Thus is established *her* otherness against the Castle's insiders, who are themselves outsiders.

Within the Protestant variety, sub-strains cross-cut each other. One such is the Northern Irish, from whom, as Conradi has pointed out, Murdoch's family on both sides largely sprang. Unlike its southern counterpart, northern Protestantism was characterised by a strong sense of local majority, a literalist religiosity, faint remnants of a radical political tradition and an industrial economy. Yet if Murdoch possessed an Irishness it was predominantly of the southern style. In her early communist sympathies and her post-Second World War work with the United Nations Relief and Rehabilitation Administration what comes through early on is a southern Protestant recognition of otherness and the reflection of a strong individualistic ethic. A resonance is in her relationship with Frank Thompson. Thompson, who idealised (and idolised) Iris as 'a poetic Irish communist',[13] subsequently operated behind enemy lines in occupied Bulgaria, and operating behind the lines is what a Protestant in a Catholic country does all the time. If by descent Murdoch is one of these quiescent fifth columnists, what forms and informs them? It is suggested that it is a concatenation of the nature of the tribe; the significance of place and its concomitant, space; and an awareness of belonging.

Mirroring Murdoch—that the path to the direct is through the indirect[14]—this essay interrogates her identity by reference to that historical southern Irish Protestant community and how it is reflected in the life and writings of her friend and contemporary Elizabeth Bowen. From the critical perspective, Murdoch's novels *The Unicorn* and *The Red and the Green* call up the sort of Irishness she may have felt she possessed.

All this follows Neil Corcoran's historicity more than Maud Ellmann's psychoanalytic or Susan Osborn's contextual deconstructions.[15]

TRIBE

The 'Protestant' tribe was never homogeneous or monolithic. Murdoch's family mélange of Presbyterians, Brethren, Baptists, Quakers, Elamites and Anglicans[16] was in many ways more typical than Bowen's much less mongrel Protestant strain. In 1911, midway between Elizabeth's and Iris's births, southern Irish Protestants amounted to 10 per cent of the population of what was to become the Irish Free State. Their spread was uneven, with a proportion of 21 per cent in Dublin—Murdoch's and Bowen's birthplace—but only 4 per cent in the west.[17] Dublin possessed not only substantial professional and entrepreneurial classes but also a Protestant working class, numbering some 10,000.[18] Within southern Protestantism there were professionals, bureaucrats, police officers and soldiers—Murdoch's people, and Beckett's people too. The true Irish gentry—Bowen's—were largely a busted flush by 1911. But while a small part of the Protestant population, they contributed a large part of the noise. Protestants economically punched far above their numerical weight; by 1926, even though the Protestant population had declined by a third since 1911 with an exodus of policemen, soldiers and civil servants in the period around independence—amongst whom was Iris's father, Hughes—it still had 40 per cent of the lawyers, over 20 per cent of the doctors and well over 50 per cent of the bankers.[19] Economic survival, especially after independence, thus dictated a necessary engagement with the Catholic universe, though reluctantly. Protestants lived within carefully ordered, internally buttressed social, religious, moral and cultural stockades. As Bowen put it, 'the unquestioned rules of our being came, in fact, from the closeness of a minority world'.[20]

In 1911 Iris's birthplace in unfashionable inner-city northside Dublin had a heterogeneous population of all occupations and religions. Blessington Street Protestants tended to be of the lower classes and were marked as such in her novel about the 1916 Rising, *The Red and the Green*.[21] Elizabeth's home on the city's Georgian south side was no less mixed religiously, but there the Catholics were mostly servants. Bowen remarked that 'I took the existence of Roman Catholics for granted but met few and was not interested in them ... They were simply "the others", whose world lay alongside ours but never touched.'[22] Southern Protestants comprised an 'internal diaspora'—in Ireland but not really of it.

While the Murdoch and Bowen worlds seldom touched, there were superficial similarities. Murdoch was perhaps not above burnishing her antecedents but a Bowen she was not. Her father's family had been landed once, but some considerable time back; her mother's was by now a lower middle-class Protestant Dublin one. Bowen's father, while of somewhat grander gentry stock with a small estate in Cork, was himself a barrister. Her mother was a scion of a prosperous and well-connected family, also from north Dublin but, through the prism of class, a universe away from Blessington Street. Elizabeth, as a child, regarded this north side of the city as '*terra incognita*',[23] so unknown that 'I took it that Sackville Street [now O'Connell Street] had something queer at the end'.

PLACE

Prosaic, dull even, southern Irish Protestants could relate to a geographical condition but rarely an imaginative one; they usually regarded Ireland as, in Joseph Hone's words, 'a country, rather than as a nation'.[24] Yet how alien would this have been to Murdoch? She expressed a connective 'Irishness' while an Oxford undergraduate, but that was an abstract, intellectualised acquisition of 'place'. Whatever about her family, her 'tribe', the obvious point about Murdoch is that, though born there, she was never of Ireland. Yes, Ireland played a part in her childhood and later, but it was never 'home' in the sense that Bowen would have understood. Iris, being Iris, was capable of creating an Irish Protestant sense of 'place'—metaphoric in *The Unicorn*, realist in *The Red and the Green*[25]—but could not achieve the experience of the direct, could not speak to the formative expressed by Elizabeth in *Seven Winters*, for instance[26]—'where is there perfection but in memory?'[27] Thus to place Iris's Irishness—if indeed it is Irishness—requires something else. Apparent to Conradi, he emphasises Murdoch's sense of absence from something—her otherness, and how her family was unassimilated into English life.[28] Yet place could be tyrannous, too; and Murdoch, unlike Bowen trying to cope with subversive plumbing and surly servants, was thankfully free of this.

SPACE

Anglo-Irish southern Protestants are the inheritors of great spaces as well as great places and are acutely aware of having that—and of losing that.[29] In Lennox Robinson's 1926 play *The Big House*, Kate Alcock muses that 'we are shrinking, aren't we? Do you remember the first winter of the war we shut up the north wing … now the drawing-room's gone and the music-room too, I suppose. Soon we'll be reduced to a single bed-sitting room.'[30] And Bowen's case is again illustrative. If, as Roy Foster maintains, '"placing" Elizabeth Bowen remains difficult',[31] it is perhaps because it is *space* that truly defines her, creating an edginess which is the impetus for much of her writing. Unlike Rainer Rilke, to whom 'trees are magnificent, but even more magnificent is the sublime and moving space between them', Bowen is unquiet when confronted with emptiness.[32] *Contra* Beckett's 'Every word is like an unnecessary stain on silence and nothingness', Bowen writes furiously as a 'sculptor of the void'.[33] Danielstown in *The Last September* is roomy, indeed empty, where

> in the dining-room, the little party sat down under the crowd of portraits ... spaced out accurately round the enormous table ... each so enisled and distant that a remark at random, falling short of a neighbour, seemed a cry of appeal ...[34]

Like Bowen, Murdoch uses tactility, time and olfactory colour as a means to format space: Gaze's drawing-room 'smelt broodingly of the past', and even a lavatory seat 'seemed warm from a generation of incumbents'.[35] Danielstown is somehow both empty and delimited, suburbanised to the villas of Bowen's youth and old age by the cooking smells that pervade it.[36] The house Montefort in Bowen's *A World of Love* had 'a ceaseless kitchen'.[37] Murdoch's formatting is often Bowenesque, from the high and wide 'water and sky and heather and silence' of the Scarren[38] through the sudden small, private, liberating space that emerges in Tim Reede's escape route from Mrs Mount in *Nuns and Soldiers*.[39]

Even where space may indeed seem filled, the southern Irish Protestant characteristic is only to be aware of that within its comprehension or on its wavelength. The significance of that is that even Catholic spaces can easily be Protestantised; Andrew Chase-White in *The Red and the Green* feels that his family 'occupied or pervaded Ireland, managing to inhabit most of its corners'.[40] Notions of sufficient, insufficient, over-abundant or pointless space abound in Bowen's writings: in *A World of Love*, the village of Clonmore 'not only provided no place to be, it provided no reason to be'.[41]

BELONGING

Finding a 'reason to be' within the amorphous concept of nation was not easy for Irish Protestants, even for their inanimate houses—in *The Unicorn*, Gaze Castle is 'belonging yet not belonging'[42] to the landscape of which it is a part. Maybe Irish Protestants didn't want to belong. For Murdoch, the Ciceronian republican motto *Ubi libertas, ibi patria* seems to have meant internationalism and a form of communism which was more Beveridge than Marx. Perhaps southern Irish Protestants are more comfortable belonging to 'ideas' because they are not allowed to belong to a nation. They have none but friends and fellow-exiles, Wild Geese and Huguenots all, lost in *The Unicorn*'s 'nothingness and nowhere' of the desolate unmapped bog at the centre of the story.[43] That bog may stand as a metaphor for an Ireland that Murdoch wished to understand and belong to but could not.[44] There is a poetic symmetry between the 'appalling landscape'[45] of which the bog was a part and the dreary architecture of the Englishman Effingham's soul (with Iris's grandfather's name) who is sucked into it. He was 'in this place, an intruder',[46] but is perhaps closer to it than he can admit. He stands for those who, in the words of a 1916 Irish Protestant novelist, were seen as 'illegitimate children of an irregular union between Hibernia and John Bull',[47] coerced into an Ireland that most rejected, in part if not in whole.

Edward Said's argument is that 'nations are themselves narrations. The power to narrate, or to block other narratives from forming and emerging, is very important.'[48] By the time of Bowen's birth in 1899, the cascading effect of land agitation, Parnellism, resurgent Catholicism and—above all—the Gaelic cultural revival had already led to an Ireland whose narrative maddeningly and inexplicably demanded Protestants' adherence to the nation and their exclusion from it at one and the same time. The *Protestant* narrative, on the other hand, eschewed even lip-service to inclusiveness. Thus there is a self-contained interior existence in which social ritual—often pointless and tedious—was acted out as if to a script. Murdoch has an ear for this Anglo-Irish stage-weariness: 'Days seemed of immense length and their simple pattern already seemed … monstrous, as if the monotony were inherent and not cumulative'.[49] This was a world that involved a great deal of class- and gender-consciousness and in which 'family trees were meticulously composed'. Hermione Lee describes it as a society in which 'grandeur has become snobbery, fanaticism has dwindled to eccentricity'.[50] And yet it had an inherent ordinariness about it, too, exemplified by the busy, structured lives of Edith Somerville at Drishane and the Leeson Marshall family in a remote Kerry Big House between the wars.[51]

Alleviating monotony by watching was one response. It is contagious, and necessarily incestuous: in *The Unicorn*, Marian's first instinct on arrival at Gaze is to focus—with her new binoculars—on the *other* Big House across the valley. And she is uneasy when stared back at,[52] mirroring a Bowen character's disquiet at 'the uncanny attentiveness of the country'.[53] An overdeveloped sense of being watched and, as a consequence, becoming excessively self- and group-aware often results in a withdrawal from the world, as echoed in *The Sea, the Sea*. It is in *The Unicorn*, an Ireland as Mervyn Peake's Gormenghast, almost impossible to escape from. It is in Bowen's *A World of Love*, where flight is into the past. Who would want such an identity? Perhaps the fabulous and the fantastical are the pressure-release valves for a forced interior life?[54]

An attachment to Crown and empire, a feeling of belonging to a wider majority, put off the evil day; once these were gone, though, in Bowen's words, 'in the life of the new Ireland … the lives of my own people become a little thing'.[55] At the time of Iris's birth in 1919 southern Protestants were already in a precarious position. By 1922 the Church of Ireland felt it necessary to assert that 'we are Irish and Ireland is our home'.[56] At first reading this seems unexceptionable; it could even have been subscribed to by advanced republicans. But Protestants and Catholics were then divided by a common language; that simple declaration contained a minefield of begged questions of what was meant by 'we', 'Irish', 'Ireland' and 'home'.[57]

This last—'home'—is a particularly interesting word. Yet the idea of Bowen's Big House as a refuge for those who seek belonging in an emotional sanctuary was devastatingly jolted in the period from 1919 to 1923. The IRA, perhaps subconsciously, knew what it was doing. Then the houses suffered the same pain as their inhabitants, victims of war and its collateral damage. Home dies. There are dead houses in Murdoch; in *The Unicorn*, Marian notices these on her journey to Gaze, but those deaths had been more prosaic, less romantic—the victims of taxation rather than torching.[58]

Belongingness works both ways. 'I see now that my father wanted me to belong somewhere, because he did not', says Portia in Bowen's *The Death of the Heart*. So place has a claim over its people too. In *The Red and the Green* Murdoch's Rathblane, with its 'formidable sinister stillness',[59] is keeping a beady eye on its occupants; and in *The Unicorn* Murdoch establishes Gaze as a 'big, self-absorbed house'[60] yet a dangerously observant one too, with its 'staring windows'.[61]

CONCLUSION

In *The Red and the Green* Iris suggested that

> history seems like a brightly lit and faintly clamorous procession, while the present is a dark rumbling corridor off which, in hidden shafts and private rooms, our personal stories are enacted.[62]

From at least the 1900s southern Irish Protestants were expected to process in the past, quietly, while Catholics colonised the corridor of today. Many duly obliged, accepting the script. Against the Gaelicising busyness and cloying Catholicity of the new state in the 1920s and 1930s, Protestant navigation was by nostalgia, which quickly became normative. Any hint of Protestant reluctance to abide by the unarticulated rule was seen as subversive. Protestants asserting a claim on the present Ireland were barely tolerated.

Bowen's 1929 novel *The Last September* should have disturbed the narrative, but it did not. Why? Possibly because—written a mere decade after the Irish War of Independence—it was already judged as, in Bowen's own description, 'fiction with the texture of history',[63] southern Protestants now knowing their place. Bowen's *A World of Love* comes closest to insubordination with its wistful references to the 'real' (i.e. British) army, Lilia's articulated mistrust of Ireland and a less than flattering portrayal of an Irish village.[64] Murdoch should have disturbed the narrative, too, in the 1938-dated epilogue to *The Red and the Green*, where Frances's English husband sets out a most condescending critique of the Irish Free State. But that novel, though also fiction with history's texture, did not at its publication in 1965 challenge the Catholic-Irish possession of that present; by 1965 the Catholic narrative was already starting to move on. *The Unicorn* does not threaten for the same reason, and for its interior generic focus—despite Murdoch's occasional casual libels on the Irish lower orders.[65]

After all this, then, what can we say of Murdoch's Irishness? There are no easy answers. There are no easy questions! Ontologically, southern Protestant Irishness could be defined as an experience of the conditional and peripheral—an ability, as has been said, 'to slip in and out of Irishness'.[66] If that were all, both Bowen and Murdoch would pass the entrance test. Yet, though Murdoch may have seen her identity as 'Anglo-Irish', her writings might be better characterised as Hiberno-English in style, tone and character. Murdoch's determined intellectualism is alien to the Irish literary tradition, and certainly to Bowen. Writing to Charles Ritchie after Iris's 1956 visit to Bowen's Court, Elizabeth opined that 'only half her mind goes into her writing, and … she's frightened of the other half being left in a vacuum. She really, deep down, is an intellectual, in the sense that I'm not.'[67]

This is where Bowen and Murdoch probably part company. Despite many concordances with the southern Irish Protestant mind-set, to follow Auden about Yeats, mad Ireland didn't much hurt Murdoch into writing. Her intellectual well-springs essentially lay elsewhere. In her literary journey, Murdoch only sporadically had, in the words of Chase-White in *The Red and the Green*, 'an atavistic urge to return to the soil of Ireland'.[68] Ireland offered nothing to her philosophy. It is perhaps illuminating that in 1956 when she expressed the fear of a loss of identity to Elizabeth Bowen it was to do with her impending marriage, not her nationality.[69] At the last, then, we might surmise that while her *Irishness* provided an anchor in an unknown sea for her, what really counts for the rest of us is her *Irisness*.

That 'ish' her nation.

12

WHAT MAKES IRIS MURDOCH'S IRISH SHORT STORY *SOMETHING SPECIAL* SPECIAL[1]

There is more than meets the eye in Iris Murdoch's only short story, *Something Special.* Short stories can be categorised as self-contained—Elizabeth Bowen's *Hand in Glove,*[2] contemporaneous with Murdoch's, is one example—or they can be episodic, like *Something Special.* It is generally accepted that the short story is a more difficult genre to handle successfully, if for no other reason than that it demands a particular skill of imaginative extension in the writer. Think of it as a 'phrase in ellipsis'; in a small space the writer has to conjure up befores and afters. Writers such as Murdoch like plenty of space, it seems. And it may go some way towards an explanation of why she did not persist in the short story genre—although it could be argued that some of her more complex novels, especially the 'baggy monsters' of the 1980s, could be disassembled into 'short stories' if one were so inclined to read them thus.

The story itself seems to have been written in or around 1954 or 1955. Murdoch's two drafts are interleaved with what appear to be early notes and fragments of *The Sandcastle*; Peter Conradi speculates that it was produced by Iris after a trip to Glengarriff in west Cork.[3] *Something Special* was not published until 1957 in an anthology, *Winter's Tales No. 3*,[4] and later in Japan in 1959. Chatto and Windus produced it in the UK as a small book in 1999, with woodcut illustrations by Reynolds Stone from Iris's book of poems *A Year of Birds*. It appeared in the USA in November 2000 by Norton, with illustrations by Michael McCurdy.

To claim that *Something Special* is close to prototypical later Murdoch—containing within it the strands of construction, contingency, characterisation, disruptive fictions, unlikeable females, placement and dialogical techniques that are found in Iris's later writing—is probably an exegesis too far, although in embryo it has power figures (Yvonne's mother, her boyfriend Sam) and a predisposition to sudden violence. But in some respects we can see in it something of a template in miniature for much of what was to follow. It is about five and a half thousand words in length; here is a précis in 158:

> It's early 1950s Ireland. Yvonne Geary, 24 years old, is still living with her poorish Protestant mother and uncle in a small, dark shop in Dún Laoghaire (formerly Kingstown), a prosperous seaside town about seven miles south of Dublin. Yvonne, tall, not unattractive, has a lacklustre relationship with the rebarbative Jew Sam Goldman, an apprentice tailor. She sees him as nothing special. They go out for a night in Dublin city centre. Sam is trying to muster the courage to propose, but Yvonne provokes a diversion into a rather brutal working-class world of beer and fallen women. Fallen trees seem more to Sam's taste. He drags Yvonne to a closed city-centre park to show her one. He believes it beautiful, special; she is unimpressed. Yvonne flees home, but after reflection says that she's going to marry Sam. In the bed which she shares with her mother, she starts to cry, silently. 'The long night was ahead.'[5]

The story has not exactly attracted a great deal of scholarly attention. It fits uneasily into the bourgeois settings so typical of the later Murdoch. In 1993 an essay by Alexander Gonzalez concentrated on aspects of gender perspectives. Vivian Valvano Lynch read an illuminating and witty paper to the American Conference of Irish Studies in 2002 which examined the story largely in terms of its perceived Joycean structure and references.[6] In a brief 2010 discussion, Priscilla Martin and Anne Rowe focused on its particular setting and characterised 'This small-scale abnegation of hope' as 'a rather depressing picture of Ireland and the Irish'.[7] Though well below the radar in Murdochian studies, it seems that Eng. Lit. students rather like *Something Special*[8] (maybe its shortness helps) and those who 'get' its message become quite fond of it, as you would of a small dog.

Unsurprisingly, the critics, where they have noticed it, are less than impressed. Stephen Amidon reviewed the American edition for the *New York Times* in November 2000 and suggested that it was 'hard to see what makes this brief tale special enough to merit a volume of its own'. The damns aren't even faint: he wrote that it 'reads like an outtake from Joyce's *Dubliners*' and that Yvonne Geary was 'too familiar a type to evoke much sympathy'.[9] The respected *Kirkus Reviews* in the same year was even blunter: 'This thoroughly unremarkable short story … won't add anything to the deservedly high reputation of the … late author'. It dismissed it as containing little but 'a few faint echoes of Joyce's "The Dead"' but, interestingly, it did pick up on 'Murdoch's gift for locating worlds of implication in commonplace quotidian dialogue, and for an occasional flash of the kind of understated animism that graced her later fiction'.[10] Elizabeth Jane Howard in 2001 tactfully suggested that its appeal would be to hard-core Murdochistas rather than the general public.[11]

Whatever about the professional critics, there are a number of online comments from ordinary readers.[12] This one, for instance, misses the point entirely:

> Pretty terrible really. Disliked the main female character, thought her parents and would-be husband were annoying too. Nothing happens and even if it had, I probably wouldn't have cared.

And this:

> There's nothing like Irish lit to leave me scratching my head after the last page … But that's the beauty of it. It's completely unpredictable and grants you the opportunity to write your own conclusion in your head, based on your experiences, philosophies, and even your current mood.

And finally the Goldilocks gambit:

> Just right. Short but compelling. A quick read that keeps your mind reeling long after you put it down.

Perhaps the time is ripe, though, for a further 'quick read'. Belying Murdoch's oft-repeated claims that she did not write from the personal, some neglected aspects merit examination.[13]

Something Special performs two antithetical services to the Murdochian canon. At one and the same time it captures Iris's sensitive sense of Irishness to a much greater extent than her avowedly 'Irish' novels *The Unicorn* and *The Red and the Green*, while also filtering out the *specifics* of that Irishness to leave exposed (albeit in miniature, model form) the great questions that inform her later writings—the primacy of good, the nature of morality, the temporary providence of myth, the plight of outsiders, the purgatory of isolation, the helplessness of life on a railway track. And while the story is often interpreted as a sort of *après*-Joyce whimsy (or even a send-up of the great man), it is argued here that this may be a partial reading and that it is another Protestant Irish writer, Samuel Beckett, who carries as much weight in how the story is constructed and balanced.[14]

The historicist approach to *Something Special* is encapsulated in Peter Conradi's interpretation. He sets its genesis firmly within Iris's life and family and implies that the story is almost some sort of homage to or acknowledgement of her presumed cousin Eva Robinson, with whom she spent time in Dublin. In this reading it embodies Eva's world—albeit with some time-shift and embellishment—through that of the anti-heroine Yvonne Geary.[15] If it is homage, it moves in a slightly mysterious way; that is to say, while it carries a grainy verisimilitude by virtue of Baedeker-like geographic and contemporaneous reference—an apparent 'Joyceiness'—it hides conceits and deceits. It may indeed be an illusion imagined for the sake of consolation.

James Joyce, in *Dubliners*, and in *Ulysses* in particular, is forensically accurate about the Dublin he portrays. His was not just Elizabeth Bowen's 'fiction with the texture of history':[16] it was closer to *Lonely Planet 1904*. Joyce's cartographic precision was taken up by Beckett in his most Joycean novel-play, *Murphy*. And to Murdoch, 'Beckett's novel called *Murphy* became a sort of sacred text'.[17] That's the literary genealogy. In *Something Special* Murdoch, who had been introduced to Beckett's work by the later Labour politician Denis Healey in 1938,[18] revels in 'All these demented particulars', as the novel's own Mr Kelly puts it despairingly.[19] *Something Special* has its own set of 'demented particulars'—Joyce compounded by Beckett, as it were. Especially the former: as Lynch writes, Murdoch is 'every bit as precise as Joyce'[20]—'the rocks beyond the Baths'; 'Isn't it the like of the bloody English to win the Sweep again this year?'; 'a large pale moon rising over Howth Head'; the Geary shop located at a real-life address, Upper George's Street, and so on.[21]

Be careful, though, not to rely on *Something Special* as one would on the Ordnance Survey or Google Maps. Murdoch explicitly places the story in a Dublin celebrating what was known in Irish as *An Tóstal* or

'Ireland at Home', a sort of festival for tourists and returning emigrants. This dates it as having been written no earlier than 1953, a quite precise Joycean-type fixing. We would expect—and, indeed, we get—the same precision in much of the other real-life allusions in the story, except for one important proto-Joycean reference that is central to *Something Special*: the trams.[22]

These rattling cans both carry and represent Yvonne's and Sam's railway-track lives, as they both travel from the suburbs to the city centre's bright lights and as Yvonne does alone, back again to the terminus of a life going nowhere. The imagery in the story would not work anything as well without the tram. It's as if Murdoch took literally novelist Maeve Binchy's much later double-meaning instruction to budding writers: 'Readers expect to go on some kind of journey. Take them there.'[23] All this is fine and it works, except that it contradicts the 'demented particulars' in one significant respect: the tram from the city centre to Dún Laoghaire was no longer running in 1953, having been replaced by a much more un-Joycean, prosaic and, above all, unfixed bus service in 1949. This, of course, could indicate an unawareness of the change, or it could be mere untidiness—Murdoch could be a sloppy writer and famously refused to be edited. But this is one Joycean reference that Murdoch *had* to include, whatever the reality.

There are lots of other Joycean echoes in *Something Special*, even down to the bed scene at the story's end, redolent of *Ulysses*. There's a line from a song 'The moon hath raised her lamp above'[24] from an opera *The Lily of Killarney* which gets three mentions in *Ulysses*, a reference that Murdoch added into the final draft.[25] In particular, as Lynch points out, Murdoch develops threads through the short narrative 'in much the same way as motifs such as dust in "Eveline" or the pubs in "Counterparts" are a feature of Joyce's literary construction'.[26] In Murdoch's story the recurring motifs are continual references to 'special' and to flowers, whether they be roses on a Christmas card that Yvonne is trying to get her mother to buy from a salesman or geraniums plucked from the public hanging baskets by a drunken poet serenading the young woman as Sam and Yvonne flee a rumbustious pub.

The exterior levels—outsiderness, isolation, internality—are pretty much pure Beckett, reflected also in Murdoch's setting of words at right angles to actions. Murdoch could have created a simple otherness in Yvonne by the well-understood bipolarity of Protestant and Catholic, one that was at its zenith at the time this story was written.[27] But she's too subtle for just that; Yvonne is much more complex. There are resonances of *Murphy* in the character of Yvonne as she seems to retreat from a repugnant outer reality more and more into her own inner world, where perhaps she can find a sort of self-acceptance.[28] Murdoch thus confuses and catches the observer off guard, as Beckett so often does.

There's a similar sort of wrong-footing for the observer in Yvonne's outer world, the Geary household; like Demoyte's character in the contemporaneous *The Sandcastle*, we are not quite sure what we're faced with. It is not immediately obvious who they are—that is, in the traditional Irish sense, Protestant or Catholic. Yvonne's former schoolfriends have decidedly Catholic names, Burke and Nolan, although her mother speaks of them being in the same 'form' as Yvonne, giving a clue as to school: the Catholic word here would be 'class'. Her uncle, presumably her mother's brother, is an O'Brien, another 'Catholic' name, yet later on the 'Protestant' names Stacey and Batey crop up.[29] Yvonne herself talks of 'Kingstown'—a typically southern Protestant kick against its post-British name, Dún Laoghaire, emphasised all the more by Murdoch's use of the latter everywhere else in the story. 'Kingstown' is the parallel southern Protestant reality, from which reference we can, just, infer that the Gearys are Anglican, but there still hangs about them a Beckettian ambiguity, an aura of the unsettled, the half-Jew of Leopold Bloom in *Ulysses*.[30]

Murdoch progressively strips away that ambiguity; there are more Protestant signposts as the story develops. Yvonne and Sam go walking on a very Protestant peregrination set by reference to the real-life Protestant Mariners' Church and Ross's Hotel. When Yvonne rashly heads off to a rather dodgy public bar in Dublin it is obvious that, despite being not a lot better off than the clientele, she is unfamiliar with the milieu. Even if as poor as church mice, middle-class Irish Protestants were genteel and not normally frequenters of low-life public houses (although they'd frequent posh ones).

But Murdoch goes one step further to catch us off guard. We learn not only that Yvonne's former boyfriend was English but also that her current one is a Jew. Following through the centrality of Jewishness in *Ulysses*,[31] Murdoch uses this in *Something Special* to almost over-emphasise a Beckettian sense of minority, of the outsider and the excluded, one inside the other, like Russian dolls. Between drafts she changed Sam's surname to the more Jewish-sounding 'Goldman' from 'Freeman', while at the same time removing some of the cruder stereotypical descriptions of him as 'foreign-looking' and displaying 'oriental gestures'.[32] In an Irish context Sam Goldman's Jewishness is decidedly exotic. He really is a rare bird; there were no more than 1,500 Jewish males in Dublin in 1953, of which very few would have been single and of marriageable age.[33] The comparable number for Dún Laoghaire was a mere thirty-five; if he lived there he would have been close to unique.[34] Logically, following the Joycean 'accuracy' trope, Murdoch should have had Yvonne meeting a suitable boy from within the 1,900 or so Church of Ireland males in the town. And yet Murdoch here characterises the Jew—as seen from the majority Catholic perspective—as a sort of 'honorary Protestant', as just another member of the marginalised non-Catholic 5 per cent. She duly has Yvonne's uncle happy that Sam would 'bring the children up Church of Ireland'.[35] Murdoch appreciates the sense of camaraderie-in-adversity that this could lead to, each side able to poke gentle irony at religious differences between them—'I always observe Christmas just as you do, Mrs Geary', says Sam. 'I take it as a sort of emblem.'[36] The cleverness in using Jewishness in a southern Irish context is that it doubly underscores a sense of extreme minority, thus exaggerating Yvonne's and Sam's otherness and alienation from the world around them. 'We're not the public, you and me', declaims Sam to Yvonne.[37]

Finally, what of the fallen tree, which Sam finds 'so beautiful'?[38] This carries a significance within the context of Sam's religious world and its meaning. The image transmits an important symbolic message. Murdoch knew Jews and knew about Jewishness.[39] In rabbinic thought, trees serve as a symbol and metaphor for the spiritual choices of individuals. Trees are among the most dependable and useful vessels to guide people to be steadfast in the face of challenges both hidden and revealed, particularly in moments of transition. When they behave properly, people are compared to the lasting physical and spiritual stature of trees, as indeed they are also when God fells them with a thundering crash for behaving badly. Humanity's failure of the moral litmus test at the Tree of Life in the Garden of Eden may well have set humankind on its journey into the world beyond paradise, but the Tree of Life of the Torah emerges as the source of protection, sustenance and proper living that allows humankind to continually reconnect with its highest self.[40] So, is the fallen tree in St Stephen's Green a judgement on Yvonne or on Sam, or on both? If it holds as a metaphor for their future, then truly it is a bleak, Beckettian conclusion. Yvonne's final words in the story—'oh, it's a sad thing'—run into the buffers. The tram has terminated. It has no further to go.

IV

NARRATIVES OF WAR AND REBELLION

13

'THE UNREASONING ADVENTURE': WHY THE IRISH GENTRY WENT TO WAR[1]

Captain Norman Jerome Beauchamp Leslie, the Rifle Brigade, of Castle Leslie, Glaslough, Co. Monaghan,[2] was killed at Armentières, northern France, on 18 October 1914. Norman was a gambler and something of a *roué*: in Germany in 1903 learning the language, his grandfather suggested to him that there was 'No better way to learn a foreign tongue than to practise with a young lady'. Norman practised with quite a lot of young ladies. A notorious womaniser, he was reputedly the last British officer to fight a duel—typically, over the affections of an already-married Turkish princess. Yet he was also a Renaissance man—an accomplished musician, a collector of ancient Greek coins, an aspiring politician and, although not in his brother Shane's literary class, showing some promise as a lyrical writer. He had harboured hopes that he could have chronicled the war for others; he wrote in his last letter to his father, never posted, found in his cigarette case, 'There's so much to write and so little time you'll have to wait for most of it at the end of the war in my diary'.[3] But it was not to be—'We live our little lives and die', as he had put it.[4]

Norman Leslie was a professional soldier. His last letter to his mother reflected that, as well as the airy immortality of youth—he was 28 when he died.

> I can't see that our losses have been heavy at all. What are 2,000 killed and 8,000 wounded out of a force of 80 or 90,000 British who repelled 200 or 300 thousand Germans. Its [*sic*] wonderfully small ... only 2½% killed. One would imagine it would be much more like 10%.[5]

War was what he did. But the Great War—a catastrophe for him and a tragedy for his family and friends—also had ramifications for the class of which the Leslies were members, the upper tiers of mostly Protestant society in Ireland, the gentry and aristocracy, the erstwhile Ascendancy.

Much has been written about the Anglo-Irish and the Great War. The war in all its facets—its individual heroisms and its call to duty, as well as its sense of 'grand tragedy'—dovetails with the narrative of decline and decay of that community that has fascinated novelists, memoirists, poets, historians and sociologists. These were the 'People of the King'. They suffered for their loyalty and their stories are irresistible. Terence Dooley's seminal book *Decline of the Big House in Ireland* has perceptively focused on the psychological effects of the war on the gentry. This essay builds on that sure foundation, using not only their history as written by scholars such as Dooley, George Boyce, Peter Martin, Patrick Buckland, Heather Jones, Keith Jeffery and R.B. McDowell[6] but also their literature from such as Shane Leslie, Lennox Robinson, Elizabeth Bowen, Molly Keane and Lord Dunsany. The aim is to interrogate the meaning of the war to this peoplehood and how it shaped their self-regard and self-perception into the turbulent post-war period.

Numbers often deaden our humanity, flattening out the vital vistas of the hills and troughs of unique lives—as Stalin reputedly said, 'One death is a tragedy; a million deaths is a statistic'—but they set the all-enveloping environment within which the gentry experienced and perceived the Great War. As regards participation by the Irish gentry, the war was on a scale hitherto unexperienced in any previous military engagement. Its reach was huge. Some three quarters of the families listed in *Burke's Peerage and Landed Gentry* (from Abercorn to Wolseley) to whom Ireland was still significant had close military connections with the conflict[7]—Lady Charles Beresford's comment that she entertained 'in a quiet way … not having any blood relations at the War' was untypical.[8] This marked the class as fundamentally different from what Joe Lee has suggested was the 'relatively weak sense of identity with the war effort' that existed amongst the Irish generally.[9] As a caste, it bore a higher casualty rate than any other marked-out group, even the generality of southern Irish Protestants.[10] About one in four or five families suffered fatalities,[11] compared to just one in thirty in Irish families generally.[12] The corollary of this, however, was that some three quarters of these families did not suffer deaths and the headship of most survived. Of the Irish-connected families in *Burke*, only six or seven heads, or one fiftieth of the total, lost their lives. The succession was not unduly disrupted. While twenty-four families lost eldest sons, all but three had either brothers or that son's son to succeed. In any case, the quality of what they succeeded to was moot. The Big Houses were already in a precarious economic position for reasons that had little to do with the war. Dooley has succinctly summarised their parlous state: 'An economic entity can survive the loss of its management structure; but management cannot survive bankruptcy'.[13] It is arguable, indeed, that death *duties* wreaked more havoc on gentry families than death itself.[14]

But the raw numbers do not comprehend the logarithmic power of death within a small, interrelated, interbred caste which meant that a loss for one family was also a loss for many. Everyone knew everyone else. Only a couple of months after the war's outbreak, Norman Leslie's father was found writing to his wife with a catalogue of the casualties that had already occurred amongst those they knew: 'Cecil Leslie's son wounded in the eye ... Lady Erne is perfectly satisfied that Harry Crichton is alive. I hope he is.' As it turned out, Harry, heir to the Earl of Erne, did not come home; he was killed a fortnight after Norman, on 31 October 1914.[15] In 1915 Douglas Hyde wrote in a much-quoted piece:

> Nearly everyone I know in the Army has been killed. Poor Lord De Freyne and his brother were shot the same day and buried in one grave ... MacDermott of Coolavin, my nearest neighbour, has lost his eldest son shot dead in the Dardanelles. All the gentry have suffered. *Noblesse oblige*. They have behaved magnificently.[16]

If the gentry appear to have fallen in disproportionate numbers, one reason may have been that many were of the officer cadre and thus notable and noted. Norman Leslie had the benefit of a Monaghan memorial service presided over by the Church of Ireland primate and another in a fashionable London church, breathlessly reported on, appropriately enough, by the *Lady* magazine. In addition, required by honour and tradition to lead men over the top, these gentry officers could not escape that first scythe of bullets from German and Austrian industrial killing-machines.[17] The obsolete weaponry of older wars was of no use in this new dispensation of gas and tanks, enormous guns and shrapnel. It may say something about how the gentry perceived war that Norman Leslie died with the blade given to him by his mother's devoted friend the Duke of Connaught,[18] while in fiction Edith Somerville's Dan Palliser, in her 1921 novel *An Enthusiast*, expires with his father's Crimean sword uselessly in his hands, but this time against domestic enemies.[19]

The Great War was different from all previous conflicts. In its enveloping totality it made all of them its prisoners. Yet, if they were, they were often willing ones and their prison was an open one. Thomas Henn of Paradise, Co. Clare—scion of an Irish gentry family and later an academic—was quite coolly analytical about what he called the 'self-contained and quasi-feudal world' of Paradise, but he did not really question the motives and imperatives of his people in joining the war effort.[20] Similarly, Norman Leslie's father bore his loss stoically. Jack Leslie had served in Egypt and South Africa and, although nearly 60 in 1914, was heavily involved, playing his part in training men in Donegal as a temporary lieutenant-colonel in the Reserve Battalion of the 12th Inniskilling Fusiliers.[21]

War was an existential part of what the Irish gentry was. Almost half of all their eligible young men born between 1830 and 1929 who survived to adulthood were commissioned into the armed forces.[22] Alongside this was a further social and familial reinforcement, as men married women from strongly military families. The class was always one of potential warriors; it was what they did, a knightly cadre still psychologically ready for battle on behalf of the Crown—and for Ireland, too, even if the Ireland that it knew was not one recognised by many of its countrymen. Increasingly the gentry were Edith Somerville's 'landless landlords'[23] after the 1903 and 1909 Land Acts: they needed place and purpose. With the Church of Ireland, the Army and Royal Navy had always been how they earned their crusts, and acquired and held status and meaning. Yet there was a paradox: the novelist George Birmingham (pseudonym of Home Ruler and Church of Ireland Canon James Hannay) suggested that the close involvement of the gentry in military and imperial service, 'dazzled with England's greatness and the prospect of Imperial power', resulted in a destructive moral and mental absenteeism more lethal than spending the season in London or on English estates.[24]

And, like the prospect of war in all ages and places, there was always excitement. Tom Henn was a schoolboy in July 1914. He remembered his brother and cousins joining up immediately 'for the unreasoning adventure of it', as he wrote.[25] Even Norman Leslie caught the bug, writing sarcastically to his mother in September 1914, 'what fun it will be in November lying with our Mackintosh in a frozen turnip field!'[26] Norman's vision was of a *Boy's Own* war: a simple polarity, them and us, mirroring the nature of a football match between Emyvale and Glaslough Church Lads' Brigades recounted by him to his mother in the 1890s.[27] All this had its origins in how the gentry lived; the manoeuvring of military men was significant and exciting in the rituals and theatre of Big House living, such as the extensive 1899 Army exercises which were held on the borders of Kilkenny and Queen's County and which went on for upwards of two weeks. That was a great social occasion, more than just pretend war, setting the boundaries of friendship and formality, even marriage prospects and possibilities. An evocation of that organic interaction and connection between gentry and military is in Elizabeth Bowen's novel *The Last September*, where the central character, Lois, is defined not only by Ireland but by her relationship with a young British officer. In another sense, the war opened out the gentry psychologically, too, making the Western Front, in Terence Brown's formulation, 'a site of complex sexual and class alliances that cement mysterious male solidarities'.[28]

According to David Fitzpatrick, the motivation for enlistment was seldom on the basis of ideology or, indeed, a rational assessment of risks and rewards.[29] Duty and honour trumped common sense. The brothers Ross-Lewin from a minor gentry family in County Clare captured this simple credo in a very bad poem, *In Britain's Need*:

> But our little Western Island
> Could never stand alone.
> And we share in the greatest Empire
> That the world has ever known.
> To Celt and Scot and Saxon
> That Empire was decreed—

> 'Tis guarded by Irish soldiers
> Who fight in Britain's need.[30]

And as Leslie wrote in 1914,

> let us forget individuals and let us act as one great British unit, mixed and fearless. Some will live and many will die, but count the loss not. It is better far to go out with honour than survive with shame.[31]

There were some—very few—dissenting voices, heard at the time in such as the pacificism of Lady Constance, daughter of the northern Irish Earl Annesley,[32] and later in the words of the fictional Kate Alcock, heroine of Lennox Robinson's play *The Big House*, written less than a decade after the war had ended. Robinson has Kate's brother killed three days away from the Armistice, and she lashes out at her conventional father: 'You and your King and your Empire! Much good they ever did Ulick, or me, or you.'[33] Echoing this in other fiction is Sidney Royse Lysaght's character who declares that 'This war … would disgrace hell … you might as well call smallpox heroic', or poet Robert Graves's 'War was foundering of sublimities'.[34] All this led some to wonder, like that self-styled 'inglorious soldier' Monk Gibbon, a suburban southern Protestant, whether ultimately the war had any purpose or objective other than prestige for some and subservience for most.[35] Yet in a perverse way it provided a species of psychological bedrock for the gentry. In that wholly negative sense the war re-energised their sense of purpose.

War had always had the capacity to sharpen identities and loyalties; that which broke out in August 1914 did not spring unformed on the Irish gentry. The earlier war against the Boers between 1899 and 1902 was the Great War's John the Baptist; the conflict in South Africa changed the gentry's relationship with Ireland. It is at one with the Great War; both are brought together in such as the memorial by and to Percy

Francis Gethin in Sligo's Church of Ireland cathedral. The Gethins were landowners in and around the town. Percy Gethin was killed in 1916; the memorial tablet in the cathedral states that the altarpiece was painted by him in memory of his brother Reginald, who had died in South Africa in 1899.[36] For the gentry, the war against the Boers was fought for high motives. By 1899, however, it was fanciful to assume that Irishmen, whatever their political differences at home, would continue to join together in the common defence, let alone in aid of an overriding imperial idea.[37] What the South African war provoked in Ireland had not been experienced before: an open, widespread, popular nationalist sympathy for those standing against the empire—occasioning riots in central Dublin, a brigade of advanced nationalists fighting on the Boer side, posters applauding the Boer generals De Wet and Botha plastered on walls and lampposts, and the flag of the Transvaal republic flying defiantly in many Irish villages.[38]

All at once, this set the vast mass of Irish Protestants, the gentry in particular, apart from the rest, questioning their sense of nationality and identity. What was disturbing to them was overt outright disloyalty, a defiant consorting with the queen's enemies. Whether as regular soldiers or auxiliaries, to those who had taken oaths of fealty to the sovereign this was nothing short of treason. It had the effect of opening eyes as to how in a Home Ruled Ireland nationalists might see and judge the loyal minority. The epithet 'Traitors' Gate' applied by some nationalists to the Royal Dublin Fusiliers' memorial arch at St Stephen's Green seemed a dangerous signal of what might be to come—and it was read as such.[39]

Around that time the language of identity began to change too, erecting further barriers between the ethnicities in Ireland. If 'West Briton' became a pejorative term of abuse by nationalists, this only strengthened its wearing as a badge of honour by the Other, exemplified by R.S. Ross-Lewin entitling his 1907 book of excruciating but heartfelt doggerel *Poems by a County of Clare West Briton*. The term 'Anglo-Irish'—relatively new, and rarely used by the Irish gentry—began to change its meaning.[40] They became a people poised precariously on a hyphen. All this is why the Great War was so significant to the gentry's sense of belonging, since—however temporarily—it restored an empathy, or at least the hope of empathy, with a seemingly sympathetic Ireland fired by the nationalist leader John Redmond's moral, religious and imperial vision.[41] Here was the possibility of transcending the divisions that had emerged during the South African conflict. The war 'cemented with their blood a new brotherhood of Irishmen all the world over, imbued with new thoughts, and new inspirations during the defence of their common Empire'.[42] It seemed that Ireland had moved back into the sort of 'Dunraven moment' that had in 1902 facilitated the beginning of the end of the land question into a new commonality in which class and religion in Ireland could be reforged into something else in the fiery crucible of the front line.[43] But it could not be sustained. By the war's end, all this was in utter ruin.

The opening days of the war changed the rules of engagement. Certainties were the first casualties: a Guinness leaving the Kildare Street Club was moved to enquire 'Which do you think will win?'[44] That which had loomed large was now little; that which was small had grown large. On 4 August 1914 Lady Constance Annesley was staying with the Kilmoreys in County Down. 'Everything was pandemonium', she wrote. 'Everyone was leaving for somewhere. Gone was the jolly little game of Carson's Rebellion.'[45] Jennie Churchill, Winston's mother, wrote to her sister Leonie, Norman's mother, that 'Ireland seems to have sunk out of sight for the moment'.[46] In Cork Norman Leslie was awaiting embarkation for France. From his barracks he wrote a letter to his mother about his financial affairs and, typically, asked her to ensure that certain ladies received some little mementos.[47] Yet normality was difficult to dislodge. On 5 August in west Cork, Castle Townshend's harbour was bedecked with flags; it was the annual regatta and, as usual, an occasion for the gathering of the Irish gentry. On that day too 'The atmosphere was the same' at Mitchelstown Castle, where a garden party was to be held.[48] The war was—and remained—remote for many.[49] Leonard Strong captured the sense of distance in his Dublin suburban memoir: 'In Sandycove the prospect of war had seemed fantastic'.[50] Writing of Protestant life in small-town Galway, Frances Moffett detailed how little the war affected her family.[51] Its horror was only really brought home in the destruction of central Dublin during the 1916 Rebellion—the Western Front in miniature, a mirror to the greater all-consuming conflagration.

What the war meant to the Protestant mind required voicing, supplemented with and mediated through the voices of sympathisers and empathisers—poets, historians, playwrights and purveyors of McGonagallish bad verse. In particular, it needed the eye and ear of the novelist to capture the incongruity of trivial domesticities set against existential disaster. Elizabeth Bowen was just 15 at the war's outbreak. Writing many years later, she pits stark light against contrapuntal darkness, everyday detail a small bright jewel that only emphasises the cataclysmic shaking of the foundations of the world that they had known:

> August 5th was a white-grey, lean, gritty day, with the trees dark. The newspaper did not come ... about eleven we drove down the avenue in the large pony trap ... At Rockmills, my father—whose manner, I do remember, had been growing graver with every minute—stopped the pony and went into the post office. There was a minute to wait, with the pony stamping, before I again saw him framed in the low dark door. He cleared his throat and said: 'England has declared war on Germany.' Getting back into the trap he added: 'I suppose it could not be helped.' All I could say was: 'Then we can't go to the garden party?'[52]

Her 'verbal painting'[53] of that first day is theatrical, structured, consciously literary—the Irish gentry are frequently aware of acting in their own drama. Another illustration of that sense of staginess is Shane Leslie's discovery of his brother's hastily buried body on the Western Front. He wrote to their mother that 'He lies about a mile behind the trenches occupied by his regiment and within sound of the guns of both armies whose shells pass daily above his head ... the sky was ripped with the flashes of the guns, while a gigantic German searchlight threw the surrounding countryside into sepulchral relief'. The grave, he said, 'seemed to rock with the thunder of the gunfire'.[54] When men from Norman's Rifle Brigade opened it, his clothes were unsoiled and clean; his hands were white and pink at the edges and rested on the wound that killed him. To fit the body into a new pine coffin they had to remove Norman's footwear; Shane wrote that he did not cry until he saw 'that lonely pair of boots' sitting on the wretched earth. Norman seemed to have borne 'no trace of suffering or contortion ... and ... as one who had reached his appointed end with credit and dignity'. 'Poor dear Norman—he is well away—for his spirit was not there and I had no feeling of his presence.'

It's a poignant piece. However, the point is that in the Leslie Papers there are a number of drafts of this letter; Shane was apparently quite consciously creating a literary memorial for Norman, even if a private one. This mirrors Elizabeth Bowen's suggestion about 5 August 1914: 'It was an afternoon when the simplest person begins to anticipate memory',[55] amplified and coloured by the fact that *her* perspective on it was written some thirty-six years later from within a greater, more immediate war. Bowen was one of the most expert exponents of the literature of 'grand tragedy'—the notion that the Anglo-Irish carried within their DNA a gene labelled 'great disaster'. Building on this sense but hanging it on the Great War was the emergence of a seductive and subversive literature, both fiction and memoir. It speaks to regretful loss and, above all, a pre-ordained sense of the gradualness of inevitability—Dostoyevsky meets the Dardanelles.

Why does the First World War figure so prominently in the Irish gentry's story, still overshadowing the almost equally proportionate southern Irish Protestant participation in the Second? Perhaps the earlier war, as the epitome of heroic awfulness—'the youthful dead shouldering past the old through St Peter's Gate'[56]—offered an irresistible foundation myth. Bowen has one of her characters say 'I can't imagine myself without a war'. The nationalist blood-sacrifice of 1916 was matched by the Somme and Armentières. The implication is that, in a sort of symmetry with the 1916 rebels, war and its sacrifice were necessary. It validated the loyalist existence and was nurtured and amplified by an iconography of sacrifice after 1918 that was all around Irish Protestants in a way that it was not for Catholics.[57] Every Sunday was a little Remembrance Day, as at services in their churches and cathedrals those who were left eyed the tablets and rolls of honour and came up time and again against the names of those who had died. Maybe, as Heather Jones has suggested, it was because the later remembrance of the war came to stand proxy for something else.[58] The four years of the Great War were followed by four more years of a lesser war in Ireland. That lesser one did more demographic and social damage than the greater. Standing behind the war dead, then, were the many more ghosts of those who later suffered by death, burning and flight from the land they called home.

Ghostliness, predetermination and predestination are everywhere. Molly Keane wrote in 1937:

> It was November 1915 and the War had been going on for a year and four months, when Cynthia heard the news that Desmond had been killed. She had never really expected him *not* to be killed. She had felt quite fatally certain about it from the first ... They had each known quite well and each tried quite futilely to hide from the other the foreknowledge

> that this was going to happen. Cynthia had made herself hard over this so often that when she read the telegram and said, 'There's no answer,' she only felt a sort of dizziness.[59]

Echoing this, the daughter of a Church of Ireland cleric, Mrs Victor Rickard, wrote about the isolated loyalist gentry of Kerry: 'nothing had come to them but loss, and again loss'.[60] The novelists and memoirists from the 1920s engender emphasis by repetition. If Jennifer Johnston, perhaps the mistress of this genre, admits that she is often seen as telling 'the same story … over and over again',[61] it should be acknowledged that saying it over and over again does have an effect, not just on the listener and reader but on the storyteller too.

It is tempting to see the gentry as almost a disembodied state of mind, visible only by virtue of what clung to them—loyalty, little isolated and isolating islands of demesne land, low Protestantism, huge useless houses that leached off them but that they could not let go. They are ghosts. Through a specific imagery of ghostliness they are transformed into ethereal, wraith-like creatures. Bowen wrote of August 1914 in north Cork: 'The bye-roads had dried in the wind and were glaring white; the War already gave them an unreal look'.[62] In this one spare image the white-dried roads are made to stand for the bleached bones of the yet-to-be-dead, and the ghosts that were to come.

Those who fashioned the war in the frozen sculpture of the word could not rid themselves of the haunting either.[63] Molly Keane was in little doubt that 'The names of most of the young soldiers who had come and gone and fallen, at Puppetstown, in and out of love with Aunt Brenda, were the names of young ghosts now'.[64] The boy Ulick in Lennox Robinson's play is a ghost even before he dies, appearing to his sister on the day that he enlists. It is said that Norman Leslie too was seen as an apparition at Glaslough a week before he was killed.[65] Lord Dunsany even has the phantoms assailing the Kaiser in his short story

'The Punishment'.[66] Every one of the 1,561 days between the declaration of war and the Armistice held the dark prospect of the dreaded orange telegram; the torture of the war was in its seeming eternity. This was Shane Leslie's 'nightmare which has no end or meaning possible'.[67] The war was literally 'bloody terrible'.[68] Life on the Front was nasty, brutish and often short. Language itself suffered; like the wrecked soldiery, it was traumatised and shell-shocked as it cowered in the short poem, the vignette, the one-act plays of the endless streams of obituaries from these terrible theatres. Lord Dunsany's *Tales of War*, written before war's end, are thus, with no scene longer than three or four pages. It is as if anything bigger, greater, is tempting the sniper, the enemy shrapnel, the screaming shell. The dead are everywhere and yet nowhere. Daisy, Countess of Fingall, recounted that

> I used to think and say, during the War, that if ever that list of Dead and Wounded could cease, I would never mind anything or grumble at anything again. But when the Armistice came at last, we seemed drained of all feeling. And one felt nothing. We took up our lives again, or tried to take them up. The world we had known had vanished. We hunted again, but ghosts rode with us. We sat at table, and there were absent faces.[69]

It was as if her sort almost invited immolation, *wanted* the ghosts.[70]

A common reaction was to bury emotion in the bland busyness of conflict. Walter Guinness's war diaries record no personal feelings or thoughts; his son felt that 'it was not for years after the War that I felt him to be free from the strain of what he and so many others had undergone'.[71] Maybe they had seen too many other burials, or were like Lord Dunsany, in his writings after the war, jolted out of fantasy and into reality,[72] or like Edith Somerville, author of the humorous *Irish RM* stories, infused with a new and terrifying seriousness.[73] The war stopped them dead in their tracks. Writing to his father a few days before coming across

Norman's grave, Shane Leslie philosophised about war, rather than *the* War. He had 'nothing against it', he wrote,

> except that the human body suffers too much. It is like a fine fretted tabernacle in it's [*sic*] acoustic resonance to pain. Warfare throws everything out of the ordinary and natural. Everything become [*sic*] extraordinary or subternatural … everything in war becomes heroic or ridiculous … the forces of war are not intended to be under human control. Powers sinister direct all, envelop all, destroy all … war is simply waste, waste of limb and life, waste of time and talent, waste of heroism and prudence, waste of all things useful and beautiful. And the same iron rain—it raineth upon the fit and the unfit alike.[74]

Later, in a bitter little poem called 'Finis', he even inverted what he called our 'little life' into a representation of death:

> Life, where is thy boasted sting?
> Where thy victory, O Day?[75]

And thus the war had become monstrous, acquiring a malign life of its own, shuffling around like Frankenstein's creature, out of control. In the Greek myth Theseus was really fighting the labyrinth, not the minotaur. In the same vein, the true enemy came to be not the Hun, or old Fritz, or Abdul; it was, ultimately, war itself.[76] At the end, those still left standing had to cling to some promise of light. In the immediate aftermath, despite grief, there was a transcendental feeling; on Armistice Day, Jack Leslie wrote to his wife: 'I wish I was with you to embrace you … I feel excited almost to insomnia. The news is the most wonderful since the world began.'[77] Shane found what he called 'solace and oblivion in the rhythm of words'.[78] Lady Constance Annesley returned in the 1920s to a decayed Castlewellan in County Down, 'all speaking of lean years and of a hard struggle: of self denial and meagre living'.[79] Yes, but we must take note of her valedictory: 'We were home. Was there any fulfilment comparable to that?'[80] Yet there were many who would never come home; those who were left had had to postpone the pilgrimage to their graves. Thus it was for the Leslies. Shane's advice to his mother in November 1914 had been to 'Stay at Glaslough where Norman's memory is vivid in the minds of all whom you meet … stay there where the whole atmosphere yearns for him and where his name will outlive ours'.[81] But once the guns had fallen silent and stillness had crept over the cemeteries those from home could not stay away. At Norman's memorial service in London four years previously the *Lady* magazine had described his mother as 'overwhelmed … she carried a beautiful bunch of violets, and stopping before the lectern, she tenderly laid down her floral tribute'.[82] A few days after the Armistice Jack Leslie suggested to Leonie another floral tribute:

> I should like to go to Armentières in the Spring, not in cold dreary winter, and lay spring flowers on our boy's grave, both of us together. His spirit knows what is going on, and that his life was not lost in vain.[83]

To know that lives had not been lost in vain was central to the loyal Irish gentry's pysche. In November 1918 that seemed a reasonable proposition. It was not so evident in the succeeding years. Lord Dunsany's very short story 'England' has a group of soldiers speaking of the land they love. It is idyllic; it is Rupert Brooke. At the end, though, the reader learns that they are marooned far behind enemy lines with no hope of rescue.[84] The Clare soldier Bindon Blood could not even bring himself to write of that Great War and his part in it because of the betrayal he felt.[85] This could stand for the sense of hopelessness of the Irish gentry, abandoned behind the lines of a lesser war, the bastard child of the Greater.

And if service was their *leitmotif*, on 12 June 1922 purpose finally died and that betrayal was complete. Despite the many who had served, and continued after Irish independence to serve, in non-Irish and non-territorial regiments, it was the indigenous Irish regiments—the South Dublin Horse, the Leinsters and Munsters, the Royal Irish, the Connaughts and the Royal Dublin Fusiliers—which stood for an Irish patriotism within an imperial and British nexus. Yet it was British War Office bureaucrats who finally accomplished what Kaiser, Emperor and Sultan had failed to achieve—their destruction. They were disbanded in the aftermath of the Treaty.[86] A funereal ceremony was held at Windsor Castle as the regimental insignia were surrendered for the last time into the bosom of the king's protection. Even *he* caught the bewilderment, remarking that the regiments were 'called upon to part with them to-day for reasons beyond your control and resistance'. Major Bryan Cooper was moved to elegise the flags:

> From Guillemont flashes our glory,
> And the Serbian mountains reply.
> You may rot: in our hearts we still cherish
> The Colours that never will die.

But die they had. For many it was perhaps the last great death of the Great War. In all but name the ceremony at Windsor *was* a funeral.[87] The *Irish Times* wrote that 'The band in the quadrangle played plaintive airs' and the regimental representatives 'were entertained to luncheon on the completion of their pathetic errand'. The leader-writer hoped vainly for a Christ-like resurrection, but it would never come.[88] The formalities represented the withdrawal of a certification of identity; in some indefinable way, the gentry had become a lesser community, rootless, stateless even. As the provost of TCD, John Henry Bernard, had put it ruefully a few days after the Anglo-Irish Treaty in December 1921, 'I confess that I don't like to think of myself as a "Colonial"! Yet that is what it has come to.'[89] In the same vein, Major Somerset Saunderson of Cavan sighed to Hugh Montgomery 'Now … I have no country'.[90]

This essay has attempted to evoke the very real sense in which war defined the essence of the Irish gentry and the way in which 'the war to end war' carried that to its logical conclusion. War is cathartic; it interrogates notions of identity, belonging and place, physical and metaphysical. The Great War came to be seen in hindsight as embodying a point at which the gentry's coherence was finally dismantled; the jigsaw could not be put back together again. That dismantling had been long in gestation. As far as the gentry were concerned, revolution in Ireland had not started in 1916 or 1919. The southern Protestant community and its gentry leadership had become ciphers long before a shot had been fired in the war of independence. From their perspective it had kicked off in 1871, when the church of the vast majority of their members was disestablished. All the purposeful parts of their place in the country—parliamentary representation, managing local government, owning land and having cultural relevance—then gradually disappeared until nothing was left except a Cheshire Cat's disembodied grin of an abstract loyalty.

Yet it seemed that the war also temporarily energised them, from knitting socks at home to dying in the Dardanelles. It also raised awkward political and cultural questions, probed motivation, provoked self- and community examination. That occurred on both sides of the divide in Ireland. It still does. While we have matured in our understanding of what motivated such as the Irish gentry to cling to their concept of loyalty, and the historical narrative has reclaimed those who fought for king as well as country, the Royal Irish Constabulary and the Dublin Metropolitan Police are not yet allowed to share the national space. This speaks to what patriotism actually means and how we define the nation. In that regard, minorities such as the gentry have become useful laboratory rats in the interrogation and understanding of what we mean by 'identity'. Often seen as a problem, they were also

> part of the solution—not only because their existence forced nationalists to reckon with diversity and pluralism, but also because their historical analysis can help historical analysts to understand the making of a pluralist society and a functioning democracy.[91]

The gentry still presented a confident face to the world. But it was in large measure a Potemkin village—a community progressively disengaged, an engine running but in neutral gear. Granted, they were still the arbiters of style and innovation—nobody could do parties like them. But increasingly this was vacuity, filling in time between birth and death. In the introverted miniature worlds of Somerville & Ross's stories of *The Irish RM* and *The Real Charlotte*, the denuded-landed classes wove Mark Bence-Jones's intricate social filigree and indulged, amongst themselves, in genealogical speculation and esoteric activities.[92] The one area of life that still offered purpose and point was that of the military. Yet it was always a two-edged sword. Mark Bence-Jones's apocryphal characterisation of 1914 for the gentry as 'not just the beginning of a war, but the end of a nation'[93] points up the essential paradox. Too little war and the gentry's *raison d'être* was further eroded; too much and they would be destroyed. None at all, and what was the point? These complexities and contradictions were captured in the garden party at Mitchelstown Castle on 5 August 1914 that the young Elizabeth Bowen was so anxious to attend. She later wrote:

> Almost every one said they wondered if they really ought to have come, but they had come—rightly: this was a time to gather. For miles around, each isolated big house had disgorged its talker, this first day of the war. The tension of months, of years—outlying tension of Europe, inner tension of

> Ireland—broke in a spate of words. Braced against the gale from the mountains, licking dust from their lips these were the unmartialled loyalists of the South. Not a family had not put out, like Bowen's Court, its generations of military brothers—tablets in Protestant churches recorded deaths in remote battles; swords hung in halls. If the Anglo-Irish live on and for a myth, for that myth they constantly shed their blood. So, on this August 1914 day of grandeur and gravity, the Ascendancy rallied, renewed itself.

Here they had rediscovered purpose. Or they thought they had. Here they were again, regrouping in the face of those who stood against them, reliving other, remoter wars—1641, 1688, 1798, 1867; India, Afghanistan, South Africa. Ireland. Here they finally perished. And here, appropriately in Bowen's words, we take our leave of the illusion that sustained the Irish gentry in those first hours of their finest days:

> The unseen descent of the sun behind the clouds sharpens the bleak light; the band, having throbbed out God Save the King, packs up its wind-torn music and goes home.[94]

14

A YEAR OF WAR: CORK PROTESTANTS IN 1916[1]

INTRODUCTION

This essay is an exploration of atmosphere, an interrogation of identity and belongingness, an evocation of community psychology and communal connectivity at an existential moment,[2] seen through the eyes of the *Cork Constitution* newspaper—the journal of the Protestant classes. Many Cork Protestants might not have read it at all, preferring the *Irish Times* or the London newspapers or, indeed, the *Cork Examiner* and the *Cork Free Press*. The *Constitution*, however, was not only a record of Cork Protestant activity and opinion but also, by gathering it together in one space, was itself the creator and confirmer of the *idea* of a cohesive and significant Cork Protestant world. That world was in flux in 1916. While processes of societal change were slow, and not always patently observable or, indeed, obvious, the tectonic plates were shifting: on the island, looming Home Rule; far away, the Great War as a huge unseen engine but with an insistent background hum.

PROTESTANT SOCIETY IN 1916 CORK

In 1916 the Protestant population of Cork city and county numbered some 34,000, about 7 per cent of the population—predominantly members of the Church of Ireland but with groups of Methodists, Presbyterians and smaller denominations. This average masked differing proportions: of about 11 per cent, or 8,000 people, in the city; of higher concentrations in such as the towns of Bandon, Kinsale and Youghal, and in the valleys of the rivers Ilen and Bandon; and again much lower in the north-western areas of the county around Kanturk and Macroom. Cork city's built environment was, like Dublin's, still a recognisably Protestant one, with one cathedral, twelve Anglican churches, two Methodist and three Presbyterian, together with less visually obvious congregations of Baptists, Congregationalists, Unitarians and the Society of Friends.[3]

Despite small numbers, the Protestant communities could have laid claim to the status of a dominant minority, albeit one subsiding like a very slow puncture. Dominance manifested itself in the forms of 'soft' and 'hard' power. 'Soft' power was exercised primarily in the economic and social spheres, but also in the cultural and ethical. In the city, private Protestant economic power was quite evident: a trawl through *Guy's Directory* for 1916 underlines the significant position they still held within Cork's mercantile and business nexus. The principal representative bodies of capital—the Incorporated Chamber of Commerce and the Employers' Federation—'were considered unionist bodies'.[4] Public economic power was somewhat different. While Protestants held some positions of direction and control, such as chairman of the Carnegie Library, the superintendent of the fire brigade, the solicitor to the county council[5] and so on,[6] in general it was Catholics who actually had the lion's share of these positions. The Protestant community had the resources to fund expensive traditional pastimes, such as hunting and yachting, but also modern ones. With some considerable gusto, it took on new pursuits such as photography and flying, telephones and typewriters. If we have to pick an iconic manifestation of relative wealth and the embrace of the new, it is in the list of 'motor car owners' in *Guy's Directory* for 1916. Of the 500 in Cork city and county, 300 or so—or about 60 per cent—were Protestants.[7]

This people was embedded into local society in three modes, which might be designated as *overlay*, *tribal association* and *admixture*. These were not mutually exclusive but could be mixed and matched as it became necessary or congenial to do so.

Overlay is evidenced in what *Guy's Directory* called the 'Establishment'. This was a *British* establishment—the outward and visible sign of the regime. In turn, it was composed of three elements: appointed, elected and employed. The *appointed* element—appointed essentially by the Crown administration in Dublin Castle—was still overwhelmingly Protestant and unionist. There were few green shoots of greening here, even by 1916.[8] It gave Protestants a rather false sense of place and position that was wholly out of synchronicity with the contemporary political tempo. Its titular head was the lord lieutenant of both city and county, the staunchly unionist Earl of Bandon. In the city, of the six deputy lieutenants, five were Protestant. Of seventy-six magistrates, about twenty-five, or one third, were Protestant. The county establishment was even more one-sided in 1916, with all the deputy lieutenants Protestant, and well over 50 per cent of the justices.[9] Even where Home Rulers received favour, a significant proportion were Protestants, such as Henry Dale and Richard Tilson.[10] As against this, the *elected* establishment was overwhelmingly O'Brienite, Redmondite and Catholic; but the point is that, largely following the rules and operating the system, it was deemed to be constitutional and thus legitimate in the eyes of those who would not have agreed with the nationalist politics of those who ran it. The *employed* establishment sat somewhere between these poles. Its composition was a function of the hangovers from the pre-1899 local government system (Protestant jobs) and afterwards (Catholic ones). In a perverse way it was even-handed. Despite the efforts of the Local Government Board and similar central bodies to stamp it out, institutional jobbery and nepotism on both sides produced a sort of collusive corruption.[11]

One important element in this overlay was semi-detached: the presence of the military. As befitting its size, position and extensive coastline, Cork had a substantial naval and military presence, consisting of thirteen garrisons and camps in 1916, along with all the necessary ancillary operations (such as pay offices, army service corps and chaplains).[12] In peacetime the officer class provided Protestant cannon-fodder for parties, flirtations and marriages. In wartime the armed forces attempted to bond with the locality by means of sports days, parties and concerts. In 1916 these were such events as the 'usual weekly concert' in connection with the 3rd Battalion of the Royal Munster Fusiliers, held in the YMCA Hall at Aghada, and the annual Christmas fête organised by the 3rd Connaught Rangers at Kinsale, which included children's entertainments.[13]

Tribal association may almost be a cliché at this stage, but clichés are clichés for sometimes good reasons. To take the example of Cork city, of its Protestant population of some 8,000 in 1916 about 6,500 were members of the Church of Ireland.[14] Even that small population, though, supported an infrastructure that permitted an urban Protestant *sans* Big House or acres to live a Protestant life, and die a Protestant death, without necessarily much troubling the other side. That often suited the other side, too.

Admixture sometimes has to be inferred rather than directly evidenced. Even where it is evident at an institutional level, that does not necessarily imply anything other than pragmatic co-operation for mutually self-interested reasons. It cannot be taken as a particular desire for social interaction or interpersonal relations. In a society polarised on politico-religious lines, it might be more appropriate to see it as occurring in demilitarised zones rather than on some form of imagined common ground. That demilitarisation occurred along a spectrum of involvement. At one end it seemed to work best where shared beneficent and economic interests were at stake. It emerges, for example, in the Cork Fishery Conservators, the Cork Ratepayers Protective Association,[15] mutual institutions like the Cork Permanent Building Society[16] and some of the local agricultural societies and shows, in Mallow,[17] Newmarket, Midleton and Clonakilty.[18] Economic development in particular was a safely neutral space, and so, despite republican infiltration, the Cork Industrial Development Association had representatives from the Protestant young men's associations on its standing committee,[19] and Protestants and Catholics (even some clerics) served together on such as the Cork Advisory Committee for Juvenile Employment, in which the Quakers Henry Beale and S.H. Newsom were prominent,[20] and the Cork Technical Instruction Committee.[21]

In the middle of the spectrum lay interaction in the cultural sphere, in the Cork Literary and Scientific Society and the Cork Historical and Archaeological Society, where disharmony was avoided through a careful and structured system of rules on what could and could not be discussed. And while hospitals were largely denominational, publicly supported ones with a predominantly Catholic clientele—such as the North and South Infirmaries and the Fever Hospital—had religiously mixed committees of management.[22] Very occasionally Protestants and Catholics found themselves in a 'holy alliance', as when an application in January 1916 by two cinemas to open on Sundays was opposed both by the Catholic diocese and by Daniel Williams, a Cork evangelical loyalist.[23] Women-run organisations such as the local branch of the Society for the Prevention of Cruelty to Children and the Munster Women's Franchise League seemed to gel better; though led by Protestants, they demonstrated considerable admixture in their memberships. Charitable activity was another area in which denominational mixing could safely take place. The Penny Dinner depot[24] in Cork city was one institutional example, while, in the sphere of ephemeral events, a Christmas fête in Clonakilty workhouse in January 1916 was funded by a local Protestant doctor and Lady Carbery but assisted by the nationalist chairwoman of Clonakilty Board of Guardians, Minnie McCarthy, and the master of the workhouse.[25]

Protestant Cork was an entity that in effect minimised and moderated potential conflict by tribal association and class interests where it really mattered and judicious admixture where it didn't. This allowed Protestant soft power to flourish. Where hard power was at stake things were somewhat different. In the mid-1890s local unionists, operating off a restricted franchise and exploiting a bitterly divided nationalism after the Parnell split, had held such a pivotal position in municipal politics that they were enabled to elect their leader—Sir John Scott—as lord mayor in 1895.[26] That turned out to be the late century high-water mark of city unionism. By 1916 the game was up. Despite Scott's success in riding the tiger of nationalist splits in 1890s Cork city, a unionist party had in effect ceased to exist as a political force. The Unionist Association could be noisy, but by 1916 formal unionist representation on the city Corporation had shrunk to three in a fifty-six-member body, less than half than that warranted by the size of the city's Protestant population and in stark contrast to their over-representation in other spheres of life in the county.

This highlights a developing trend that was to continue into independent Ireland. Denominational identification—rather than political empathy—seems to have been the dominant consideration for Protestant voters. The south centre city ward had a high Protestant population, and here we duly find in 1916 that four of the eight councillors and aldermen were Protestant, but only one—Daniel Williams—was an avowed unionist.[27] Where politically active, broadly Protestants emerged as independents, ratepayers' representatives and, prefiguring later support for Cumann na nGaedheal, some as supporters of William O'Brien's All-For-Ireland League.[28] By sidestepping the larger national question unionists found refuge in a role as 'local nationalists'. Stemming from unionist and anti-Parnellite manoeuvres in the early 1890s, the nationalist *Cork Examiner* claimed not to be fooled, forever seeing unionists and Protestant political perfidy under every bed. The lack of formal unionist representation did not imply Protestant political aloofness or an unwillingness to become involved. It merely meant that they were willing to operate in a much fuzzier environment than a simple bipolarity of Protestant equalling unionist and Catholic equalling nationalist.

There were three principal forces at work. First, there was a small but highly visible Protestant nationalist group, exemplified by High Sheriff Henry Tilson and the National Volunteer commander Maurice Talbot-Crosbie.[29] Second, Cork unionists, learning from their successes in the 1890s, had become political chameleons, shape-shifting to maximise their advantages. Thus O'Brien's All-for-Ireland League was inherently congenial not only because of O'Brien's conciliatory stance but also because anything that would divide nationalism carried political advantages. Third, while Cork had its die-hards—a leading light was the proprietor of the *Constitution* and the Dublin *Daily Express*, Henry L. Tivy[30]—and even a few invisible Orange lodges,[31] the point is that by 1916 a significant element, if not a silent majority, of Cork Protestants had probably recognised that some form of Home Rule was inevitable, and that accommodation rather than antagonism was the practical way forward if they were to maintain their economic, educational and social privileges in any new Ireland. Such men included the brewers Richard Beamish and Arthur Sharman Crawford in the city[32] and, perhaps rather surprisingly, Lord Barrymore in the county. The former Arthur Hugh Smith Barry—a formidable leader of landlords during the late nineteenth-century land war—had spoken in the House of Lords in 1913 on the Home Rule Bill, at last recognising its inevitability.[33]

A final point about Protestant engagement in the political process was that the more local, the more successful. In 1916 there were no Protestants on Cork County Council,[34] but they surfaced here and there in the lesser bodies of urban and rural district councils and on the boards of Poor Law guardians. In 1916 there were about twenty-one in the county; notable were David Acton, chairman of Kinsale Urban District Council, Mrs Lucy Acton as a guardian for Kinsale, and Mrs Jane Marlow Burke as vice-chairman of Mallow Board of Guardians. The point is, though, that these numbers, as on Cork Corporation, were a substantial under-representation when compared to the population proportion and socio-economic status of Protestants. Either they were not opting in to the system or had been frozen out. Where they did participate, though, they seemed to have been held in some regard: when Francis Weldon, a member of Charleville RDC, died in early May 1916, the members, while noting that he differed from them in religion, nevertheless praised him for being 'independent and honest'.[35]

THE YEAR 1916 THROUGH PROTESTANT EYES

On 1 January 1916, if the *Constitution* had thumped down on a cold, early morning hall floor, how did it present the world, Britain and Ireland to the Protestant Cork businessman reading it before breakfast? The war seeped in everywhere. The year was to see that war as truly a world one, with the defence of Verdun, the fall of Kut, the Battle of Jutland, the Somme offensive (on the first day of which five Cork Protestants died), the entry of Romania into the conflict, the first use of tanks on the battlefield and airplane air raids. Yet if the newspapers are to be credited with reflecting the relative significance of what would interest their readerships, we might note that the war did not overshadow everything. The form of the paper was comfortingly familiar: the cover page was much as it had been, with commercial and personal advertisements. Only in the 'Deaths' section did the war overly intrude upon a familiar countenance. Thus ordinariness and extraordinariness sat side by side.

On that New Year's Day the *Cork Constitution* reported *in extenso* the sermon given on New Year's Eve by the newly enthroned Church of Ireland bishop of Ossory, John Allen Fitzgerald Gregg. Gregg—the grandson and nephew of former bishops of Cork, Cloyne and Ross, and himself a contentious cleric in Cork city between 1899 and 1911—talked about God causing a 'moral convulsion', evidenced, he said, by the war. He positioned Irish Protestantism in a more encompassing context: 'Our thoughts should have a wider reference—we should remember how we are citizens of a great Empire ... I feel that on a day like this, we ought not to think of ourselves alone.'[36]

That Protestant sense of being part of something greater than Ireland is everywhere in early 1916. A report on the work of the Church of Ireland Diocese of Cork, Cloyne and Ross for 1915 spoke of the war 'being uppermost in the minds of most people' and commended 'the splendid and sustained efforts which both clergy and laity are making to promote the efficiency of our forces'.[37] The Church was active in organising intercession services, and various prominent clerics were outspoken in their support for the war effort.[38] It is fair to say that at this stage the pattern of war support was one of Protestant leadership but not-inconsiderable Catholic participation; the *Constitution* was fond of pointing up what it called the turnout of 'all grades, creeds and classes' at recruiting meetings.[39] As a particular instance, at one in early January in east Cork the schoolhouse was made available by the local parish priest, who presided 'and expressed his full sympathy with the objects of the meeting'—but there was a considerable Protestant attendance, too.[40] Protestants may have felt that they should have led such recruiting meetings but this was tempered by the reality that the cannon-fodder was going to be overwhelmingly Catholic.[41]

Sending men to the front was important but, as far as this relatively small Protestant community was concerned, war support work, largely the preserve of women, was equally significant. 'The Munster Flag Day Fund' tapped into cross-denominational geographical patriotism in its aim to supply comforts for 'Munster Men fighting at the Front and POWs in Germany'. It was run by a group of Catholic and Protestant women.[42] Its joint patrons were the Protestant Countess of Bandon and the Catholic lady mayoress. If it was a symbolic mix of religions, nationalist and unionist, city and county, the one thing in common was its solidly middle-class base. The effectiveness of this prosperous alliance was demonstrated in its raising of £1,000 by the beginning of 1916. In contrast, the donations for the local branch of the British Red Cross in January 1916 came mostly from Protestants.[43]

The war imposed itself upon young and old Protestants alike. Those whom Elizabeth Bowen characterised as being in 1914 'the unmartialled loyalists of the south'[44] had become quite martial two years on. The Rising and its fallout did not deter an 'energetic Mallow War Committee' from issuing certificates of honour to relatives of men serving at the front at a public meeting in Buttevant on 26 August 1916.[45] For the young, the effect was seen on the local Church of Ireland's Young Men's Association, with the number of members dropping sharply and a consequent financial crisis. Some 240 members out of a total of 980 had joined up by the autumn of 1916.[46] At the other end of the age spectrum, connectivity with the war effort and an overt demonstration of loyalty could be had by joining the Volunteer Training Corps. This 'Dad's Army'—a group of which was famously attacked at Beggar's Bush during the Rising—had been established nationally in 1915; the Cork Corps was founded in May 1915. It had started with 100 volunteers and, in a mark of enthusiasm, by February 1916 had reached some 200 men.[47]

Side by side with the war effort life went on. While the war could impinge on money and food, weddings and golf,[48] ordinariness was always there, in such as the press reports of the day-to-day work of the county, rural and urban councils, the city Corporation, the police office, boards of Poor Law guardians and so on. The Cork Show went ahead as usual in July,[49] while the secretary of the All-Ireland Donkey Protection Society was much exercised by the potential mistreatment of animals in the summer entertainment season in August.[50] Not all Protestant activity was directed towards the war. On 19 January 1916 the Methodist church in Schull held a 'sacred concert', the proceeds of which went towards its renovation rather than the war effort. In Brinny Church of Ireland parish in October the offertory at the annual harvest service 'was devoted, as usual, to the Protestant Orphan Society'.[51] Sometimes the war's influence was more subtle. Despite its militaristic image, a New Year message from the Boys' Brigade didn't mention the war directly but enjoined the boys to 'be grateful, be wise, be careful'.[52] The message, though subliminal, would have been comprehended.

The balance between the ordinary and the exceptional is seen in the Protestant Cork Grammar School's magazine for 1916. Here the war is ever-present, of course: the frontispiece is a photograph of the school's Officers' Training Corps, there are notes on the Corps' activities, the inevitable, poignant roll of honour, a picture of a former pupil killed, and a long, heroic, anti-German poem entitled 'Kultur'. Nevertheless, while 'we are not forgetting the War', the editorial is evenly split between the conflict and the ordinary activities of the school. In contrast to the horrors of the front are reports of academic successes, changes in the teaching staff, cricket, hockey and swimming notes, and the debating society subjects, none of which was war-related.[53]

Whatever about how the war was seen and dealt with by Cork Protestants before it, there was a sea change after the Rising. The *Cork Constitution*'s offices were stoned during the rebellion and proprietor

H.L. Tivy reported death threats against him.[54] The year was turning into a game of two halves. The Rising had three principal consequences. The first, as in Dublin, was the hope that it would cement rather than fracture a national consensus. And the nationalist establishment, and its leadership, conformed initially to that hope—that is, unconditional condemnation. It seemed that the merchant princes of Cork were on the same side. As early as 29 April the AGM of the Cork Free Buffet for travelling soldiers and sailors—a body patronised by a mix of the upper echelons of city and county society, Protestant and Catholic—heard an alliterative condemnation from the Catholic Sir Stanley Harrington of 'these mad, mischievous and murderous deeds'.[55] In Cork, as in Dublin, that condemnatory mood began to change, and change very quickly, as the executions proceeded.[56] The increasing calls for clemency[57] did not strike much of a chord with die-hard loyalists,[58] although the Incorporated Chamber of Commerce, with several Protestants present, did vote for it on 12 May. Significantly, though, this was coupled with a strong denunciation of the rebellion.

More than the calls for clemency, the refusal of some public bodies to pass resolutions of condolence for the casualties suffered in the naval Battle of Jutland at the end of May seems to have enraged Cork Protestants and fractured any identity of interests even between the upper echelons of Protestants and Catholics. A vitriolic letter published on 12 June from Dr William Donovan captured the Protestant *Zeitgeist*: 'Can the loyalists of the city and county be expected to accept men like this as our future rulers?'[59] Another in October from 'a loyal corporator' decried the absence of the royal toast at the lord mayor's recent dinner.[60] This last points up an important development in Protestant political and cultural consciousness over 1916. Political unionism was almost imperceptibly being supplanted by a cultural sense of loyalism, of an almost abstract royalism, encapsulated in excessive references to the king, loyal addresses and the singing of the national anthem—that is, *God Save the King*—at every opportunity.

A second major consequence was indirect. It was not necessarily the 1916 Rising *per se*, nor the increasing nationalist empathy for its aims, but rather Lloyd George's attempts in June 1916 to find a partitionist solution in its immediate aftermath that exercised Cork political unionism. The war had kicked the Home Rule can down the road—and partition with it—but here was an attempt to bring it back up front. Unionists reacted predictably. Lord Barrymore attended a meeting in Dublin to impress upon the administration the unionist opposition to any new form of Irish government.[61] A special meeting of the committee of the county and city of the Cork branch of the Irish Unionist Alliance in mid-June, with Lord Bandon in the chair, excoriated the proposals as a 'reward for disloyalty and outrage', while the Cork women unionists expressed similar sentiments.[62] It is significant that these resolutions were passed not at public gatherings but rather in private meetings. It was probably wise to keep a low profile. On 23 June a public meeting held by William O'Brien and Maurice Healy quickly turned into a pro-Sinn Féin near-riot. The mob, passing through the city, hissed the unionist city club.[63] Later in the year Dr Dowse, bishop of Cork, Cloyne and Ross, addressed his diocesan synod. Seeing things from a British perspective yet demonstrating a strong sense of *patria*, he suggested that 'Rebellion has humiliated us ... We long for settlement ... we long for some scheme that may unite North and South ... but this result can hardly come from dividing our country.' Directly addressing his Cork Protestant flock in the post-Rising world, Dowse wondered whether 'a further measure of self-government would mean for us a still further ostracisation from our country's life and management'.[64]

The third consequence for the Protestant sense of belonging was that nationalist support for the war rapidly began to contract. Overt support began to be almost exclusively—though still not totally—a Protestant phenomenon. There were no Catholic equivalents of the Church of Ireland Young Men's Choral & Orchestral Society's self-styled 'patriotic concert' on 7 December 1916, at which 'patriotic' was defined wholly in terms of support for soldiers and sailors.[65] Up to the aftermath of the Rising, the flow of Redmondite and O'Brienite nationalism, broadly war-supportive, was in harmony with Cork Protestant sentiment. However skin-deep, the sense of being on the same side was quite powerful. From mid-1916 that sense began to vanish. The polarisation of society was emphasised and strengthened.

One incident captures the increased sourness and sectarian tensions unleashed by the rebellion. It relates to the case of the appointment of a Protestant nurse to Cork workhouse. On 7 April, just *before* the Rising, the Cork Board of Guardians discussed the appointment of a nurse for the Protestant section of the district hospital. The problem was that the salary proposed was lower than for Catholic nurses; while the Church of Ireland representative, Canon Nicholson, had been asked to identify a suitably qualified Protestant nurse at that salary, he couldn't find one and he protested at the apparent discrimination. The Board agreed to increase the salary range, and Nicholson was again tasked with finding a suitable candidate. Significantly, it was immediately after the Rising that the matter came again before the Board. This had already developed into a sectarian spat between Nicholson and an elderly O'Brienite, John Dorgan. It was considerably worsened when Nicholson again reported his inability to get a suitable Protestant nurse, whereupon the Board proceeded to appoint a Catholic. Nicholson walked out of the meeting. This had consequences for Dorgan; in February 1917 Nicholson shopped him to the authorities in a prosecution under the Defence of the Realm Act that resulted in a conviction.[66]

CONCLUSION

On the surface it would seem that, whatever about the nationalist-Catholic-republican communities, it would be hard to argue for a revolutionary mind-set within the stolid Cork Protestant nexus. Cork Grammar School's motto—*Deum timete, regem honorificate* ('Fear God, honour the king')—is perhaps an apposite summation of the Cork Protestant world-view in 1916. But what *was* revolutionary about 1916 was not necessarily the Rising but the war. All previous remembered conflicts when compared to this one were essentially newspaper ones—remote, unchallenging to the social and political order.[67] The Great War was different. Despite the overarching censorship, cinema, illustrated papers, photographs and oral testimony brought the exceptional hurtling into the ordinary. The war made everyone its prisoners, especially those willing ones, like the vast majority of the Cork Protestant communities, who had empathy with its objectives and aims. It comes as no surprise that, just as the *Cork Constitution*'s first editorial of the year was on the prosecution of the war, so too was its last. On 31 December the Church of Ireland observed a day of thanksgiving and prayer, with offertories given to the Red Cross.[68] Thus this war, localised and personalised, book-ended the year and enveloped it.

Few were in any doubt about the significance of what they were living through. The fact was that the war *did* change everything, creating a sense of life and existence as unexpected and contingent. Consuming itself through a sort of auto-cannibalism, it was already producing major and fundamental change within society, from the emergence of women and conscientious objectors, through the industrialisation of death and killing and the unleashing of populism and violent nationalisms, to unprecedented control of their citizens by state apparatuses. Given their enthusiastic embrace of the greater war effort and the enormous changes it perforce already in 1916 carried in its slipstream, is it too fanciful to suggest that the likes of Cork Protestants were in some senses more 'revolutionary' than the dreamers, idealists and poets of that lesser revolution? If so, it might be held that this 'revolutionary conservatism' would continue to be a significant part of the Irish Protestant make-up and would influence the trajectory of their social and cultural evolution in the decades that followed 1916.

15

'A SINISTER AND HATEFUL MEMORY': THE 1916 REBELLION THROUGH THE EYES OF PROTESTANTS IN DUBLIN[1]

INTRODUCTION

There were very few dissonant voices in the centenary remembrance of the 1916 Rebellion. The overwhelming sense of the citizens of today's Irish republic is that the Rebellion was a good thing. One hundred years of propaganda, bad or non-existent history and Hollywood have had their effect in retrospectively giving the Rebellion a form of legitimacy despite its profoundly anti-democratic nature and moral dubiousness. It was flawed in conception, suffering from—in Eoin MacNeill's words—'the vanity of thinking ourselves to be right and other Irish people to be wrong'.[2] And on the eve of the Rebellion those other Irish people formed the vast majority, part of which would have been the Protestants of, and in, Dublin. Mostly politically unsympathetic to looming Home Rule, they would have found the notion of anything further along the road to total separation abhorrent. This essay sees the Rising through their eyes and attempts an evocation of their afterthoughts in the days of May and June 1916, a topic not much discussed *per se* in the histories.

We have to be mindful of distinguishing between the experiences *of* Protestants in the Rebellion and their experiences *as* Protestants. In many instances their involvement had no necessary causal connection with their religious beliefs or practices, or even their loyal politics. The privations visited upon them, their suicidal forays into the theatres of violence, their being shot at by both sides—all these things happened to Catholics and Jews and atheists as well. Nevertheless, insofar as prominent Protestants and institutions such as TCD, the unionist press, the churches and the administration were caught up in the conflict, it is legitimate, from what happened to them and how they reacted, to seek a specifically Protestant 'take' on the Rising.

ENTANGLEMENT

If for no other reason than social geography Protestants in 1916 Dublin could not escape the Rebellion. The city was still very 'Protestant', with its significant civic and public architecture that of eighteenth- and nineteenth-century Ascendancy, and its economy likewise, with businesses such as Jacobs, Guinness and the Bank of Ireland, the railway and steamship companies, shops, insurance agencies and engineering firms. With about 20 per cent of the total population,[3] Protestants were overrepresented in the upper social classes and professions, with around half of doctors and lawyers, for instance. There was a Protestant lower middle/working class, consisting of about 20 per cent of the Protestant population, but in 1911 only 3 per cent of the 17,000 general labourers were Protestants.[4]

Unlike Belfast, settlement was along class rather than religious lines. However, while the bourgeoisie of both religions clustered together south of the Liffey and in the northern enclaves of Clontarf, Howth and Malahide in areas of relative salubrity,[5] intermixing between them was limited. Novelist Elizabeth Bowen's Edwardian Dublin childhood memories were of a Protestant bubble, in a small but comfortable house on the south side of the city at Herbert Place, close to the Grand Canal. Here Catholics were in 'a world that lay alongside ours, but never touched';[6] the people that they mingled with were almost exclusively Protestant. Of her parents, Elizabeth wrote that 'their friends were drawn from the Bar, from TCD, from amongst the prelates of the Church of Ireland or landed people living quietly in town'.[7] Even odours seemed sectarianised: the Molesworth Hall, where she learned dancing, 'had a Protestant smell'.[8] And Dublin definitely had a 'Protestant smell' in 1916.

A universe away from Bowen was a different sort of odour and a different sort of admixture, typified by Seán O'Casey's Bessie Burgess in his play about 1916, *The Plough and the Stars*. A loud-mouthed, drunken, unionist working-class Protestant harridan, Bessie lives in the same tenement building as the Catholic Nora Clitheroe. While seemingly forever baiting her nationalist neighbours—'Has th' big guns knocked all th' harps out of your hands?'[9]—O'Casey has Bessie siding with Nora when disaster strikes and class and gender solidarity is called for. But we should not be overly seduced by his wishful invention. Looking at a typical north city Dublin street in the 1911 census—in this case North King Street, an area of fierce fighting in 1916—only 31 residents, or 2 per cent, were Protestants in a total population of some 1,600. Like anxious Irish Catholic ecumenists in the 1960s wondering whether there'd still be enough Protestants to be ecumenical *with*, the actual opportunities to practise O'Casey's form of solidarity may have been thin on the ground. Of those Protestants, the occupations largely matched those of the Catholic population in the midst of which they lived—baker, dressmakers, slater, house-painters, draper's assistant. There were two Protestant schoolteachers identifying themselves as Gaelic: Maighread and Proinnsias Ni Chinnseamain.[10]

Dublin's Protestant working class was one already in a sharp decline that had begun in the nineteenth century; it did not originate in the revolutionary period. The causes are complex but are due to such as manufacturing decline, emigration by skilled workers to Britain and further afield (and not being replaced, as Catholics were, by migration into Dublin from rural Ireland) and the social ones of increased intermarriage with Catholics and the itinerant military. Pockets of the Protestant working class were scattered here and there, often dependent on special factors, such as the coterie of domestic servants employed by the substantial Protestant bourgeoisie in the south city, county and township areas and beyond, or the skilled working-class Protestants in the south inner city. The 1911 census reveals that in Inchicore, one of the few areas where the Protestant population was growing, only 23 per cent of the Protestant households that had featured in the 1901 census were still in the area. Many of those working in Inchicore were employed in the railway engineering works. It is unlikely that in depressed Dublin very many of these skilled workers moved elsewhere in the city.

If the Rebellion bore a distinctly 'Catholic' tinge, it wasn't manifested in religious warfare. There was little, if any, targeting of Protestants *per se*. This was not Belfast. That much was admitted by the *Church of Ireland Gazette*. After the Rebellion the paper was at pains to point out that it had not been a sectarian conflict:

> the religious element did not enter in any way into this unfortunate rebellion. We heard no whisper of old sectarian feuds. It was no case of Roman Catholice [*sic*] *versus* Protestant. The rebels did not hesitate to seize a Convent which occupied a position of considerable strategic importance,

licanism fired largely by the Gaelic revival (Constance Markievicz and Kathleen Lynn).

Outside the direct area of fighting were activists attempting to ameliorate the lot of civilians. On Friday 28 April the rather alarmingly named 'Clontarf Committee of Public Safety' was formed. Its leaders—the stolid Alderman James Moran, JP, a moderate nationalist and hotel-proprietor, and Revd J.L. Morrow, a Presbyterian clergyman—were no Robespierre and Saint-Just. Its main (indeed, its only) claim to a sort of fame was what was breathlessly triple-headlined[17] by the Dublin *Daily Express* as

Relief from the North
Adventurous Motor Ride to Belfast
In Search of Food for Starving Clontarf

David Barry, general manager of the B & I Steam Packet Company, and Jack Hickey, 'that capable motorist', set forth with what Barry described as a 'semi-military pass' signed by E.A. Aston, a Methodist Home Ruler[18] and secretary of the Public Safety Committee, and endorsed by the Royal Irish Rifles officer-in-command at Clontarf bridge and an officer of the Durham Light Infantry at Dollymount School of Musketry. In a 'fine Talbot car', they headed north towards Belfast to purchase provisions—a destination probably not unconnected with Barry's Presbyterianism. Their *faux* pass got them through military and police cordons at Balbriggan, Drogheda, Castle Bellingham and Dundalk. Nerves were on edge, marinated in a fine sense of personal preservation from Mr Barry:

> While cautiously rounding a quiet rural corner, with eyes and ears alert, what seemed like a shot suddenly rang out. I gathered myself into as small a bulk as possible and quickly whispered to my friend, the driver, 'Drive on, drive on.' Instead, he laughed and reassured me that it was only a tyre that had burst.

Having started at 7 p.m., they were travelling in darkness much of the time. Their lights failed, and they got lost. The journey took ten hours. On reaching the north, they arranged for the purchase of 10,000 loaves, bacon and butter and for the dispatch of the viands to Dublin via a special van attached to a Great Northern train. All ended well, reinforcing this derring-do episode as being as much a 'Boy's Own' adventure as a humanitarian exercise.[19] Other attempts in the north city to organise forces of 'loyalists' to prevent looting seem to have been stillborn,[20] although Howth also had a relief committee, led by the local squire, J. Gaisford St Lawrence, and a Catholic priest.[21]

Clontarf may have been starving in early May 1916 but in that comfortable suburb it was temporary. Who could eat, anyway, what with the excitement and the adrenalin? Beneath the stories of delicious middle-class privations there were real hidden ones which only can be divined from secondary evidence. On 5 May a small notice appeared in the *Irish Times* advising the clergy and Protestant members of boards of Poor Law guardians that they could obtain vouchers from the Association for the Relief of Distressed Protestants 'for distribution amongst the Protestant poor who are in distress, caused by the recent disturbances'.[22]

Moving further along the spectrum from active to passive participant was Henry Hanna, KC. Hanna was one of the party of elderly loyalist reserve soldiers known as the 'Gorgeous Wrecks'—a play on their badges, which bore the name of the king (Georgius Rex). This 'Dad's Army' of volunteer militia were attacked as they returned from manoeuvres to their barracks at Beggar's Bush on Easter Monday. Hanna escaped unscathed and later became a spectator from his house at Lansdowne Road. He had a grandstand view of the action along the railway line to beyond Bath Avenue Bridge, a hot spot of rebel activity. He helped with food for the troops at Beggar's Bush Barracks and trying to find a way of delivering it. The house next door was taken by the rebels and there was always the threat of being caught in the crossfire. On Thursday 27 April he narrowly missed being shot.[23]

Passive participants were usually just in the wrong place at the wrong time, such as Lord Dunsany, an army officer captured by the rebels, or the cars of Sir Horace Plunkett and the Earl of Donoughmore being 'riddled with bullets' because they tried to travel through rebel hot spots.[24] Other such accidental incidents involving Protestants in the city veered between the farcical and the serious. On Easter Monday the bishop of Tuam was travelling around St Stephen's Green when he was held up by heavily armed rebels who demanded his car for a barricade. On his explaining who he was, he was 'treated with civility', according to the *Church of Ireland Gazette*, but his car was nevertheless commandeered. At this the bishop, 'realising things were serious, gave his card to the *Sinn Feiner* and asked him to bring it to his superior officer' with a view to returning the car. He was permitted to retrieve the vehicle but only on condition that he provided a substitute for the barricade, which he did—it's not clear whether that involved the sacrifice of some other hapless Protestant's motor.[25]

Active spectators seemed determined to precipitate a premature death. One such was Sir John Irwin, an elderly Presbyterian magistrate. On Easter Monday he was at the tram terminus at Rathfarnham when a judge told him that a 'Sinn Féin rebellion' had broken out in Dublin and that there had been bloodshed. Despite this warning Sir John continued into the city, where, following some 'miraculous escapes', he proceeded down one of the most hazardous routes via Harcourt Street, past the Royal College of Surgeons, down to Trinity College and into Sackville Street to see for himself. After dining in the fashionable Red Bank Restaurant in D'Olier Street (amazingly still open), he tried to hire a taxi home but was informed by the taxi proprietor that he was ceasing operations 'as the last car which returned to the garage was covered with blood'.[26] There are another three newspaper columns of this, as Irwin describes his adventures during Easter Week. Perhaps it was a sort of substitute for not being able to participate in the 'proper' war.

The testimony of Revd Gordon Clements, a Presbyterian minister who crisscrossed the various bridges on the south side under fire, also demonstrates foolhardiness, although in his case it seems to have been engendered as much by the necessity of pastoral duties as by simple curiosity.[27] Some shooting was still continuing on 1 May—the chimney of his manse was hit—but, despite that, the next day he ventured into town to see what had been happening.[28] The provost of Trinity, Dr Mahaffy, trapped in his college residence, was visited by an intrepid lady, Lilly Stokes, who had come into town just to see what was going on.[29]

Passive spectators were further along the spectrum. They almost revelled in a sense of exhilaration once danger was safely passed. In the *Dublin Daily Express* of 9 May was

> *The Ballsbridge Battle*
> *A Resident's Story of Exciting Events*

This anonymous eyewitness account described soldiers working their way down Serpentine Avenue, 'followed by a great crowd that moved on with them … one would have thought that nothing was happening, that they were looking on at an exciting football match or race'.[30] The 'Armagh Lady's Adventures' in the *Express* of 16 May recounted that she was alternately 'mistaken for Countess Markievicz' and 'chased by rebels';[31] another account of the 'Burning of Sackville Street' was subheadlined 'A lady's graphic narrative' and 'Three-hour journey from Wicklow to Dublin'.[32]

Most tried to carry on a normal life as the fighting raged around them, but it wasn't easy. Isabel Fleming, a Church of Ireland spinster living in Northumberland Road, witnessed the attack on the Gorgeous Wrecks, in which five of the elderly men were killed and seven wounded.[33] 'Of the six men by the tree only one is now standing—the others must have lain down—but no, they have fallen on their backs, one over another—they are all wounded! Oh, the horror of it all—what does it mean?'[34] Candidates turned up at Trinity College on Easter Tuesday for examinations and were marooned.[35] Mahaffy, in a forced break with hallowed tradition, had to share his lunch-table with them. For him that was probably more traumatic than any rebellion.

All along the spectrum, from Wylie to Mahaffy, people tried to make sense of what they were seeing and hearing. Henry Hanna chronicled the glow of burning Dublin, the noise, the feeling that sniper fire could come from anywhere and, above all, the necessity to try and find out what was actually going on.[36] Nervous energy and the constant swirl of rumour and gossip during Easter Week seemed to engender a sense of unreality but also vivid memory, as an eyewitness of the defence of TCD attested:

> All the details and incidents of that first night will live in the memories of those who were present. The uncertainty, the suddenness of the outbreak, the lack of proper equipment and commissariat, the various incidents, tragic and comic, that seemed to fill each moment, form a phantasmagoric memory.[37]

On 5 May the *Church of Ireland Gazette*'s editor, W.B. Wells, a Liverpudlian of Irish extraction (and later a chronicler of the Rebellion in one of the first accounts to appear in print), attempted—in what was headlined as a 'study in psychology'—an analysis of what it felt like to be caught up in the Rebellion. He noted that seemingly important things—in his case, eagerly awaiting a consignment of furniture—suddenly diminished in significance as the prospect of 'stopping a bullet' shot into the foreground. Being on edge all the time meant that little food was eaten, never mind tasted; there was a 'stimulus supplied by that zest of adventure … a certain feeling that if one came through it would be pleasant to talk intimately in future years about the Irish Rebellion'. But this, according to the writer, was succeeded by 'a mood of intense and profound weariness' when little things—like hurried meals in friends' houses and the lack of a tram service—began to irritate and loom larger than they should have. And, as for those at the front, there was always the dread of being struck down by the *last* shot in the war.[38]

THE REBELLION'S EFFECT ON PROTESTANT INSTITUTIONS

If the recollection of one rebel forty years later was that in Wexford 'the houses of nearly all the loyalists were visited by parties of Volunteers and motor cars and arms seized', this does not seem to have been the case in Dublin to any significant extent—at least if the absence of any such reports in the Protestant press and eyewitness statements is anything to go by.[39] But that does not mean that the Rebellion had no effect whatsoever on the city's specifically 'Protestant' institutions. Many duly did what might have been expected of them. On 4 May 1916 the Kildare Street Club's managing committee solemnly recorded taking what it called the 'emergency steps during the Sinn Féin Rising'. This, though, was not the stalwart defence of its premises *à la* TCD but rather the entertainment of army officers with copious quantities of food and drink and their admission as guests and honorary members.[40]

As the dominant Protestant denomination, the Church of Ireland was fortunate to emerge virtually unscathed; the Dublin *Daily Express* reported on 13 May that 'no serious damage was done to the fabric of any of the Dublin churches in the recent disturbances'.[41] Reflecting what the *Gazette* wrote on 5 May about the non-sectarian nature of the conflict, where churches and clerics did suffer it was a matter of collateral rather than purposeful damage. The churches seem to have been considered by the rebels purely in the light of their strategic importance—such as St James's, which overlooked the Royal (now Collins) Barracks.[42] Church life thus continued on, with the archbishop of Dublin requesting that services should be held on Low Sunday, 30 April. It was reported that many churches did so, though under difficult circumstances. Resident in St Stephen's Green, the archbishop gave 'a little address of cheer'[43] in his local parish church of St Ann's, Dawson Street, although the situation, in the military argot, was 'unhealthy'. His palace, located on the side of the Green opposite the Royal College of Surgeons, was 'uninjured save for two bullet holes in my daughter's bedroom window'.[44]

The situation was more perilous elsewhere. That Sunday at Christ Church, Leeson Park, soldiers were firing from its steps and the service had to be abandoned. At the Pepper-Canister Church, St Stephen's, there was 'fighting very close to church during service' when '3 bullets hit Ch[urch]', and only three persons turned up for the service.[45] According to the preacher's book, the school and the parochial hall were seized by rebels on Easter Monday and recaptured by the military two days later. The synod hall at Christ Church Cathedral was apparently occupied by the rebels for a short time but no serious damage was reported.[46] Marsh's Library, though not a church-run organisation, had links, physical and institutional, with St Patrick's Cathedral, against which it abutted. Close to the fighting at Jacob's biscuit factory, the librarians escaped unscathed, but some books were later found to have bullets lodged in them.[47]

Casualties amongst clerics were rare. One such was the rector of St Catherine's church in the Liberties, who was wounded in the leg by a stray bullet;[48] another was Revd H.J. Clarke, lately a curate in one of the city churches but on Easter Monday a recently appointed chaplain to the armed forces. He had the misfortune to be strolling down the quays in his uniform, albeit with a clerical collar. Captured by the rebels, he was lodged as a prisoner in the Four Courts, suffering culinary torture rather than anything worse: 'fed on bread and cold Bovril', with Worcester sauce 'a welcome condiment'.[49]

The Presbyterians and the Methodists were less fortunate. Both had premises in Abbey Street which were destroyed. Adelaide Road Presbyterian church noted the death in the Rebellion of one of its former members.[50] Methodists also reported two child casualties connected with Dolphin's Barn on the south side of the city—one killed and one badly injured.[51] The secretary of the Christian Union Buildings, an official of the Dublin branch of the Methodist Bible and Colportage Society, Abbey Street, was also shot.[52] The Dublin synod of the Methodists had to postpone its regular meeting because of the Rebellion,[53] and the General Synod of the Church of Ireland had to be deferred until June.

One very prominent manifestation of the city's Protestant culture was its newspapers: the Dublin *Daily Express*, the *Irish Times* and the weekly *Church of Ireland Gazette*. The staunchly unionist *Daily Express*'s offices were at the top of Parliament Street, just opposite the City Hall and contiguous to Dublin Castle. Seemingly for strategic rather than political reasons, it was occupied early on by the rebels. Its recapture by troops was recounted in greatly relished detail in its issue of 9 May. The following day, one of the more colourful accounts of the business came from its racing correspondent, whose principal complaint was that the horse-racing form books—the essential bible for a turf correspondent—had been stolen, and that the Rebellion was likely to have had an adverse effect on the Irish horse-breeding industry.[54]

The *Irish Times* escaped occupation or destruction, despite being sandwiched between the strong rebel force in the GPO and the considerable corps of British troops billeted in TCD, each a few hundred yards from the newspaper's offices. Alone amongst the Dublin papers, it more or less continued publication during Easter Week, but carried almost nothing of value; it is arguable that the exigencies of military censorship, the lack of access to telegraph and telephone communications and instructions not to light the building were more annoying and unconducive to proper journalism than the threat of a rebel take-over.[55] The *Church of Ireland Gazette* at 61 Middle Abbey Street had 'a remarkable escape from the fire which devastated the Sackville street area ... Our side of the street, up to and including no. 62, is gutted ... the fire stopped immediately short of this office, which is untouched except for some slight damage to the roof.' From the Wednesday in Easter Week access to the offices was 'altogether impossible' and its editor was marooned in the building.[56]

One particular Protestant institution was centrally involved in combating the Rebellion and, more so than a defiant press and unscathed church, became the symbol of Protestant loyalty and active resistance in the Dublin of 1916. That institution was Trinity College. Its defence achieved iconic status in the eyes of many Protestants.[57] While depleted because of Easter, a detail of its Officers' Training Corps was on hand to defend the College. By the evening of Easter Monday some two dozen of the corps had been located and, under the command of E.H. Alton, a fellow (later one of the university's TDs and provost), rifles were obtained from the armoury and windows were sandbagged. The defenders were augmented by regular army personnel on leave in the city, including a number of ANZACs and Canadian troops.[58]

That first night was nerve-wracking, as the defenders attempted to secure the College's sprawling 37 acres. The staff particularly rallied round; the only one who didn't was the provost's chauffeur, who stayed away for eight days and was promptly dismissed on his return.[59] Chief Steward Joseph Marshall wrote his account in June 1916:

> There were six porters on duty within the College ... In the course of my rounds, I heard that the Sinn Feiners had seized the General Post Office and other public buildings in the city. I immediately directed Porters Halpin and Wilson to shut and lock the Front Gate ... I took from my

> office a large padlock ... and put it on the gate myself, together with arming the Porters with Fenian Pikes, which I had seized while in the DMP in 1867.[60]

The next afternoon, regular Army reinforcements arrived from the Curragh. The College then became a billet for troops to be deployed against the insurgents elsewhere in the city. As a student Officer Training Corps cadet, Robert Tweedy, pointed out, they were not there necessarily to defend the College, although its garrison—loyal, Protestant Dublin—might have liked to think so.[61] Some participants and observers, though, were adamant that the defence of TCD was vital in breaking the links between the rebels in the Sackville Street–Abbey Street area, north of the river, and their redoubts in and around St Stephen's Green.[62] Businessmen—many Protestant—in the surrounding streets were in no doubt that the actions of the OTC and College servants in securing the College had prevented the sort of destruction visited upon Sackville Street and the adjoining area.[63]

In recognition of this, £700 was raised by subscription for two large cups, a number of replicas and the sponsoring of a bed in Sir Patrick Dun's hospital, with an illuminated address presented to the garrison members. The elaborate Celticism of the address in contrast to the lack of overt national symbols or even typescript on the 1916 Proclamation exemplified the sorts of cultural complexities that were swirling around in the gun-smoke of 1916. Just as the General Post Office came to symbolise heroic defiance for the republicans (and later the mass of the nationalist population), so the resistance of TCD performed much the same function for the city's loyal Protestants, resonating with the shutting of the gates of Derry in 1689 against the Catholic King James II.

AFTERTHOUGHTS

In the aftermath of the Rebellion, newspapers, diarists and letter-writers were not quite sure what had actually happened. Had it been a 'war' or was it strictly a civil conflict? The authorities seemed clear enough; as set out in the indictments against the rebels, it had been 'an armed rebellion and … the waging of war against his Majesty the King'.[64] But to some it was perhaps more comforting to see it as a season of 'riots' and 'disturbances'; to the likes of Isabel Fleming and the *Gazette*, it carried echoes of the French Revolution when it was described as 'the Terror'—maybe the Clontarf Committee of Public Safety wasn't so off-the-wall after all. The *Gazette* comprehensively covered the outbreak and its immediate aftermath,[65] with the military operations described, perhaps tellingly, by its 'War Notes' contributor (Wells).[66] Eventually it settled on the more neutral 'Rebellion'. The *Daily Express* characterised it as 'The Revolt'. The Methodists described it as a 'disloyal movement'.[67] Death notices in the Protestant papers spoke of killings in the 'Dublin Riots';[68] some such notices were placed in the usual 'Deaths' section, whilst others were in the 'Killed in action' special section for the Great War.[69] Perhaps mindful of their mixed customer base, Protestant businesses in Dublin attempted to avoid a terminological minefield; grocers Alex. Findlater & Co. carefully apologised to its customers 'for the inconvenience caused them during the last fortnight'.[70] Jacob's biscuit factory, an epicentre of the Rebellion, in its notice of resumption of business merely referred to the 'recent disturbances in Dublin'.[71] Reading these, the apocryphal visitor from Mars might have been forgiven for thinking that nothing much had happened at all.

Initially Protestant Dublin concentrated on the material damage occasioned by the Rebellion. Many businesses suffered badly, although most seemed to get back on their feet fairly quickly. The question of compensation for loss and damage exercised them early on, and it is arguable that the bitterness expressed towards the government in the immediate aftermath was due in no small measure to its initial refusal to accept financial responsibility for the consequences of the Rebellion. On 6 May the *Irish Times* had already editorialised about 'Compensation',[72] to be followed by the Incorporated Law Society, a largely Protestant body, seeking action 'for compensating adequately all loyal subjects who have suffered by reason of the outbreak',[73] and on 19 May by the *Church of Ireland Gazette* on a similar tack.[74]

During the Rebellion, and for a short period afterwards, nationalist and unionist Ireland alike condemned it out of hand. It had passed into 'a sinister and hateful memory', asserted the *Gazette* on 5 May.[75] Almost universally, loyalists would have wholly agreed with the assessment of one newspaper, also on 5 May, which spoke of the 'stunning horror of the past ten days'. Nowhere

> was there the slightest evidence of a hope that the insurrection could succeed, or of any belief that the … 'proclamation of the Republic' was anything but gas. The waste of life was known and realised to be a barren thing even by those who were flinging it criminally away. Despair sat by the mad enterprise in its cradle and followed it to its grave.

These sentiments would have been expected to have surfaced in the *Irish Times* or the Dublin *Daily Express*, but in fact these particular comments were the trenchant, if temporary, views of the *Freeman's Journal*, the organ of the Irish constitutional nationalist movement.[76] It could be held that, in this commonality of condemnation, in a wholly ironic way the Rebellion had produced—albeit briefly—a unity of classes and creeds that was one of the leitmotifs of the 1916 Proclamation.

For a moment, then, Protestant loyalism and Catholic nationalism seemed to march in almost perfect step. But even by that 5th of May elements of uncertainty as to the future were beginning to be evident.

The *Church of Ireland Gazette* was in no doubt that in the 'upper and middle classes of all creeds the rebellion is generally regarded as both a blunder and a crime'. But while the paper felt that 'Dublin was not with the rebels' and that 'we did not get the impression that the rebellion was popular with the working classes', it expressed some misgivings, shrewdly noticing that 'the crowd cheered the unfortunate men and lads who were marched as prisoners from the College of Surgeons' on St Stephen's Green.[77] And thus unity in obloquy was to vanish like snow in summer. While loyalists consistently continued to vilify the rebels, the elongated and distasteful parade of executions rapidly produced revulsion amongst nationalists, and 'By the end of May, opinion had settled on the rebels' bravery'.[78] And by that time Protestant and Catholic opinion had firmly—and fatally—divided.[79] And that was that.

Why, according to the Protestant narrative, had the Rebellion happened? The *Church of Ireland Gazette*'s editorial comment was unequivocal as to where the blame primarily lay—in 'the criminal negligence and worse of the Irish Executive and ultimately of the Imperial Government'[80]—and it damned the Rebellion as 'the most melancholy and discreditable chapter in the history of Irish administration'.[81] The *Irish Times* was glad to see the resignation of Chief Secretary Augustine Birrell: 'It is a public blessing, but it has been purchased at a terrible cost to Ireland'.[82] The archbishop of Dublin was no shrinking violet either; at the postponed General Synod of the Church of Ireland in June, he condemned Chief Secretary Birrell's legacy as 'a wrecked and ruined Dublin and a *damnosa hereditas* of mourning and strife … for those who come after'.[83] On Sunday 14 May the Church of Ireland dean of Ossory, preaching to a captive congregation of the establishment at the Chapel Royal, Dublin Castle, harangued them about the duty of the civil government 'to protect the lives, liberty and property of those under their care', and demanded that the government should 'take the sternest measures to stamp out once and for all rebellion from amongst them'.[84]

The assembled grandees must have shuffled uncomfortably in their seats. Anglican cleric Revd Ernest Bateman, self-described as 'a Christian, a citizen of the Empire and an Irishman',[85] was so enraged that he went so far as to ascribe nobler motives to the rebels than to the Irish government:

> The careless ones who sat at ease
> In the high councils of the land,
> And heeded not the warning hand
> Which, everywhere and openly,
> Wrote of the dawn that was to be.
>
> Who would not rather be with those
> Who in that mad rebellion rose,
> And died like men, than those whose shame
> Will last as long as stands their name;
> Who, plight by each [?] and paid to rule,
> Pouched the rich fee and played the fool?

Other clerics had a field day—biblical texts were tailor-made for sermonising on the apocalypse. On Sunday 30 April the Presbyterian minister Gordon Clements preached on 'Scornful men set a city in a flame, but wise men turn away wrath', a text from Proverbs. He read from 2 Samuel chapter 30, the revolt of Sheba, 'a story very pertinent to the present situation'.[86] Revd J. Denham Osborne, speaking at Rutland [Parnell] Square Presbyterian church, took no less than two texts for his address: 'Why standest then far off, oh Lord, why hidest thyself in times of trouble' and 'There standeth one amongst you whom ye know not'—references to the sense of abandonment felt by many Protestants, and perhaps an unease that they really had not known of what their neighbours were capable.[87]

From the Anglican side, the archbishop of Dublin preached to the Female Orphan School on 7 May 1916 with the text 'Comfort ye, my people, saith your God'. He said that 'This is the message of the prophet to us today. We are thinking of the same thing. Our hearts are full of the tragedies of the past fortnight—the devastation of the city, the blood and the wounding and the tears which the mad revolt has brought.'[88] He listed a hierarchy of casualties—soldiers, policemen, innocent civilians. Unlike, though, the uncompromising condemnation from the Presbyterians and Methodists,[89] he ended with the vaguest hint of reconciliation:

> And we are sad, too, when we think of the wretched men who have lost their lives trying to stir up a revolt that could never have succeeded. We are sorry, for they are and were our countrymen, wanton and wicked as their treason was ... Let there be no bitterness.[90]

Cesca Trench, writing in her diary on 9 May 1916, was unimpressed: 'the Archbishop is making worse statements than the British. He would like to have vengeance on "the forces of anarchy", the "wretched men" ... Shame on him!'[91]

Trench's reference was probably to Archbishop Bernard's characterisation of the violence as not between Roman Catholic and Protestant or unionist and nationalist but between the abstractions of authority and anarchy. For the archbishop, who had lost a son at Gallipoli in 1915, this was a moral conflict, just as was the Great War. On Easter Sunday, the day before the Rebellion broke out, in Christ Church Cathedral Bernard had preached on the war—a 'great crusade', as he characterised it. Down the road in St Patrick's Cathedral, the dean had said that 'we are face to face with the prospect that nothing but more and more ruin and destruction can be the only preliminary to the advent of peace ... the inner meaning of the war is spiritual'. Nearly two years in, in April 1916, with tens of thousands of Irishmen serving and thousands already killed and maimed, it was seemingly going nowhere. Apart from strolling military men on leave and telegrams announcing death or wounding, it was a newspaper and newsreel war, relatively remote and unthreatening. But in 1916 the Rebellion brought the Great War to Dublin in a way it hadn't to the other cities of the kingdom. Thus the treachery of the Rebellion was seen as in stark contrast to the essential morality of the Great War.

For Dublin Protestants that war was never far away. The imagery of the devastation wreaked by the Rebellion only reinforced the immediate resonance with northern France. When the fighting ceased on 29 April, the centre of Dublin resembled the flattened towns on the Western Front, a fact not lost on Gordon Clements: 'The first sight of Lower Sackville Street', he wrote in his diary, 'reminds one of the pictures of some of the desolated cities of Belgium'.[92] 'The soldiers home from the Front say that what *was* Sackville St is now like Ypres', commented Julia Taylor to Marie Elizabeth Savage Armstrong on 4 May,[93] echoed by visiting English cleric Canon Lord William Cecil at St Bartholomew's on 7 May when he noted that the destruction of Dublin was 'similar to what he had seen in France'.[94] The nurses of Sir Patrick Dun's Hospital, which treated many casualties from nearby Mount Street Bridge, were praised as having 'a fortitude and calmness not to be surpassed by any sisterhood in the most storm-swept zone of the French battlefield'.[95] At the so-called 'Battle of Ballsbridge', a witness account wrote of people being ordered out of their houses and likened the exodus to 'the pictures of the refugees from Verdun'.[96] 'Barbed wire' across Sackville Street added to the illusion that this was a piece of Ireland that was forever Flanders.[97]

The *Gazette* claimed that 'the soldier is popular in Dublin now … And Dublin felt that the rebellion was stabbing the soldier in the back.'[98] This was what was uppermost in most Protestant minds. As regards trying to understand what made the rebels tick, there seemed to be little inclination to look past a notion of disingenuousness, of simple men and women misled by a manipulative and malign Germany, 'the plot of which our countrymen were the dupes', as Archbishop Bernard put it;[99] 'preaching rebellion to a lot of silly boys', in William Wylie's words. As the Dublin *Daily Express* asserted, 'the Sinn Féin revolt was part of a German plan to divert the energies of Britain from the supreme task of beating the Central Powers'. Perhaps it was comforting to their sense of identity to think that the whole business might *not* have been instigated by the Irish.

Moved by the bringing of the body of a 20-year-old rebel into TCD, John Joly, professor of civil engineering, pondered what had motivated him; he concluded that it was 'listening to the insane wickedness and folly preached by those older and who ought to be wiser than he' that had led to the young man's death. He speculated that the rebel was only carrying to its 'logical conclusion the long crusade against English rule which for generations has kept peace from Irish hearts',[100] and concluded by asking 'When will England appreciate the Irish temperament? When will our rulers learn that these rash and foolish sons of the Empire require quiet and resolute government, sane education, and protection from the fanatic and agitator, to whose poison they are at present exposed from their earliest years?'[101]

The *Church of Ireland Gazette* was more critically reflective. In two articles on 19 and 26 May 1916 one of its regular columnists endeavoured to educate the *Gazette*'s readership into understanding the Easter Rising in more transcendental terms.[102] In 'Sentimentalism and Rebellion', the correspondent blamed the 'literary cult of the Rebels of the past' for firing the enthusiasms of the 'sentimental dreamers, visionary enthusiasts, of romantic young men living in a fanciful realm'. But while ridiculing the ineptitude of this and previous rebellions, he was prescient enough to suggest that eventually

> The hundreds of slaughtered Irish people, the blackened ruins of Sackville Street, the agony and the brutality will be forgotten. Hectic lyrics will tell of the high souled aims, the unselfish devotion of the young poetic spirits that once again unsheathed the sword for Ireland. Pearse and MacDonagh and

> Plunkett will take their place in the Irish pantheon with Wolfe Tone, Lord Edward, and Robert Emmet.[103]

This theme was continued a week later, with an examination of the poetry of MacDonagh and Plunkett in an attempt to ascertain what moved them. It was not a sympathetic analysis, emphasising what it saw as a mania for martyrdom, an unhealthy obsession with death and dying, an unwillingness to join in co-operative enterprise for the material good of the country, nothing but 'twilight shadows of plaintive imaginings'. The writer wondered how such ineffectual poets 'deceive themselves and others into thinking they were capable of the task of overturning the greatest of empires?'[104]

The association of advanced nationalism with outright rebellion and treason, as most Protestants would have seen the events of Easter 1916,[105] posed problems for those whose identities were more muddied. The Church of Ireland had its 'nationalist' wing—the Irish Guild of the Church, whose *raison d'être* was to assert and emphasise the 'Irishness' of the Church of Ireland. It did this through art, literature and the use of Bible, prayer-book and hymnal in the Irish language. It was broad enough to contain moderate advanced nationalists like Cesca Trench and committed republicans like George Ruth, James Deakin, George Irvine, Harry Nicholls, Ernest Blythe and James Duncan,[106] as well as clerics like Canon Day and Dean Geddes who would have had little truck with treason. But it had to tread a delicate path through these interests after the Rebellion. Speaking of 'the unhappy stirring up of the bitter party feeling which they had hoped was disappearing', the Guild publicly deplored the Rebellion, more in sorrow than in anger, hoping for 'the restoration of peace and good-will among the people of Ireland',[107] but only after an acrimonious internal discussion, which was *not* reported in the press. From Trench's diary entries, it is obvious that the Church of Ireland Irish-language group was broadly sympathetic to the aims of the rebels, if not to their methods.[108]

AT THE END ...

In September 1916, W.B. Yeats privately published a poem, 'Easter, 1916', that has come to embody the idea of the Rebellion, with its famous lines:

> All changed, changed utterly:
> A terrible beauty is born.

But Yeats had been beaten to it. An earlier piece, 'Easter Week, 1916', written under the pseudonym 'Sybil', had appeared in the Dublin *Daily Express* on 16 May.[109] In their exploration of the genesis of the Rising there is a counterpointed complementarity about the poems. Yeats explained the rebels' motivation as coming from the inside, from the dreams of the revolutionaries' 'vivid faces':

> Hearts with one purpose alone
> Through summer and winter, seem
> Enchanted to a stone
> To trouble the living stream.

'Sybil', on the other hand, saw it as the result of outside forces—government and Germans in collusion—and all the time delusion:

> A Government that doth not govern
> Is truly worse than none
> Then bribery by German gold
> And aid of German gun

Our poor deluded brothers were
Lured on, and so undone.

Perhaps they were both right. Where they agreed was in wondering whether it had all been worth it:

Was it needless death after all?
For England may keep faith
For all she had done and said.

'Sybil' wrote:

Now must they bear the bitter fruit
Of folly—for 'tis true
That sin and sorrow hand in hand
The world go journeying through

Apart in quality, they are perhaps closer in sentiment.

The disruption and physical damage to the persons, properties and businesses of Dublin Protestants in 1916 were repaired easily enough. Less so the psychological. Being caught up in it, however unwillingly, it was *their* Rebellion too. And yet in one highly significant sense it wasn't. The *Gazette*, perhaps unwittingly, had put its finger on the unease of 1916 for Protestants, pointing out that there would be no Protestant ghosts to match those of Tone, Fitzgerald and Emmet, and of Grattan, Butt and Parnell, of course. Unlike virtually all other patriotic nationalist and rebellious movements in Ireland since the 1780s, this one had no significant Protestant leadership, and quite early on a cloying Catholicity began to adhere to it stubbornly, like fluff to chewing-gum. That was one more reason for Protestants to see it in a wholly malign light.[110] The longer-term effect of the Rebellion was to propel these southern Irish

Protestants into a mode whereby because of their almost unquestioning loyalty they became ever more identified with the British regime in southern Ireland. Furthermore, even though they had excoriated the government for allowing the Rebellion to happen, 1916 was a stark reminder, if they needed it, that the ultimate guarantor of their lives and livelihoods was the British *military* presence. That perception of dependence would have consequences. Southern Protestants would be marooned on the wrong side of the tracks and their acceptance of and into the state that emerged after 1922 would be stunted and delayed. The 1916 Rebellion was an unmitigated disaster for the unity of the Irish people, not just between north and south but also between the peoples that would make up 'Home Rule' Ireland. It would take many decades for the fires of memory to die down and a new form of southern Protestant Irishness to emerge from the ashes.

V

THE TRAUMA OF PARTITION AND REGIME CHANGE

16

THE BIRTH OF PARTITION: THE SOUTHERN PROTESTANT EXPERIENCE THROUGH THE LENS OF THE *CHURCH OF IRELAND GAZETTE*[1]

The *Church of Ireland Gazette*'s masthead stated that it was 'A church paper for church people'. Although not the official organ of the Church, it was inevitably often seen in that light. By the early twentieth century it denied that it was still only 'a clerical paper for clergy' or that 'the trail of clericalism is visible in our Editorial notes'.[2] Founded as the *Irish Ecclesiastical Gazette* in 1856, it had reported on the vicissitudes and turbulences—institutional, political and theological—that had rocked the Church since then. In particular, disestablishment of the Church in 1871 had been traumatic and challenging but ultimately rejuvenating, and the *Gazette*'s own fortunes mirrored that. It expanded to become a weekly paper in the 1880s and became much more a conduit of information for the laity. Fifty years after disestablishment, the Church was faced with another potential crisis, as the island was split into two political jurisdictions. Three quarters of the Church's membership and clergy were in the new Northern Ireland. This essay looks at how partition—established by the Government of Ireland Act which came into force on 3 May 1921—was seen through the prism and pages of the *Gazette*'s heavily southern orientation at the time.

Historian Daithí Ó Corráin has written of the churches in Ireland that 'the advent of the border did not occasion ecclesiastical partition, or make obligatory a new organisational beginning, or compel a sharp break with the past'.[3] However, that masked the subterranean partitionism that already existed in the Church of Ireland long before the parcelling of the island into two states. It was recognised in the nineteenth century that the Church in the north-east of the island was always more literal, more biblical, with a strong evangelical and anti-Roman Catholic streak—the Irish bible-belt, in other words. Archbishop Charles D'Arcy of Armagh averred in 1934 that the Church of Ireland in Northern Ireland reflected 'a community with a character and history of its own'.[4] Southern churchmen often struggled with the northern psyche; in 1938 Archbishop John Gregg of Dublin, on the occasion of his (first) election to the see of Armagh, confided to his diary: 'nor did I think that at age 65 I should ever be able to find N. Ireland anything but a strange land spiritually and politically'.[5] Archbishop of Canterbury Cosmo Lang agreed that the 'political Protestantism of the North' might make Gregg's position difficult if he were to accept the position.[6] As the *Church of Ireland Gazette* put it in a reflective editorial in December 1920 after the passage of the Government of Ireland Act, 'The partition of Ireland is now permanent, not because it is on the Statute Book, but because it is engraven on the tablets of the heart'.[7]

In particular, the 'prosperity and Protestantism'[8] reflected in the rapid growth of Belfast and its environs as a result of industrialisation posed challenges of a missionary and pastoral nature that were hardly felt in the isolated rural communities and comfortable suburban neighbourhoods of the south and west. In addition, the Church's main opponent in Ulster was the various forms of Presbyterianism—a rivalry that could, and did, include poaching and proselytising. In the south and west it was a different situation. There, Anglicans and Presbyterians were more or less on the same side, warily keeping their distance from a resurgent political Roman Catholicism but having little interaction with it.

Southern Anglicans and unionists were vociferous in their anti-Home Rule rhetoric; John Henry Bernard, bishop of Ossory, spoke for many in the southern Church in 1912 when he averred that 'loyalty is not a monopoly of Ulster'.[9] For a long time there existed a veneer of all-Ireland loyalism in organisations such as the Irish Loyal and Patriotic Union (founded in 1885 and later, in 1891, becoming the Irish Unionist Alliance) and the Unionist Clubs. But the truth was that, politically powerless in the face of democratisation and Irish nationalism, southern unionists relied on the Ulster card to frustrate Home Rule for the whole island. It was a dangerous and unstable gamble which ultimately did not pay off. Increasingly, Ulster unionism began to find its own regional voice and political structures separate from southern loyalism—the Ulster Unionist Council's foundation in 1904–5 was a seminal moment in the split between the two unionisms. The 1912–14 crisis over the third Home Rule Bill further demonstrated Ulster unionism's go-it-alone tendencies.[10]

The Irish Convention in 1917 and 1918—that last attempt to bring together a representative body to try and hammer out a common political destiny for the island—exemplified the political dilemma faced by the Church of Ireland in holding itself together in the face of Ulster unionist exceptionalism. The Convention's membership included John Henry Bernard, the archbishop of Dublin, and John Baptist Crozier, the archbishop of Armagh; each symbolised his 'Church of Ireland'—Crozier the northern version, Bernard the southern. And each was under pressure from die-hards in their respective communities not to 'give an inch'.[11]

The Convention was an important catalyst—after the traumas of the 1916 Rebellion and the Great War—in crystallising the deep splits within nationalism and unionism. Recognising the weakness of the southern unionist position, Bernard and Lord Midleton had tried to broker a scheme of all-Ireland self-government with the nationalist Redmondites. It failed; the Ulster delegates insisted on exclusion from the compromise. Southern Irish unionism sundered, with the 'accommodationists', led by Midleton, setting up the Unionist Anti-Partition League in January 1919, focusing on the benefits for the southern minority in having Ulster in an all-Ireland settlement.[12] But that was going nowhere. Finally, in March 1920, the scales fell from southern unionist eyes. The Ulster Unionist Council decided not to oppose the Government of Ireland Bill, which effectively admitted a partitionist solution to the 'Irish Question'. On 27 May 1920 the final betrayal took place: the Council declared support for a six-county, not nine-county, parliament. Unionists from Donegal, Cavan and Monaghan resigned from the Council in protest.[13]

Yet, if southern unionists were to be thrown to the wolves of a nationalist and Catholic state, it might be held that the institutional Church of Ireland at least offered a haven, a sense of continuity and connectivity with the *ancien régime* and their religious compatriots in an all-island body.[14] In any case, with disestablishment the Church had already had its own 'Home Rule' moment. Unlike what was now on offer in the political sphere, *its* governance was an all-Ireland system, with comfortably recognisable British parliamentary procedures and administrative rules,[15] as well as a legal and court system. That was not to be jettisoned lightly, no matter what separatist tendencies might lie dormant in the breasts of northern Church members.

One such member who exhibited a strong northern exceptionalism was Charles D'Arcy, briefly archbishop of Dublin in 1920 and archbishop of Armagh in the period of partition from 1920 to 1938. He was a very 'political' bishop, the fourth signatory to the Ulster Covenant in

1912, and later an unashamed protagonist of partition and partisan for Northern Ireland as against the Free State.[16] D'Arcy said prayers at the first session of the parliament of Northern Ireland and its State opening by George V on 22 June 1921—marking, he wrote, 'the triumphant close of a long struggle', giving 'to Ulstermen a position secure from the ceaseless agitations of the past and with power to live in peace, protected by their own lawful guardians'. With hindsight, in 1934 he went further, suggesting that partition had actually strengthened the overall position of the Church on the island—'It would give to the Protestants of Ireland a secure foothold in their country'—and evidencing this by reference to the spate of church-building in Belfast.[17] That sense of the Church standing apart from, or even above, temporal politics was articulated by Archbishop Gregg on the occasion of his (first) election to Armagh in 1938; he wrote in his diary that 'his main concern was not with forms of government but with the welfare of the Church'.[18]

The determination to keep the Church united no matter what politics threw up is the key to the public reaction in Church circles to looming partition in 1920 and 1921. Despite its strong editorial line in favour of Irish political unity, there was already a partitionist 'feel' to the *Gazette*, with a special section, 'Belfast Notes', often across two or three pages, contrasting with the relative paucity of news from the southern dioceses.[19] It was the most punchy part of the paper and occasionally the overtly political nature of the northern Church rose to the surface—for example, an Empire Day service in May 1921 turned into a unionist election rally, with a message read from Sir Edward Carson stating that every vote for unionist opponents was for the breakup of empire, the Union and Ulster. The *Gazette*'s editor could not resist pointing out that that was a bit rich, 'seeing that the Belfast Parliament stands on a broken up Union, and a broken up Ulster'.[20]

That editor was the Dublin-based Revd George Ashton Chamberlain, rector of Clondalkin, Dublin. He took a strongly anti-partition editorial line, mirroring the Midletonite Anti-Partition League's policy. Leading up to the Government of Ireland Bill's passage through parliament in late December 1920, the *Gazette*'s reportage and comment were almost exclusively about the conflict in Ireland and the rumours of interventions and truces;[21] as the Bill progressed, however, it commented extensively on the prospective dispensation.

The *Gazette* under Chamberlain's editorship had a number of consistent lines on the relationship between partition, the Church and the southern minority. From its perspective of the best interests of the minority outside Ulster, the journal excoriated partition as 'an irrevocable calamity'.[22] It pointed out that 'We have always opposed the [Government of Ireland] Bill, on the ground that any measure which postulates the partition of Ireland is rotten at its core'. The *Gazette*'s argument was that 'it places Southern Unionists in a hopeless position from the start'. The paper suggested that 'the vital fact of the Irish problem' was 'that Ireland is a unit, politically and economically, and that any artificial attempt to divide it must in the long run lead to a disastrous failure'. Ulster had accepted it 'because it is feared that, if it rejected this chance to get out from under a Dublin Parliament, it might not get such a favourable opportunity in a hurry again'. The *Gazette* felt that 'Nobody in Ireland thinks that it is a good Bill … Ulster will get its Parliament, and make a success of self-government, while Southern Ireland will enjoy the blessings of Crown Colony administration for the next twenty years'.[23] The *Irish Times* took a similar view: the Bill did not have 'a single friend in either hemisphere, outside Downing Street'.[24]

On 24 December 1920 (the day after the Bill became law) the *Gazette* continued its crusade. What is striking is the southern-centric tone of its editorials, almost as if the north was already a foreign country: 'Here we are in Southern Ireland. Ireland is our home. An Act of Parliament is about to separate us from the great Northern province for ever.'[25] How this may have gone down with its northern readership can only be imagined; most Anglicans there would almost certainly have been perfectly happy with the prospect of partition. On the last day of the year the *Gazette* was in bitter mode: 'It would be silly to act like a dog in the manger and begrudge Ulster the Parliament that her ceaseless efforts have won for her', but 'For us in the South of Ireland the outlook is very bleak'.[26] And while the editorial headline read 'Ireland' on 26 March 1921, it was actually about the increasing level of violence in the southern and western areas of the island.[27]

The *Gazette*'s angle in this was often to see both Church and state as living, developing organisms. That exegesis could at least lead to expectations of better times for both. Thus in the dark days at the end of 1920 it looked to hope in a parallel 'Transition' in both state and Church. If the 1920 Act marked profound political change, it was mirrored by equally important changes in Church finance, organisation and administration that had been approved by a Special Synod in 1920,[28] and 'the conscience of the Church awoke to the fact that she must change in a changing world'.[29]

Another way of dealing with this was to hope that, even if 'Partition, against which we, in common with all other Southern Unionists, have protested all along the line, is now an accomplished fact', it might, with goodwill on all sides, be temporary.[30] In its editorial on 14 January 1921 the *Gazette* argued that partition should not be seen as set in unchanging and unbreakable stone, and that the way to get rid of it was by way of the Council of Ireland. (The framers of the 1920 Act, while recognising the reality of the here and now, actually saw it as a step towards unity in the provisions for a transfer of powers to the Council.)[31] The suggestion of a 'constituent assembly' (deriving from the Irish Convention) was mooted from time to time by the journal.[32]

Challenging Sinn Féin, the *Gazette* suggested that only by precept—southern Ireland taking up the challenge of working the Act—would there be any chance of Ulster ever deciding to throw in its lot with the rest of Ireland.[33] With the elections for the Northern Irish parliament, though, the paper had to admit that '"Ulster" is definitely out of it, so far as the British Government is concerned'; 'the *fait accompli* in Belfast has completely changed the whole political problem of Ireland's future'. It is doubtful, however, that the *Gazette*'s conclusion—southern-centric to the last—that 'the barrier of Partition will become permanent and Ireland's ruin will become complete'[34] would have caused the Church's northern unionist members many sleepless nights. Elsewhere in the paper that week, its 'Belfast Notes' section was blatantly political, crowing over unionist victories and that 'Socialism and Sinn Féinism were so completely spurned'.[35]

While in hindsight Archbishop D'Arcy could maintain that 'our Church of Ireland was strong enough and united enough to hold her own in spite of change', Archbishop Bernard of Dublin, according to D'Arcy, feared that 'a very grave division in the ecclesiastical sphere might follow the political separation'.[36] In February 1921 the *Gazette* was concerned about this, too: 'it is important that the Church should be kept from drifting apart across the secular frontiers'.[37] After the elections for the Northern Ireland parliament in May 1921 the paper noted that, 'With the establishment of two Legislatures in our country, many regard with apprehension the possibility of interest and organisation tending to revolve around two centres, and a consequent drifting apart of two sections of our Church'.[38] Despite its strong line against partition and its integrationist approach to southern politics, the *Gazette* may have been somewhat optimistic in seeing itself as a unifying force, as a sort of common forum: 'it is a meeting place where Northern and Southern Churchmen may exchange views, strengthen sympathy and feel that they are one in the cause they have at heart'.[39]

Yet the *Gazette*'s coverage of, and comment on, the process of partition in late 1920 and through 1921 is quite sparse. Apart from the editorial and comment pieces mentioned above, letters on the question of Ulster and partition, generally from southern readers, accept the principle that if nationalist Ireland could claim self-determination, so could Ulster.[40] But even they were few and far between; none was published in the months following the passage of the Act in December 1920. Partition is not mentioned in the weekly 'Diocesan News' section from those dioceses which were split by the new border—Armagh, Derry and Raphoe, Clogher and Kilmore.[41] In its 'The Week' comment on 6 May 1921, three days after the Government of Ireland Act came into force, the *Gazette*, using its favourite French phrase, contented itself with the simple reportage that 'The Home Rule Act is on the Statute Book, and whether we like it or not, partition is a *fait accompli*'. Its principal editorial in that issue was on 'Germany in default'. There were no letters on the topic of the Act, or its consequences.[42] The Church's General Synod was publicly quiet; Primate D'Arcy's address in May 1921 detailed acts of violence (two members of the Synod had been murdered) but did not reference partition. There was no hint that a Bill introduced in Synod in 1921 to allow it to alter diocesan boundaries would be used to align them with the new political dispensations.[43] At the 1922 General Synod D'Arcy conferred equal legitimacy on both jurisdictions ('Northern Ireland and Southern Ireland') by asserting that the clergy and laity would 'obey the law of the State to which they belong'.[44] Ultimately, the Church of Ireland safeguarded its religious unity by not making political legitimacy an issue, quietly keeping its head down while adjusting its administration, finances and procedures to life in two states rather than one.[45]

The *Gazette* in this period took the line of unity between north and south as being ultimately best for the country—and the Church. Reporting on the first sitting of the Northern Ireland parliament, it emphasised the principles of precept and consent in ending partition:

> If we want 'Ulster' to throw in her lot with the rest of the country; in other words, if we want to avoid the permanent partition of Ireland, we must win her over, not by bombs, bullets, or boycotts, but by convincing her of our desire to share the blessings of peace and our genuine intention to

> work for the future good of the country which is dear to her as well as to us.[46]

Over a century later, we are still on that journey.

17

'A TUGGING AT THE HEARTSTRINGS': THE PLACE OF THE 1922 DUBLIN CASTLE HAND-OVER IN THE SOUTHERN LOYALIST NARRATIVE[1]

One week before Dublin Castle was handed over to the Provisional Government of the Irish Free State, the *Irish Times* was fearful for the 'southern loyalists' now beached on the wrong side of a revolution. They, overwhelmingly Protestant and Anglican,

> face the future with anxious hearts. All their old landmarks have disappeared. They have reached a point where they must break with traditions that were very dear to them. They are forced to adjust their minds to an entirely new set of ideals and ideas.[2]

This essay sets the existential change—that of 'ideals and ideas', represented by the Castle hand-over—in the continuum of a narrative that chronicles the slow seeping away of the substance of power from the latter part of the nineteenth century, increasingly replaced by the symbols of a hollow loyalism. The brutal reality was that the taking over of the Castle marked the confirmation of a truth that the minority had long recognised in its heart—that it was becoming peripheral in Irish affairs. The loyalists increasingly were bystanders, not participants. With an 'inevitability of gradualness', Church disestablishment in 1871, the effective demise of parliamentary representation in the south after 1885, the dismantling of their position in local government in 1898 and the transfer of land ownership in the early century, élite loyalism became a sort of strutting peacock, a display of sentimental attachment to Crown, military and empire preserved in the aspic of elaborate social rituals centred around Big Houses and the Viceregal Lodge, acting out Polly Devlin's 'minutiae of the last days of the Irish Raj'.[3] Wars in Africa and Europe temporarily gave purpose, especially to the gentry and nobility, but the main healthy abstract was all but gone.

Unionism for a long time paid lip-service to the notion of an all-island repudiation of nationalism. But the truth was that, politically powerless in the face of democratisation and Irish nationalism, southern unionists—like a small boy in a hostile playground protected by a larger one—relied on the Orange card to stymie Home Rule for the whole island. It was a dangerous and unstable gambit which ultimately did not pay off. Northern unionism's jettisoning of three Ulster counties in 1920 was the final break with its southern counterpart. Some astute southern unionists had been reading the runes before then; even that arch-enemy of the Plan of Campaign during the latter stages of the Land War, Lord Barrymore of Cork, admitted in 1913 that 'if Home Rule is forced upon us we shall have to bow under it and get on as best we can'.[4] That was a world away from a northern 'No Surrender'. The southern unionists led by Archbishop Bernard of Dublin and Lord Midleton tried to fashion a compromise with the Irish Parliamentary Party at the Irish Convention in 1917–18. Already, though, the Midletonites were arguing yesterday's solutions with yesterday's men; Sinn Féin was the coming force, and nothing eventually emerged.

Truce and Treaty seemed to offer an end to an extremely disturbed and disturbing few years for the loyalist minority which had featured murder, burnings, intimidation and flight.[5] Militants may have perceived *their* actions as against those who supported the authorities or betrayed them, but many Protestant loyalists thought that they were being targeted merely as Protestants.[6] While no rerun of 1641 or Scullabogue in 1798, Church of Ireland diocesan synod reports capture that sense of unease and despair in 1920 and 1921.[7] Depopulation was already obvious through reduced church and school attendance, although it would take the 1926 census to reveal its true extent.[8] Perception often trumped reality. As Charles Townshend has written, 'Protestants' own sense of persecution should not necessarily be taken at face value—insecurity is more a psychological than a physical state …'.[9] Southern unionist historian R.B. McDowell thus concluded that 'hardships sustained by the southern loyalists were on the whole not excessively severe nor long-lasting'.[10]

However defined—Protestant, unionist, loyalist, Anglo-Irish, West British—the minority is often placed in an enduring trope of descendancy and grand tragedy; for the likes of J.C. Beckett, Patrick Buckland and Terence de Vere White, the Treaty and its aftermath loom large, exemplified in the title of Buckland's final chapter in his book *Irish Unionism 1*: 'The End, 1922'.[11] For McDowell, a self-confessed 'neo-ex unionist', the change of regime ushered in a rather zen-like sense of stasis, of 'semi-assimilation', as he put it.[12] After the Truce and the negotiations which followed it, the provost of Trinity College asked whether the southern unionists were 'to be ignored'.[13] The answer was yes, more or less; they were an irrelevance to a British government which by mid-1921 had lost its southern unionist ideological supporters like Walter

Long and Lord Lansdowne. They were fatally divided and their leaders incompetent; at critical junctures they failed to press for specific binding commitments on such as land purchase, double taxation, compensation, continuation of the grant for TCD and protection for ecclesiastical property. The inconvenient truth that the southern loyalists had to face was that once the Ulster issue had been 'settled' they became a complete cipher.

The southern unionists got a couple of scraps from the Treaty's table. In November 1921 Arthur Griffith gave a written assurance that they would benefit from representation in the upper house of the new Parliament;[14] Article 2 implied a right of appeal to the privy council if the Treaty were violated, and Article 16 guaranteed educational and religious rights. However, ultimately these concessions were due to sensitivity towards keeping the minority's money in the country more than to southern unionist pressure. All their attempted high-politicking resulted in thin gruel.

Loyalist reaction to the end of violent hostilities was a mixture of 'relief, shocked surprise, pessimistic acquiescence and the intention of making the best of a *fait accompli*'.[15] Relief was probably the predominant emotion.[16] At a debate in Sligo Corporation on 29 December 1921 a unionist councillor stressed the importance of the peace that the Treaty would bring.[17] In asking his clergy to offer prayers of thanksgiving, Bishop Godfrey Day of Ossory welcomed the cessation of hostilities not because it represented an ideal solution but because it gave respite.[18] In early January 1922, speaking at a County Sligo Farmers' Association meeting, Sir Malby Crofton saw peace and the restoration of law and order as now the prime concerns.[19] Revd Dudley Fletcher probably spoke for more than himself when he opined that 'I am in favour of the Treaty chiefly because of the tragic and ghastly failure of the old system; but I by no means expect a new heaven and a new earth'.[20]

Not all public voices of loyalism were fatalistic. As the *Church of Ireland Gazette* editorialised in January 1922: 'Unionism has, in any practical guise, ceased to exist in practical politics … We regret its passing unreservedly, but practical men must face facts.'[21] Likewise, the *Irish Times* briskly offered a prospectus for the southern ex-unionists:

> they must be up and doing. It is in their interest that the Free State shall be an administrative and economic success … apart from the quality of their attachment to the Empire and to Imperial traditions, Southern Unionists will have the same broad policy in future as the constitutional Nationalists.[22]

When Lord Mayo organised a meeting on 19 January in Dublin of the southern minority's élite, mainly ex-landed gentry, to face what he called 'a cold douche'[23] of reality, he too looked for positives: 'no matter what Government might be in power in Ireland, England was their best customer, and they would always have to trade with their best customer'.[24] Public declarations of loyalty to the new regime were now almost *de rigeur*. In return for an outward acceptance of the constitutional dispensation, the loyalists had expiated their former sins; the responsibility for Irish history was no longer theirs to bear. The extent, though, to which these declarations were purely tactical rather than representing a Damascene conversion is open to very considerable doubt. Church of Ireland Archbishop Gregg of Dublin was publicly prepared to accept the change 'as a constitutionalist', but privately he felt banished from the Garden of Eden.[25] Presbyterians were more positive: 'with our democratic training, [our members] will be willing and ready to take their part in the promotion of the peace and of the prosperity of our native land'.[26]

Many looked for some optimism amidst ruined hope. A *Church of Ireland Gazette* correspondent opined that the coming change 'will not be without distinct elements of gain'. The emphasis will shift from 'internecine political warfare with various governments in England' to grappling with the practical problems of state-building and management.[27] Historian and TCD professor Alison Phillips saw in the settlement the best chance the country had of restoring peace and prosperity, because a native government would have the legitimacy and clout to impose law and order.[28] It could be interpreted as liberating for the minority, offering the prospect of a new and different engagement with Ireland. However unrealistic, the *Church of Ireland Gazette* identified opportunities in the moral and spiritual sphere: 'The function of the Church with regard to government in any country should be to so permeate the life and thought of the people with the ideals of the Kingdom of God … It seems as if our Church can worthily take a new position of spiritual leadership in the new Ireland.'[29] In the secular world, the president of the Dublin Chamber of Commerce, Andrew Jameson, was optimistic that business could now have a more immediate influence on government—hitherto it had been a story of pointless deputations to an uninterested London.[30]

Yet if it suited Sinn Féin to present the nascent dominion as inclusive and tolerant,[31] it was unlikely to offer anything other than symbolic gestures to the minority. Thus the *Church of Ireland Gazette*'s call in late December 1921 for southern loyalists to be brought more generally into the Provisional Government on the basis of their patriotism, business acumen and administrative experience was not taken up.[32] Even as the *Gazette* in January 1922 urged Protestants to realise, 'no less than by the majority, that they are an integral part of the State',[33] the Treaty debates in Dáil Éireann revealed an undercurrent of hostility towards and distrust of the loyalists. Lorcan Robbins claimed that 'We want the Southern Unionists and we want every Irishman (hear, hear)', but Constance Markievicz excoriated her class as 'traitors and oppressors', and Art O'Connor said that 'These people have stood in our way every time we tried to make a little advance'.[34] Ever optimistic, though, the

Irish Times downplayed 'the wild abuse of southern loyalists which came from one or two excited speakers in the *Dáil*'.[35]

And so we come to the moment when a rude reality finally intruded a few days after the Treaty's ratification. On 16 January 1922, Michael Collins and his colleagues arrived at the Castle and were formally shown to the privy council chamber—as if Collins didn't already know every inch of the building! The withdrawal of British forces and the hand-over of Dublin Castle to the new government were tangible reminders that the old order was in the process of vanishing before the minority's eyes. Sir Henry Robinson, vice-president of the Local Government Board, saw it simply as the surrender of the government to Sinn Féin, with the heads of the Irish departments, as he put it, 'sitting on one side of the under-secretary's room, and the Sinn Féin leaders sitting opposite, glowering at each other'.[36] While admitting that 'the Castle' was identified with dark deeds, the *Church of Ireland Gazette* suggested that 'some of us are left which will regret its passing'.[37] 'No Irish loyalists can watch the departure of the British garrison without a tugging at the heartstrings', sadly opined the *Irish Times* on 14 January.[38] 'The great fact', it wrote, 'is that the 16th January, 1922, will be written in history as the day on which the old *regime* ceased to exist and the Irish Free State took possession of Dublin Castle.'[39] But for some the 'old regime' was already disintegrating. Rosamond Stephen's informant told her that 'the discipline in Dublin Castle is what you never would believe. Drink, Idleness, gambling, and the most extreme form of flirtation between the young men and maidens ... to feel that chaos is in the Castle too is depressing.'[40]

The very manner of the hand-over was not lost on Protestant observers, critical wherever possible. A perceived lack of class (in every sense) in the victors seeps through loyalist commentary. The Methodist *Christian Advocate* claimed that 'the Lord Lieutenant ... appears to have been kept waiting for some time'.[41] The *Gazette* reproduced the *Irish Times*'s put-down that the Castle had been handed over to 'eight gentlemen in three taxi-cabs', hardly the stuff of a heroic victory.[42] The *Irish Times* also criticised the triumphalist tone of the hand-over's official report by the Irish side: 'The members of *Rialtas Sealadach na hEireann* received the surrender of Dublin Castle at 1.45 pm today. It is now in the hands of the Irish nation.' The paper commented that 'The phrase contrasts ungraciously with the Lord Lieutenant's courteous language to Mr Michael Collins and his colleagues'.[43] It emphasised the civility on the British side: 'the Lord Lieutenant congratulated Mr Collins ... he wished them every success in the task they had undertaken and expressed the earnest hope that ... the ideal of a happy, free, and prosperous Ireland would be attained'. Nevertheless, hopefully seeing a glass half-full, it suggested that the word 'surrender' was more about the Treatyites establishing their credentials against republicans than 'a desire to hurt the feelings of Irish loyalists'.[44]

But loyalist Rosamond Stephen's feelings were certainly hurt. Loitering outside the Castle on the day of the hand-over, her reaction was a mixture of loss, fatalism and alienation:

> I stood in Dame Street and watched with the crowd for the giving over of the Castle to the Provisional Government. It has haunted me ever since ... it was horrid beyond words ... then some of them said that the sun was shining, and that it was a great day, and Ireland was coming into her own after centuries of oppression. And I said it was very amusing to watch a crowd, but I had to go unfortunately. So I left them.[45]

If that last comment captured a Protestant sense of 'leaving' the new Ireland, perhaps Ireland had already left them. In 1916 they had been characterised as 'the illegitimate children of Hibernia and John Bull'.[46] The new reality found many not now knowing what they were—or, indeed, what others expected them to be. Major Somerset Saunderson of Cavan lamented 'I have no country'.[47] Lord Oranmore and Browne and the provost of Trinity feared that they were now colonials.[48] Edward

Gwynn of TCD wrote that 'this last year has made me feel for the first time that I am essentially English and not Irish in spite of certain sympathies and antipathies'.[49]

That southern minority—a term which started to come into common currency in early 1922—was not a ripe fruit just waiting to fall into Cathleen Ni Houlihan's capacious apron; its sense of identity was quite tenacious and it was never mysteriously going to change overnight. Indeed, over succeeding decades southern Protestants became a species of inner diaspora, living in an open prison of their own construction, inventively imagining a community for themselves within the bounds of the new polity—one which we might call the *Protestant* Free State. It was one way in which belonging to what *was* could be squared with what loyalists wanted to belong *to*.

And the change of regime symbolised by the nationalist take-over of the Castle and the constitution that followed in itself did not require the minority immediately to choose between competing allegiances. As Nora Robertson later wrote, 'In respecting new loyalties it had not seemed incumbent upon us to throw our old ones overboard'.[50] The *Church of Ireland Gazette* maintained that while Protestants were 'as good Irishmen as any … they will still be loyal Britons'.[51] How those parallel loyalties could be reconciled was summed up by Revd Dudley Fletcher: 'I am proud of my British blood and name. I allow the same privilege to my Gaelic neighbour. We both want to be proud of being Irishmen.'[52] That was encapsulated in the wider British citizenship and membership of the Commonwealth in which Sinn Féin had acquiesced—'to come within the Empire', as one *Irish Times* correspondent put it.[53] The gates to imperial service in the colonies and the British military had not been slammed shut either.

The settlement allowed loyalism—that is, a sense of cultural and royalist Britishness—to linger on.[54] A Dublin Anglican cleric could thus reassure his flock that 'Over the Irish Free State we are still to have our

King'.[55] It enabled loyalists and ex-unionists to imagine themselves still in a game of thrones, subjects of His Majesty in this revived 'Kingdom of Ireland', a reimagination of Repeal. The position of the monarch in the polity legitimised flying the Union flag and singing 'God Save the King'. Symbolising this, the *Irish Times*'s 'Court and Personal' column carried on as if nothing had changed: it was important to show that the viceregal lodge was still functioning. And so on 11 January 1922 it reported that Lord and Lady FitzAlan of Derwent attended a lecture in the RDS.[56] Next day, Lady FitzAlan was discussing the question of a wedding gift to Princess Mary from 'the women of Ireland'.[57] On the day of the hand-over itself, the viscountess visited Miss Hamilton's exhibition of paintings in Dublin. It was almost as if there was a determination to show that nothing much of consequence had happened.[58]

***

The Castle had always been, in the *Irish Times*'s words, 'the centre and symbol of British authority in Ireland',[59] pejoratively described by the *Freeman's Journal* as a 'sinister symbol of alien rule'.[60] Like the Ascendancy's Big Houses, it had never been a native Irish redoubt; even the *Times* admitted that 'always the Castle has been a place apart from the Irish people'. Like those Big Houses, it was 'the stronghold of a class which … remained a garrison'.[61] From Chapel Royal to Throne Room to Privy Council chamber, its architecture, function or symbolism had little meaning for the 'Irish nation' now in charge. But the Castle's sturdy continuance contrasted with the fate of the other elements of the *ancien régime* most closely connected with Britishness in Ireland—the Irish privy council, the honorary offices of hereditary chief butler and hereditary lord high steward, the Order of St Patrick, the Royal Irish Constabulary and Irish regiments, the position of governor-general, the Irish representative peers and ultimately the monarch himself.[62] The

Castle itself was never under threat from the new dispensation. It radiated power, and that is what the Provisional Government had to project, too. The new regime showed practicality in how it subsequently used and managed the sprawling estate. Many of the offices that were there on 16 January 1922 remained there. And is it perhaps whimsical to suggest that the Castle's essential otherness is reflected in its still being the headquarters of an entity equally as feared as its former occupants—that of the tax-gathering Irish Revenue Commissioners?

18

LOOSE ENDS? THE 1925 BOUNDARY COMMISSION AND THE PROTESTANT BORDER COMMUNITIES[1]

DEFINING INTERNATIONAL BOUNDARIES AFTER THE GREAT WAR

The question of national boundaries bedevilled much of Europe and, indeed, other parts of the world after the First World War. The great empires—German, Austro-Hungarian, Russian, Ottoman—had created multi-ethnic, multi-cultural and multi-faith entities. When the imperial glue was dissolved and successor states emerged, borders in Europe faced realignment and reordering. With a new thrust towards self-determination sponsored by the United States, a number of plebiscites were held in areas bordering Germany and the former Austria-Hungary after 1918.[2] Apart from the return of Alsace-Lorraine to France by annexation, these resulted in the transfer of relatively small parcels of land. Importantly, they did not solve many of the ethno-religious disputes that had led to their triggering.[3]

The Irish boundary question was of a somewhat different character. It emerged from the 1920 Government of Ireland Act, which set up two subsidiary parliaments within the United Kingdom. The relationships between the two jurisdictions on the island changed with the War of Independence and the subsequent Anglo-Irish Treaty of 6 December 1921. Article XII of the Treaty attempted to address the thorny question of the border between the United Kingdom and the soon-to-be-independent dominion, the Irish Free State, but it contained inherent flaws which were ultimately its undoing. It possessed a particular resonance for questions of identity and belonging of particular concern to those Protestants living in the borderlands of Donegal, Cavan and Monaghan, now tantalisingly beached on the 'wrong' side.

THE ORIGINS OF THE BOUNDARY COMMISSION

The history of the Boundary Commission is complex. The most comprehensive analysis is to be found in Paul Murray's book *The Irish Boundary Commission and its Origins, 1886–1925*, published in 2011. At first glance, it might be asked why the border question needed to be addressed at all: hadn't the fateful decision of the Ulster Unionist Council to go for a 'defensible' six-county solution, subsequently endorsed in the 1920 Act, settled the issue? But there was a recognition that it was a messy and somewhat chaotic border, with enclaves of both communities—unionist/nationalist, Protestant/Catholic—stranded on the wrong side. Some unionists were aware of the problems that this could cause; as early as December 1919, northern unionist leader James Craig, in a 'long conference' with members of the British government, was 'strongly in favour of the proposed Boundary Commission'.[4] Craig's purpose was to rectify anomalies with the aim of making Northern Ireland more governable, not less. In the circumstances of late 1919, though, the Cabinet decided not to take the Boundary Commission proposal further.

During the Treaty negotiations in 1921, the idea of a Boundary Commission was resurrected by British Prime Minister Lloyd George, so often the master of getting out of a hole by apparently giving people what they imagined they wanted. The Sinn Féin side thought that a commission would see the transfer of most of Fermanagh and Tyrone and parts of Armagh, Londonderry and Down to the Free State.[5] Kieran Rankin asserts the centrality to the Treaty of the article that constituted the Boundary Commission: 'Without the expectations [Michael] Collins had expressed on it, Collins would not have signed the Treaty and without his assent no Treaty would have been signed at all'.[6] While virtually nothing was said in the Treaty debates in Dáil Éireann about the boundary question, those expectations about Article XII that it 'would deliver vast tracts of nationalist areas to the South'[7] were a silent subtext. But between Craig's original idea of tinkering and Collins's and Griffith's hope of effectively rendering Northern Ireland unviable there lay a chasm that, as we shall see, could not be bridged.

CONSTITUTING THE COMMISSION

What did Article XII of the Treaty say?[8] It allowed Northern Ireland to opt out of the Irish Free State by an appropriate address to the king, and in that case the provisions of the 1920 Act would continue to apply there. If *that* happened, then a Commission of three persons—one nominated by the Northern Ireland government, one by the Free State government and a chairman by the British government—would be set up. The purpose of the Commission was to

> determine in accordance with the wishes of the inhabitants, so far as may be compatible with economic and geographic conditions, the boundaries between Northern Ireland and the rest of Ireland.

It is important to note that from the outset the Commission felt that its purpose was 'not to reconstitute the two territories [of Northern Ireland and the Irish Free State], but to settle the boundaries between them'.[9] 'Explicit in its ambiguity',[10] it did not address the issue of how the 'wishes of the inhabitants' were to be ascertained, and it left open the question as to whether 'economic and geographic conditions' could override those 'wishes'. That ambiguous drafting of the clause was ultimately to be its undoing.

Accepting the idea of altering the boundary was a headache for all sides. The British government wanted to see only minor changes; anything wider would place the whole Treaty settlement in jeopardy. The Northern Ireland unionists had not been a party to the Treaty. While they could afford to treat anything emanating from it with disdain—Charles D'Arcy, Church of Ireland archbishop of Armagh and staunch northern unionist, was particularly hostile—the unionist fear was that the Commission might damage the nascent northern statelet[11] and that something unpalatable might be decided without their participation. While Irish nationalists, north and south, were against the whole notion of partition, they had effectively conceded the principle by setting up customs controls in 1923. In addition, the Free State needed to present the Commission as engaging in large changes; small ones, by removing anomalies and discontents, might have the effect of making partition more rather than less secure. That was recognised by no less than the anti-partitionist editor of the *Church of Ireland Gazette*. He was dead set against the Boundary Commission—it would be 'a calamity for the whole country'—arguing that it would postpone Irish unity for another century or plunge the country into civil war again.[12]

And it was the original Civil War that fatally delayed the Commission's establishment: that delay gave vital time for Northern Ireland to 'bed down'.[13] It was not set up until October 1924, by which stage each side had differing expectations of what it was actually going to achieve.[14] Despite Lloyd George's assurances to northern premier James Craig after the signature of the Treaty in December 1921 that 'mere rectifications of the Boundary are involved, with give and take on both sides',[15] the Northern Ireland government was intensely suspicious, seeing it as a mechanism by which substantial territorial transfers might be made to the Free State. To everyone's surprise, however, Michael Collins and Craig met in January 1922 and apparently agreed a pact to settle the boundary question without British interference. Craig's motivation might have been a desire not to concede by default. But yet again the 'agreement' seemed to have been based on what Lloyd George had said to each, separately; and when Craig saw that Collins had a map implying that the latter had already been promised 'almost half of Northern Ireland, including the counties of Fermanagh and Tyrone, large parts of Antrim and Down, Derry city and Enniskillen and Newry', all bets were off for the northern unionists.[16] Any award of that quantum would provoke violent loyalist resistance.[17] That finally persuaded the unionist government to have no formal contact with the Commission, although, through the evidence presented by unionist bodies to the Commission and coordinated by the Ulster Unionist Council, it had a useful but deniable channel of communication with it.[18] In the context of the relatively 'settled' long-term nature of the Northern Ireland population breakdown by religious denomination—in the fifty years between 1861 and 1911, the change in religious denomination varied only by between plus and minus 3.8 per cent[19]—it was likely that even small adjustments would be heavily opposed.

Since it had not been contemplated that a Northern Ireland representative would fail to be nominated, the Irish and British governments concluded a supplementary agreement on 4 August 1924 which allowed the British government to nominate a commissioner on behalf of the northern side.[20] Despite this essentially eviscerating and delegitimising the Commission before it even sat, on 31 October 1924 it was officially established. The chairman, appointed by the British government, was a distinguished South African judge, Richard Feetham, who turned out to be dominant in how the Commission interpreted its mandate and carried out its work. The Free State representative, Professor Eoin MacNeill, was a 'largely indifferent, ineffectual Commissioner'.[21] He did not keep the Irish government informed of significant developments. The 'Northern Ireland' representative—appointed by the British government—was Joseph R. Fisher, a barrister, former foreign editor of the *Daily Chronicle* and editor of the *Northern Whig*, a Belfast unionist newspaper. Fisher was close to Craig and in 1922 had advised on a more radical exchange of territory involving Donegal, south Armagh and north Monaghan, the objective being 'to take in a fair share of the people we want and leave out those we don't'.[22] Fisher kept unionists well informed; he was their 'representative', doing a much better job for his side than MacNeill did for his.

THE COMMISSION'S WORK

The Commission invited submissions from the Irish, Northern Irish and British governments as soon as it was set up. The Irish government complied; the British declined to give any observations, as—predictably—did the Northern Irish government.[23] The Commission decided that its work should be confidential and that it should gather evidence before deciding on any principles. It made a preliminary scoping visit to Northern Ireland in December 1924; its travels did not stray far from the existing border, which perhaps was an early indication that its remit would be narrowly circumscribed.[24] Between March and July 1925 it took formal evidence in Northern Ireland; again, its failure to hold hearings in the Free State was perhaps evidence of the direction in which its thinking was heading. Those hearings heard oral evidence based on written submissions. They were held *in camera*, with only the barest details released to the press and public. The Commission gave the appearance of thoroughness: 575 witnesses were heard—ten individuals and the remainder witnesses from fifty-eight organisations.[25] The difficulties inherent in ascertaining the 'wishes of the inhabitants' consequent upon seriously out-of-date statistics (the last census was 1911) and marrying this with current 'economic and geographical conditions' were somewhat ameliorated by these hearings, although it has been suggested that they were merely cosmetic, designed to give the appearance of meaningful consultation rather than informing the commissioners' deliberations.[26]

The Commission proceeded on the basis that Protestants equated to unionists and Catholics to nationalists. In the context of the times, it was probably a reasonable working assumption. The chairman[27] also decided that the statistical units used to decide on the 'wishes of the inhabitants' should be the smallest for which information was available. That was always going to point the Commission in the direction of small rather than large changes. In the absence of European-style plebiscites—ruled out by Feetham as not mentioned in Article XII[28]—this effectively scuppered anything but tinkering. Nationalists' vision that whole counties would be considered was never in the frame. Furthermore, the chairman's distinction between undefined 'bare' and 'substantial' majorities when determining potential transfers undermined any pretence at democracy.[29]

The Boundary Commission's report was thorough and extremely detailed, covering 155 printed pages and a further 109 of appendices and schedules, together with a series of maps. The Commission's secretiveness had possibly led to a 'bubble' mentality. This applied particularly to the Free State commissioner, MacNeill, who was prepared to sign the 'Award', as it was called, on the basis that 'it would serve the great ultimate object of avoiding further controversy'.[30] On 25 October 1925 the three commissioners agreed a draft outline of the Award. Fisher, however, had been in correspondence with northern unionists all during the Commission's existence and, while there is no direct evidence, he may have been responsible for a leak of a map of the proposed Award to the ultra-unionist *Morning Post* newspaper, published on 7 November 1925. It showed that, despite the work put into it, the outcome was little more than an exercise in minor adjustments; nationalist expectations of wholesale transfers of large areas to the Free State were completely dashed. Two decisions in particular rankled: over 30,000 acres of Donegal were awarded to Northern Ireland to bolster Derry's economic hinterland, while Feetham insisted that Newry, where 75 per cent of the inhabitants were assessed as wanting transfer to the Free State, fell within the economic ambit of Belfast and that therefore 'economic and geographical' factors should override the inhabitants' wishes.[31]

The leak provoked a political crisis in Dublin. On 20 November 1925 MacNeill resigned as commissioner. The Free State's engagement with the Boundary Commission 'was badly handled from beginning to end'.[32] The *Irish Times*, in 'told-you-so' mode, wrote of the 'inevitable collapse' of the Commission.[33] The *Church of Ireland Gazette* excoriated MacNeill: he was 'unfitted to his post … he never took the trouble to examine in detail the evidence placed before the Commission, or the lines of the projected report'.[34] The remaining two commissioners ploughed ahead, but it was now clear that any transfer of land in either direction would be political dynamite. The British and Irish governments hastily convened talks which culminated in an agreement on 3 December. It was much broader than just dealing with the Boundary Commission. Registered with the League of Nations, it gave permanent recognition to partition.[35] Irish liabilities for Great War debt were waived, but the Free State agreed to assume liabilities arising from the War of Independence and Civil

War. The Council of Ireland was abolished. It was agreed to confirm the *status quo* and suppress the Boundary Commission's report.[36] It was considered so sensitive that it was not released into the public domain until 44 years later.[37]

THE REACTION OF THE PROTESTANT BORDER COMMUNITIES

Scholarly discussions of the episode by such as Hand, Rankin and Murray have tended to focus on the high politics involved. But the Boundary Commission provoked intense debate, hope, worry and fear amongst the border communities of both traditions. The Commission noted that witnesses wanted to be 'in their own country', where there were no 'Special Police', where they would get 'fair play'. Each side saw brighter prospects, a cheaper cost of living and better employment in the jurisdiction to which they aspired to belong. But the inherent paradox in any adjustment of the border is that there would still be a border, somewhere; 'witnesses on both sides freely said that their real wish was that there should be no boundary either political or fiscal'.[38] Whatever about the politics, it had been the Free State that imposed the customs border in 1923 that effectively made partition a lived and unpleasant reality for many, and which was not formally removed until 1992 with the institution of the EU's Single Market. It was expensive, annoying and bureaucratic. Alexander Bryce, an east Donegal Protestant farmer, told the Commission that, 'if we are cut off from Londonderry, we have no other market town … we all feel the grievance in our district. It is not altogether a matter of sentiment, it is a matter of business and economy.'[39]

Bryce's comment was typical. In its report, the Commission stated—and a reading of the evidence presented to them confirms—that most witnesses spoke more about economic than about political or religious aspirations. For instance, of sixty-one witnesses from east Donegal (a Protestant area), fifty-four laid 'primary stress' on the inconvenience of being separated from their market towns.[40] The other side expressed similar views: 'A wholesale trader, who was asked whether he wished his town to be in the Free State if one half of its market remained in Northern Ireland said, "as an ex-politician, yes. As a merchant, no".'[41] Protestants tended to emphasise their economic clout, and to use this to counter simple measurement of heads.[42] In its detailed consideration of the Derry/east Donegal situation, the Commission concluded that transferring Derry to the Irish Free State 'would make economic conditions worse instead of better'.[43] The east Donegal Protestants had some success, though; the Commission agreed that a portion of east Donegal contiguous to Derry should be transferred to Northern Ireland.[44]

In general, the evidence given to the Commission by Protestants north of the existing border could be summed up in the phrase 'not an inch'. A Fermanagh rector was an extreme example; he advised that 'all Protestants should get out of the Free State as quickly as they can'. He would immediately resign his living if his parish was transferred to the Free State, since he could not be loyal to it—'I can't get over my bringing up'.[45] Most other witnesses were less extreme, and they tended to stress the lack of economic connections with the Free State as the principal reason for not wanting change.[46]

Southern border Protestant evidence reveals a more nuanced mindset four years after partition and demonstrates some essential differences between how they viewed their world and that seen and experienced by Protestants elsewhere in the Free State. But we would not want to exaggerate these differences. Most significant, perhaps, is that the border Protestants—north and south—had a breadth and depth of support networks that were largely border-blind. Their kinship and friendship connections, their churches and particularly the Orange Order probably all acted to make the border less relevant in cultural and political terms, whatever about the economics.[47] One feature of much of the Protestant evidence was its assertion that, as against migrant Catholic labourers and short-term tenants, it had a deeper and more embedded stake in the landscape and economy and contributed proportionately more to overall prosperity.[48]

Indeed, the border perhaps gave them options that other Protestants in the Free State didn't have. The evidence given to the Commission by loyalists often highlighted that one reason they wanted a shift to Northern Ireland was the language issue.[49] By 1925 the Gaelicisation policy of the Free State government was in full swing. It was claimed that compulsory Irish had encouraged east Donegal Protestants to send their children to primary schools over the border, with a consequent weakening of Protestant national schools in Donegal[50]—'we cannot see any benefit in teaching our children Irish. We do not see it will be any benefit to them in after life, and it is a matter of losing their time.' 'Those of us who have children at school feel hurt about the Irish language being forced on them', as Samuel Condell, a County Monaghan farmer, put it.[51]

Perhaps what is most striking about the submissions to, evidence given and comments on the Irish Boundary Commission by Protestant commentators is what wasn't said as much as what was. Declarations of royalist loyalty rarely featured. Sectarian opinions were wisely kept silent. There was a recognition that the economic privations, costs and annoyances resulting from the border were common to all who lived and worked in its shadow. Moving the border this way or that would only shift the problem somewhere else and visit it on a different set of similarly disgruntled people. 'We none of us give evidence in any spirit of hostility to the Free State', said the secretary of the Donegal Protestant Registration Association,[52] and the Protestant desire to be moved into Northern Ireland was often expressed in terms of specific dissatisfactions—the issue of compulsory Irish being a prominent example—rather than a fundamental rejection of the southern state. Enquiries like those from the rector of Clogh, a parish straddling the border, that 'large numbers of Protestant residents' in that part of the parish in Monaghan wanted to find out whether their area could be transferred north revealingly asked whether 'the fact of these people trying to get out of the Free State might afterwards injure them'.[53] This does not necessarily, then, signify a fundamental rejection of the Free State—after all, it was always open to individuals to sell up and relocate if they so wished. And some did, but the vast majority stayed put and made the best of things. As Orangeman Alexander Haslett of Monaghan had asserted in 1923, 'We are not going to be sulky in a corner. We have to live in this country and we are going to make the most of it.'[54] They participated in civic life, albeit in a limited way; under proportional representation Cavan, Monaghan and Donegal had 'Protestant' TDs elected up to the 1940s and, in Eoin MacNeill's words, Donegal had 'a very competent member' of Dáil Éireann in Major James Myles.[55]

CONCLUSION

The Boundary Commission always had the potential to cause more harm than good. In May 1925 the *Church of Ireland Gazette* opined that 'The Boundary Commission can settle nothing'.[56] After the Commission's failure, reflecting transfers of land in post-war Europe not solving embedded ethno-religious disputes, the paper's columnist 'Boreas' felt that it had 'threatened dire disturbance and civil war' but in its demise had 'actually led to the promotion of long absent friendliness'.[57] What was still wanted a mere four years after the Treaty was stability and certainty. One Protestant submission to the Boundary Commission was probably the most far-seeing and prescient. It was from Bolton C. Waller, a researcher for the North Eastern Boundary Bureau, a body set up by the Irish government in 1922 to prepare for the Boundary Commission. Waller was an internationalist, an enthusiast for the League of Nations and a fervent proponent of Irish unity, and later (1932) an Anglican cleric, where Protestant church unity became his abiding interest. Waller's submission argued that three things had to happen to allow the island to find peace with itself: a customs union which would mitigate the worst economic effects of the border; the satisfaction of legitimate grievances of the minorities, north and south; and co-operation between the two jurisdictions.[58] It took until the 1990s for all these three conditions to be met even in part, and post-Brexit arrangements have to an extent seen some retreat. We still do not have the sort of Ireland that Waller imagined it could be if they had been met in full.

VI

RELIGIOUS DISPUTATIONS

19

A VISION OF CHURCH OF IRELAND DISESTABLISHMENT AND WHERE IT MIGHT LEAD[1]

In 1868, with the debates about disestablishing the Church of Ireland in full swing, Richard Chenevix Trench, newly instituted Anglican archbishop of Dublin, set out a *Charge* to the clergy of his province and diocese.[2] In it he formulated an apocalyptic vision of what Irish Church disestablishment would mean for Ireland in the next half-century: 'the seeds of the future are wrapped up in the present, and wise men may read to what these seeds will grow; nor need they any gift of prophecy to discern what the course of events in the next half-century is likely to be'.[3]

One of Trench's recent biographers points out that Trench is perhaps remembered more today for his poetry than for his politics, and his early romanticism, exemplified by his journey to Spain in 1830 in support of a revolutionary. He fits 'uncomfortably into what has come to be accepted as the natural trajectory of Irish history, a path leading inexorably to national sovereignty'.[4] This essay examines Trench's view of historical determinism, and how an intelligent and well-informed outside observer (he was Irish but was brought up and educated in England) could take an event—the looming disestablishment and disendowment of the Church of Ireland—and read the tea-leaves. It contextualises Trench's views on what might be called 'the inevitability of gradualness' within the process and completion of disestablishment, and how he saw in it the elements that would shape a particular vision of Ireland into the future.

What happened to the Irish Church 150 years ago has resonated with the turmoils over Brexit. A long and entwined union was suddenly undone by a political upheaval in Britain. A determined prime minister soldiered on in the face of all sorts and conditions of opposition, internal and external. The process was complex, slow and uncertain. There were extremists on all sides, minorities often vociferous but with no clear alternative to what was being proposed. One side saw the sunny uplands of freedom beckoning; others predicted a plague of unicorns and the end of the world as they knew it. Then, after the dust had settled, it turned out that life went on much as before. The world did not stop turning. The parallels are not perfect—the Irish Church did not leave its union with the Church of England voluntarily—but the *process* of separation bears an uncanny parallel to what happened in these islands after the UK's referendum in 2016 to leave the European Union.

It is perhaps worth noting that while British Prime Minister W.E. Gladstone later claimed that his 'conversion' to disestablishment had been a long time in gestation and was based on principle,[5] one of his admirers ascribed it to a rather less high-minded 'restlessness at being out of office'.[6] That thoroughly temporal concern was reflected in the disestablishment process—primarily about money, governance and resources. Disestablishment had more to do with Mammon than with God.[7] While it had some knock-on effects in the theological sphere, the core faith did not have to strike off on a different path on 1 January 1871. Thus the arguments were often conducted within a concept of the temporal, which explains Trench's placing of disestablishment and its consequences firmly within Ireland's perceived political, rather than spiritual or religious, trajectory. And that emerged from the entanglement of Church and State in a dense, Erastian and oftentimes Faustian bargain, from the State deciding the number of sees, through appointments of bishops and deans, tithes, functions in relation to the union of parishes, the use of burial-grounds and the promulgation of special days of prayer,[8] to an archbishop and three bishops sitting in the House of Lords. The *Irish Ecclesiastical Gazette* even employed a lawyer who replied, month after month, to detailed and complex queries on the State's long and deep reach into the Church's legal and personnel affairs.

Trench's views on where the Church—and Ireland—was heading after disestablishment was inevitably coloured by its existing power, privileges and position. Increasingly, and not just by radicals, the Church of Ireland—in the context of its position on the island—was seen as an anachronistic institution. Radical Robert Lowe characterised it thus in an 1839 parliamentary motion:

> The curse of barrenness is upon it; it has no leaves; it bears no blossoms; it yields no fruit. 'Cut it down; why cumbereth it the ground?',[9]

while whig Lord John Russell hoped to take some of its money and expend it on 'secular' projects in Ireland. As early as 1844 Disraeli described the Church of Ireland as an 'alien Church'. As Catholics and Dissenters came to be accepted—reluctantly and gradually—as members of the *polis*, as part of the notion of 'citizen', the concept of an exclusive religious and denominational basis for membership came under attack.

What finished Church establishment off was the Victorian passion for facts and statistics. The religious censuses of 1821, 1831 and 1834 were unreliable, but they pointed to an undeniable reality: that Anglicanism was the belief system of a minority of the island's people. There were explicit prohibitions on religion questions in the legislation authorising the 1841 and 1851 censuses in Ireland, but by 1861 political pressure for information on the denominational breakdown was irresistible. The decisive tipping-point against establishment, in demographic terms at any rate, occurred as a result of that census; it showed conclusively that Irish Anglicans comprised less than 12 per cent of the island's population.[10] In March 1868 Gladstone carried resolutions in the House of Commons against the minority Conservative government of Lord Derby, seeking disestablishment and disendowment but with vested interests protected.[11] This acted as a rallying-point for the Liberals, and the government was ejected from office at the subsequent general election in late 1868; the phoney war had ended, and the scene was set for a marathon on disestablishment. Gladstone's policy forced the Irish Church not so much to try to stop disestablishment in its tracks as to negotiate for the least-worst outcome. At the level of the upper clergy that was tactical rather than strategic. They had much to lose and didn't want to lose it. The laity, not for the last time (*vide* the 'State Prayers' controversy of 1949),[12] were more hard-line than the clerics and attempted to set up a representative assembly to oppose disestablishment.[13] That went nowhere.

What became 'An Act to put an end to the Establishment of the Church of Ireland, and to make Provision for the Temporalities thereof, and in respect of the Royal College of Maynooth', was passed by the Commons in May 1868, but then faced a much more ferocious opposition in the Lords. At the end, though, the archbishop of Canterbury's aim was to 'make this a good bill, though I grant it will be very difficult'. The Lords effectively conceded the Bill's principle but worked hard to give the disendowed Church more money. That was contested by British liberal and Irish Catholic opinion. Eventually a compromise, brokered by the Liberal Lord Granville and the Conservative Lord Cairns, was agreed.

Proponents of establishment suggested that the Church might have two possible missions. One was as a national church. The 1861 census, however, definitively confirmed the failure of the Church as a missionary movement in Ireland (it was more successful overseas); indeed, it was claimed that establishment had in fact 'created about 4½ millions of the most determined Catholics in the world'. The second argument was for the Church as an instrument of political power for the regime. Those in favour of disestablishment pointed out, though, that since the 1830s at least (mentioning the tithe wars in particular) establishment acted as a running sore, and thus a permanent irritation to Catholics, increasing instability rather than the reverse—in one critic's words, 'it must necessarily prove not an assistance but a serious impediment in the way of administration'.[14]

The case for establishment based solely on numbers and politics was indefensible. Consequently, its defenders had to fall back on Edmund Burke's dictum that 'it would be a bad day for mankind when great principles come to be decided by numerical majorities'. Trench's take on this—that 'We are the Established Church because we are the Church which the State believes to be true'[15]—may have been philosophically coherent but was politically irrelevant in 1868.

The archbishop's *Charge* to the clergy of his diocese was delivered in early September that year. This was a time when it was becoming obvious that disestablishment would happen. Trench's take in the *Charge* in this politically fraught atmosphere was to see in this 'end of days' a seamless connectivity and continuity with the future of the Union and with the Protestant position in Ireland generally. In this he was not unique. His sense of historical determinism was interesting, though. What he argued was that, as he put it, 'In the historic life of nations there is no escaping the dominion of the past … If it be attempted to ignore its verdicts, to reverse its decisions, to undo what it has done, a far larger task will have to be taken in hand than merely the overthrow of the Establishment.'[16] So, it is not the 'overthrow of the Establishment' *per se* that will trigger undesirable change but rather the negating of the flow of history of which the establishment was, well, an *established* part. He was arguing for a form of stasis on the basis that change will always trigger change, and not necessarily for the better. That was an intriguing conceptual view coming from a beneficiary of the Reformation and the Glorious Revolution!

Trench then looked at the logical consequences of suborning history, as it were. If the Established Church was a 'badge of conquest',[17] where did this leave the other badges of conquest, such as Protestant possessors of seven eighths of the soil? The viceroyalty, and royalty itself? 'Where is a movement like this to stop?', was his rhetorical question. 'This much is certain', he went on to write, 'that, if once allowed, it will not stop exactly where those desire and intend to have set it agoing, any more than the rock which has been detached from the mountain-top will pause upon its side exactly where he who first impelled it may desire.'[18] What Trench was implying was that, while the destination might not be precisely determinable, the journey itself would be in little doubt. In this reading Trench does fit 'into what has come to be accepted as the natural trajectory of Irish history'.[19]

But Trench's view was not that the process would be entirely random. He was perceptive in getting the sequence broadly right, as it turned out: the order in which the dominoes would fall would be Church, land, union. Trench was what Charles D'Arcy, archbishop of Armagh, writing in the 1930s, characterised as one of the 'discerning minds' that saw in disestablishment the seeds of political revolution that would lead to political independence[20]—except that Trench, from the perspective of a Britain at arguably the apogee of its imperial reach, could not envisage that that last stage could or would be reached. England simply would not allow it. In his *Charge*[21] he wrote that

> at last, a day will arrive when the democracy of England, moved in part by the sufferings of the Protestants, from which they will have long wilfully

> hid their eyes, but far more by the determination to maintain, at all costs, the unity of the Empire, and angry and fierce as only a democracy can be, will turn and stand at bay; and, having long shrunk from the struggle, yet will not shrink from it to the end. What the issue of a conflict between the strength of England and the weakness of Ireland will be, it is easy to foretell; but in the course of that struggle what an Iliad of woes will have been poured out on Ireland; and that day will be one to fill the hopeful with despair, when, perhaps, some new Cromwell stands amidst the smoking ruins of the civilization and prosperity of this land, to begin once more a work which is ever beginning, but is never brought to a successful end.

Predictably, threatening Ireland with a 'new Cromwell' did not go down well in Catholic circles; Trench wrote to his wife that the *Freeman's Journal* had mounted a 'furious attack on the *Charge*', menacing the archbishop with 'no compensation for [our] vested rights' if he continued in this vein.[22]

Trench may have got the future broadly correct. As it turned out, however, when landlordism, control of local government and the British administration itself all went, it is piquant that the trigger for his vision—the Church of Ireland—survived remarkably well. 'The Irish Church Act 1869' came into effect on 1 January 1871.[23] The practicalities worked surprisingly smoothly. The Church's financial position was generally secured. Before then, as soon as the Act received royal assent in July 1869, the Church set out to form a governance structure for itself. A General Synod met in September 1869 and a General Convention was called in February 1870 to draw up a constitution.[24] It is broadly the constitution that governs the Church of Ireland today. It has stood the test of time, which speaks to its robustness.

What Trench perhaps didn't, or couldn't, foresee was that the trajectory of the Church of Ireland itself—the repository of political unionism—was, in many respects, the precursor of what 'Home Rule' might actually look like. The Irish Church Act could be held to have been one of the first 'land acts'. The General Synod aped parliamentary structures and language. The select vestries formed the Church's 'local government'. Parishes had to be self-reliant (and, broadly, were). In an echo of later Sinn Féinism, the Church had its own courts. It was democratised, as the laity's voices were increasingly heard, not always to clerics' liking: parochial nominators of rectors for vacant parishes came in for special opprobrium, 'better fitted to be judges of a *horse*, a *dog* or even a *pig*', as one disgruntled rector complained.[25]

R.B. McDowell summed up the whole affair succinctly: 'when Victorian political presuppositions, the contemporary political climate, Irish discontent and Irish population statistics are all taken into account, Disestablishment was inevitable'.[26] Nevertheless, while what was not inevitable was its effect on the Church itself, Trench in 1868 broadly understood its consequences for the bigger picture. In its editorial of 20 March 1868, the *Irish Ecclesiastical Gazette*, commenting on Earl Russell's suggestions for ending the Church of Ireland's establishment, was in desperation mode. 'She will be left an easy prey to the wiles and machinations of her foes ... the Church of Ireland is to have a cruel, a real, a permanent injury inflicted upon it.' On 1 January 1871, when disestablishment became operative, a newly penned, despairing hymn by Mrs Cecil Alexander sung in Derry Cathedral captured the feelings of many:

> Look down, Lord of heaven, on our desolation!
> Fallen, fallen, fallen is now our Country's crown,
> Dimly dawns the New Year on a churchless nation,
> Ammon and Amalek tread our borders down.[27]

Some thought that disestablishment would result in economic ruin for the Church; others feared schism and internal breakup, and distance from other Anglican churches. None of this happened. A decade after his gloomy *Charge*, Trench—still archbishop—would have read an editorial in the *Irish Ecclesiastical Gazette* which cheerfully stated that 'the Church seems to have passed beyond the spasmodic and sensational epoch that followed hard on the first shock of Disestablishment, and to have settled down to a quiet recognition of its new status'.[28] The paper went on to list the positives, including church and cathedral restoration, less slovenly services and a revived associational culture. Gladstone's charge to the Church—that 'it should come to place its trust in its own resources, in its own great mission, in all that it can draw from the energy of its ministers and its members'[29]—seemed to have largely been realised. A voluntarist church was actively engaging (sometimes tetchily and acrimoniously, but at least engaging) with its members, and with a sense of liveliness and hope. It had revealed, in Trench's own words in 1865, 'sources and secrets of strength which only the day of trial will reveal'.[30] Indeed, the *Gazette* itself manifested the new interest in, and energy of, the Church. From January 1880 it became a penny weekly, effectively quadrupling its size; its new subtitle—'A church paper for church people'—reflected its transformation from an intelligence sheet primarily for the clergy to a newspaper for the laity.[31]

Fifty years after the Act another senior Church of Ireland cleric looked backwards, much as Trench had looked forward. In 1920 the bishop of Cork, Cloyne and Ross assessed what had happened:

> The dark clouds of Disestablishment were gathering thickly round the Irish Church in the 'sixties; men's hearts were failing them for fear; many were asking with apprehension, 'What of the future?' 'Can the Church of Ireland survive?' 'Can she retain her position deprived of State connection, and of State support?' But faith triumphed.[32]

All was not rosy, of course, but the fact remains that disestablishment turned out to be an unmitigated blessing for the Church. It had to stand on its own feet. While it did not take politics out of the Church (vestries and synods were vociferous in their espousals of political unionism in 1886, 1893 and 1912), it effectively took the Church out of politics. That was important in an age when the Protestant community's visibility in Ireland was increasingly problematic. Archbishop Trench's vision of a 'new Cromwell' had echoes in the 1920s Black and Tans and in Churchill's threats. Just as well, then, that the Church/State connection had been severed in 1871. Anglicans in a 'Protestant establishment' in 1920 would not have been in a good place.[33]

20

BENEATH THE PULPIT, ABOVE THE PARAPET? THE CLERICS IN THE IRISH CONVENTION, 1917–18[1]

INTRODUCTION

In many respects the Irish Convention was a throwback. It had an old-fashioned feel about it, from its meeting in the august surroundings of Trinity College and glimpses of the old Irish parliament building from the windows, through glittering receptions in grand houses on St Stephen's Green, to the chairman addressing letters to 'My Lords and Gentlemen'. It is hard to square it with the membership, a mere couple of years later, of the first Dáil. Not the least incongruous element in this nostalgia-fest was the presence of the clerical-collared classes. The last time that they had sat in an assembly which included representative Irishmen was in 1869, when Irish Anglican bishops had had seats in the House of Lords. Nearly half a century on, it seemed as if nothing much had changed. As observer Shane Leslie put it, 'The hidebound lines of division in Irish politics and religion were marked by due delegations'.[2] The Convention contained seven senior and seasoned clerics from the three most numerous religious groupings on the island. The Roman Catholic hierarchy was represented by one archbishop and three bishops (Archbishop John Harty of Cashel, and Bishops Patrick O'Donnell of Raphoe, Denis Kelly of Ross and Joseph MacRory of Down and Connor); the Church of Ireland by its two archbishops (John Baptist Crozier of Armagh and John Henry Bernard of Dublin); and the Presbyterian Church in Ireland by its moderator (Rt Revd John Irwin). There were only lay Methodists. There were no Jews or Quakers. Sinn Féin, William O'Brien's All-for-Ireland League and Labour refused to participate.

Apart from the eponymous account by R.B. McDowell, the Convention has had few mentions in scholarly history. Here and there it has had supporting roles and bit parts in articles and books such as Patrick Buckland's *Irish Unionism 1*, David Miller's *Church, State and Nation in Ireland*, Thomas Hennessey's *Dividing Ireland: World War I and Partition*, Jerome aan de Weil's *The Catholic Church in Ireland, 1914–1918* and Conor Mulvagh's *The Irish Parliamentary Party at Westminster.*[3] Its proceedings were subject to a press blackout under the Defence of the Realm Act.[4] While following parliamentary procedure in a sort of way, there was no daily verbatim report *à la* Hansard. For contemporary accounts we are reliant on the chairman Horace Plunkett's periodic reports to King George V; letters written by him to Irish Parliamentary Party leader John Redmond; Archbishop Bernard's, Bishop O'Donnell's and Lloyd George's correspondence; sporadic notes made by such as Provost Mahaffy of TCD and others; later memoirs from participants such as the Earl of Desart, Viscount Midleton and Stephen Gwynn; and comment from privileged informants Shane Leslie and W.B. Wells.

This essay approaches the involvement of the clerics and denominational representatives as thematic questions:

- How were they chosen?
- Why these particular representatives?
- What were their characters and backgrounds, and how might that have coloured their participation?
- Within their respective ethnicities, what strands of political and religious opinion did they represent?
- Was sectarian feeling an issue in the Convention?
- What roles did the denominational representatives assume? Did they see themselves as constructing a state or imagining a nation?
- What freedom to manoeuvre did they possess?
- What was the nature of clerical influence?

The Convention has not had a particularly good press—or, indeed, much of a press at all. According to McDowell, it 'conspicuously failed'; it was little more than a 'rhetorical irrelevance on the margins of Irish history'.[5] Dermot Meleady, biographer of John Redmond, suggests that 'the Convention was a nobly-inspired venture to avert Partition … it was doomed to fail … because a 32-county home rule settlement was not available and anything less was unacceptable to nationalists'.[6] And its genesis, as so often with political initiatives in Ireland before 1922, lay as much in the exigencies of domestic British politics as in anything Irish.

Pacifying Ireland in the face of existential threats to the larger island was as imperative in 1917 as it had been in 1588, 1652 or 1798. Increasing Irish unrest and Lloyd George's desire to neutralise the Irish question while the United States was brought safely into war against the central powers were the main drivers in its establishment. In the aftermath of the 1916 Rebellion it had proved well-nigh impossible to keep juggling the mutual antagonisms of confident northern unionists, depressed southern unionists, a rattled Irish constitutional nationalism and various shades of resurgent republicanism, never mind shadowy and not-so-shadowy sponsors and idealists in the United States and the British cabinet.[7] The

Convention seemed a ripping wheeze to keep the balls up in the air for as long as possible.

That may be overly cynical, of course; in the spring of 1917 a domestic consensus *was* emerging outside republican and some labour circles that perhaps a private forum of interests might be able to plot a way forward between the Scylla of nationalism and the Charybdis of unionism. Archbishop Bernard was an early adopter, signalling his considerable interest in the idea.[8] The Catholic Bishop Kelly, an establishment figure, had been consulted by Irish Chief Secretary Duke in early May about the make-up of a convention. Kelly favoured a small, workmanlike group—below seventy, preferably fifty.[9] The idea of a convention gathered traction. The prime minister wrote to John Redmond on 16 May suggesting one on the lines of that which had formulated a constitution for the Union of South Africa in 1908, and on 21 May Lloyd George announced that 'Ireland should try her hand at hammering out an instrument of government for her own people'.[10]

COMPOSITION

Whatever about his ulterior motives, the prime minister was careful to give at least the appearance of genuinely wanting an assembly that would be representative of 'all leading interests, classes, creeds and phases of thought in Ireland'.[11] It was apparently Redmond who suggested that representatives of the churches should be included. A telegram of 24 May 1917 from nationalist MP T.P. O'Connor to Redmond, Dillon and Devlin about an imminent announcement of the membership indicated that it would consist of sixty men. There would be three Catholic Church representatives, to be nominated by Cardinal Logue, archbishop of Armagh, with one each from the Church of Ireland, Presbyterians and Methodists. Ultimately this schema was not adopted, although the Convention might have marched on at a brisker pace if it had. As we shall see, various windbags might have not had the opportunity to stretch out the proceedings, and certain interests may not have had as much wind behind them either.

If sixty was too few, Redmond's suggestion of 171—opposed by the bishop of Ross—was too many.[12] Eventually, it was decided that the Convention should consist of ninety-five members.[13] The Catholic Church's participation was never really in doubt, although on 14 June 1917 Bishop O'Donnell told Horace Plunkett (who was to become the Convention's chairman) that the Church might not send a delegation. Nevertheless, the archbishop of Cashel was fearful of the consequences if they didn't.[14] A week later the Catholic hierarchy, meeting in Maynooth, duly agreed to nominate four representatives.

Like the Catholics, the Church of Ireland delegation represented balance, on geographical as well as political lines. The northern wing had (or thought it had) the archbishop of Armagh, J.B. Crozier, onside; the champion of the southern and western members of the church, facing a very different situation in the event of self-government, was the archbishop of Dublin, J.H. Bernard, invited by Lloyd George on 13 June 1917 to become a member.[15] Unlike the bishops, the Presbyterian moderator only had a year's tenure. This inevitably affected how his involvement in the Convention would be structured and perceived. The fourth most populous religious denomination in Ireland was Methodism, but the 62,000 Methodists on the island had no clerical representation.

CHARACTER AND CALIBRE OF THE CLERICS

CATHOLIC

Overall, they fitted Lytton Strachey's description of Cardinal Manning: 'He belonged to that class of eminent ecclesiastic—and it is by no means a small class—who have been distinguished less for saintliness and learning than for practical ability'.[16] Wells & Marlowe in 1918 wrote that 'A very notable feature of the Convention was the amount of ability which resided in the delegations from the two Churches'.[17] From the Catholic side, Shane Leslie concurred: the 'Catholic phalanx ... could not be bettered'. And, indeed, they brought quite a lot to the party—not necessarily confessional or denominational, or spiritual or ethical either, even if Horace Plunkett confided to John Redmond in October 1917 that some of their fellow-nationalists regarded John Harty (1867–1946) and MacRory (1861–1945) as 'politically dummies'.[18] That seemed harsh, especially as regards MacRory, who possessed sterling qualities as a debater and logician, evidenced in his later magisterial public exchanges with the Church of Ireland's Archbishop John Gregg on St Patrick in 1932,[19] but he often gave the impression of a man carrying a cross. As Plunkett put it, 'a Roman Catholic prelate with Belfast in his diocese may be somewhat sorely tried'.[20] Harty was more politically quiet, a supporter of Redmond, but moving towards the Sinn Féin position.[21]

Shane Leslie, colour-writing for American newspapers, eulogised O'Donnell of Raphoe (1856–1927), 'who for a quarter of a century has been silvering his locks defending the land and language of the Gael in Donegal'.[22] He was perhaps the most astute and worldly in a group that was already astute and worldly. Another contemporary remarked that O'Donnell was the only native Irish-speaker in the Convention, and 'more of a democrat and an enthusiast, a very fine politician'.[23] O'Donnell was the Irish Parliamentary Party's 'strongest and most loyal supporter within the Catholic hierarchy'.[24] That did not survive the Convention. Characterising the bishop of Raphoe as a horny-handed son of toil and a man of the people may have been what audiences composed of Irish-Americans wanted to hear, but it is set against McDowell's assessment of O'Donnell as 'of princely presence and gracious manners who had for years played a leading part in the counsels of the nationalist party'.[25] Bishops, like—and, indeed, as—politicians, were quite capable of shape-shifting and matching their political and social colours to whatever happened to be the surrounding advantageous environment.

Denis Kelly of Ross (1852–1924) had, in Shane Leslie's rather catty remark, a 'tiny diocese' which 'has afforded him the time to become an expert economist'.[26] He was 'a student of Irish statistics and finance'.[27] He had already published extensively on economic and social matters, such as the war and Ireland's food supply, the position of women in Ireland's industrial life and, perhaps of most relevance to the Convention, *The Practical Application of Christianity to the Lives of the Irish People Today*, written in 1906.[28] A later historian described him as 'a staunch nationalist and a remarkably able man'.[29] Kelly had a better feeling for the trajectory of opinion in Ireland than O'Donnell, writing in July 1917 that 'Ireland was travelling frightfully fast ... The younger population have no moorings and the old generation are rapidly losing theirs.' Kelly was convinced that this could only be prevented 'by a strong measure of Home Rule for all Ireland'.[30] Whatever about his politics, his socio-economic views would have chimed with those of Horace Plunkett. As a quasi-establishment figure—Kelly had been a member of Sir Henry Primrose's Committee on Home Rule Finance in 1910 and had excoriated the 1916 Rebellion as 'a senseless, meaningless debauch of blood'—he might have been expected to see positivity in the Convention.[31] Yet even he early on seemed not to believe that it could result in a 'decent settlement'.[32] Likewise, Stephen Gwynn, a Convention member, was 'very uncertain what will happen'.[33]

Kelly and O'Donnell were seen as particularly dangerous by their opponents. Writing in June 1917, Hugh de Fellenberg Montgomery, a caustic member of the backroom advisory council to the northern unionist delegation, emphasised the necessity of that delegation to be comprised of men 'who will be able to flatten out clever, plausible gasbags like the Roman Catholic bishop of Ross'.[34]

In nominating the prelates it did, the hierarchy stuck to its traditional formula of *una voce*. Horace Plunkett was not deceived: 'they are evidently badly split', he confided to his diary.[35] This split was apparently between, on the one side, Redmond's 'two chief clerical supporters'[36] (O'Donnell and Kelly) and, on the other, Harty and MacRory, who 'represented fairly accurately the feeling of Independent Nationalists'—code for a viewpoint closer to Sinn Féin than to the Irish Party.[37] O'Donnell and MacRory were at loggerheads very early on in the Convention, when the latter was reported as making 'a speech in which he awoke some bitter memories of the Anglo-Irish conflict in the nineteenth century'. But he was out of tune with the Convention, at least as it comported itself in its early optimistic phase. Plunkett reported to the king that 'It was noticeable … that the revival of past controversies was not very cordially received by the Nationalist members of the Convention' and that 'his reverend brother, the bishop of Raphoe, seized the earliest opportunity to place his views before us in an altogether conciliatory way'.[38] Another incident in January 1918 underscored differences between MacRory and Kelly: the former rubbished the proposals from southern unionist leader Lord Midleton, while Kelly strongly advocated acceptance 'for the sake of a settlement'.[39] Ultimately, though, even Kelly and O'Donnell parted company on this issue.

CHURCH OF IRELAND

No one particularly wanted to cede the field to the opposition by not turning up—hence the Catholic hierarchy's somewhat unenthusiastic participation, and also the Church of Ireland's: in June 1917 Crozier recognised that the Home Rule Act, dormant on the statute book so long as the war lasted, 'gives an overwhelming advantage to the enemy and makes it absolutely necessary for us to attend'.[40] The 'us' here, though, were Ulster unionists, not the Church of Ireland *per se*. And this points up the dilemma common to many of the clerics. What, or who, exactly did they represent? Crozier exemplifies this confusion. In one reading he was a unionist first and foremost, having, as Wells & Marlowe pointed out, 'joined the No-Surrender campaign before the War'.[41] His ecclesiastical jurisdiction and political sympathies lay in and with Ulster. But his position as head of an all-Ireland church meant riding two horses: 'he has preserved in the Convention his independence of action', wrote Horace Plunkett carefully to the king; he was one of the few who 'resisted firm alignment with any of the parties'.[42] On 14 March 1918 he made an impassioned speech declaring his own 'absolute independence'. He did not sign the Ulster unionists' final report, instead opting to align himself with Provost Mahaffy in a short, idiosyncratic but politically pointless note, stating that the majority view of the Convention was unacceptable because it involved either 'the coercion of Ulster, which is unthinkable', or 'the partition of Ireland, which would be disastrous'.[43]

If the coercion *of* Ulster was unthinkable, coercion *by* Ulster unionists was not. The northern unionist bloc raised tactical fence-sitting—and taciturnity—to a performance art form during the Convention. They had little choice; the verdict of a Belfast source in mid-October 1917 was that 'they have their Sinn Féiners outside just has Redmond has, and they must "walk delicately"'.[44] This policing duly produced paranoia. Hugh de Fellenberg Montgomery brusquely warned Crozier in September 1917 that the Ulster unionists were becoming 'uneasy and suspicious' of the archbishop.[45] Crozier's failure to sign the Ulster unionist final report must have confirmed their doubts of his soundness, despite his voting with the Ulster unionists in favour of exclusion. He abstained in the final division of the Convention on 5 April 1918, 'That the Report as a whole be adopted'.[46] His split loyalty to church and tribe left him unable to be as staunch—in the unionist meaning of the term—as his private comment in June 1917 indicated. With this, Crozier more or less self-neutralised any influence he might have had in the Convention. He was never really close to the centre of the Ulster unionist bloc in the Convention in the same way that Bernard was in relation to the southern unionists. Crozier, though, made a couple of good speeches, and he was co-opted to the Convention's Grand Committee.[47] His principal contribution was his chairmanship of the committee appointed to draw up its procedures;[48] Wells & Marlowe claimed that its standing orders were modelled on those of the General Synod of the Church of Ireland.[49]

If Crozier turned out to be a rather damp squib, the same could hardly be said of Archbishop Bernard, a former TCD academic, professor of divinity and churchman who later resigned his archbishopric in 1919 to become provost of the College. Shane Leslie described him as 'a moderate high churchman and a rare combination of orator and scholar'.[50] McDowell characterised him as having 'patience, lucidity and decisiveness … common sense … gravitas' which gave him 'immense weight in council'.[51] Buckland has him as 'a man of affairs with an acute brain, quicker than most … to see the potentialities of a given situation and anxious that he or the institutions he served should play a leading role in modern life'.[52]

It helped that Bernard carried with him an aura of personal courage and travail. His son had been killed in the 1915 Gallipoli campaign. Throughout the 1916 Rebellion, resident in St Stephen's Green, he had been conspicuous in his leadership of the Anglicans of Dublin. He was in contact in both public and private forums with those who governed Ireland. On 12 May 1916 he dined with Lord Lieutenant Lord Wimbourne and Prime Minister Asquith; on 23 May he entertained General Sir John Maxwell; he wrote to Lloyd George in June; in September he dined with the king and queen; in November he was found commenting to the viceroy on a set of proposals produced by the government.[53] Lord Midleton would later describe him as 'probably the most distinguished Irishman of the day', and he was an early mention for chairman.[54] Seeing the 1916 Rebellion and the Great War as essentially moral conflicts between the forces of anarchy and order, Bernard would have found the idea of the Convention attractive.

If Crozier had nobbled himself as an overt Ulster unionist supporter, what about Bernard? Apart from the obvious interests of the southern Church of Ireland, he mainly represented the metropolitan academic and professional worlds in which he moved. He was acutely aware of his status. Lloyd George was advised to address him as 'archbishop' and not as 'Dr Bernard, as he does not like it'.[55] Robert MacCarthy suggests that Bernard allied himself 'entirely with the Irish peerage, of which he seemed to think he was an honorary member', symbolised by his move around the Green to stay in Lord Iveagh's house when the Convention was sitting. And, indeed, it may have been socially and culturally delightful to be in a house party that consisted of every gradation of the peerage—the Duke of Abercorn, the Marquess of Londonderry, the Earls of Desart and Mayo, Viscount Midleton and the 3rd Baron Oranmore and Browne.[56] This social dalliance, though, should not distract from the reality that the Convention was first and foremost a political gathering and Bernard was there above all because of his political acumen, ability and influence.

PRESBYTERIANS

Like Crozier, the moderator of the General Assembly of the Presbyterian Church in Ireland had, in theory, to tread a careful path. But in practice a fully paid-up member of the northern unionist bloc, the extent to which he could be held adequately to reflect the 20,000 or so General Assembly Presbyterians[57] outside Ulster is open to considerable question. Dr John Irwin was described by Wells & Marlowe as a 'stern Covenanter' and by Shane Leslie more diplomatically as representing 'the silent and solid virtues of the Scotch Irish'.[58] The moderator was not entirely silent, though; Plunkett records that he was amongst those who made 'interesting and important' speeches during the Convention's early days in August 1917.[59] It is a pity that we have no details. In the heel of the hunt, Irwin followed his tribe; he seconded the Ulster unionist leader Barrie's motion in March 1918 on the exclusion of Ulster[60] and he was found voting with his fellow Ulster unionists on almost every issue, eventually signing their minority report.

METHODISTS

With no clergymen, Methodists had to be content with lay representation. The two Methodist lay members were Captain William Doran, the nationalist chairman of Louth County Council, erroneously described by McDowell as a Presbyterian,[61] and the eminent Belfast consulting physician Sir William Whitla, who was a government nominee.[62] The latter was a strong supporter of the Ulster unionist position. Along with virtually every other member of that delegation, he rarely broke ranks—thus compounding the impression that was powerfully made upon the other groupings of the discipline, obduracy and single-mindedness of the northern unionist delegates, in contrast to the more fluid and open southern unionists and nationalists.

CLERICAL INVOLVEMENT IN THE CONVENTION'S WORK

How attentive were the clerics and the lay Methodists? One quantitative measure was obviously their presence at the sessions. The maximum number attended by any member of the Convention was fifty-one. The clerics recorded two of these—not surprisingly, O'Donnell and Bernard. Plunkett admiringly informed Redmond in October 1917 that 'Dr O'Donnell came all the way from Letterkenny, whither he has to return immediately, to help save an awkward situation, and he did, as usual, splendidly'; O'Donnell himself claimed that he had given the summer of

1917 to the Convention.[63] Of the remainder, Crozier attended 50 sessions, Doran 48, MacRory and Irwin 45 each, Harty 44, Whitla 40 and Kelly 21. The latter's poor showing was primarily due to his ill health from December 1917 onward. It may be noted that John Redmond attended twenty-nine sessions.[64] A sporadic attendee even in its early phase, he effectively opted out after early January 1918.

As regards the clerics' participation in the work of the Convention, a list of their activities gives an indication of their qualitative contribution:

CATHOLIC

John Harty, archbishop of Cashel
Member, Grand Committee [GC]
Signatory, report of 22 nationalists

Patrick O'Donnell, bishop of Raphoe
Member, GC
Member, GC subcommittee of nine to assess schemes
Member, delegation to confer with the cabinet
Signatory, report of 22 nationalists

Denis Kelly, bishop of Ross
Member, GC
Member, GC subcommittee on land purchase
Non-signatory of any Convention report

Joseph MacRory, bishop of Down and Connor
Signatory, report of 22 nationalists

CHURCH OF IRELAND

John Baptist Crozier, archbishop of Armagh
Chairman, Preliminary Procedure Committee [standing orders]
Member, GC
Signatory of a Note with Provost Mahaffy
Non-signatory of the Ulster Unionist report

John Henry Bernard, archbishop of Dublin
Member, GC
Member, GC subcommittee on the franchise and electoral systems
Member, delegation to confer with the cabinet
Signatory, southern unionist report

PRESBYTERIAN

John Irwin, moderator of the General Assembly
Member, GC
Signatory, Ulster Unionist report
Seconder of Barrie's 'exclusion' resolution

METHODIST

Captain William Doran, chairman [Redmondite], Louth County Council
Member, GC subcommittee on defence and police
Signatory, report of the majority of nationalists
Sir William Whitla, physician, Belfast
Signatory, Ulster Unionist report

SECTARIAN DISPUTATION

All this evidenced the seriousness with which Convention members approached their task. To make the Convention work at all it was essential—whatever about tribal, political and cultural differences—that sectarianism should not become a fault line. While it was always there subliminally, it was striking that overt religious disputation as such seldom intruded into the Convention's deliberations—surprising, perhaps, for this was a period of quite antagonistic Catholic–Protestant relations. It was as if it was accepted that the conventions of the Convention precluded any serious discussion of religious matters unless they touched upon secular notions of government and democracy. Plunkett reported early on to the king that 'one good sign was that the Protestant and Catholic bishops spontaneously sought adjoining seats' at the opening session.[65] Catholic convert Shane Leslie, writing in the *Chicago Tribune* at the end of April 1918, well after the effective collapse of the Convention, suggested that 'religious friction was speedily abated by the proximity in which the bishops of the rival churches found themselves'.[66] In one official picture of the Convention, taken on 21 August 1917 at TCD, all the bishops are seated in the front row. Three of the Catholic prelates are safely separated from the Church of Ireland archbishops by the solid figures of Mahaffy and Redmond and the slighter one of Plunkett.[67] O'Donnell and Irwin are seated together at the end of the row—the body language is slightly uneasy, however.

Even allowing for Plunkett's optimism, a feature of his reports to King George V was the absence of anything significantly resembling sectarian argument and dispute. Plunkett found only three or four incidents worthy of mention. An early speech in September 1917 from 'that old fool' Mahaffy (Plunkett's description) feared that Protestants would suffer discrimination in the same way as Catholics had done in Penal Law times—he cited an Irish test for county council scholarships as a means of discouraging Protestant candidates from applying.[68] On a lighter note, Charles McKay, a labour representative from Belfast, 'much to the amusement of the Convention, if a little to the consternation of the clerical side of it', wrote Plunkett, 'produced his remedy for the Ulster difficulty. Take away religion and Belfast will be alright.'[69]

A more substantial incident concerned the recent papal edicts *Ne Temere* (1907) and *Quantavis Diligentia* (1911), the first placing serious obstacles in the way of mixed marriages and the second concerning excommunication of those in legislative assemblies and administrations who curtailed the rights and liberties of the Catholic Church.[70]

These issues were raised by Belfast Orange Grand Master, Downpatrick solicitor and Boer War hero Colonel Robert Wallace with, according to Plunkett, 'a complete avoidance of tact'. Wallace was a dyed-in-the-wool Ulster unionist, the organiser of the James Craig-inspired Orange Grand Lodge of Ulster in 1911, a crucial building-block of the partitionist edifice.[71] He was also one of the founding committee members of the Ulster Unionist Council in 1905, and in 1911 an initiator of the legal permissions that would allow 'military exercises, movements and evolutions' for what became the Ulster Volunteer Force.[72] Wallace's blunt points were answered politely by Bishop O'Donnell in an urbane and silkily slick performance. Plunkett cheerily averred that 'On the whole, no ground was lost by the introduction of the religious controversy, and many apprehensions were dispelled by the good temper in which it was argued'.[73]

The bishop of Raphoe may have seen off Wallace easily but the Methodist Sir William Whitla was of another calibre and of greater subtlety. Ostensibly on the subject of education but in reality about the denominational apartheid that was a defining feature of Irish society, Sir William spoke of the value of a mixed education. Recognising what he reckoned would be the reaction, Whitla said that 'he made no appeal to the heads of the Church … to reverse their decision. But he would remind the right reverend prelates that the working of denominational education in recent years had made vastly more difficult the prospect of agreement on the national question.' According to Plunkett, he ended 'by suggesting that the Protestant and Roman Catholic prelates, the Moderator, and a few lay members of the Convention should informally meet to discuss frankly and freely this great and vital problem'.

The right reverend prelates were having none of this. 'At once', Plunkett reported to the king, 'Dr Harty, the Archbishop of Cashel, rose to reply.' One of Harty's rare interventions in the Convention's plenary sessions, his speech was initially conciliatory. He said that while Catholics in Belfast were well provided for educationally, he regretted that there was considerable educational deprivation on the Protestant side. It was a principle of Catholic educational teaching that there must be a mingling of the religious and the secular—but only within the denominational redoubt. He went on for some time more, but made it absolutely plain that, in Plunkett's words, 'educational progress along undenominational lines was, for the present, barred'. And that was that. No more was heard of Whitla's suggestion.[74]

Plunkett was not going to risk any descent into sectarian confrontation or, indeed, one between the secular and the religious. Political friction was a different matter. Irish politics was as much about public theatre and playing to one's gallery, and therefore common socio-cultural sympathies often had to remain somewhat below the radar. Although it is unlikely that, say, Bishop MacRory and the moderator would have found much common political ground, ultimately both these men had an interest in conservatism, order and good government. As such, there was a shared if narrow ground of Victorian values. To take one instance, in October 1916 Bernard had set out his political views in the *National Review*. On the recent Rebellion he was not afraid to state that many of the younger Catholic priests 'favour the rebellion of Easter week'. But one older one who didn't was Bishop Denis Kelly. 'I am delighted with your Grace's article', he wrote to Bernard. 'It is wise and courageous. Only an extremist can take offence.' But he couldn't resist a dig—'Of course you are too impartial as between Ulster and Dublin rebels!'[75]

CONSTRUCTING A STATE OR IMAGINING A NATION?

The clerics may not have been able to advance their professional vocations in dogmatic theology and denominational disputation in the

Convention, but that did not mean that they were passive participants. Far from it. Indeed, two bishops emerged as key players in the schemes-and-negotiation phases that commenced in late September 1917. O'Donnell for those nationalists who insisted on full fiscal autonomy and Bernard for the accommodative southern unionists occupied pivotal political roles in their respective camps.

The bishop of Raphoe was a consummate politician, carrying real political clout and influence in the constitutional nationalist camp. Since the late 1890s he had been a key ally of Redmond, and was treasurer of the United Irish League, the organisation on the ground of the Irish Parliamentary Party. As early as September 1917 he had been put up by Redmond to suggest a self-government scheme. George Russell was also a possible drafter, but Plunkett wrote to O'Donnell saying that 'Redmond and I would rather you did it'. With some show of *faux* resistance, O'Donnell eventually did table a scheme in early October, the crucial element of which was full control of customs, as well as internal taxation.[76] In an attempt to mollify the northern unionists, fearful of any Irish administration but especially one whose scraggy tail would be wagged by an agricultural dog, Lord Midleton for the southern unionists proposed that the control of customs should remain with parliament at Westminster. But by the end of December O'Donnell had not moved—on the basis, Plunkett felt, that the government would, in McDowell's words, 'sweep away unionist resistance'.[77] It might have been able to do so in the case of the southern wing, but Ulster was a different matter. And *contra* Plunkett, O'Donnell was clear-sighted enough to see that. Writing to Redmond on 22 December 1917, he somewhat airily dismissed the southern unionists as merely 'our helpers in this matter [that is, fiscal autonomy]'; 'any compromise', he continued, 'that is not with the North is no good for an agreed settlement'.[78] If the north came in, however, anything was possible. Plunkett reported a conversation with the bishop in late December 1917 in which O'Donnell indicated that if the Ulster unionists had fallen in with the Midleton scheme the situation for the 'fiscal autonomy' nationalists would have been much different.[79]

William Martin Murphy, proprietor of the *Irish Independent*, was no natural ally of O'Donnell's; even though identified by Murphy as 'a whole hogger' on the taxation issue, the bishop nevertheless expressed some misgivings on 22 December 1917 that, 'if Redmond bolts, he will probably follow'.[80] Redmond proposed in January 1918 that he would accept the Midleton proposal on customs if the government would immediately legislate for a self-government package, but this compromise failed. O'Donnell's attitude turned out to be critical. Stephen Gwynn felt that the bishop would not support it, not least because of his friendship with northern nationalist MP Joseph Devlin, who was opposed.[81] In early January 1918 O'Donnell duly decided that he could not back Midleton's scheme as amended by Redmond on the basis that, unless the Ulster unionists agreed, it was pointless giving away external fiscal autonomy.[82] That, in effect, scuppered the Midleton–Redmond compromise.[83] Harty and MacRory—though not Kelly—stood behind O'Donnell. Redmond was bitter that his party treasurer had failed to support him. Writing to Lloyd George, he maintained that, 'largely owing to the action of three of the Irish Catholic bishops, my efforts were absolutely futile'.[84] It marked an irrevocable rift between Redmond and one of his most trusted supporters.

What of Kelly, the second most influential Catholic prelate? John Blake Powell, a southern Catholic unionist, reported an encouraging conversation with Kelly ('the brain-carrier of the sane nationalists') to Lord Midleton on 1 December 1917. Powell felt that the bishop would give way to the Midleton idea if pressed,[85] but by this stage any influence that Kelly possessed within the nationalist nexus was waning. He was not well, and in any case his forte lay more in articulating the issues, often at great length and in mind-numbing detail, than in promulgating potential solutions.[86] Yet Stephen Gwynn thought that his absence through illness in the latter stages of the Convention was a critical factor in the rejection of the Midleton–Redmond compromise.[87] In the end, Kelly stuck by Redmond's memory; he was the only one of the Catholic clerics not to sign the nationalist reports of the Convention.[88]

For the southern unionists, Bernard's position was somewhat analogous to O'Donnell's. His principal biographer suggested that while *de jure* he played second fiddle to Lord Midleton in the southern unionist bloc of nine, *de facto* he was at the least the co-leader of the group.[89] Plunkett indicated to the king that he was their ablest representative.[90] His numerous letters, interventions, participation in meetings and discussions—with the likes of Redmond, Lloyd George, Curzon, Joseph Devlin, O'Donnell and the archbishop of Canterbury, detailed in McDowell's book—evidence a man at the centre of the Convention.[91]

All this politicking raises an important point about motivation as well as performance. Is there any meaningful sense in which it is useful to see the clerics in general, and these two prelates in particular, as anything *other* than politicians? It is perhaps paradoxical that those most concerned in their professional lives with the supernal and the transcendental seemed to be the cheerleaders for little more than designing and engineering a workable practical constitutional machine. In Shane Leslie's formulation, 'There was an inter-change of views on the subjects that do not involve future reckonings'. 'The main controversy', he wrote, 'centered not on theology but on taxation.'[92] In other words, this was all about constructing a state, not imagining a nation. O'Donnell for the nationalists and Bernard for the southern unionists came wearing rational politicians' top hats rather than episcopal mitres. The clerics on both sides kept well away from the Cathleen Ni Houlihan school of mystical nationalism. Church of Ireland cleric Dudley Fletcher had summed it up in June 1917 by pleading for support for the Convention from those who 'live in the world of reality, and not of romance',[93] and it generally avoided the bear-pit of what Edward MacLysaght described in a letter to Lloyd George in February 1918 as 'the growing self-consciousness of nationality … the growing force of a religion, with the carelessness about death, suffering or material loss which we find among the devotees of a religion'.[94]

And on the few occasions when such notions intruded they were often less than helpful. One instance is a reply drafted by nationalists, including O'Donnell, to practical questions from Plunkett. All seemed rational and mechanical, but at the end of it the nationalists could not resist couching their advocacy of complete fiscal control in terms of national self-determination. Plunkett reckoned that all it achieved was to alarm the Ulster unionists.[95] In the end it might have been safer to stick to the minutiae of voting systems and the powers of the lord lieutenant.

THE CLERICS' FREEDOM TO MANOEUVRE

It might seem self-evident that, because the prelates did not have to answer to any particular constituency, they had the advantage of flexibility and a relative freedom of action. But that was illusory. In a number of ways they were fenced in. Cardinal Logue, writing to a US bishop in mid-February 1918, claimed that it was the intransigence of 'Unionists in the North East corner of Ulster … determined to come to no settlement' who sunk the Convention.[96] He was right, but he failed to acknowledge the contribution to intransigence located within his own camp. If, as was reported in July 1917, the archbishop of Cashel 'enters the Convention determined to accept anything', it was the following phrase, 'short of partition …',[97] that did the damage. The critical point is that Cashel's position reflected what the clerical representatives had agreed with their colleagues in Maynooth on nomination. The Catholic bishops were as pledge-bound to oppose partition as the northern unionists were to achieve it. This, David Miller has suggested, the prelates interpreted disastrously narrowly—as an instance opposing federal or cantonal systems[98] and unwilling to contemplate special committees or some form of 'parliament within a parliament'; and, in O'Donnell's case, attempting the absurd jerry-building of gerrymandered representative constructions to placate minorities.

The Church of Ireland bishops had to keep looking over their shoulders too. As we have seen, the archbishop of Armagh was dogged by suspicious Ulster unionists. Bernard had more freedom to manoeuvre, but even he came in for severe criticism at the Standing Committee of the Church of Ireland's General Synod in January 1918 for allegedly diluting the pure spirit of unionism—not just from northern churchmen but from southern ones as well, presaging a split that would eventually occur in southern unionism in 1919.[99] Within the Protestant camp, tenure and longevity of power offered little protection against the popular voice, thus putting the bishops in a similar position to the moderator—an acquiescent, if temporary, prisoner in the Ulster unionist camp.

A familiar problem for the historian is how to judge actors in a situation where we know that everything is about to change but they are still for the most part moored to familiar policies and principles. In the case of the Convention, though, this issue is unusually clear-cut. The discontinuity between what was being debated there and the contemporary political mood was very obvious. Thus the northern unionists, like the proto-Sinn Féiners, saw themselves as the coming force, looking forward. The Redmondite constitutional nationalists were yesterday's men, and many knew it: the representative nationalists in the Convention, the county council chairmen, had been elected in 1914 and were now out of political synchronisation with their electorates, evidenced by the victories of Sinn Féin in parliamentary by-elections in May, July and August 1917, even before the Convention had got into its stride. The southern unionists were also yesterday's men, and they knew it too. This led to a recognition between these 'two endangered species of Irish politics',[100] the Redmondites and Midletonites, that if they couldn't try and swim some distance together they would probably both sink. That was the psychological, if not political, basis of their attempts at *rapprochement.*

THE NATURE OF CLERICAL INFLUENCE

The prelates occupied a unique position because of the innate nature of their calling. With the legitimacy of the Irish Parliamentary Party slipping away and a vacuum developing in the nationalist leadership, the bishops were well placed to step in. Anchored in firm and ageless belief systems, and the permanent apparatus of rock-solid institutions, they had tenure. At the last, O'Donnell, Kelly, Harty and MacRory—and Crozier and Bernard too—would still be bishops after the next general election, no matter what the outcome for Redmond or Carson or Midleton. They might have to—and did have to—come to terms with new polities in Ireland, but that was not disastrous. Influence could always be exercised through different modalities and channels.[101]

This had the potential to give the prelates a sense of power and lordly disconnection with political reality and aspiration. Perhaps the surprise is that not all exhibited such traits. O'Donnell was the most egregious example of those who did. After Redmond effectively bowed out of the Convention in early 1918, the bishop of Raphoe became the *de facto* leader of the fiscal autonomy nationalists. As such he became a powerful figure—'the nationalist dictator' Plunkett called him in March 1918.[102] He rather enjoyed his new-found position.[103] Not every nationalist was happy. For instance, Plunkett noted on 13 January that

> a lot of the County Councillors came to me and said they would leave the bishops to go their own way and would insist in supporting Midleton.[104]

On 26 February 1918 Plunkett reported on a 'long wrangle' between 'the Bolsheviks led by the Bishop of Raphoe and [William Martin] Murphy, and some County Councillors … who wish to go ahead and settle on Midleton-cum-Lloyd-George lines'.[105] Plunkett criticised O'Donnell's 'domineering tone' in the nationalist counsels. After Redmond's death on 6 March, Plunkett reported that the majority of the nationalists felt that 'they must not tolerate the dictation of the bishop any more'.[106] Some bishops had bees in their bonnets—Kelly's obsession with facts and figures, somewhat missing the point about transcendental nationalism, is one. Another is a vignette of Lord Midleton, after a well-lubricated party at Lord Granard's, being walked round and round St Stephen's Green until two in the morning by a Catholic bishop—almost certainly MacRory—who harangued the hapless peer about the possibility that England would ruin Irish trade as it had done in the eighteenth century.[107]

At the last, the clerics were willing to engage, to put their heads above the political parapet. That was perhaps not unexpected from Erastian Anglican prelates who had had to deal with the fallout from Church disestablishment and Catholic bishops politicised by the Parnell split. In particular, the Catholic hierarchy's initial brief hesitancy to participate in the Convention was in spite, not because, of their political profile since the bruising they had received during the Parnell imbroglio and its long finish. Ultimately they exhibited a willingness to shape history and engage with the world that was not only modern but startlingly *pre*-modern. The Catholic view of history at this time was still bound up with

> viewing the Church as the *societas perfecta* and the view of revelation as divine truths becoming visible in time. In that older model 'history' was acknowledged as equivalent to time's movement—the ticking of the clock—rather than history as real change which is the result of human activity.[108]

Not until Pope Paul VI's encyclical *Ecclesiam Suam* nearly half a century after the Convention did the Church begin to acknowledge that it 'bears in mind the actual situation in which human society finds itself today'.[109] That the Catholic bishops appeared in the Convention to be 'Irishmen first and Catholics second'—to invert John A. Costello's infamous formulation—is then surprising. But if they were, this extremely public politicisation was something of an aberration. What the Convention demonstrated—yet again—were the limitations of disintermediation for the clerics. In 1917 the lesson of the then-raging Great War was that to stick one's head above the parapet invited immolation. In this reading it was perhaps as well for the bishops that the Convention *was* a failure; if it had 'succeeded'—however that might be defined—they might have been politicised to the point of endangering their status and position. Instead, the lesson learnt was that achieving their objectives by working through their flocks, if less efficient in theory, was just as—if not more—effective in practice. Ultimately, pulpits could—and would—trump parapets.

21

A LETTER FROM THE ARCHBISHOPS: THE CHURCH OF IRELAND AND THE DOGMA OF THE ASSUMPTION, 1950[1]

INTRODUCTION

On the Second Sunday in Advent, 10 December 1950, at Morning Prayer in all churches of the Church of Ireland clergymen read a pastoral letter from its archbishops and bishops. This was a relatively unusual event. Anglican bishops issued (and still issue) pastoral letters, but a general letter in the name of all the prelates of the Irish Church was rare—indeed, virtually unheard of—so this must have been on a subject that particularly exercised the Church of Ireland. And perhaps it is no real surprise that it concerned the Virgin Mary. Outlined here is the reaction of that Church to the promulgation of the dogma of the Assumption, setting it in the context of the perceived position of Anglicans in southern Ireland a year after the establishment of the Irish republic.

THE CONTEXT

The theological context in which the dogma was proclaimed is briefly as follows. According to the doctrine and traditions of the Catholic Church, the Blessed Virgin Mary, 'having completed the course of her earthly life, was assumed body and soul into heavenly glory'.[2] Catholics generally believe that the promises of Christ as regards eternal life and resurrection of the body were fulfilled in Mary. The doctrine of the Immaculate Conception defines Mary as conceived without original sin and as having lived a sinless life. If Mary was thus free of original sin, she should not have had to suffer the consequences of that sin, namely death. At death our souls and bodies are parted, to be reunited only after the Day of Judgement. In Mary's case, because of her freedom from original sin, this process was short-circuited, as it were, and she was transported into heaven with her body and soul united.

With popular devotional pressure building for a declaration of the Assumption as an article of faith,[3] together with pleas by bishops and clergy, an obvious opportunity presented itself in 1950. As Pius XII stated,

> We rejoice greatly that this solemn event falls, according to the design of God's providence, during this Holy Year, so that we are able, while the great Jubilee is being observed, to adorn the brow of God's Virgin Mother with this brilliant gem, and to leave a monument more enduring than bronze of our own most fervent love for the Mother of God.[4]

In mid-August the Vatican City newspaper *L'Osservatore Romano* carried an announcement[5] that 'We have been informed that His Holiness has in mind the holding of a secret consistory next October 30 to announce his intention to proclaim on the following Wednesday, the dogma of the Assumption of the Blessed Virgin Mary into heaven'. Commenting on the pope's reasons for choosing this particular time to define this teaching, the newspaper stated that,

> Filled with fear of new and more tremendous catastrophes and while the world denies us every hope, once again we raise our eyes to heaven, imploring Our Lady, Mother of Mercy, with those words which Pius XII gave us: 'that the Virgin, moved to pity by the massacres of her children, by so many wounds and so many anxieties, may strengthen souls, extinguish hatreds and rancour, obtain concord and may cause to shine that Christian peace under which alone all nations, both victors and vanquished, united not in violence but in justice and equity, can enjoy lasting and fruitful tranquillity.'

'New and more tremendous catastrophes' referred to what was perceived then as a dangerous and unstable world. Cardinal Mindszenty had been imprisoned in Hungary. The Korean War was in full swing, and the possibility of nuclear exchanges was not discounted. A godless communism was sensed to be rampant and almost unstoppable.[6] In Ireland the advance of Marxism was to be countered by ostentatious popular Catholic devotion; the 1940s and 1950s saw a whole range of activities aimed at the conversion of Russia. The *Pax Christi* crusade of prayer was one of the most prominent, but it is significant that many efforts were based on the Marian cult; there were special devotions to the Immaculate Heart of Mary and Our Lady of Fatima, and always the ubiquitous rosary crusades.[7]

The reaction of the Church of Ireland to the dogma—trumpeted by the *Irish Catholic Directory* as the 'greatest Catholic event of the century'[8]—cannot properly be understood without a comprehension of the then political context. From 1922 (and to a certain extent before it) southern Protestants had made 'successful failure' into close to an art form. As a defence mechanism it had generally proven remarkably effective. In that 'failure' of southern Protestantism possibly lay the seeds of its relatively successful survival. It was crucial that the significant legacy of the British administration (not consciously planned) was that the great issues—land, local government, education, the Church—had been effectively settled by 1921. This left Protestants at once less visible and less important; in Roy Foster's words about the poet's family, 'The Yeatses had had money, social influence and a history in Ireland. By the later nineteenth century all they were left with was the history.'[9] And that history was, essentially, religion and loyalty, all that remained as the badges that marked out Protestants from the rest. Each was underlain by a strong sense of past glories, not future aspirations.

Loyalty lingered on right up to, and beyond, the foundation of the republic in 1949. It enabled a slow transition to take place. It sidestepped southern Irish Protestantism having to maintain a separate, irredentist and aggressive political identity. To those for whom the Irish Free State was anything but free—economically, socially, culturally—departure was the only option, and many did leave. But those who remained found that they could manage. Freed from an incubus of history, they got on with things, inventing a sort of hybrid state for themselves, a 'Brireland'. Thus symbol—relatively harmless—took the place of substance. Spontaneous renderings of *God Save the King* at Armistice Day remembrances in the Phoenix Park in 1931 and 1950 were rare public manifestations of a loyalty usually kept close to the chest.[10] The Church of Ireland's *Church Hymnal* still contained the hymn *God Save the King*; it did not acquire a rubric—'For use in Northern Ireland'—until the year 2000.

'White mice' was one description applied to southern Protestants in this period; and when the likes of Cardinal MacRory declared in 1931 that the Protestant Church in Ireland was not a part of the Church of Christ at all, one could probably see why.[11] The 1932 Eucharistic Congress, held shortly after Fianna Fáil's accession to government, seemed to symbolise the conflation of cultural Catholicism and political nationalism in the Free State. By this measure, southern Irish Protestants had, despite Yeats's protestations in 1925, simply become unnoticed and their remaining public functions were close to vanishing point. Amplified by the strident voices of Catholic triumphalism in the 1920s and 1930s, as evidenced by legislation in favour of the Irish language and censorship and restrictions on liquor sales, divorce and contraception, southern Protestants were encouraged to keep a low—even a cringing—profile. It helped that through the 1920s, 1930s and 1940s it was still possible to live an interior Protestant life without necessarily entering a Catholic world. Some Church of Ireland clerics and laity attempted to embrace Irishness through such as a devotion to the language, but it could not be said that they were representative.

From the perspective of the early 1920s, mere survival could have been considered a kind of triumph. It is not surprising, therefore, that with a few exceptions—columnists in the *Irish Statesman*, *The Bell*, the *Church of Ireland Gazette*, the writer Hubert Butler, Yeats and some prominent, but totally atypical, churchmen—southern Protestants chose not to confront and engage. Indeed, in the 1920s and 1930s their public representatives had often displayed a rather distasteful fawning attitude to the Free State.[12] An essential obeisance to the current power? Yes, in part. They had much to lose and had nearly lost it. Perhaps, as a later writer has put it, 'as a vestigial population in the new nation-state' they instinctively felt that 'their citizenship was a matter of indulgence and not of right'.[13] But it may have been a little more than this. At least up to the 1950s many southern Protestants were not much less illiberal than Catholics when it came to matters like divorce and abortion. If the likes of Yeats and Hubert Butler—as far removed from many of their co-religionists as from the mass of Catholics—imagined that they led an army, it was, in the main, a conscript one, reluctant and uncomprehending.[14]

Nevertheless, if their political position was somewhat quiescent, religious disputation still bubbled and occasionally broke the surface. Four specific issues that erupted in the years before 1950 were calculated to inflame Anglican reaction further. The first, the question of 'State Prayers', emerged as a consequence of the sudden declaration of the Republic in 1948. Prayers for the king at Anglican services had been acceptable so long as southern Ireland remained within the ambit of the Commonwealth, but the question had to be addressed following Ireland's departure. While Archbishop Gregg of Armagh acted to defuse the controversy and to ensure that the Church moved on,[15] there was a strong feeling amongst southern Anglicans against removing prayers for the king.[16] The second issue was the sensitive one of hospital control. In 1949 enthusiastic Roman Catholic doctors had engineered a management putsch in the Quaker-founded Meath Hospital. Several Protestant medics subsequently resigned or were sacked. Even for devout Catholics this was a step too far. It took a hasty combination of Catholic Archbishop McQuaid of Dublin and a Private Member's Bill in Dáil Éireann to repair the damaged relations.[17]

Whatever about the symbolism of 'State Prayers', it is perhaps significant that just before the dogma was promulgated a serious matter of substance had erupted between Catholics and Protestants involving the essence of the relationships between them. The Ernest Tilson case in 1950 sent a shiver down Protestant spines, intimately connected as it was with the very survival of the caste. Tilson, an Anglican who had signed the promise to bring up his children as Roman Catholics, wished to renege on that undertaking on the breakdown of his marriage. His wife sought the return of their children, whom Tilson had placed in a Protestant Home. In the High Court, Judge Gavan Duffy, allowing Mrs Tilson's claim, cited Article 44 of the 1937 Irish Constitution as the *raison d'être*, thus apparently enshrining Roman Catholic canon law in Irish jurisprudence. And thus it was seen by Irish Protestants, north and south, despite a later judgement of the Supreme Court which upheld it on the basis of the rights of the family and as an establishment of the principle that parents 'have a joint power and duty in respect of the religious education of their children' and that it marked the establishment of the legal equality of the sexes in guardianship matters.[18]

And finally, of little practical significance but hugely symbolic, as a mark of the Holy Year the Angelus began to be broadcast on Irish radio. During the late 1940s the secretary of the Department of Posts and Telegraphs, León Ó Broin, had discussed the idea of a daily broadcast spoken Angelus with Archbishop McQuaid. Charles Kelly, the director of Radio Éireann, was also consulted but was not in favour of this proposal. After further discussion, they concluded that 'the introduction of speech would be a mistake and we should experiment further simply with a bell'. Archbishop McQuaid suggested that it would be appropriate to commence on the Feast of the Assumption, 15 August 1950, and so it was done.

THE BULL

The bull *Munificentissimus Deus* was promulgated by Pope Pius XII on 1 November 1950. It declared infallibly that the Assumption of the Blessed Virgin Mary was a dogma of the Catholic faith. A dogma is a truth appertaining to faith or morals, revealed by God, transmitted from the Apostles in the Scriptures or by tradition and proposed by the Church for the acceptance of the faithful. This is the initial problem, so far as Anglicans are concerned. They have a difficulty with the acceptance of the whole concept simply because of its teleology, irrespective of its possible intrinsic merits. It contradicts a fundamental Protestant tenet, that there be no mediation between God and man save Christ, as revealed in holy Scripture.

Academic criticism had gathered pace during 1950 with the publication of *The Assumption of Our Lady and Catholic Theology* by two Roman Catholics, Raymond Winch and Victor Bennett,[19] and a scathing attack in the *Manchester Guardian* on 5 August 1950 by the senior lecturer in ecclesiastical history at the University of Manchester, Clifford Dugmore. The authoritative Anglican reaction came from the archbishops of Canterbury and York even before the promulgation of the dogma itself. Quick off the blocks on 15 August, the Feast of the Assumption, the two primates issued a joint statement in the name of the Church of England. It was uncompromising:

> We must at once state publicly that the Church of England does not and cannot hold this doctrine to be a necessary part of the Catholic faith ... there is not the smallest shred of evidence in the Scriptures or in the teaching of the early Church of belief in the doctrine of her bodily assumption.[20]

Getting their retaliation in first, Archbishop Geoffrey Fisher of Canterbury spoke of 'doctrines altogether outside of the Bible and the ancient universal creeds' and of the dogma being 'quite irrelevant to the saving of men in Christ', while on 12 October 1950 Archbishop Cyril Garbett of York dealt extensively with the arguments against the dogma. His speech was reproduced in full in two sequential issues of the *Church of Ireland Gazette.*[21] It is a learned speech and was doubtless read carefully by Archbishop Gregg of Armagh as he pondered the Church of Ireland's response.

The *Gazette* continued to run with the story after the promulgation of the dogma on 1 November 1950. An editorial, strong against the papacy, appeared in its 3 November issue, and on the same day the *Gazette*'s usual contemplative column, 'In quietness and confidence', belied its title by a vitriolic attack. Broadening the debate into one on the perceived excessive Mariology in the Catholic Church, it proclaimed that 'There are no grounds for the extravagant honours which the Roman Church pays to the Blessed Virgin, endangering as they do the doctrine of the Holy

Trinity', and 'the Assumption is a complete fiction without a shred of historical evidence'.[22] The *Gazette*'s issue of 17 November quoted from the British *Church Times*:

> To assert as historical an event for which there is no historical evidence is folly. To exalt a pious but unscrupulous opinion into an essential dogma is heresy. To disguise expediency as an act of Providence is near blasphemy. And on Wednesday Rome finally insisted on doing all these things.[23]

This was pretty strong stuff: for the mainstream voice of the Church of Ireland, albeit by second-party quotation, to call the pope unlearned, a heretic and a blasphemer ran counter to much of the way in which Irish Protestantism had conducted itself since the 1920s.

Reading the *Gazette* and its secular counterpart the *Irish Times*, what is striking is not the extent, depth and range of the adverse comments on the dogma but rather their relative absence.[24] The aforementioned Tilson case attracted much more attention, with extensive reports in the *Gazette* in the issues of 18 August, 25 August and 8 September, and numerous letters in the *Irish Times* during the last quarter of 1950.[25] Why was this? The obvious reason is that the issue of the Assumption was esoteric, the arguments based on obscure early church history and difficult theology, not the sort of stuff that would be the staple of loyalist pub-chat on the Shankill Road, nor even Saturday-night dinner parties in south Dublin—in a phrase, not likely to sell newspapers.

Again, in a conflict between the opportunity of some Catholic-baiting and the sensible desire to keep heads down, the latter possibly predominated. There is some fascinating, though inconclusive, evidence that the *Irish Times* may have deliberately decided to keep out of the controversy: one churchman complained in late 1950 that the newspaper had failed to publish a relevant letter to the editor. And the complete absence of any letters from the public is a little odd, to say the least—though a simpler explanation might be that Smyllie, the legendary, chaotic editor, may have simply mislaid any such letters.[26] The *Times* was content to report, but it seemed reluctant to comment or even allow comment. While it did publish the archbishops' pastoral in full, it was not placed on the front page but on page 4, suspiciously juxtaposed with Myles na gCopaleen's satirical column 'Cruiskeen Lawn'.[27] Maybe the newspaper had taken to heart a previous archbishop of Dublin's admonition in 1920 at a time of great tension that 'Singularity is never popular'.[28] That archbishop was John Gregg, now thirty years later archbishop of Armagh and primate of All Ireland and to be the author of the Church of Ireland's official response to the dogma's promulgation.

On 26 October the *Irish Times* reported that the Dublin Diocesan Synod had met on 25 October, a week *before* the official promulgation of the dogma. A motion was proposed by Canon W.G. Proctor in which he asked the 'appropriate authorities' to make a statement 'which will re-affirm the basis of our Church's faith and teaching, namely the Holy Scriptures and the practice of the Primitive Church'. The chairman, Archdeacon Sullivan, revealed that the matter had been raised in the previous week at the Standing Committee of the Representative Church Body (the Church of Ireland's executive board). A grant of money had been sought for the preparation of a pamphlet on the dogma. Archbishop Gregg, who had presided at that meeting, 'at once said that this was a very deep theological question and could not be dealt with by any member of the committee, but must be dealt with authoritatively when the right time came. The Primate had disapproved of any people other than the real theological authority of the Church making any pronouncement on the doctrine.' As if to ram the point home, the archdeacon stated that the Diocesan Synod was not there to define doctrine and he was going to rule the motion out of order. That ended the discussion. Gregg's biographer confirms this: he states that, after the promulgation, the archbishop sent letters to his clergy 'peremptorily forbidding any of them to reply to it … he would deal with it himself'.[29]

And so he did. We do not now know whether a specific Church of Ireland response to the dogma was the result of a plan or of pressure. The episcopal pastoral letter was due more to Archbishop Gregg's character, interests and antecedents than to any real necessity to set out a separate Church of Ireland stall. Certainly, Canterbury's and York's pronouncements would seem to have done the job more than adequately. Nevertheless, the letter ranks as one of Gregg's finest theological expositions. This was by no means the first time that he had expostulated publicly against the tenets of Roman Catholicism. When rector of Blackrock, Cork, in 1909, he had delivered a series of Lenten sermons entitled 'The Primitive Faith and Roman Catholic Developments' which dealt with such matters as papal supremacy and infallibility, indulgences, the invocation of saints—and the Assumption of the Virgin Mary. While couched in more vigorous terms than in 1950, there were to be found all of Gregg's later arguments, lucidly expounded.[30]

THE LETTER

The 'Pastoral Letter from the Archbishops and Bishops of the Church of Ireland to be read at Morning Prayer in all the Churches of the Church of Ireland on the Second Sunday in Advent' was considered by the House of Bishops in draft on 15 November 1950 and approved for publication with an embargo of 10 December 1950.[31] It was signed by Gregg and Arthur Barton, archbishop of Dublin, but it had Gregg's fingerprints all over it. It began:

> Dear Brethren in the Lord
>
> It is probable that you expect to receive some official guidance from your Church concerning the recently defined Dogma of the Roman Catholic Church on the Assumption of the Virgin Mary.
>
> If we ask what historical evidence has come down to us that, as a fact, such a taking-up into the heavenly glory of the Mother of Jesus, body and soul, did actually occur, the only answer that can be given is that there is no historical evidence whatever. The death of the Blessed Virgin, whensoever and wheresoever it took place (and, undoubtedly, it must have taken place some time before the later books of the New Testament appeared) is entirely without contemporary record whether within or without the New Testament …
>
> Acceptance of the belief proceeded with an ever-intensifying fervour, as pious meditation, not unmixed with fancy, occupied itself with the venerated figure of the Mother of our Lord.
>
> As the ages passed, an uncurbed religious sentiment came to exalt her to a position in the heavenly world, entirely different from, and out of all proportion to, that which is accorded to her in the New Testament and in the earlier centuries of the Church's life.
>
> Far from being pressed on our notice in the New Testament, it would seem that, apart from those crucial passages in the Gospels where her place in relation to the Incarnation of the Eternal Word brings her into special prominence, her personality has very little emphasis laid upon it, as distinct from that of others …

Here Gregg gives a set of biblical quotations to prove his point. He goes on to set out what in the Anglican view is the veneration proper to the Virgin:

> Her place and function in relation to the taking of flesh by the Eternal Word are unique. She stands solitary in the mysterious privilege with

> which she was favoured. It can be shared by no other. High honour is due, and rendered, to one so chosen as to give Him birth and to pass some thirty years in His company in the life of the home.

The archbishop then deals with the development of Mariology in the Roman Catholic Church, as he sees it:

> over-busy sentiment has not allowed her to make way for, and be lost sight of behind, the Son, who is the sole reason for her high renown and whose Divine glory is reflected upon her ... Further, veneration of her person has come to concentrate devotion upon her cult, almost as if she held a position in her own right, so that she can even be styled Co-redeemer and Mediatrix of all graces—until this Marian exaltation has attained such dominance, that theology is called in to justify it.

And then the broadside:

> When Pope Benedict XIV in 1740 stated that the most ancient fathers of the primitive Church are silent as to the Bodily Assumption of the Blessed Virgin; while the same Pope wrote that the Assumption ... is not an Article of Faith ...; Pope Pius XII asserts in 1950 that it is a truth revealed to the Church by the Holy Ghost. And so, we now learn that a doctrine now embodying what must have been, if it actually occurred, a fact in time and place, can dispense altogether with historical evidence, and the grave step has been taken of defining the result of devout speculation and inference as a truth divinely revealed.

Finally, Gregg answers those Catholics who 'may say that this is no concern of ours'. His initial sentence in this section is, on first reading, an admission that that is the case:

> In a sense—and alas! in a growing sense—this is true.

But then he continues:

> By its various enlargements of the ancient Catholic Creed to contain the twelve new articles of Pope Pius IV's creed, the two new articles of Pope Pius IX in 1854 [the Immaculate Conception] and 1870 [papal infallibility], and this new Dogma of 1950, the Roman Church is shutting itself further and further away from the rest of Catholic Christendom into being a self-enclosed corporation—a sectarian organisation, governed by its own private and self-determined Rule of Faith, which those who are content with the ancient Rule of Faith and the primitive Church Order, can only reject as heretical … it misrepresents the Catholic Faith and exposes it to ridicule, to define this dogma as an Article of Faith, to be believed by all Christians.

The pastoral was necessary, Gregg maintained, 'to make our public protest' against the pronouncement of the article of faith. Crucially, he sees it, essentially, as 'the penalty, both for the Pope and for his Church, of the absoluteness of the papal claim to Infallibility'.

Gregg ends with a magisterial cry:

> This grave event should teach us this lesson. Christianity centres upon the ever-living Christ, God made Man, Crucified, Risen, Ascended, Exalted; our Eternal High Priest in the Heavenly Temple.
>
> If the truth of His Glorified Manhood becomes obscured for us … it will be no wonder if we find the Gospel … insufficient for our needs, and are tempted to overlay it with all that fabric of supplication and doctrine which has taken shape in Roman Catholic Mariology.

In short, papal authority cannot, and should not, trump biblical authority.

THE AFTERMATH

The pastoral letter was published in the *Irish Times* on 11 December and in the *Church of Ireland Gazette* on 15 December 1950, each without comment. Gregg's learned piece required no further exposition, or so it seemed. On 10 November the *Gazette* published a satirical attack on the pope's reported comments that the promulgation of the dogma would help the poor, the weak, and those without a roof over their heads.[32] On 22 December a long article by 'J.B.S.' appeared in the *Gazette* which in popular and often vulgar language paraphrased the pastoral. It was ironic and satirical and made resonance with Ireland in a way that was instantly recognisable, as the following extract shows:

> Up to and including 31 October 1950, you were free to hold what opinion you wished on the subject, but on 1 November if you didn't hold the truth of this new Dogma the gate of Heaven was slammed in your face, like the gate of Derry on a famous historical occasion … It stands on the same level of authenticity as that famous classic, Jack and the Beanstalk.[33]

More strong stuff, then. The writer (Canon J.B. Shea, a retired cleric of Tuam) added to and amplified Gregg's reasons why Anglicans should be concerned: truth for its own sake was congenial; the Protestant is jealous to defend the honour and dignity of Christ; if this so-called 'resurrection' is proved only to be myth, then there is a danger that belief in Christ's true rising will be weakened.

Roman Catholics did not let these attacks pass unremarked. Indeed, it could be held that the Catholic reaction to the Anglican comments was more extensive and vitriolic than the Anglican reaction to the original cause. This may have been because of considerable doubts within much of the Catholic theological community at the time as to the validity of the new Article of Faith. Anglican criticism touched a somewhat raw nerve.[34] Monsignor Ronald Knox, who, as the son of a Church of England bishop, knew the Anglican mind better than most, had in 1927 had an ingenious argument for the right of the Catholic Church to declare Articles of Faith which was deployed on the occasion of the dogma's promulgation:

> the Protestant had no conceivable right to base any arguments on the inspiration of the Bible, for the inspiration of the Bible was a doctrine which had been believed, before the Reformation, on the mere authority of the Church ... Did they suppose that Biblical inspiration was a self-evident fact, like the axioms of Euclid?[35]

In Ireland one doughty defender of the new article of faith was Alfred O'Rahilly, professor of mathematical physics and registrar (later president) of University College Cork. He was as dismissive of Protestant religiosity as his contemporary Cork academic Daniel Corkery was of Protestant culture. In a series of thirteen articles in the Catholic *Standard* newspaper between 1 December 1950 and 23 February 1951 he 'raked over the embers of opposition to the Dogma', much to the annoyance and boredom of many of his colleagues in UCC.[36]

It has to be said that O'Rahilly spread his vitriol evenly, criticising what he saw as atheistic articles in the left-wing British *Daily Worker* and *New Statesman* and right-wing anti-Catholicism in the conservative *Spectator*. But if he had one greater hatred than Protestantism it was a godless Marxism, and he regretted the division in Christianity that was occasioned by the Assumption controversy. On 22 September 1950 he wrote hoping that, if Anglicans 'would stop their sneering at

Rome, we would work together more efficiently against Moscow'.[37] He returned to the theme three months later, expressing disappointment at the appearance of the pastoral, which was prompted not by agnosticism and communism, he claimed, but rather by simple sectarianism.

On the Catholic side, there was also an occasional descent into something more than abstract theological criticism of the Anglican position. 'A certain nervousness has characterised their utterances ... they have not essayed to meet argument with argument', wrote an anonymous columnist in the *Gazette* on 3 November 1950.[38] In his Lenten Pastoral in February 1951, the nonagenarian Roman Catholic bishop of Cork, Daniel Coholan (scrupulously in line with Pope Leo XIII's 1896 declaration of Anglican orders as invalid), suggested, rather mischievously, that the archbishop of York and the archbishops of Armagh and Dublin were not qualified to discuss the finer points of Catholic theology, being mere laymen.[39] And, as the Holy Year was drawing to a close, O'Rahilly wrote disparagingly of 'the prelates of this little man-made Church' who 'could only be regarded by their flock as convenient officials under the constitution of 1870'.[40]

And so the debate petered out in acrimony and mutual misunderstanding early in 1951, with a late flurry provoked by Roman Catholic bishops' Lenten pastorals. Professional meetings of the Church of Ireland diocesan clergy held over the period did not, as far as can be ascertained, discuss the controversy. Nor did Methodists or Presbyterians join in. It was reported on, briefly, by Gregg at the Church of Ireland's General Synod in May 1951. Interestingly, Gregg bracketed the dogma controversy and the Tilson case together.[41] It resurfaced in 1954 when, as a reaction to a series of lectures in the Queen's University of Belfast organised to mark the centenary of the promulgation of the Immaculate Conception, the Anglican dean of residences reissued the pastoral letter. Gregg's position had not softened in the interim. In reply to a letter from the dean at the time, he observed that 'It is difficult to limit pious speculation, but to make it official doctrine is nothing short of heretical ... we have to distinguish between the Mary of history and the Mary of faith'.[42]

CONCLUSION

Reading through the controversy, it seems that what really exercised the Anglican protagonists was not the Marian dogma in itself but in a deeper sense the exercise of Church authority and particularly the process of papal infallibility that facilitated it. This is emphasised in the archbishop of York's statement to his convocation on 12 October 1950, where he pointed out that error in a bishop of the Church of England is his alone and does not bind the faithful, whereas in the Church of Rome it can. As he said, 'The Pope represents an authority overriding every other. Conscience, creed and Christian history go for nothing once the papal edict has gone forth ... the ordinary Roman Catholic finds himself with no defence, no appeal to reason, no freedom to protest.'[43] Of course, that misses the whole point about the Catholic Church's magisterium.

Opposition to Mariology was on safer ground. Gregg had written in 1909 that 'Next to the supremacy of the Pope I do not think there is anything which makes all right-minded Anglicans so afraid of Romanism as the worship of the Virgin Mary'.[44] Forty-one years later, the promulgation of the dogma of the Assumption brought together his two worst fears. But perhaps Gregg's distaste of papal infallibility stemmed from how infallibility might be manipulated rather than the concept of infallibility itself. As he had written in the pastoral letter,[45]

> Infallibility has received a mandate and proceeds to obey it. The voice of the people appears to have been approved as the voice of God. But can the popular voice be relied on as a sure guide to the Truth?

Pope Pius IX's declaration in 1870 that 'I am the Tradition'[46] would have confirmed Gregg in his view of papal infallibility as inherently capricious and potentially dangerous, capable of being exploited by a malign or ignorant 'popular voice'. Yet he had shown that he was quite prepared to control *his* Church's reaction with a rigid discipline that would have been the envy of many popes. Clearly seeing himself as 'the real theological authority of the Church', he was, in this sense, more papal than the pope—not prepared to accept popular sway over matters of doctrine.

Gregg would have taken especial exception to O'Rahilly's description of him as a 'convenient official' of his 'little man-made church'. While legally founded on a United Kingdom Act of Parliament and a constitution adopted by a Convocation of the whole Church in 1870, the Church of Ireland would to the primate have seemed much less prone to the whims of devotional fashions than the Roman Catholic Church, not to mention the often contradictory pronouncements of oligarchic popes. The tenets and principles of the Church of Ireland are set out in the Preamble and Declaration at the head of its constitution 'as being essential to its identity'.[47] But while the rest of the constitution may be changed by the Church's due legislative process, significantly its framers were careful not to include this Preamble and Declaration. This 'fundamental law' informs all that the Church of Ireland stands for; it certainly informed Gregg's 'constant witness' against one of those 'innovations in doctrine and worship' which he perceived 'this grave event', the promulgation of the dogma of the Assumption, to be.[48]

Let us end on a somewhat lighter note. To put it kindly, neither Gregg nor O'Rahilly were renowned for their sense of humour. Nevertheless, while opposed on practically everything else, they managed to alight on the same joke—a pun, really, and probably the only one applicable to the controversy. In O'Rahilly's case, he was the butt of the humour, while the archbishop, rather implausibly, was the humorist. After yet another wearisome diatribe in the UCC Common Room against the Anglican divines, it is reported that O'Rahilly provoked one of his colleagues, Professor John Busteed, to make an observation which was somewhat similar to that later made by Gregg on the dogma. 'After all', the archbishop had ventured, 'it is only an *assumption*.'[49]

AFTERWORD

Alan Ford

> 'Attended a conference paper in the morning, by a young man from Peterhouse … He is a bright and pleasant young man, D'Alton by name (and a Protestant)'—J.C. Beckett, diary, November 1972–November 1973 (PRONI MS D4126/A/30), entry for 23 March 1973.

It's tough being an Irish historian. Caught in a no-man's-land between literature and science, subjectivity and objectivity, Catholic and Protestant, revisionism and anti-revisionism, it is sometimes a challenge to decide not just where you are coming from but also what it is that you are actually doing. You could, on the one hand, take refuge in the rigour of science. There is the confident, much-quoted statement by the early twentieth-century Roman historian J.B. Bury (son of a Church of Ireland cleric, as it happens) that, 'though history may supply material for literary art or philosophical speculation, she is herself a science, no less and no more'.[1] And, of course, the launch of *Irish Historical Studies* by Robin Dudley Edwards and Theo Moody in the 1930s is often claimed to represent a firmly 'scientific' turn in twentieth-century Irish history.[2] But even Bury soon rowed back from such an extreme claim, admitting that 'the presentation of the results of historical research' was also an art, and, for all their scientific rigour, the backgrounds of Edwards (Catholic and nationalist) and Moody (Quaker and pacifist) still shine through in their writings.[3]

You can, of course, go to the opposite extreme and see yourself as an artist, taking the literary turn and viewing what you write as a subjective story, with one person's tale as good as another's. Hayden White, most famously, has explored the way in which historians use literary tricks to plot their narratives.[4] But this approach, while attractive to literary theorists, has never had much traction amongst those who actually write history. As Richard Evans demonstrated so devastatingly, post-modern exculpations of David Irving run into an inescapable fact: Hitler and the Nazis killed millions of Jews.[5] 'Emplotment' and the Holocaust are uneasy bedfellows.[6]

As you can see from reading these collected essays, Ian d'Alton makes no grand claims about the theoretical significance of his writing. He is, after all, another example of that distinguished blood-line of Peterhouse-Irish, cross-bred historians whose doctoral training essentially consisted of no training at all. As another Cambridge academic, R.B. Wernham, put it when asked about his attitude towards theory, 'I'm a simple man'.[7]

And yet ... as you read Ian's essays, a rather sophisticated and far from simple underpinning emerges. Yes, he is indeed true to his Cambridge empiricist breeding—after all, he started off working on nineteenth-century Cork elections. But—and this is an important 'but'—he never went down the route of the tenured professional historian: his work isn't the product of the need to secure research grants, the desire for academic promotion, the endless (well, in English universities, anyway ...) pressure to publish. What he writes about is what piques his interest and, as you have by now found out, piques the reader's interest too. That is a precious, liberating freedom.

More than that, because he is not constrained within an academic department or specialism he has an enviable disciplinary flexibility, in particular his seemingly effortless (though I am sure it is not) ability to straddle history and literature. He can, as he shows in his work on Iris Murdoch, 'do' literary criticism, but always uses the literary artefact to explore and enlarge the 'parallel southern Protestant reality', as when he unpicks the essential 'Protestantness' of Yvonne in Murdoch's *Something Special*. Or take his masterful account of the Irish gentry in World War I in Chapter 13, which opens by doing due statistical diligence with *Burke's Peerage and Landed Gentry*, counting up the human cost to the Protestant gentry, but then deepens the examination of the impact of the war by moving from letters and reminiscences through autobiography to fiction, finally bringing home to us the complexities of the Anglo-Irish responses, the contrast between the 'existential disaster' and 'trivial domesticities'.

All this is illuminated by the most precious gift of all—one not granted to most academics—of lightness of touch and stylish phrase-making. 'War was an existential part of what the Irish gentry was.' When it came to enlistment, 'Duty and honour trumped common sense'. The vacuity of post-war existence as the 'ennui of a perpetual Protestant afternoon tea'. The Yogic concept of 'Catholic transcendental nationalism'. The band playing at Windsor Castle as the Irish regimental insignia were surrendered for the last time—'the last great death of the Great War'. 'All the purposeful parts of their place in the country … gradually disappeared until nothing was left except a Cheshire Cat's disembodied grin of an abstract loyalty'. Not to mention Norman Leslie's horizontal approach to language-learning …

University academics tend to be rather coy about the personal baggage they bring with them to scholarly writing. Their natural instinct is to preserve the illusion of that objectivity to which all historians aspire: we are simply and straightforwardly telling you 'what really happened'. In this case, as we can see from Ian's opening essay, there is no such fear of subjectivity: the personal leads directly and honestly to the history. As he himself says, he is a southern Irish Protestant, and that is what he has chosen to study. More than that, as Felix Larkin points out, Ian is a product of a particular time, when Protestantism no longer cast doubt on your Irishness, but rather it was possible, as J.C. Beckett almost said, to be Irish (and Protestant). And you can add to that that he grew up at another turning-point: when the inbred religious hatred of Catholics and Protestants, cemented in the Irish psyche for over three hundred years, was beginning to crack under the influence of ecumenism, modernity and secularism. He can thus look back at the old cast-iron anti-Catholic certainties of Archbishop Gregg and his attack on the Assumption and at that wonderful(ly awful) 'Hate Counter' in the Hibernian Bible Society's bookshop, but also look forward to the new Ireland where secular liberalism has replaced religion as a driving force in public and private life.

As new possibilities loom for a united Ireland, this book also points to a sobering perspective on a largely neglected topic: the disunited nature of Irish Anglicanism, north and south. Ian is quite clear that he is '… *not* a northern Protestant—there *are* differences between the northern and southern varieties, to put it mildly!' Rather he offers a distinctly southern perspective on twentieth-century Protestant history, markedly at odds with the view from the north. Liam Kennedy has had fun at the expense of nationalist historians who insist that the Irish are the Most Oppressed People Ever.[8] Ian d'Alton has extended the trope by applying it to those Northern Irish Protestant historians who continue to be convinced that their 'Free State' brethren, labouring under Rome rule, *must* be the Most Oppressed Protestants Ever, taking to heart the hope of Hugh Montgomery in 1918 that Church of Ireland members, safe in their northern redoubt, would be able to provide 'help to southern brethren threatened with oppression under a rebel and priest-ridden parliament in Dublin'.[9] The charge sheet is familiar: *Ne Temere*, the Mayo librarian fracas in the 1930s, the Tilson case, the Fethard-on-Sea boycott and so on. But the reality was more nuanced and far less hostile. As both Ian and his fellow southern Protestant Ida Milne have repeatedly shown, the lived—or, in both their cases, the lived-in—southern Protestant experience looks very different when viewed from south of the border.

What we have in this delightful book is the weaving together of history, politics, literature and identity at which southern Protestants have proved so adept. It is, in short, yet another example of that favourite Anglo-Irish genre, the thought-provoking essay, witty and charming, but with a sharp, perceptive undertow. It sits—very comfortably—in the noble tradition of twentieth-century southern Irish Protestant historians, from that neglected master St John Seymour through Hubert Butler to Roy Foster and, now, Ian d'Alton.

NOTES AND REFERENCES

***Felix M. Larkin*: Ian d'Alton: historian of a 'confident minority'**

1 Ian has contributed essays to three volumes that I have edited or co-edited, and I have an essay in I. d'Alton & I. Milne (eds), *Protestant **and** Irish: The Minority's Search for Place in Independent Ireland* (Cork, 2019).

2 D'Alton & Milne, *Protestant **and** Irish*, p. 1.

3 E. Bowen, *Seven Winters: Memories of a Dublin Childhood* (London, 1943), p. 11.

4 Response by I. d'Alton to an address by Dr M. Mansergh to the Modern Irish History Seminar, Sidney Sussex College, Cambridge, 15 October 2014 (unpublished).

5 I. d'Alton, 'A perspective upon historical process: the case of southern Irish Protestantism', in F.B. Smith (ed.), *Ireland, England and Australia: Essays in Honour of Oliver MacDonagh* (Canberra and Cork, 1990), p. 89.

6 J. O'Neill, *Blood-dark Track: A Family History* (London, 2000), p. 327.

7 Review by I. d'Alton of R. Bury's *Buried Lives: The Protestants of Southern Ireland* (Dublin, 2017), *IT*, 4 March 2017.

8 I. d'Alton, '"No country"? Protestant "belongings" in independent Ireland, 1922–49', in d'Alton & Milne, *Protestant **and** Irish*, pp 32–3.

9 The title of Bishop Butler's sermon on the eve of the General Synod of the Church of Ireland, 13 May 1963, quoted by D. Ó Corráin, *Rendering to God and Caesar: The Irish Churches and the Two States in Ireland* (Manchester, 2006), p. 70.

10 D'Alton, 'Protestant "belongings" in independent Ireland', p. 33.

11 [R.S. Ross-Lewin], *Poems by a County of Clare West Briton* (Limerick, 1907), p. 7.

***Ian d'Alton*: Protestant *and* Irish: seeking identity through history, biography and literature**

1 For a recent example of an Irish Protestant journey of 'identity through history' (and vice versa) see P. Brown, *Journeys of the Mind: A Life in History* (Princeton, 2023).

2 R.B. McDowell, 'Memories: an afterword', in *Crisis and Decline: The Fate of the Southern Unionists* (Dublin, 1997), pp 197–211.

3 H. White, *Tropics of Discourse. Essays in Cultural Criticism* (London, 1978), cited in T. Dunne, 'A polemical introduction: literature, literary theory and the historians', in Dunne (ed.), *The Writer as Witness* (Cork, 1987), p. 4.

4 E. Bowen, *Collected Impressions* (London, 1950), pp 249–63.

5 E.A. Chase, 'Counting the dead as "one" and "one again" in the fiction of twentieth-century Irish women novelists' (unpublished Ph.D thesis, Emory University, 2012), p. 65.

6 For discussions on why and how the Catholic élite, such as it was, had to navigate Protestant 'blocking' of its progress, see C. O'Neill (ed.), *Irish Elites in the Nineteenth Century* (Dublin, 2013), and *Catholics of Consequence—Transnational Education, Social Mobility, and the Irish Catholic Elite 1850–1900* (Oxford, 2014).

7 Jeremiah 29:11 (Revised Standard Version).

8 J. Buchan, *The Causal and the Casual in History* (Cambridge, 1929), p. 7.

9 T. Dunne, *Rebellions: Memoir, Memory and 1798* (Dublin, 2010), p. 66.

10 E. Norman, *A History of Modern Ireland, 1800–1969* (London, 1971).

11 Cork, 1980.

12 Norman, *A History of Modern Ireland*, preface, n.p.

1. Cork city's Protestant culture in the eighteenth century

1 A version of this essay was published as 'Cork City's 18th-century Protestant culture', in J. Crowley, R. Devoy, D. Linehan, M. Murphy & P. O'Flanagan (eds), *Atlas of Cork City* (Cork, 2005), pp 160–7.

2 J. McGuire, 'The Church of Ireland and the "Glorious Revolution" of 1688', in A. Cosgrove & D. McCartney (eds), *Studies in Irish History Presented to R. Dudley Edwards* (Dublin, 1979), pp 138–42; D. Hayton & G. O'Brien, *War and Politics in Ireland 1649–1730* (London, 1986), p. 124.

3 *Cork Mercantile Chronicle*, 3 January 1827.

4 J. McCracken, 'Protestant Ascendancy and the rise of colonial nationalism', in T. Moody & W. Vaughan (eds), *A New History of Ireland* (Oxford, 1986), IV, pp 105–22; J. Hill, *From Patriots to Unionists: Dublin Civic Politics and Irish Protestant Patriotism 1660–1840* (Oxford, 1997), pp 19–41; M. McCarthy, 'The historical geography of Cork's transformation from a late medieval town into an Atlantic port city, 1600–1700' (unpublished Ph.D thesis, UCC, 1997), pp 570–8.

5 A. Fahy, 'A social geography of nineteenth-century Cork' (unpublished MA thesis, UCC, 1981), pp 63–4.

6 Alexander the Coppersmith, *Remarks on the Religion, Trade, Government, Police, Customs, Manners, Maladies of the City of Cork* (Cork, 1737), p. 2.

7 T. Barnard, 'The political, material and mental culture of the Cork settlers, *c.* 1650–1700', in P. O'Flanagan & C. Buttimer (eds), *Cork: History and Society* (Dublin, 1993), p. 347.

8 *Ibid.*, p. 351.

9 J. O'Brien, 'Population, politics and society in Cork, 1780–1900', in *Cork: History and Society*, pp 700, 718;

R. Day & W. Coppinger (eds), *The Ancient and Present State of the County and City of Cork, by Charles Smith MD* (2 vols) (Cork, 1893–4), I, p. 459; C.B. Gibson, *The History of the County and City of Cork* (2 vols) (London, 1861), II, pp 208–11; J. Keane, 'Four tales of a city: the transformation in the social, economic and political geography of Cork City 1780–1846' (unpublished MA thesis, UCC, 1990), p. 194.

10 Fahy, 'A social geography', p. 58.

11 *An Abstract of the Number of Protestant and Popish Families in the Several Provinces and Counties of Ireland Taken from the Return made by the Hearthmoney Collectors ... in the years 1732 and 1733* (Dublin, 1736; repr. 1786), p. 5. These returns have to be treated with circumspection.

12 O'Brien, 'Population, politics and society', pp 699–704.

13 *CC*, 24 October 1833, evidence of Joseph Hayes given to the commissioners appointed to inquire into the municipal corporations in Ireland; D. Dickson, 'Second city syndrome', in S.J. Connolly (ed.) *Kingdoms United? Great Britain and Ireland since 1500* (Dublin, 1998), p. 105.

14 D. Dickson, 'The Cork merchant community in the eighteenth century: a regional perspective', in L. Cullen & P. Butel (eds), *Negoce et Industrie en France et en Irelande aux XVIIIe et XIXe siècles* (Paris, 1980), p. 47; S.J. Connolly, *Religion, Law and Power: the making of Protestant Ireland, 1600-1760* (Oxford, 1992), p. 148.

15 Hayes, evidence to the corporate commissioners.

16 O'Brien, 'Population, politics and society', p. 703.

17 T. Barnard, *A New Anatomy of Ireland: The Irish Protestants, 1649–1770* (Yale, 2003), p. 258; D. Dickson, *New Foundations: Ireland 1660–1800* (Dublin & Portland, 2000), p. 133; Dickson, 'The Cork merchant community', pp 47–9; Keane, 'Four tales', p. 57.

18 J. O'Donovan, 'The Volunteer movement in Cork and other southern counties, 1745–85' (unpublished MA thesis, UCC, 1980), pp 68, 70–7, 86; Connolly, *Religion, Law and Power*, pp 125–8; Barnard, *New Anatomy*, p. 330; Gibson, *History of... Cork*, II, p. 215; Barnard, 'The political, material and mental culture', pp 349–50.

19 Fahy, 'A social geography', pp 98–101, 269–72.

20 Barnard, *New Anatomy*, p. 19; *First Report of Commissioners of Public Instruction*, appendix 124c, 136c, 138c, 140c; Keane, 'Four tales', p. 121; P. Jupp & S. Royle, 'The social geography of Cork City elections, 1801–30', *IHS*, vol. 29 (1994), pp 31–2.

21 T. Newenham, *A View of the Natural, Political and Commercial Circumstances of Ireland* (London, 1809), appendix xviii; *Second Report of Commissioners of Irish Education Enquiry*, appendix 22, parochial abstracts, pp 1000–23 (HC 1826–7 (12.) xii.1.); Hill, *From Patriots to Unionists*, pp 24–32, 39–41; Barnard, *New Anatomy*, p. 15.

22 Revd W. Neligan to Sir R. Peel, 28 January 1845 (BL Add. MS 40,558, 307); minutes of St Peter's vestry, Cork city (NLI MS 764); *CC*, 7 November 1844; Keane, 'Four tales', p. 82.

23 E. Wakefield, *An Account of Ireland, Statistical and Political* (2 vols) (Dublin, 1812), II, p. 303.

24 See Connolly, *Religion, Law and Power*, pp 160–1.

25 R. Harrison, *Cork City Quakers, 1655–1939* (privately printed, 1991), p. 4; Barnard, *New Anatomy*, p. 113; *First Report of Commissioners of Public Instruction*, appendix, 124c, 136c, 138c, 140c.

26 P. Kilroy, *Protestant Dissent and Controversy in Ireland 1660–1714* (Cork, 1994), pp 171–213; Connolly, *Religion, Law and Power*, p. 156; G. Goldberg, *Jonathan Swift and Contemporary Cork* (Cork, 1967), p. 26; Barnard, *New Anatomy*, p. 17.

27 Goldberg, *Jonathan Swift*, p. 23; O'Donovan, 'The Volunteer movement', p. 49.

28 E. Wetenhall, *A Brief and Modest Reply to Mr Penn's Tedious, Scurrilous and Unchristian Defence against the Bishop of Cork* (Dublin, 1699), p. 9; Goldberg, *Jonathan Swift*, p. 24; Harrison, *Cork City Quakers*, pp 4, 5; J. Falvey, 'The Church of Ireland episcopate in the eighteenth century' (unpublished MA thesis, UCC, 1995), p. 29; Easter vestry reports, Holy Trinity parish, in *CC*, 21 April 1829, 13 April 1830 and 5 April 1831.

29 Dickson, 'Second city syndrome', pp 103, 104; M. Costello, 'A symbolic geography of church construction in Cork City from the early seventeenth to the mid-nineteenth century' (unpublished MA thesis, UCC, 1994), pp 136–45; D. Dickson, 'Huguenots in the urban economy of eighteenth-century Dublin and Cork', in C. Caldicott, H. Gough & J.-P. Pittion (eds), *The Huguenots and Ireland: Anatomy of an Emigration* (Dublin, 1987), p. 322; A. St Leger, *Silver, Sails and Silk: Huguenots in Cork 1685–1850* (Cork, 1990), pp 9–13, 26–9.

30 Gibson, *History of… Cork*, II, pp 189, 271–2; Dickson, 'The Cork merchant community', p. 49.

31 *The Freeholder*, 15 July 1827.

32 *Southern Reporter*, 28 February 1832.

33 Day & Coppinger, *The Ancient and Present State*, I, p. 433; I. d'Alton, *Protestant Society and Politics in Cork 1812–1844* (Cork, 1980), pp 92–3, 97.

34 J. O'Shea, 'A transcription and extension of an index of the council books of the Corporation of Cork from 31 Oct. 1710 to 25 Oct. 1841' (typescript in the possession of Cork City and County Archives), pp 328, 374; *Appendix to the First Report of the Commissioners Appointed to Inquire into the Municipal Corporations in Ireland* (southern, midland and western circuit), HC 1835 (27) xxvii, 169, pp 33–5; Gibson, *History of… Cork*, II, p. 183; D. Franklin, 'Extracts from the Letter Book of Joseph ffranklyn, Mayor of Cork in 1708', *JCHAS*, vol. 1 (1895), p. 50; R. Caulfield, *The Council Book of the Corporation of Cork, from 1609 to 1643, and from 1690 to 1800* (Guildford, 1876), pp 294, 488; Day & Coppinger, *The Ancient and Present State*, I, p. 393.

35 Hill, *From Patriots to Unionists*, p. 28; d'Alton, *Protestant Society*, pp 92–3.

36 Gibson, *History of… Cork*, II, p. 189; Caulfield, *Council Book*, pp 431, 433, 729.

37 Hill, *From Patriots to Unionists*, p. 43.

38 D'Alton, *Protestant Society*, pp 93–6; Keane, 'Four tales', pp 93–9; K. Milne, 'The Irish municipal corporations in the eighteenth century' (unpublished Ph.D thesis, TCD, 1962).

39 Evidence of J. Besnard given to the commissioners appointed to inquire into the municipal corporations in Ireland, *CC*, 8 October 1833.

40 Day & Coppinger, *Ancient and Present State*, I, pp 403–4, 461–2; F. Tuckey, *The County and City of Cork Remembrancer* … (Cork, 1839), pp 312–13; O'Shea, 'A transcription', pp 30–1.

41 T. Evans, 'Notes of the Besnard family', *JCHAS*, vol. 39 (1934), p. 95.

42 Connolly, *Religion, Law and Power*, pp 74, 87; P. Jupp, 'Urban politics in Ireland 1801–1831', in D. Harkness & M. O'Dowd (eds), *The Town in Ireland* (Belfast, 1981), pp 110–11; d'Alton, *Protestant Society*, pp 99–100; Connolly, *Religion, Law and Power*, pp 74, 87.

43 R. Gillespie, 'The religion of Irish Protestants: a view from the laity, 1580–1700', in A. Ford, J. McGuire & K. Milne (eds), *As by Law Established: The Church of Ireland since the Reformation* (Dublin, 1995), p. 89.

44 D. Hayton, 'Did Protestantism fail in early eighteenth-century Ireland? Charity schools and the enterprise of religious and social reformation, *c.* 1690–1730', in Ford, McGuire & Milne, *As by Law Established*, pp 166–7.

45 A. Winnett, *Peter Browne: Provost, Bishop, Metaphysician* (London, 1974), p. 61; T. Barnard, 'Improving clergymen, 1660–1760', in Ford, McGuire & Milne, *As by Law Established*, pp 174, 184; M. Conlon, 'Some old Cork charter schools', *JCHAS*, vol. 48 (1943), pp 86–9; S. Pettit, 'The Rev. Henry Maule of Shandon and the Charity School Movement', *JCHAS*, vol. 77 (1972), pp 107–16; P. McCann, 'Cork City's eighteenth-century charity schools: origin and early history', *JCHAS*, vol. 84 (1979), pp 102–11; S. Ó Coindealbháin, 'Schools and schooling in Cork City 1700–1831', *JCHAS*, vol. 48 (1943), pp 44–8.

46 *First Report of Commissioners of Public Instruction*, appendix, 124c, 136c, 138c, 140c.

47 Costello, 'A symbolic geography', p. 92.

48 S. Hood (ed.), *Register of the Parish of Holy Trinity (Christ Church), Cork 1643–1669* (Dublin, 1998), p. 9; Costello, 'A symbolic geography', p. 83; Gibson, *History of … Cork*, II, p. 301.

49 Costello, 'A symbolic geography', p. 88.

50 C. Webster, *The Diocese of Cork* (Cork, 1920), p. 149.

51 E. Bolster, *A History of the Diocese of Cork from the Penal Era to the Famine* (Cork, 1989), *passim*; Costello, 'A symbolic geography', p. 99.

52 Keane, 'Four tales', p. 194; Costello, 'A symbolic geography', pp 99, 103.

53 Hill, *From Patriots to Unionists*, p. 22.

54 R. Caulfield, *Annals of St Fin Barre's Cathedral, Cork* … (Cork, 1871), p. 67; Costello, 'A symbolic geography', pp 99 *et seq.*, 103–7.

55 J. O'Shea, 'The churches of the Church of Ireland in Cork city', *JCHAS*, vol. 48 (1943), pp 30–5; Gibson, *History of … Cork*, II, p. 313.

56 C. Maxwell, *Dublin under the Georges* (Dublin, 1997), pp 57–88; Day & Coppinger, *The Ancient and Present State*, I, p. 376; O'Donovan, 'The Volunteer movement', p. 59.

57 A. Acheson, *A History of the Church of Ireland 1691–1996* (Dublin, 1997), pp 36–7; Winnett, *Peter Browne*, pp 54, 60, 62–3, 190.

58 Costello, 'A symbolic geography', p. 100.

59 Acheson, *History of the Church of Ireland*, pp 85–8; Costello, 'A symbolic geography', pp 170–3.

60 J. O'Donovan, 'The anatomy of the Volunteers in Cork 1775–1782', *JCHAS*, vol. 87 (1982), pp 27–39, and 'The Volunteer movement', pp 32–3; C. MacLeod, 'A toasting glass of the Cork True Blue Volunteers', *JCHAS*, vol. 87 (1982), pp 45–7; Gibson, *History of… Cork*, II, p. 217; Day & Coppinger, *The Ancient and Present State*, II, pp 318, 323–5.

61 M. Bric, 'Ireland and Colonial America', in J. Devlin & H. Clarke (eds), *European Encounters: Essays in Memory of Albert Lovett* (Dublin, 2003), esp. p. 146.

62 Goldberg, *Jonathan Swift*, pp 25–6; O'Donovan, 'The Volunteer movement', pp 69–72; Connolly, *Religion, Law and Power*, p. 72.

63 Dickson, 'Second city syndrome', pp 102–4; Goldberg, *Jonathan Swift*, pp 25–6; S. Pettit, 'The Royal Cork Institution: a reflection on the cultural life of a city', *JCHAS*, vol. 81 (1976), pp 70–90; D. & M. Coakley, *Wit and Wine: Literary and Artistic Cork in the Early Nineteenth Century* (Dún Laoghaire, 1985), *passim*.

2. Keeping faith: an evocation of the Cork Protestant character, 1820–1920

1 A version was published in P. O'Flanagan & C. Buttimer (eds), *Cork: History and Society* (Dublin, 1993), pp 755–92.

2 D. Dickson, *Old World Colony* (Cork, 2005), p. 499; J. Chatterton to Sir R. Peel, 13 August 1837 (BL Add. MS 40,424, 63–4).

3 James Morgan to Sir R. Peel, 27 December 1843 (BL Add. MS 40,537, 298–9).

4 [R.S. Ross-Lewin], *Poems of a County of Clare West Briton* (Limerick, 1907), p. 27, 'Lament of a West Briton'.

5 D. Bowen, *The Protestant Crusade in Ireland 1800–70* (Toronto, 1978), p. 314.

6 K. Bowen, *Protestants in a Catholic State* (Quebec, 1983), p. 217.

7 A. Daunt to W.E.H. Lecky, 9 December 1895 (Lecky Papers, TCD MS 1113).

8 O. MacDonagh, *The Nineteenth-century Novel and Irish Social History: Some Aspects* (Dublin, 1970), p. 11.

9 L. Fleming, *Head or Harp* (London, 1965), p. 36; 'Corinthian' [H.P.F. Donegan], *History of Yachting in the South of Ireland 1720–1908* (Cork, 1909), pp 70, 85, 98, 102; I. d'Alton, '"Aquatic gentlemen …"—the sport and status of sailing in the gentry's world from the 1830s to the 1920s', in T. Dooley & C. Ridgway (eds), *Sport and Leisure in the Irish Country House* (Dublin, 2019), pp 86–101.

10 *Census of Ireland*, 1881, II, p. 2.

11 W.E. Vaughan, 'An assessment of the economic performances of Irish

landlords, 1851–81', in F.S.L. Lyons & R.A.J. Hawkins (eds), *Ireland under the Union—Varieties of Tension: Essays in Honour of T.W. Moody* (Oxford, 1988), p. 199; M. Bence-Jones, *Twilight of the Ascendancy* (London, 1987), p. 20.

12 Guy, *Directory of Cork, 1899* (Cork, 1899), pp 191–5.

13 A sample of Cork estate papers for the period 1900–12 (Conner, Ballineen; French, Queenstown [Cobh]; Evans, Doneraile; Newenham, Carrigaline) has numerous receipts for and references to such securities, together with applications for gilt-edged and mining stock. See also Bence-Jones, *Twilight of the Ascendancy*, pp 191–3.

14 D.O. Madden, *Ireland and its Rulers since 1829. Part the First* (London, 1843), p. 4.

15 Kingston to Lord Redesdale, 21 December 1824 (PRONI MS T3030/10/22); Lord Carbery to R. Peel, 28 November 1817 (BL Add. MS 40,276, 384).

16 J.S. Donnelly Jr, *The Land and the People of Nineteenth-century Cork: The Rural Economy and the Land Question* (London, 1975), p. 70.

17 R.D. King-Harman, *The Kings, Earls of Kingston* (Cambridge, 1957), p. 79.

18 *BC*, p. 255.

19 HC 1825 (81) ix, i, *Minutes of Evidence taken before the Select Committee of the House of Lords, appointed to Inquire into the State of Ireland*, p. 434, 1, evidence of Lord Kingston; D.O. Madden, *Revelations of Ireland in the Past Generation* (Dublin, 1848), pp 85–107.

20 *BC*, pp 255–6.

21 *BC*, p. 255.

22 King-Harman, *The Kings*, p. 81.

23 M. Scott (ed.), *Hall's Ireland: Mr and Mrs Hall's Tour of 1840* (London, 1984), pp 1, 40; King-Harman, *The Kings*, p. 82; Donnelly, *Nineteenth-century Cork*, p. 70; [N.L. Beamish], *Peace Campaigns of a Cornet* (2 vols) (London, 1829), II, p. 33.

24 *CC*, 12 December 1829; King-Harman, *The Kings*, pp 82–3.

25 Donnelly, *Nineteenth-century Cork*, p. 70.

26 A. de Tocqueville, *Journeys to England and Ireland* (ed. J. Mayer; trans. G. Lawrence & K. Mayer) (London, 1958), p. 158.

27 *CC*, 27 July 1833.

28 *BC*, p. 258.

29 *The Freeholder*, 29 September 1827.

30 Lord Kingston to R. Peel, 10 January, 10 February, 14 December and 30 December 1822, and 29 January 1823; Peel to Kingston (copies), 19 December 1822, 20 January and 13 March 1823 (BL Add. MSS 40,353, 174, 203, 243, 245; 40,354, 124; 40,355, 90, 92).

31 Kingston to R. Peel, 12 March 1823 (BL Add. MS 40,355, 91).

32 P. Jupp, 'Irish parliamentary elections and the influence of the Catholic vote, 1801–20', *The Historical Journal*, vol. 10 (2) (1967), p. 185.

33 I. d'Alton, *Protestant Society and Politics in Cork, 1812–1844* (Cork, 1980), pp 124–5.

34 See *CC*, 6 August 1829, editorial; W. Johnson (Youghal) to Lord Liverpool, 12 and 13 June 1825 (BL Add. MS 40,379, 119); K.T. Hoppen, *Elections,*

Politics and Society in Ireland 1832–1885 (Oxford, 1984), pp 309–10.

35 Madden, *Revelations of Ireland*, p. 187.

36 *The Freeholder*, 14 April 1828; the Cork and County Club, MS volume, general committee minutes, 29 July 1837 and 11 March 1840 (Cork City and County Archives).

37 *The Freeholder*, 21 April 1826.

38 Anon., *A Full and Accurate Report of the Proceedings at the Election for the City of Cork which Commenced on Friday the 17th and Terminated on Friday the 24th March, 1820* (Cork, 1820), p. 9; Callaghan to R. Peel, 21 February 1816 (BL Add. MS 40,253, 15–16).

39 Anon., *A Full and Accurate Report*, *passim*; P. Jupp, 'Urban politics in Ireland, 1801–1831', in D. Harkness & M. O'Dowd, *The Town in Ireland* (Dublin, 1981), pp 116–17.

40 *CC*, 4 July 1829; Madden, *Revelations of Ireland*, p. 219.

41 *The Freeholder*, 9 and 30 December 1826; R. Sainthill to T.C. Croker, 30 November 1826 (Croker Papers, II, p. 2, UCC Library, Cork).

42 *Cork Mercantile Chronicle*, 21 February and 10 April 1827; *The Freeholder*, 21 April 1827; Letters … relative to the Brunswick Constitutional Clubs, 1828 (NLI MS 5017, p. 1).

43 P. Madden, 'Unseating a Cork MP', *CE*, 30 August 1976; Anon., *A Full Report of the Proceedings at the Election for the City of Cork, 7th–9th July 1829* (2nd edn) (Cork, 1829), *passim*.

44 Deane to Croker, 18 April 1830 (Croker Papers, III, item 175, UCC Library, Cork).

45 Anon., *The Entire Proceedings of the Election for the City of Cork, which Commenced on Saturday the Thirteenth, and Terminated on Monday the Twenty-ninth of March, 1830* (Cork, 1830); *The Freeholder*, 13 November 1830.

46 Anon., *A Synoptical Exposé of the Proceedings of the Late City Election …* (Cork, 1818), p. 34.

47 *CC*, 3 August 1830.

48 Hoppen, *Elections, Politics and Society*, p. 485.

49 B. Walker (ed.), *Parliamentary Election Results in Ireland, 1801–1922* (Dublin, 1978), p. 264; C.T.M. Beamish, *Beamish* (London, 1950), pp 13–15.

50 Beamish, *Beamish*, p. 133.

51 *CC*, 4 April 1829.

52 W. Fagan, *CC*, 22 July 1837.

53 Diary of Capt. O. Travers, February 1832 (NLI microfilm P. 3064).

54 *CC*, 29 April 1830, 15 March 1832 and 4 January 1834.

55 J. O'Brien, *The Catholic Middle Classes in Pre-Famine Ireland* (Cork, 1979), pp 14–15; *CC*, 1 July 1837; d'Alton, *Protestant Society*, pp 100–1.

56 Bowen, *The Protestant Crusade in Ireland*, especially pp 83–192.

57 *CC*, 18, 22 and 25 July 1837; Capt. Travers's diary, January 1835.

58 *CE*, 25 October 1841; *CC*, 30 October 1841.

59 J. Bateman, *The Great Landowners of Great Britain and Ireland* (London, 1883), p. 6; *Burke's Peerage* (82nd edn), p. 194; *CE*, 1 May 1895; *CC*, 28 March and 16 May 1898.

60 E. Bowen, *Collected Impressions* (London, 1950), pp 195–200; H. Mitchell, 'Somerville and Ross: amateur to professional', in E.E. Evans

(ed.), *Somerville and Ross: A Symposium* (Belfast, 1968), pp 21–2; West Carbery Hunt Papers (TCD MS 4261–70).

61 J.H. Robb, *The Primrose League, 1883–1906* (New York, 1942), p. 228.

62 *Notes from Ireland*, no. 49 (1894), p. 214 (PRONI MS D89C/3/22); *CC*, 20 April 1891, 20 April 1892 and 27 July 1898.

63 *CC*, 14 and 20 March 1893.

64 Newenham Papers, anon., diary for 1898 (Newenham family, Coolmore, Carrigaline, Co. Cork); Fleming, *Head or Harp*, p. 36; *BC*, pp 344–5.

65 *CE*, 30 January 1891.

66 P. O Maidin, 'The Primrose League at Blarney 1891', *CE*, 18 August 1971; *CE*, 19 August 1891.

67 *Crockford's Clerical Directory* (1890), p. 23.

68 *IT*, 12 November 1885.

69 *CC*, 19 November 1885.

70 *CC*, 20 November 1885.

71 *CC*, 1 March and 24 June 1886.

72 *CC*, 27 February, 11 and 23 June and 3 July 1886.

73 Guy, *Directory of Munster 1886* (Cork, 1886), pp 364, 371, 381, 391, 400.

74 *CE*, 27 October 1891, editorial; *CC*, 7 March 1893.

75 J. Loughlin, 'The Irish Protestant Home Rule Association and nationalist politics, 1886–93', *IHS*, vol. 24 (95) (1985), pp 341–60; *CE*, 16 January 1886.

76 *CC*, 17 and 25 June 1886.

77 *CE*, 9 January 1891.

78 See a report of his lecture 'The survival of Irish nationalism' in *CC*, 17 June 1886.

79 *Burke's Peerage* (82nd edn), p. 2642; Guy, *Directory of Cork* (1899), pp 193–5.

80 P. Bew, *Conflict and Conciliation in Ireland, 1890–1910* (Oxford, 1987), pp 15–16; J. Loughlin, *Gladstone, Home Rule and the Ulster Question 1882–93* (Dublin, 1986), p. 23.

81 A. Jackson, *The Ulster Party: Irish Unionists in the House of Commons, 1884–1911* (Oxford, 1989), p. 213; L.P. Curtis Jr, *Coercion and Conciliation in Ireland* (Princeton, 1963), p. 321.

82 *CE*, 8, 10, 24 and 27 October 1891; *CC*, 24 and 29 October and 6 November 1891; *CC*, 24 August 1891 (letter from 'an old Cork Tory'); *CE*, 20 October 1891, editorial.

83 *CC* and *CE*, October–November 1891–5; *CE*, 3 December 1895.

84 J.H. Scott to G. Cox (secretary, Irish Unionist Alliance), 24 February 1893 (PRONI MS D989A/8/2, 1).

85 I. d'Alton, 'From Bandon to … Bandon: sectarian violence in Cork during the nineteenth century', in K. Hughes & D. McRaild (eds), *Crime, Violence, and the Irish in the Nineteenth Century* (Liverpool, 2017), pp 185–8.

86 Lord Castletown to W. O'Brien, 15 April 1910; R.M.D. Sanders (a Cork landlord) to O'Brien, 12 February 1910 (UCC, O'Brien MSS AR 91, 76). The 1910 municipal elections saw sixteen Protestants standing under various labels: *CC*, 29 November and 3 December 1910, editorials; *CE*, 7 January 1911.

87 Evidence of J. Hayes to the commissioners appointed to inquire into the

municipal corporations in Ireland, *CC*, 24 October 1833; *Census*, 1881, XIX, pp 296–302.

88 Revd W. Neligan to Sir R. Peel, 28 January 1845 (BL Add. MS 40558, 307).

89 J. Hutchinson, *The Dynamics of Cultural Nationalism: The Gaelic Revival and the Creation of the Irish Nation State* (London, 1987), pp 258–62; J. White, *Minority Report* (Dublin, 1975), p. 159; Bowen, *Protestants in a Catholic State*, pp 91, 93.

90 Capt. Travers's diary, December 1833; Fleming, *Head or Harp*, p. 17; *BC*, pp 192, 281, 293, 368; Bateman, *Great Landowners, passim*.

91 *CC*, 20 July 1881.

92 Secretary of the Irish Society for Promoting Protestant Schools in Ireland to J.V. Bond, principal of Ashton School, Cork, 28 May 1975 (Ashton School archives, Cork). See also D. Rudd, *Rochelle, the History of a School in Cork, 1829–1979* (Cork, 1979), and A. St Leger, *A History of Ashton School* (Cork, 2016), esp. pp 86–104.

93 *CC*, 21 July 1882.

94 Prize day reports in *CC*, 24 December 1883, 23 December 1885, 23 December 1886 and 24 December 1888.

95 *Crockford's Clerical Directory* (1911), p. 666; *ibid.* (1920), p. 668.

96 S. Farrington, 'The Grammar School under Harvey', *The Grammarian* [the past pupils' magazine], vol. 1 (4) (1953), p. 10; St Leger, *Ashton*, p. 91.

97 T.J. McElligott, *Secondary Education in Ireland 1870–1921* (Dublin, 1981), pp 168–9; K.T. Hoppen, *Ireland since 1800: Conflict and Conformity* (London, 1989), pp 155–80.

98 48 and 49 Vict., c. 78.

99 J. Coolahan, *Irish Education: Its History and Structure* (Dublin, 1983), p. 63; McElligott, *Secondary Education in Ireland*, pp 28, 45.

100 *CC*, 18 December 1895, 23 December 1898, 23 December 1899 and 19 December 1901; Intermediate Education Board for Ireland, *Reports of Inspectors* (1901–2 and 1909–10); St Leger, *Ashton*, p. 94.

101 Ashton School archives, printed list of potential subscribers; *CC*, 23 January 1908.

102 Prize day reports, end of December each year, 1888–1908, in *CC*.

103 *CC*, 21 December 1907.

104 *CC*, 21 December 1906.

105 Intermediate Education Board for Ireland, *Reports of Temporary Inspectors* (Dublin, 1903), I, p. 163.

106 *CC*, 24 December 1894.

107 White, *Minority Report*, p. 69.

108 G.C. Bolton, 'The Anglo-Irish and the historians 1830–1980', in O. MacDonagh, W. Mandle & P. Travers (eds), *Irish Culture and Nationalism, 1750–1950* (Canberra, 1983), pp 239–57.

109 Hoppen, *Elections, Politics and Society*, p. 170.

110 J. Cronin, 'Dominant themes in the novels of Somerville and Ross', in Evans (ed.), *Somerville and Ross: A Symposium*, p. 9.

111 E. Somerville & M. Ross, *Irish Memories* (London, 1925), p. 324.

112 Mitchelstown Castle was burnt down during the Irish Civil War in August 1922. Cork Grammar School still

flourishes—now as Ashton School, a State-funded 'Protestant comprehensive'.

3. Image and reality in the lives of the nineteenth-century gentry of east Cork and west Waterford

1 A version of this essay was published in *Decies* (the journal of the Waterford Historical and Archaeological Society) (2014), pp 85–102.

2 D. Murphy, 'Swept away on my own river of life', *IT*, 8 August 2011.

3 The baronies of Barrymore, Kinnataloon, Condons & Clangibbon and Imokilly.

4 M. Kiely & W. Nolan, 'Politics, land and rural conflict in County Waterford, *c.* 1830–1845', in W. Nolan & T. Power (eds), *Waterford: History and Society* (Dublin, 1992), p. 461.

5 L. Proudfoot, 'The estate system in mid-nineteenth century Waterford', in Nolan & Power, *Waterford: History and Society*, p. 521.

6 W. Vaughan, *Landlords and Tenants in mid-Victorian Ireland* (Oxford, 1994), and 'An assessment of the economic performance of Irish landlords, 1851–81', in F.S.L. Lyons & R.A.J. Hawkins (eds), *Ireland under the Union—Varieties of Tension: Essays in Honour of T. W. Moody* (Oxford, 1980), pp 173–99.

7 From D. Akenson, *Small Differences: Irish Catholics and Irish Protestants, 1825–1922* (Quebec, 1988), p. 162, appendix F; Proudfoot, 'Estate system', p. 519.

8 G. Birmingham, *The Bad Times* (London, 1914), p. 40.

9 J. Donnelly Jr, *The Land and the People of Nineteenth-Century Cork: The Rural Economy and the Land Question* (London, 1975), pp 173–4.

10 See Chapter 4 for a detailed discussion of Smith Barry.

11 Proudfoot, 'Estate system', p. 524; J. Burtchaell, 'A typography of settlement and society in County Waterford, *c.* 1850', in Nolan & Power, *Waterford: History and Society*, p. 551.

12 T. Dooley, *The Big Houses and Landed Estates of Ireland: A Research Guide* (Dublin, 2007), p. 97; Proudfoot, 'Estate system', p. 521.

13 See http://landedestates.nuigalway.ie:8080/LandedEstates/jsp/map.jsp (accessed 17 July 2011).

14 The Griffith statistics, which are of estates of over £500 valuation, are in Proudfoot, 'Estate system', pp 534–5, fig. 20.2. Hoppen has postulated that up to a quarter of estate-owned lands changed hands as a result of the operations of the encumbered estate and land courts, even if a significant proportion of such land was bought up by more solvent existing landlords—K.T. Hoppen, *Ireland since 1800: Conflict and Conformity* (London, 1999), p. 87.

15 M.J. Farrell [Molly Keane], *Two Days in Aragon* [1941] (London, 1985), pp 16–17.

16 Dooley, *Big Houses*, p. 42.

17 C. Murray (ed.), *Selected Plays of Lennox Robinson* (Gerrards Cross, 1982), pp 16, 192, 197.

18 *Ibid.*, p. 192.

19 J. Johnston, *The Gates* (London, 1974), p. 172.

20 Beatrice, Lady Glenavy, *Today We Will Only Gossip* (London, 1964), p. 115.

21 See http://www.landedestates.ie/ (accessed 30 November 2019).

22 R. Tobin, '"Tracing again the tiny snail track": southern Protestant memoir since 1950', *Yearbook of English Studies*, vol. 35 (1) (2005), p. 172.

23 L. Fleming, *Head or Harp* (London, 1965), p. 17.

24 H. Lee, *Elizabeth Bowen* [1981] (London, 1999), p. 20.

25 T. Brown, *Ireland: A Social and Cultural History, 1922–2002* (London, 2004), p. 133; E. Bowen, 'The back drawing room', in *The Collected Stories of Elizabeth Bowen* (Hopewell, NJ, 1981), p. 203; P. Conradi, *Iris Murdoch: A Life* (London, 2001), p. 447.

26 C. Webster, *The Diocese of Cork* (Cork, 1920), pp 357–9.

27 E. Broderick, *Waterford's Anglicans: Religion and Politics, 1819–1872* (Newcastle upon Tyne, 2009), pp 321–4.

28 L.P. Curtis Jr, *The Depiction of Evictions in Ireland 1845–1910* (Dublin, 2011), p. 182.

29 B. Walker (ed.), *Parliamentary Election Results in Ireland, 1801–1922* (Dublin, 1978), pp 130–6; I. d'Alton, 'Cork unionism: its role in parliamentary and local elections, 1885–1914', *Studia Hibernica*, vol. 15 (1975), p. 149.

30 Curtis, *Depiction of Evictions*, p. 139.

31 *CC*, 2 December 1885.

32 D. Murphy, 'Stuart, Henry Windsor Villiers', *DIB*, vol. 9, pp 136–7; I. d'Alton, 'A "first voice": Henry Villiers Stuart (1827–95) and the cause of the Irish agricultural labourers', in B. Casey (ed.), *Defying the Law of the Land: Agrarian Radicals in Irish History* (Dublin, 2013), pp 64–75.

33 *HC deb*, vol. 53, 21 February 1898, c. 1248.

34 D'Alton, 'Cork unionism', pp 153–7; C. Shannon, *Arthur J. Balfour and Ireland 1874–1922* (Washington, 1988), pp 99–106.

35 M. Davitt, 'Retiring the landlord garrison', *Nineteenth Century*, vol. 27 (1890), p. 794.

36 S. Brookes, 'The last chance of the Irish gentry', *Fortnightly Review*, vol. 83 (2 March 1908), p. 405; J.P. Mahaffy, 'The Romanization of Ireland', *Nineteenth Century* (1 July 1901), pp 33–4.

37 *BC*, pp 259, 436; M. Bence-Jones, *Twilight of the Ascendancy* (London, 1987); Akenson, *Small Differences*, p. 149, using the term from S. Freud, 'The taboo of virginity' (1917).

38 R. Hawkins, 'Blake, Sir Henry Arthur', *DIB*, vol. 1, pp 583–4.

39 The Marx quote is from *Eighteenth Brumaire*. See Corey Robin, 'The war on tax', *London Review of Books*, vol. 33 (16) (25 August 2011), p. 8.

40 T. McGrath, *Pictures from Ireland* (London, 1880), pp 1–3.

41 B. Dugdale, *Arthur James Balfour 1848–1905, First Earl of Balfour KG, OM, FRS* (2 vols) (London, 1939), II, p. 392; Shannon, *Balfour and Ireland*, p. 281.

42 R. Foster, *Modern Ireland, 1600–1972* (London, 1988), p. 434.

43 A. Trollope, *Castle Richmond* [1860] (3 vols) (London and New York, 1979), II, p. 297.

44 Fleming, *Head or Harp*, p. 36.

45 *BC*, p. 437.

46 Farrell, *Two Days in Aragon*, p. 17.

4. Purpose and the Irish landed gentry: the life of Arthur Hugh Smith Barry, 1843–1925

1 Published in the *Journal of Irish and Scottish Studies*, vol. 10 (1) (2022), pp 117–41.

2 G. Smith, 'The administration of Ireland', *Contemporary Review*, vol. 48 (1885), p. 4.

3 T. Dooley, *The Decline of the Big House in Ireland: A Study of Irish Landed Families 1860–1960* (Dublin, 2001), p. 44.

4 *BC*, p. 259.

5 As one instance, see the description of Owen Fitzgerald's bachelor life in Anthony Trollope's 'Cork' novel, *Castle Richmond* [1860] (3 vols) (London and New York, 1979), I, pp 1, 12–13 and 27–8.

6 'Memoir of the early life of Arthur Hugh Smith Barry later Lord Barrymore covering the years from his birth to the period after the death of his first wife Lady Mary Frances Wyndham Quin' (typescript of an unpublished MS now in the archives at Fota House, Co. Cork, p. 3 [hereafter AHSB memoir]). I am indebted to Mr Niall Foley for enabling sight of the typescript and for other kindnesses, and to Mr Robin Petherick for permission to quote from it. See also J. O'Brien & D. Guinness, *Great Irish Houses and Castles* (Dublin, 1992), p. 195.

7 J. Banville, *Birchwood* (London, 1984), p. 12.

8 L.P. Curtis Jr, *The Depiction of Eviction in Ireland 1845–1910* (Dublin, 2011), and 'Demonising the Irish landlords since the Famine', in B. Casey (ed.), *Defying the Law of the Land—Agrarian Radicals in Irish History* (Dublin, 2013), pp 20–43.

9 For example: J.A. Froude, 'On the uses of a landed gentry', *Fraser's Magazine* (December 1896); J.P. Mahaffy, 'The Irish landlords', *Contemporary Review*, vol. 41 (January–June 1882), pp 160–76; M. MacDonagh, 'Are Irish landlords as black as they are painted?', *Fortnightly Review*, vol. 73 (June 1903), pp 1030–47; Lord Dunraven, 'The land purchase deadlock', *Fortnightly Review*, vol. 78 (November 1905), pp 795–8; 'The social revolution in Ireland', *Edinburgh Review*, vol. 198 (July 1903), pp 200–30; D. Cosby, 'The hard case of the Irish landlords', *Westminster Review*, vol. 154 (August 1900), pp 194–211; Lord Castletown, 'The Land Banks (Ireland) Bill and the land question', *Journal of the Institute of Bankers*, vol. 4 (January 1902), pp 28–47; M. Sharman Crawford, 'Experiences of an Irish landowner', *Contemporary Review*, vol. 52 (August 1887), pp 263–74; Sir H. Plunkett, 'Agricultural organisation', *New Ireland Review*, vol. 1 (June 1894), pp 197–205; C.S. Parnell, 'Mr Balfour's Land Bill', *North American Review*, vol. 150 (June 1890), pp 665–70; Anon., 'The ex-landlords of Ireland, their duties and prospects', *National Review*, vol. 52 (February 1909), pp 942–51; report of a lecture by William O'Brien entitled 'The lost opportunities of the Irish gentry', 8 September 1887, in L.M. Geary, 'Anticipating memory: landlordism, agrarianism and deference in late-nineteenth-century Ireland', in

T. Dunne & L. Geary (eds), *History and the Public Sphere: Essays in Honour of John A. Murphy* (Cork, 2005), pp 129–31.

10 G. MacBeth, *Trespassing: Poems from Ireland* (London, 1991), pp 46–7.

11 'Spy' [Leslie Ward], 'An Irish landowner', *Vanity Fair*, 31 August 1910.

12 I. d'Alton, 'Barry, Arthur Hugh Smith, Lord Barrymore', *DIB*, vol. 1, pp 318–19.

13 Earl of Midleton, KP, *Records and Reactions, 1856–1939* (London, 1939), pp 227–8; *A Page from the Past: Memories of the Earl of Desart by Himself and his Daughter, Lady Sybil Lubbock* (London, 1936)—'Lord Desart and the Irish Convention, by the Earl of Midleton', pp 241–5.

14 Will, 18 June 1925 (probate 16 December 1925); *IT*, 29 April 1926.

15 J.G. Sutton, 'The political career of Arthur Hugh Baron Barrymore 1867–1903' (unpublished MPhil. thesis, UCC, 2004), p. 9 [hereafter Sutton, AHSB].

16 AHSB memoir, p. 4; Earl of Dunraven, KP, CMG, *Past Times and Pastimes* (London, 1922), I, p. 26, a story recounted by an American journalist staying at Fota and being presented with a freshly picked lemon for his hot whiskey punch.

17 J. McCrea & L. Murtagh, *Aspects of Fota: Stories from the Big House* (Dublin, n.d.).

18 AHSB memoir, p. 4.

19 Email from Ms Judith Curthoys, archivist, Christ Church, Oxford, to I. d'Alton, 6 April 2004; Sutton, AHSB, pp 10–11; AHSB memoir, p. 12.

20 Dunraven, *Past Times and Pastimes*, I, p. 96.

21 A. St Leger, *A History of the Royal Cork Yacht Club* (Cork, 2005), pp 138, 172, 190, 418; AHSB memoir, pp 12, 19.

22 Cricketing obituary in *Wisden* (1926) and his biography in A. Haygarth, *Scores and Biographies* (London, 1878), vol. 10.

23 AHSB to Mr Blake, 1 July 1868 (Cheshire County Record Office [hereafter Cheshire CRO] DCN1402/72/1).

24 C. Smith Barry [Lady Charlotte Cole, daughter of the Earl of Enniskillen, wife of James Hugh Smith Barry, AHSB's brother], *Notes on the Smith Barry Family. Written for her Son, Robert Smith Barry* (privately printed, 1933), pp 26–7; *Cambridge Chronicle*, 30 April 1886; AHSB memoir, pp 6–8, 10–11, 13, 18, 20.

25 AHSB memoir, p. 20; AHSB's appointment papers as high sheriff of Chester in 1883 (Cheshire CRO QDA12/52).

26 M.C. de Trobriand Post, *The Post Family* (New York, 1905), p. 192.

27 W. Mahood, *General Wadsworth: The Life and Times of Brevet Major James S. Wadsworth* (Cambridge, Mass., 2009); H.G. Pearson, *James S. Wadsworth of Geneseo, Brevet Major-General of United States Volunteers* (Forgotten Books, online, 2012).

28 Indenture—Declaration of Trusts 'as to trust funds invested in America pursuant to ante-nuptial settlement', 12 December 1889 (Cheshire CRO DCN1402/72/1); draft codicil to the will of Lord Barrymore, 24 February 1915, which indicates the existence of American money (Cheshire CRO DCN1402/72/2).

29 IUA, Annual Report 1891 (PRONI, MS D/989/C/4/1); *A Page from the Past*, p. 242.
30 *HL deb*, 29 July 1902, vol. 112, c. 1.
31 P. Buckland, *Irish Unionism 1: The Anglo-Irish and the New Ireland 1885–1922* (Dublin, 1972), p. 150.
32 Obituaries: *Northwich Guardian*, 24 February 1925; *Weekly Irish Times*, 28 February 1925. For portraits of Smith Barry see (1) by Walter Stoneman, bromide print, 1917; (2) by Sir (John) Benjamin Stone, platinum print in card window mount, July 1897 [1 and 2 in the National Portrait Gallery, London]; (3) portrait by William Orpen, 1915.
33 J.J. Lee, quoted in McCrea & Murtagh, *Aspects of Fota*, p. 31.
34 James Hugh Smith Barry had been appointed as a member of the Conservative committee to contest the Cork County election in 1837; *CC*, 8 July 1837.
35 *CE*, 22 February 1867.
36 *CE*, 14 February 1867, letter from a person claiming to be a tenant farmer from the Kanturk area.
37 *CE* and *CC*, 19 February 1867.
38 *CC*, 22 February 1867; B. Walker (ed.), *Parliamentary Election Results in Ireland, 1801–1922* (Dublin, 1978), p. 266. Walker classifies AHSB as a Liberal.
39 *CE* and *CC*, 13 February 1867; Sutton, AHSB, pp 11, 13.
40 *CC*, 21 February 1867; *HC deb*, 4 March 1867, vol. 185, c. 1306.
41 Sutton, AHSB, p. 29.
42 *HC deb*, 11 March 1870, vol. 199, c. 1857.
43 *Cambridge Chronicle*, 30 April 1886; *HL deb*, 11 December 1906, vol. 167, c. 36.
44 AHSB memoir, p. 16.
45 Archbishop Thomas Croke to Very Revd R. Cahill, PP, VG Tipperary, *Freeman's Journal*, 28 June 1889, in L. Geary, *The Plan of Campaign 1886–1891* (Cork, 1986), p. 116.
46 *United Ireland*, 26 October 1889; *Tipperary Nationalist*, 14 August 1889; *Freeman's Journal*, 28 June 1889; D. Marnane, *Land and Violence: A History of West Tipperary since 1660* (Tipperary, 1985), p. 110; V. Crossman & D.S. Lucy, '"One huge abuse": the Cork Board of Guardians and the expansion of outdoor relief in post-Famine Ireland', *English Historical Review*, vol. 126 (523) (2011), pp 1424–5; *CC*, 17 January 1890.
47 William O'Brien, *Evening Memories* (London and Dublin, 1920), p. 440.
48 Earl of Midleton, KP, *Ireland—Dupe or Heroine* (London, 1933), p. 73; Midleton, *Records and Reactions*, p. 228.
49 *CC*, 15 November 1887.
50 Speeches on land matters in 1896: *HC deb*, 8 June 1896, vol. 41, cc 686–7; 12 June 1896, vol. 41, cc 1017–35; 21 July 1896, vol. 43, c. 329, c. 359; 22 July 1896, vol. 43, c. 371.
51 Sutton, AHSB, p. 35.
52 Speeches on evicted tenants: *HC deb*, 29 March 1893, vol. 10, cc 1444–8; on the 'disturbed' state of parts of County Cork in 1907: *HL deb*, 4 June 1907, vol. 175, cc 456–9; on the Irish Land Bill, where he had an amendment accepted by the government: *HL deb*, 25 October 1909, vol. 4, cc 331–2.
53 E.g. *HC deb*, 16 June 1899, vol. 72, cc 1354–5; Smith Barry to Mr Blake (solicitor), 23 November 1867, re his future wife's financial settlement

from Lord Dunraven (Cheshire CRO DCN1402/72/1); 22 June 1873, concerning the merits of investing in consols or railway stock (Cheshire CRO DCN1402/72/1).

54 F.S.L. Lyons, *Ireland since the Famine* (London, 1971), p. 213; *HC deb*, 23 November 1908, vol. 196, c. 1866; S. Warwick-Haller, *William O'Brien and the Irish Land War* (Dublin, 1990), p. 224.

55 D.D. Sheehan, *Ireland since Parnell* (London, 1921), p. 91; *HL deb*, 13 June 1904, vol. 135, c. 126.

56 *HL deb*, 17 June 1907, vol. 176, c. 102; 6 August 1907, vol. 179, cc 1751–2; *HC deb*, 11 June 1917, vol. 94, c. 612.

57 T. Dawson [Town Clerk], *Tipperary Urban District Council Housing Schemes. Lord Barrymore and the Tipperary UDC. The Relations Explained* (pamphlet, n.d. but probably 1917).

58 *HC deb*, 7 May 1891, vol. 353, c. 330.

59 Barrymore Estate Act 1905 (5 Edw 7 cap.1P, assented to 11 July 1905), 'To enable the Baron Barrymore to restore certain forfeited leases in the town of Tipperary, and for other purposes' (Cheshire CRO DCN/72–77, 1857–1919). Papers relating to the Act's passage are in the UK Parliamentary Archives, HL/PO/PB/1/1905/5E7c1 and HL/PO/JO/10/10/221 Item 166 a) and b).

60 *Cambridge Chronicle*, 2 April 1886.

61 *Cambridge Chronicle*, 30 April 1886; *Hunts Guardian*, 25 June 1886; *Hunts County News*, 30 June 1886; *Hunts Post*, 2 July 1886; *Hunts Post*, 5 July 1902; R.H. Mair (ed.), *Debrett's House of Commons and Judicial Bench* (London, 1886), p. 33 (for Thomas Coote); *Cambridge Chronicle*, 16 July 1886; *Hunts Post*, 30 June 1895; Sutton, AHSB, p. 114.

62 A. Jackson, *The Ulster Party* (Oxford, 1989), p. 173.

63 *Northwich Guardian*, 25 June 1892: 'Great Unionist Demonstration at Northwich' in honour of AHSB.

64 Marquess of Salisbury to Earl Cadogan, 7 November 1896 (Cadogan Papers, UK Parliamentary Archives, CAD/938).

65 *HC deb*, 9 March 1888, vol. 323, c. 753.

66 These figures are derived from a search of the (incomplete) online *Hansard* at https://hansard.parliament.uk/search?endDate=2024-01-09&partial=False&searchTerm=Arthur%20Hugh%20Smith%20Barry&sortOrder=1&startDate=1800-01-01 (accessed 9 January 2024).

67 *HC deb*, 13 March 1900, vol. 80, cc 707–10; *Northwich Guardian*, 25 June 1892.

68 *HC deb*, 7 March 1887, vol. 311, cc 1380–1; *HC deb*, 11 May 1898, vol. 57, c. 957.

69 *CC*, 15 July 1886.

70 *Cambridge Independent Press*, 21 November 1885; *Cambridge Chronicle*, 7 May 1886.

71 *Cambridge Independent News*, 21 November 1885; *Cambridge Chronicle*, 25 June 1886. From a local East Anglian perspective, Home Rule was seen primarily in terms of potentially provoking a flood of Irish immigration to Britain, undercutting local labour.

72 *Northwich Guardian*, 25 June 1892.

73 *CE* and *CC*, 28 September 1885; Property Defence Association, *Annual Report of the Committee* (Dublin, 1881–7), *passim*. Its Cork branch (of which Smith Barry was the largest subscriber in 1880—see 1881 *Annual Report*, p. 22) was the most active.

74 *CC*, 25 October 1885.

75 Balfour to C.M. Davidson, 15 May 1888 (Balfour Papers, BL Add. MS 49,826, 508).

76 *CC*, 19, 20 and 26 October 1885; *CE*, 31 October 1885. It was alleged that the Church of Ireland bishop of Cork was a member and had 'encouraged' his clergy to do likewise: speech of Sir John Brunner, *HC deb*, 12 September 1887, vol. 321, cc 413–14.

77 The first reported case of the CDU aiding a boycotted person was in *CC*, 16 October 1885, when a threshing machine was delivered to a Protestant tenant farmer in west Cork.

78 G. Pellew, *In Castle and Cabin* (New York, 1887), p. 83; *CC*, 3 May 1886.

79 CDU, *Boycotting in the County of Cork* (Cork, 1886), p. 1, objects of the CDU; Smith Barry, letter in *The Times*, 15 October 1885, reprinted in *CC*, 16 October 1885; D.C. Savage, 'The Irish Unionists, 1867–1886', *Éire-Ireland*, vol. 2 (3) (1967), pp 86–101; J.G. Sutton, 'The emergence of the Cork Defence Union, September 1885–March 1887', *JCHAS*, vol. 112 (2007).

80 *CC*, 28 September 1885; on the Ponsonby estate—copy of a letter (n.d. but probably 1890) of Neville Chamberlain, Inspector General, RIC, to the Earl of Bandon, President, CDU, relating to an incident wherein a Mr W. Hanna, described as secretary of the Cork Defence Union, saved a policeman from serious injury at an eviction at Mitchelsfort, 12 October 1890 (?) (copy in the possession of Ian d'Alton); Curtis, *The Depiction of Eviction*, p. 177; *CE*, 25 October 1886.

81 *CC*, 3 May 1886.

82 J. Donnelly Jr, *The Land and the People of Nineteenth-Century Cork: The Rural Economy and the Land Question* (London, 1975), pp 329–30; Savage, 'Irish Unionists', p. 95; CDU, *Boycotting in the County of Cork*, p. 13.

83 *The Times* obituary, 23 February 1925, noted that his 'name was associated with the Irish Nationalist agrarian movement known as "The Plan of Campaign", from 1888 to 1891'; F.M. Larkin, 'Keeping an eye on Youghal: the *Freeman's Journal* and the Plan of Campaign in east Cork, 1886–92', *Irish Communications Review*, vol. 13 (2012), pp 20–6.

84 C.W. Talbot-Ponsonby's principal residence was Langrish House, Petersfield, Hants. He subscribed to AHSB's testimonial at Northwich in 1892—see bound copy of 'Great Unionist Demonstration at Northwich', 23 June 1892, list of subscribers, p. 6 (Cheshire CRO D2802/25).

85 F.M. Larkin, 'Canon Keller of Youghal', in Casey, *Defying the Law of the Land*, pp 155–63.

86 Balfour to E.A. King-Harman, 19 November 1887 [copy] (BL Add. MS 49,840, 57); Balfour to Sir West Ridgeway, 13 March 1888 (BL Add. MS 49,826, 377); J.V. O'Brien, *William O'Brien and the Course of Irish Politics, 1881–1918* (Berkeley, 1976), p. 72.

87 King-Harman to Balfour, 21 and 22 November 1887 (BL Add. MS 49,840, 59–62, 69–71).

88 *HC deb*, 17 February 1890, vol. 341, c. 535. Donnelly, *Cork*, p. 357, puts Smith Barry's intervention in Ponsonby's finances in 1887; Geary, *Plan of Campaign*, pp 105–6; L.P. Curtis Jr, *Coercion and Conciliation in Ireland 1880–1892: A Study in Conservative Unionism* (Princeton, 1963), pp 180–1.

89 Geary, 'Anticipating memory', p. 136.

90 See a draft of a letter to an unnamed duke, *c.* April–May 1889, in B. Dugdale, *Arthur James Balfour, First Earl of Balfour, KG, OM, FRS, 1848–1905* (London, 1939), p. 132.

91 Balfour to Lord Courtown, 2 May 1888 (BL Add. MS 49,826, 483).

92 Viscount De Vesci to Balfour, 27 January 1889 (BL Add. MS 49,821, 161–3); Geary, *Plan of Campaign*, p. 110.

93 O'Brien, *Evening Memories*, p. 427.

94 Geary, *Plan of Campaign*, p. 114.

95 Larkin, 'Canon Keller', pp 162–3; Donnelly, *Cork*, p. 359.

96 Warwick-Haller, *William O'Brien and the Irish Land War*, p. 116.

97 O'Brien, *Evening Memories*, p. 425.

98 J.G. Sutton, 'New Tipperary revisited: the case of Arthur Hugh Smith-Barry', *Tipperary Historical Journal* (2005), pp 155–73.

99 IUA, *Mad Tipperary*, leaflet no. 49 (October 1891); Donnelly, *Cork*, p. 375; O'Brien, *Evening Memories*, pp 432–8.

100 *HC deb*, 20 July 1894, vol. 27, c. 642; *HC deb*, 17 February 1890, vol. 341, cc 535–8.

101 *HC deb*, 17 February 1890, vol. 341, cc 537–8.

102 Smith Barry, *Notes on the Smith Barry Family*, p. 29.

103 *HC deb*, 3 August 1905, vol. 151, c. 208.

104 O'Brien, *Evening Memories*, p. 421; Marnane, *Land and Violence*, p. 102; Warwick-Haller, *William O'Brien and the Irish Land War*, p. 17.

105 Larkin, 'Canon Keller', p. 160.

106 'Instructions for settlement of the fortune of Miss Smith Barry, daughter of Arthur Hugh Smith Barry, Esq., MP, on her intended marriage with H. Overend, Esq.' (n.d.), solicitor's note that AHSB is a 'tenant for life of estates in the Counties of Tipperary and Cork which are entailed in the usual mode' (Cheshire CRO DCN1402/74/1); also Barrymore Estate Act, p. 5.

107 Smith Barry, draft will, 5 July 1912, lawyer's annotation: Has AHSB 'any of his *own* land in Ireland?—No' (Cheshire CRO DCN1402/72/2).

108 Marnane, *Land and Violence*, p. 114; *HC deb*, 13 April 1891, vol. 352, cc 389–90.

109 Sutton, AHSB, p. 96.

110 *HL deb*, 6 August 1907, vol. 179, cc 1751–2.

111 *CC*, 22 April 1886.

112 P. Maume, *The Long Gestation: Irish Nationalist Life 1891–1918* (Dublin, 1999), p. 109.

113 O'Brien, *William O'Brien*, p. 203.

114 O'Brien, *Evening Memories*, pp 439–40.

115 Warwick-Haller, *William O'Brien and the Land War*, p. 261; O'Brien, *William O'Brien*, p. 212.

116 *CoIG*, 12 April 1912, 'The Week'.

117 *CC*, 22 April 1912; *HC deb*, 15 January 1913, vol. 46, cc 2103–224.
118 *HL deb*, 30 January 1913, vol. 13, c. 770–3.
119 See http://www.merseyforest.org.uk/foam/wp-content/uploads/2012/10/Section-1-Families-Associated-with-Marbury-HallRev5.pdf (accessed 9 January 2024); J. & C. Hamlett, *A House with Spirit: A Dedication to Marbury Hall* (Northwich, 1997).
120 *HL deb,* 6 August 1907, vol. 179, cc 1751–2.
121 S.R. Lysaght, *My Tower in Desmond* (London, 1927), p. 95.
122 Geary, 'Anticipating memory', p. 130.
123 Curtis, 'Demonising the Irish landlord', in Casey, *Defying the Law of the Land,* p. 31.
124 AHSB memoir, p. 4.

5. Southern Irish Protestantism: a perspective on historical process

1 Published in F.B. Smith (ed.), *Ireland, England and Australia: Essays in Honour of Oliver MacDonagh* (Canberra and Cork, 1990), pp 70–91.
2 O. MacDonagh, 'The nineteenth-century revolution in government: a reappraisal', *Historical Journal,* vol. 1 (1958), p. 52.
3 John Buchan, *The Casual and the Causal in History* (Cambridge, 1929), p. 10.
4 T. Dunne, 'A polemical introduction: literature, literary theory and the historians', in T. Dunne (ed.), *The Writer as Witness* (Cork, 1987), pp 1–9.
5 H. White, *Tropics of Discourse: Essays in Cultural Criticism* (London, 1978), quoted in Dunne, 'A polemical introduction', p. 4.
6 T. Arnold, *Introductory Lectures on Modern History* (London, 1843), p. 299.
7 Dunne, 'A polemical introduction', p. 6; E. Bowen, *Collected Impressions* (London, 1950), pp v, 249–63; also M. Doyle, 'Redefining Irishness' [an interview with Roy Foster], *Irish Post,* 6 November 1993.
8 J. Coolahan, *Irish Education: Its History and Structure* (Dublin, 1981), pp 63, 65, 71; J. Hutchinson, *The Dynamics of Cultural Nationalism: The Gaelic Revival and the Creation of the Irish Nation State* (London, 1987), pp 261–3.
9 K.T. Hoppen, *Ireland since 1800: Conflict and Conformity* (London 1989), p. 299.
10 S.J. Connolly, 'Religion and history', review article in *Irish Economic and Social History,* vol. 10 (1983), pp 66–7; P. Buckland, *Irish Unionism 1: The Anglo Irish and the New Ireland 1885–1922* (Dublin, 1972), p. 288.
11 D. Boyce, '"One last burial": culture, counter-revolution and revolution in Ireland, 1886–1916', in D. Boyce (ed.), *The Revolution in Ireland, 1879–1923* (Dublin, 1988), p. 126; R.F. Foster, *Modern Ireland 1600–1972* (London, 1988), p. 290; J.C. Beckett, *The Anglo-Irish Tradition* (London, 1976), pp 87–97.
12 I. d'Alton, *Protestant Society and Politics in Cork, 1812–1844* (Cork, 1980), pp 7–8; S.J. Connolly, *Religion and Society in Nineteenth-century Ireland* (Dublin, 1985), pp 3–5; I. Budge & C. O'Leary, *Belfast: Approach to Crisis. A Study of Belfast Politics 1613–1970* (London, 1973), p. 50;

D. Bowen, *The Protestant Crusade in Ireland 1800–70* (Dublin, 1978), p. 29.

13 A. Jackson, *The Ulster Party: Irish Unionists in the House of Commons, 1884–1911* (Oxford, 1989), pp 15–16, 325; R.B. McDowell, *The Church of Ireland 1869–1969* (London, 1975), pp 52–3; Beckett, *Anglo-Irish Tradition*, p. 90; P. Buckland, 'Irish unionism and the new Ireland', in Boyce, *The Revolution in Ireland*, pp 80–1, 88–9.

14 O. MacDonagh, *States of Mind: A Study of Anglo-Irish Conflict 1780–1980* (London, 1983), p. 70.

15 Foster, *Modern Ireland*, p. 290.

16 R.F. Foster, 'Towards an inclusive definition of nationalism', *IT*, 7 March 1989.

17 K. Bowen, *Protestants in a Catholic State: Ireland's Privileged Minority* (Dublin, 1983), p. 210; Beckett, *Anglo-Irish Tradition*, p. 152.

18 Dunne, 'A polemical introduction', pp 3–4.

19 Bowen, *Protestant Crusade*, p. 314.

20 Buckland, *Irish Unionism 1*, pp 1–28; Beckett, *Anglo-Irish Tradition*, p. 118.

21 Eagleton, quoted in *IT*, 25 August 1989; Foster, 'Towards an inclusive definition of nationalism'; Boyce, '"One last burial"', pp 117, 119–21, 133.

22 Boyce, '"One last burial"', p. 135.

23 F.S.L. Lyons, 'Yeats and the Anglo-Irish twilight', in O. MacDonagh, W. Mandle & P. Travers (eds), *Irish Culture and Nationalism 1750–1950* (Canberra, 1983), pp 218–20; T. Brown, *Ireland: A Social and Cultural History 1922–1985* (London, 1981), pp 120–4; D.W. Miller, *Church, State and Nation in Ireland 1898–1921* (Dublin, 1973), *passim.*

24 E. Longley, 'The separation of political Irishness and culture in Ireland', *IT*, 9 August 1989; J.H. Whyte, *Church and State in Modern Ireland 1923–1979* (Dublin, 1980), *passim*; F.S.L. Lyons, 'The minority in the 26 Counties', in F. MacManus (ed.), *The Years of the Great Test 1926–39* (Cork, 1967), pp 93–103.

25 J. Hill, 'The Protestant response to Repeal: the case of the Dublin working class', in F.S.L. Lyons & R.A. Hawkins (eds), *Ireland under the Union—Varieties of Tension: Essays in Honour of T.W. Moody* (Oxford, 1980), pp 48–9; d'Alton, *Protestant Society*, pp 200–14.

26 Foster, *Modern Ireland*, p. 434.

27 S. Day, *The Amazing Philanthropists* (London, 1916), p. 16; MacDonagh, *States of Mind*, p. 106.

28 [R.S. Ross-Lewin], *Poems by a County of Clare West Briton* (Limerick, 1907), p. 7.

29 I. d'Alton, 'Cork unionism: its role in parliamentary and local elections, 1885–1914', *Studia Hibernica*, vol. 15 (1975), pp 143–61; Buckland, 'Irish unionism and the new Ireland', p. 85.

30 C. O'Halloran, *Partition and the Limits of Irish Nationalism* (Dublin, 1987), p. 80; White, *Minority Report*, p. 96.

31 D. Pearce (ed.), *The Senate Speeches of W.B. Yeats* (London, 1961), p. 99; see also Hoppen, *Ireland since 1800*, p. 242.

32 F.S.L. Lyons, *Culture and Anarchy in Ireland 1890–1939* (Oxford, 1979), p. 177.

33 M. Bence-Jones, *Twilight of the Ascendancy* (London, 1987).

34 For instance, rural poverty: J.W. Kingston, *These Miracles did Jesus in*

Ireland (London, n.d.), pp 24–9, 118; Beckett, *Anglo-Irish Tradition*, p. 91.

35 I. d'Alton, 'Southern Irish unionism: a study of Cork city and county unionists, 1884–1914' (unpublished MA thesis, UCC, 1972), *passim.*

36 *BC*, pp 258–9.

37 Beckett, *Anglo-Irish Tradition*, p. 88; Lyons, 'Yeats and the Anglo-Irish twilight', p. 213.

38 Revd H.T. Newman to G. Daly, 9 January 1822 (SPO Dublin, registered papers, 2342/11 [now the NAI]); G. Bennett, *The History of Bandon, and the Principal Towns in the West Riding of County Cork* (Cork, 1869), pp 297–301, 409, 450–1, 508. A later work is I. d'Alton, 'From Bandon to … Bandon: sectarian violence in Cork during the nineteenth century', in K. Hughes & D. MacRaild, *Crime, Violence and the Irish in the Nineteenth Century* (Liverpool, 2017), pp 178–81.

39 E. Bowen, 'The Big House', in *Collected Impressions*, pp 195–200, and *The Last September* [1929] (London, 1998), p. 312; Beckett, *Anglo-Irish Tradition*, p. 95; O. MacDonagh, *The Nineteenth-Century Novel and Irish Social History: Some Aspects* (Cork, 1970), p. 15.

40 Bence-Jones, *Twilight of the Ascendancy*, p. xv; Lyons, *Culture and Anarchy*, p. 71, and 'Yeats and the Anglo-Irish twilight', p. 213; Beckett, *Anglo-Irish Tradition*, p. 150; White, *Minority Report*, pp 2, 10.

41 R. Fanning, review in *IT*, 28 October 1972; Buckland, *Irish Unionism 1*, pp 1, 272; J. White, review of Bowen, *Protestant Crusade*, in *IT*, 10 October 1978.

42 Beckett, *Anglo-Irish Tradition*, p. 85.

43 K.T. Hoppen, *Elections, Politics and Society in Ireland 1832–1885* (Oxford, 1984), pp 436, 484–5.

44 Buckland, *Irish Unionism 1*, p. xxi; I. d'Alton, 'A contrast in crises: southern Irish Protestantism, 1820–43 and 1885–1910', in A. Hepburn (ed.), *Minorities in History* (London, 1978), p. 80.

45 D. Akenson, *Small Differences: Irish Catholics and Irish Protestants 1825–1922* (Quebec, 1988), p. 131; Hoppen, *Ireland since 1800*, p. 155; *SW*, p. 48.

46 Foster, *Modern Ireland*, p. 290; O'Halloran, *Partition and the Limits of Irish Nationalism*, p. 85; d'Alton, 'A contrast in crises', p. 79; Akenson, *Small Differences*, p. 148.

47 L. Fleming, *Head or Harp* (London, 1965), pp 22, 36.

48 Bowen, *Collected Impressions*, p. 198; *BC*, p. 19.

49 MacDonagh, *States of Mind*, p. 28; Akenson, *Small Differences*, p. 149.

50 G.C. Bolton, 'The Anglo-Irish and the historians, 1830-1980', in O. MacDonagh, W. Mandle & P. Travers (eds), *Irish Culture and Nationalism, 1750-1950* (Canberra, 1983) p. 254.

51 Akenson, *Small Differences*; Bowen, *Protestants in a Catholic State*; Foster, *Modern Ireland*; Hoppen, *Elections, Politics and Society*; Jackson, *The Ulster Party*; MacDonagh, *States of Mind* [and works which appeared after this essay was first published—H. Crawford, *Outside the Glow* (Dublin, 2010); R. Bury, *Buried Lives* (Dublin, 2017); I. d'Alton & I. Milne, *Protestant **and** Irish: the Minority's Search for Place in Independent Ireland* (Cork, 2019);

D. Nuttall, *Different and the Same* (Dublin, 2020)].

52 New Ireland Forum, *Report* (Dublin, 1984), pp 5, 8, 11–12, 19–20, 28, 39–40; New Ireland Forum, *Report of Proceedings*: no. 3, pp 32–49 (Prof. D. Harkness); no. 11, pp 20–30 (C. McGimpsey); no. 8, pp 9–10 (Revd Dr W. McDowell).

53 Since this was originally written, we have seen more Irish historians willing to enter the world of 'public history'—current (2023) examples are Robert Gerwarth, Diarmaid Ferriter, Brian Walker, Felix Larkin, Conor Mulvagh, Patrick Geoghegan, Linda Connolly, John Borgonovo and Sarah-Anne Buckley.

6. *The Borrowers*: southern Irish Protestant writers, cultural appropriation … and Purgatory

1 Read at a conference, 'Class and Culture in Twentieth-Century Ireland—Resilience, Resistance and Transformation', at St John's College, University of Cambridge, 18–20 April 2015. An earlier version appeared in *The Irish Review*, no. 48 (Summer 2014), pp 47–59.

2 L. MacNeice, *The Strings are False* (London, 2007), p. 282.

3 His father was a Church of Ireland bishop—see D. Fitzpatrick, *Solitary and Wild: Frederick MacNeice and the Salvation of Ireland* (Dublin, 2011); Derek Mahon's new preface to MacNeice, *Strings*, pp 6–7.

4 'The novel is practically a protestant form of art; it is a product of the free mind, of the autonomous individual'—G. Orwell, 'Inside the Whale', in *A Collection of Essays* (New York, 1957), p. 246.

5 *Archbishop Ussher's Answer to a Jesuit; with Other Tracts on Popery* (Cambridge, 1835), p. 150.

6 See Chapter 21 in this volume.

7 *The Book of Common Prayer …* (Cambridge, 1761) [no pagination].

8 H.J. Bicknell, *A Theological Introduction to the Thirty-nine Articles of the Church of England* (London, 1944), pp 347–57.

9 See V. Kreilkamp, 'The novel of the Big House', in J.W. Foster, *The Cambridge Companion to the Irish Novel* (Cambridge, 2006), p. 74.

10 D. Kiberd, *Inventing Ireland: The Literature of the Modern Nation* (London, 1996), p. 206.

11 W. Trevor, *The Story of Lucy Gault* (London, 2002), pp 84, 195.

12 Kreilkamp, 'The novel of the Big House', p. 72.

13 C. Murray (ed.), *Selected Plays of Lennox Robinson* (Gerrards Cross, 1982), p. 191.

14 'The Church of Rome holds that the justified soul departing this life in grace and charity, is not, *as a general rule*, fit for heaven until that soul has passed through the cleansing fires of Purgatory'—W. Kenny, *Purgatory and its Developments* (Dublin, 1951), p. 2.

15 J. Hughes, 'The Big House on the Hill', in *Negotiations with the Chill Wind* (Oldcastle, 1991), p. 33.

16 E. Bowen, *The Last September* [1929] (London, 1998), pp 22, 206.

17 Murray, *Selected Plays*, p. 186.

18 *Ibid.*, pp 192, 197.

19 M.J. Farrell [Molly Keane], *Two Days in Aragon* [1941] (London, 1985), p. 228.

20 Murray, *Selected Plays*, p. 17; C. Murray, 'Robinson, Lennox', *DIB*, vol. 8, pp 543–4.

21 O. MacDonagh, *States of Mind: A Study of the Anglo-Irish Conflict, 1780–1980* (London, 1983), p. 28.

22 D. Thomson, *Woodbrook* (London, 2002), p. 239.

23 J. Johnston, *The Gates* (London, 1974), p. 172.

24 J. Cronin, *The Anglo-Irish Novel* (2 vols) (Belfast, 1990), II, p. 126; O. Rauchbauer, *Ancestral Voices: The Big House in Anglo-Irish Literature* (Dublin, 1992), p. ix.

25 Bowen, *The Last September*, p. 65; G. Cronin, 'The Big House and the Irish landscape in the work of Elizabeth Bowen', in J. Genet (ed.), *The Big House in Ireland: Reality and Representation* (Dingle, 1991), pp 146–7.

26 I. Murdoch, *The Red and the Green* [1965] (London, 2002), p. 185.

27 I. Murdoch, *The Unicorn* [1963] (London, 2000), p. 16; 'the room felt watchful', p. 19.

28 Revd W. Proctor, *The Faith of a Protestant* (London, 1955), p. 59.

29 R. Tobin, '"Tracing again the tiny snail track": southern Protestant memoir since 1950', *Yearbook of English Studies*, vol. 35 (1) (2005), p. 172; E. Grubgeld, *Anglo-Irish Autobiography: Class, Gender and the Forms of Narrative* (Syracuse, 2004), p. xi; E.M. Wolff, *'An Anarchy in the Mind and in the Heart': Narrating Anglo-Ireland* (Lewisburg, 2006); A. Wessels, 'Elizabeth Bowen's "A World of Love": a "cultural analysis" of the Anglo-Irish Ascendancy in the twentieth century', *Canadian Journal of Irish Studies*, vol. 21 (1) (1995), pp 88–95.

30 Grubgeld, *Anglo-Irish Autobiography*, pp xi, xx, 4, 14.

31 Murray, *Selected Plays*, p. 192.

32 T. Brown, *Ireland: A Social and Cultural History, 1922–2002* (London, 2004), p. 133.

33 Murdoch, *The Unicorn*, p. 29.

34 *Ibid.*, p. 15.

35 Bowen, *A World of Love*, p. 17.

36 E. Somerville & M. Ross, *Some Irish Yesterdays* (London, 1906), p. 249.

37 R.M. Kain & J.H. O'Brien, *George Russell (A.E.)* (Lewisburg, 1976), pp 81–2.

38 J. Hewitt, 'Once Alien Here', in A. Bradley (ed.), *Contemporary Irish Poetry: An Anthology* (Berkeley, 1980), p. 110.

39 Brown, *Ireland*, p. 157.

40 D. Boyce, '"One last burial": culture, counter-revolution and revolution in Ireland, 1886–1916', in D. Boyce (ed.), *The Revolution in Ireland, 1879–1923* (Dublin, 1988), p. 135.

41 Murdoch, *The Red and the Green*, p. 18.

42 L. Fleming, *Head or Harp* (London, 1965), p. 36.

43 J. Hone, *Duck Soup in the Black Sea* (London, 1988), p. 238; *SW*, p. 48.

44 Murray, *Selected Plays*, p. 196.

45 R. Foster, 'Feeling the squeeze' [review of D. Fitzpatrick's *Descendancy*], *Dublin Review of Books*, no. 66 (April 2015).

46 R.B. McDowell, *Crisis and Decline: The Fate of the Southern Unionists* (Dublin, 1997), p. 2.

47 Austin Clarke, 'Burial of an Irish President', *The Dubliner*, vol. 2 (1) (1963), p. 35; R. Welch & B. Stewart, *The Oxford Companion to Irish Literature* (Oxford, 1996), p. 101. The reference in the last three lines is to the (then) different versions of the Lord's Prayer.

48 E.R. Dodds (ed.), *The Collected Poems of Louis MacNeice* (London, 1966), p. 53.

7. Projecting Irish Protestant soft power through anti-Catholicism in the early twentieth century

1 Read at an international conference on anti-Catholicism at the University of Newcastle, 11 September 2018.

2 M. Viney, 'The five per cent', *IT*, 24 March 1965.

3 R.F. Foster, *Luck and the Irish* (London, 2007), pp 37–66.

4 For the northern variety of anti-Catholicism and its theological manifestation within the Church of Ireland see A. Ford, 'Fishing for controversy: W.S. Kerr and the demise of Church of Ireland anti-Catholicism', in C. Gheeraert-Graffeuille & G. Vaughan (eds), *Anti-Catholicism in Britain and Ireland, 1600–2000: Practices, Representations and Ideas* (Cham, 2020), pp 237–54.

5 J. Nye, *Soft Power: The Means to Success in World Politics* (New York, 2005).

6 E.R. Norman, *Anti-Catholicism in Victorian England* (London, 1968), p. 18.

7 J.A.F. Gregg, *The Primitive Faith and Roman Catholic Developments* (Dublin, 1957 edn), p. 104.

8 G. Seaver, *John Allen Fitzgerald Gregg, Archbishop* (Dublin, 1963), p. 53.

9 Seaver, *Gregg*, pp 54, 312; D. Ó Corráin, *Rendering to God and Caesar: The Irish Churches and the Two States in Ireland, 1949–73* (Manchester, 2006), pp 183–4. Also see Chapter 21 in this volume.

10 Gregg, *Primitive Faith*, pp 106–7.

11 *Irish Motor Directory and Motorists' Annual, 1913–14* (Dublin, 1914), pp 329–31. The analysis is based on 1911 census returns and on surnames.

12 Saorstát Éireann, *Census of Population, 1926*, vol. 10, pp 51–2.

13 R.B. McDowell, *Crisis and Decline: The Fate of the Southern Unionists* (Dublin, 1997), p. 5; *Census of Population, 1926*, vol. 10, pp 49–57.

14 *Census of Population, 1926*, vol. 10, p. 52; R.B. McDowell, *The Church of Ireland 1869–1969* (London, 1975), pp 121–2; C. O'Neill (ed.), *Irish Elites in the Nineteenth Century* (Dublin, 2013), p. 26, and *Catholics of Consequence: Transnational Education, Social Mobility, and the Irish Catholic Elite 1850–1900* (Oxford, 2014), pp 206–7.

15 P. Campbell, *My Life and Easy Times* (London, 1988), p. 127.

16 F. Moffett, *I Also Am of Ireland* (London, 1985), pp 72–3.

17 Canon G. Chamberlain, 'The Church and Roman Catholicism', *CoIG*, 22 July 1932.

18 C. Murray (ed.), *Selected Plays of Lennox Robinson* (Gerrards Cross, 1982), p. 196.

19 E. Biagini, 'A challenge to partition: Methodist open-air work in independent Ireland, 1922–1962', *Bulletin of the*

Methodist Historical Society of Ireland, vol. 19 (2014), pp 5–44, at p. 13.

20 Gregg, *Primitive Faith*, p. 106.

21 Chamberlain, 'The Church and Roman Catholicism'.

22 *Morning Post*, 19 December 1931.

23 J.A. Gaughan, *Alfred O'Rahilly, III. Controversialist, Part 2: Catholic Apologist* (Dublin, 1993), p. 24.

24 M. O'Brien, *The Irish Times: A History* (Dublin, 2008), p. 135.

25 A. Holmes & E. Biagini, 'Protestants', in E. Biagini and M. Daly (eds), *The Cambridge Social History of Modern Ireland* (Cambridge, 2017), p. 105.

26 P. Semple, 'Previous generations would be astounded at attitudes to churches in Ireland today', *IT*, 18 November 2014. The Church of Ireland Purity Society was dedicated to purity amongst men, respect for women and a higher tone for public discourse: W. Bell & N. Emerson (eds), *The Church of Ireland A.D. 432–1932. The Report of the Church of Ireland Conference held in Dublin, 11th–14th October, 1932* ... (Dublin, 1932), p. 188; *CoIG*, 23 March 1923; Holmes & Biagini, 'Protestants', p. 105.

27 C. Webster, 'The Church since Disestablishment', in W.A. Phillips (ed.) *History of the Church of Ireland from the Earliest Times to the Present Day* (3 vols) (Oxford, 1933), III, p.422.

28 E. Somerville, *An Enthusiast* (London, 1921), p. 65.

29 *CoIG*, 30 December 1921.

30 P. Buckland, *Irish Unionism 1: The Anglo-Irish and the New Ireland, 1885 to 1922* (Dublin, 1972), pp 288–90.

31 M. Cunningham, J. Rutherford, T.J. Johnston *et al.*, *Looking at Ireland* (London, 1937), p. 51.

32 D. Hume, 'Empire Day in Ireland, 1896–1962', in K. Jeffrey (ed.), *An Irish Empire* (Manchester, 1996), p. 153.

33 'It was not in the Roman Church that those movements for the betterment of boys and girls ... had their origin'—Chamberlain, 'The Church and Roman Catholicism', *CoIG*, 22 July 1932.

34 Gregg, *Primitive Faith*, p. 106.

35 Emerson & Bell, *The Church of Ireland, 432–1932*, p. 239.

36 B. Fitzgerald, *We are Besieged* [1946] (Bantry, 2011), p. 234.

37 *The Bell*, vol. 8 (3) (1944), p. 228.

38 Emerson & Bell, *The Church of Ireland, 432–1932*, pp 182–6; articles in *The Bell* in 1944–5 on 'What it means to be a ...': Revd Matthew Bailey (Presbyterian), vol. 8 (4) (July 1944), pp 298–305; Violet Disney (Church of Ireland), vol. 8 (5) (August 1944), pp 379–87; T.W.T. Dillon (Catholic), vol. 9 (1) (October 1944), pp 12–19; Revd E. Savell Hicks (Unitarian), vol. 9 (2) (November 1944), pp 155–62; Stella Webb (Quaker), vol. 9 (3) (December 1944), pp 199–209; A.J. Leventhal (Jewish), vol. 10 (3) (June 1945), pp 207–16.

39 *CoIG*, 2 March 1923. The advertisement for the Sweepstakes in the 1932 Saorstát Éireann *Official Handbook* was the first in 150 pages of advertisements.

40 Cunningham *et al.*, *Looking at Ireland*, p. 67.

41 Chamberlain, 'The Church and Roman Catholicism', *CoIG*, 22 July 1932.

42 Emerson & Bell, *The Church of Ireland, 432–1932*, pp 191–2, 195; *Irish Independent*, 14 October 1932.
43 Seaver, *Gregg*, p. 54.

8. 'Devoted ladies': interrogating novelists Elizabeth Bowen and Molly Keane

1 The title of M.J. Farrell's [Molly Keane's] 1934 novel. This journalism piece was published online in the *Irish Times*, 16 January 2017. The biographical information therein is principally from V. Glendinning, *Elizabeth Bowen—Portrait of a Writer* [1977] (London, 1993), and S. Phipps, *Molly Keane: A Life* (London, 2017). See also I. d'Alton, 'Bowen, Elizabeth Dorothea Cole', *DIB*, vol. 1, pp 693–5, and 'Keane, Mary Nesta ("Molly")', *DIB*, vol. 5, pp 32–3.
2 Thomas McCarthy, 'Introduction' to Bowen, *Bowen's Court* (reprint edn, Cork, 1998), p. xi.
3 S. Phipps, 'Memories of Molly Keane', in E. Walshe & G. Young, *Molly Keane: Centenary Essays* (Dublin, 2006), p. 21.
4 *SW*, p. 29.
5 H. Lee (ed.), *The Mulberry Tree: Writings of Elizabeth Bowen* (London, 1986), p. 276.
6 *Ibid.*, p. 14.
7 *Ibid.*, p. 16.
8 R. Froggatt, 'Agnes Nesta Shakespeare Higginson Skrine (1864–1955): poet and writer', *Dictionary of Ulster Biography*.
9 Phipps, *Molly Keane*, pp xiii–xiv, 32–3.
10 Maryann Johnson, at https://www.flickfilosopher.com/2000/04/the-last-september-review.html (accessed 7 January 2024).
11 *The Collected Stories of Elizabeth Bowen* (Hopewell, NJ, 1981), p. 8.
12 E. Bowen, *Collected Impressions* (London, 1950), p. vi.
13 M. Sarton, *A World of Light: Portraits and Celebrations* (New York, 1976), p. 193.
14 Lee, *Mulberry Tree*, p. 15.
15 J. Parry, *The Shadowy Third: Love, Letters and Elizabeth Bowen* (London, 2021), is about the affair.
16 Glendinning, *Elizabeth Bowen*, p. 119.
17 M.J. Farrell [Molly Keane], *Mad Puppetstown* [1931] (London, 1985), pp 23, 45.
18 M. Ignatieff, *Isaiah Berlin: A Life* [1998] (New York, 1999), p. 90.
19 E. Bowen, *The Last September* [1929] (London, 1998), p. 206.
20 E. Bowen, *The House in Paris* (London, 1935), p. 63.
21 E. Bowen, *The Heat of the Day* [1948] (London, 1954), p. 248.
22 *BC*, p. 459.
23 M.J. Farrell [Molly Keane], *Young Entry* [1928] (London, 1996), p. 25.
24 E. Bowen, *Eva Trout* [1969] (London, 1999), p. 16.
25 *BC*, p. 32.
26 Lee, *Mulberry Tree*, p. 25.
27 C. Ritchie, *The Siren Years: A Canadian Diplomat Abroad 1937–1945* (Toronto, 1974), entry for 2 June 1942.
28 V. Glendinning (ed.) with J. Robertson, *Love's Civil War: Elizabeth Bowen and Charles Ritchie: Letters and Diaries 1941–1973* (London, 2009), p. 475.

29 S. Phipps, 'Molly Keane', *passim*, but esp. pp 84–8, 114–15, 142–4.
30 Lee, *Mulberry Tree*, p. 17.
31 Clare Boylan's obituary in *IT*, 23 April 1996.
32 *The Guardian*, 23 April 1996.
33 Glendinning, *Elizabeth Bowen*, p. 186.
34 For a critical view of Bowen's wartime activities see J. Lane & B. Clifford, *Elizabeth Bowen: 'Notes on Eire'—Espionage Reports to Winston Churchill, 1940–2* (Aubane, 1999).
35 *BC*, p. 453.
36 R.F. Foster, *Paddy and Mr Punch: Connections in Irish and English History* (London, 1993), p. 122.
37 E. Bowen, 'Preface to The Last September' [US edition, 1952] in Lee, *Mulberry Tree*, p. 123.
38 C. Murray (ed.), *Selected Plays of Lennox Robinson* (Gerrards Cross, 1982), p. 195.
39 Woolf to Vanessa Bell in N. Nicholson (ed.), *The Sickle Side of the Moon: The Letters of Virginia Woolf, 1932–1935* (London, 1979), pp 299–300.
40 M.J. Farrell [Molly Keane], *Devoted Ladies*, introduction by Polly Devlin [1934] (London, 1984), p. vii.
41 Farrell, *Devoted Ladies*, p. 61.
42 *The New Yorker*, 5 October 1986.
43 M. Gordon, 'Paperbacks; Vanities of the hunting class', *New York Times*, 29 September 1985, Section 7, p. 43.
44 H. Lee, *Elizabeth Bowen* [1981] (London, 1999), p. 228.

9. 'No more autumns': the Anglo-Irish and the death of the house, 1919–23

1 Read at the Annual Conference of the Centre for the Study of Historic Irish Houses and Estates, Maynooth University, 10 May 2016. The quote is from E. Bowen, *The Last September* [1929] (London, 1998), p. 206 [hereafter *TLS*].
2 *TLS*, p. 205.
3 F.S.L. Lyons, 'Yeats and the Anglo-Irish twilight', in O. MacDonagh, W. Mandle & P. Travers (eds), *Irish Culture and Nationalism, 1750–1950* (Canberra, 1983), p. 232.
4 T. Dooley, *'The Land for the People': The Land Question in Independent Ireland* (Dublin, 2004), p. 29, and *The Decline of the Big House in Ireland: A Study of Irish Landed Families 1860–1960* (Dublin, 2001), pp 127–31, 171–205.
5 V. Kreilcamp, *The Anglo-Irish Novel and the Big House* (Syracuse, 1998), p. 168.
6 D. Kennedy, 'The Big House in Irish literature: a study of Somerville & Ross, W.B. Yeats and Seán O'Casey', *Bulletin of the Irish Georgian Society*, vol. 32 (1989), p. 27.
7 G. Bence-Jones, 'Drishane', in *Ostrich Creek: Tom and Other Survivors* (New Hope International, 1999), p. 23.
8 Kennedy, 'The Big House in Irish literature', p. 27.
9 *BC*, p. 455.
10 O. MacDonagh, *States of Mind: A Study of the Anglo-Irish Conflict, 1780–1980* (London, 1983), p. 28.
11 D. Kiberd, *Inventing Ireland: The Literature of the Modern Nation* (London, 1995), p. 107.
12 See also G. Cronin, 'The Big House and the Irish landscape in the work of Elizabeth Bowen', in J. Genet (ed.), *The Big House in Ireland:*

Reality and Representation (Dingle, 1991), p. 146.

13 J. O'Brien & D. Guinness, *Great Irish Houses and Castles* (London, 1992), p. 131.

14 *Waterford News*, 19 April 1885.

15 *The Times*, 29 October 1921: '£85,000 COMPENSATION—Lord Listowel's burnt mansion'.

16 G. MacBeth, 'A conversation with Grandfather', *Harvard Book Review*, vols 17/18 (1990), p. 3.

17 Cronin, 'The Big House', p. 146.

18 C. Murray (ed.), *Selected Plays of Lennox Robinson* (Gerrards Cross, 1982), p. 137.

19 *Ibid.*, p. 143.

20 J. Cronin, *The Anglo-Irish Novel* (2 vols) (Belfast, 1990), II, p. 126.

21 G. Clark, *Everyday Violence in the Irish Civil War* (Cambridge, 2014), p. 84.

22 *BC*, p. 32.

23 M. Deen Larsen, 'Saints of the Ascendancy: William Trevor's Big House novels', in O. Rauchbauer (ed.), *Ancestral Voices: The Big House in Anglo-Irish Literature* (Dublin, 1992), p. 261.

24 M.J. Farrell [Molly Keane], *Two Days in Aragon* [1941] (London, 1985), pp 16–17, 94.

25 E. Bowen, *Pictures and Conversations* (London, 1975), p. 29.

26 G. Bachelard, *La Poétique de l'Espace* (Paris, 1957), pp 24, 51–78; Rauchbauer, *Ancestral Voices*, p. ix.

27 P. Lassner, *Elizabeth Bowen* (Savage, 1989), p. 160.

28 *TLS*, p. 7.

29 *TLS*, p. 8.

30 Cronin, 'The Big House', p. 147; *TLS*, p. 65.

31 V. Glendinning, 'Introduction' to E. Bowen, *The Last September* [1929] (London, 1998), p. 2.

32 I. d'Alton, 'Courting Elizabeth Bowen: *Elizabeth Bowen: New Critical Perspectives*, ed. Susan Osborn (Cork, 2009); *Love's Civil War: Elizabeth Bowen and Charles Ritchie: Letters and Diaries 1941–1973*, ed. V. Glendinning with J. Robertson (London, 2009)', *The Irish Review*, vol. 42 (2010), pp 128–36.

33 Kate Alcock may declare that Ballydonal was but 'bricks and stones' (Murray, *Selected Plays*, p. 196) but it is the only time in the play when the house is treated in such a brusque, inanimate way.

34 *TLS*, p. 206.

35 E. Bowen, 'The Big House' [1942], in *Collected Impressions* (London, 1950), p. 195.

36 E. Bowen, 'The Back Drawing-Room', in *The Collected Stories of Elizabeth Bowen* (Hopewell, NJ, 1981), p. 205.

37 Murray, *Selected Plays*, pp 144, 149.

38 *BC*, p. 20; Cronin, 'The Big House', p. 147; L. Fleming, *Head or Harp* (London, 1965), pp 17, 36.

39 Murray, *Selected Plays*, p. 153.

40 *Ibid.*, pp 164, 193.

41 *Ibid.*, p. 192; *TLS*, p. 58; Cronin, 'The Big House', p. 150.

42 *TLS*, pp 22, 206; W.B. Yeats, *Purgatory* (1938)—see N. Crohn Schmitt, 'The landscape play: W.B. Yeats's "Purgatory"', *Irish University Review*, vol. 27 (2) (1997), pp 262–75.

43 Clark, *Everyday Violence*, pp 70–85.

44 Murray, *Selected Plays*, p. 186.

45 Clark, *Everyday Violence*, p. 68.

46 Michael Hartnett, *Collected Poems, edited by Peter Fallon* (Oldcastle, 2001), pp 136–7.

47 See https://www.poetryireland.ie/publications/poetry-ireland-review/online-archive/view/stately-home (accessed 4 March 2019).

48 E. [Daisy] Fingall, *Seventy Years Young: Memories of Elizabeth, Countess of Fingall* (London, 1937), p. 29.

49 *TLS*, p. 66.

50 A. Coleman, 'The Big House, Yeats and the Irish context', in Rauchbauer, *Ancestral Voices*, p. 124.

51 H. McDowell, 'The Big House: a genealogist's perspective and a personal point of view', in Rauchbauer, *Ancestral Voices*, p. 286.

52 Clark, *Everyday Violence*, p. 75.

53 *Midland Tribune*, 3 March 1923, quoted in C. Reilly, 'The burning of country houses in Co. Offaly during the revolutionary period, 1920–3', in T. Dooley & C. Ridgway (eds), *The Irish Country House: Its Past, Present and Future* (Dublin, 2015), pp 126–7.

54 William O'Brien, *Evening Memories* (London & Dublin, 1920), p. 440.

55 Clark, *Everyday Violence*, p. 61.

56 'The defence of Irish country homes', produced by the Irish Unionist Alliance in 1913—a practical guide on the steps to be taken to prevent fire (PRONI MS D/989/C/1/17).

57 NUI Galway's landed estates database at http://www.landedestates.ie/ (accessed 3 June 2022).

58 J.G. Farrell, *Troubles* (London, 1970), p. 446.

59 Clark, *Everyday Violence*, p. 92.

60 Keane, *Two Days in Aragon*, p. 253; M. Elliot, 'Molly Keane's Big Houses', in Genet (ed.), *The Big House in Ireland*, p. 195: 'her nails sunk into the very body of Aragon'. See also E. Walshe & G. Young (eds), *Molly Keane: Centenary Essays* (Dublin, 2006).

61 Elizabeth Bowen was haunted all her life by images of Bowen's Court burning: V. Glendinning, *Elizabeth Bowen—Portrait of a Writer* [1977] (London, 1993), pp 40, 68.

62 Dooley, *Decline of the Big House*, pp 171–97.

63 P. Martin, 'Unionism: the Irish nobility and the revolution 1919–23', in J. Augustein (ed.), *The Irish Revolution* (Basingstoke, 2002), pp 157–8.

64 Bowen in 1929 has the Montmorencys, having moved from their house, contemplating building a bungalow—clearly a ghastly idea. Quoted in Kennedy, 'The Big House in Irish literature', p. 27.

65 See https://landedestates.ie/property/3247 (accessed 9 January 2024).

66 Murray, *Selected Plays*, p. 196.

67 F. Browne, 'The death of the Pallastown heir: Lt Robert Heard, Irish Guards', in T. Dooley and C. Ridgway (eds), *The Country House and the Great War: Irish and British Experiences* (Dublin, 2016), pp 27–8.

68 Castle Hyde near Fermoy was brought back to life by dancer Michael Flatley in the 1990s. Further down the Blackwater, near Youghal, Ballynatray was a near-ruin in the early 1980s but has since been restored as a commercial venture: see P. Cockburn, *Figure*

of Eight (Dingle, 1989), p. 20; Dooley, *Decline of the Big House*, pp 250–60.
69 Bowen, 'Back Drawing-Room', pp 209–10.
70 *BC*, p. 459.
71 Quoted in S. Curtis Brown, 'Foreword' to Bowen, *Pictures and Conversations*, p. xxxv.

10. Bowen's Court as 'an aesthetic of living': a lost mansion's significance in the imagining of the Irish gentry

1 A version of this essay was published in J. Raven (ed.), *Lost Mansions: Essays on the Destruction of the Country House* (Basingstoke, 2015), pp 63–80. The phrase is Elizabeth Bowen's, in her short story 'Sunday Afternoon': *The Collected Stories of Elizabeth Bowen* (Hopewell, NJ, 1981), p. 616.
2 H. Lee, *Elizabeth Bowen* [1981] (London, 1999), p. 260.
3 T. Dooley, *The Decline of the Big House in Ireland* (Dublin, 2001), pp 24–7 and 146–9.
4 *BC*, p. 32.
5 *BC*, p. 5.
6 *BC*, pp 14, 20.
7 E. Bowen, 'The Big House', in *Collected Impressions* (London, 1950), p. 195.
8 *BC*, pp 4–5.
9 *BC*, p. 19.
10 *BC*, p. 9. For the parish in 1837 see T. Cadogan (ed.), *Lewis' Cork: A Topographical Dictionary of the Parishes, Towns and Villages of Cork City and County* (Cork, 1998), pp 235–6. In contrast to descriptions of other houses elsewhere in his *Dictionary*, Lewis has nothing to say about Henry Cole Bowen's mansion. The house was valued at £75 at the time of Griffith's Valuation (https://landedestates.ie/property/3261; accessed 9 January 2024).
11 Dooley, *Decline of the Big House*, p. 24.
12 *BC*, pp 167–8.
13 *BC*, pp 21–8.
14 V. Glendinning with J. Robertson, *Love's Civil War: Elizabeth Bowen & Charles Ritchie: Letters and Diaries from the Love Affair of a Lifetime* (London, 2009), p. 351.
15 Lee, *Bowen*, p. 47.
16 *BC*, p. 459.
17 Glendinning with Robertson, *Love's Civil War*, p. 465.
18 C. Reid, *The Lost Ireland of Stephen Gwynn: Irish Constitutional Nationalism and Cultural Politics, 1864–1950* (Manchester, 2011), p. 245.
19 H. Lee (ed.), *The Mulberry Tree—Writings of Elizabeth Bowen* (New York, 1986), p. 125. Bowen was careful not to claim historical verisimilitude for *Bowen's Court*: 'I am, evidently, not a historian' (*BC*, p. 452). Indeed, 'She was no historian at all': Glendinning, *Bowen*, p. 64.
20 *The Bell*, vol. 1 (1) (October 1940); the essay was reprinted in Bowen, 'The Big House', in *Collected Impressions* [but dated there 1942].
21 E. Bowen, *The Last September* (London, 1998) [hereafter *TLS*], and *A World of Love* (New York, 1978) [hereafter *AWOL*]; A. Wessels, 'Elizabeth Bowen's "A World of Love": a 'cultural analysis' of the Anglo-Irish Ascendancy in the twentieth century', *Canadian Journal of Irish Studies*, vol. 21 (1) (July 1995), pp 88–95.

22 E. Bowen, 'Preface to The Last September [1952]', in Lee, *The Mulberry Tree*, p. 123.
23 H. Butler, '*The Bell*: an Anglo-Irish view', *Irish University Review*, vol. 6 (1) (1976), pp 66–72.
24 *AWOL*, pp 37, 80.
25 G. Cronin, 'The Big House and the Irish landscape in the work of Elizabeth Bowen', in J. Genet (ed.), *The Big House in Ireland: Reality and Representation* (Dingle, 1991), p. 146; also D. Kennedy, 'The Big House in Irish literature', *Bulletin of the Irish Georgian Society*, vol. 32 (1989), p. 27.
26 *BC*, p. 455.
27 C. Murray (ed.), *Selected Plays of Lennox Robinson* (Gerrards Cross, 1982), p. 139; *TLS*, p. 20.
28 E. Walshe, 'Several landscapes: Bowen and the terrain of north Cork', *Estudios Irlandeses* (2005), pp 141–7.
29 *BC*, pp 18–20, 28–30.
30 *TLS*, p. 7; Bowen, 'The Big House', p. 195.
31 *TLS*, pp 9, 24.
32 For instance S. Towheed, 'Territory, space, modernity: Elizabeth Bowen's *The Demon Lover and Other Stories* and wartime London', in S. Osborn, *Elizabeth Bowen: New Critical Perspectives* (Cork, 2009), p. 121, writes of 'Bowen's geometrically obsessed writing'.
33 Bowen, 'The Big House', p. 196.
34 *AWOL*, p. 56; see also C. Wills, '"Half different": the vanishing Irish in *A World of Love*', in E. Walshe, *Elizabeth Bowen* (Dublin, 2009), p. 135.
35 *TLS*, pp 22, 206.
36 Cronin, 'The Big House', p. 146.
37 *TLS*, p. 40; E. Bowen, *Eva Trout* [1968] (London, 1999), p. 16.
38 *BC*, p. 449.
39 R.F. Foster, *The Irish Story: Telling Tales and Making It Up in Ireland* (London, 2001), p. 150; N. Corcoran, *Elizabeth Bowen: The Enforced Return* (Oxford, 2004), p. 23.
40 *BC*, p. 451.
41 F.S.L. Lyons, 'Yeats and the Anglo-Irish twilight', in O. MacDonagh, W. Mandle & P. Travers (eds), *Irish Culture and Nationalism, 1750–1950* (Canberra, 1983), p. 232.
42 Lee, *The Mulberry Tree*, p. 126.
43 *BC*, p. 447.
44 *BC*, p. 259.
45 Lee, *Bowen*, p. 37.
46 I. d'Alton, 'Murdoch, Iris', *DIB*, vol. 6, pp 783–6.
47 M. Eatough, '*Bowen's Court* and the Anglo-Irish world-system', *Modern Language Quarterly*, vol. 73 (1) (2012), p. 73.
48 *Ibid.*, pp 72–3.
49 Bowen, 'The Big House', p. 199.
50 *BC*, p. 456.
51 *BC*, p. 437.
52 E. Grubgeld, *Anglo-Irish Autobiography: Class, Gender and the Forms of Narrative* (Syracuse, 2004), p. 154. See J. O'Neill, *Blood-dark Track: A Family History* (London, 2000), p. 327. As O'Neill notes, 'families and nations have self-serving editions of their past'.
53 M. Davitt, 'Third Draft of a Dream' (trans. P. Muldoon), in T.P. Coogan (ed.), *A Special Issue of Literary Review Ireland and The Arts* (London, 1982), pp 161–3.

11. Elizabeth Bowen illumines the *Irish* Murdoch

1 Read at the Fifth International Iris Murdoch Conference, Kingston University, UK, 10 September 2010.

2 W. Shakespeare, *The Chronicle History of Henry V*, Act 3, Scene 2, line 1251.

3 P. Conradi, *Iris Murdoch: A Life* (London, 2001) [hereafter Conradi, *IM*], pp n523 *et seqq*.

4 Conradi, *IM*, p. 29.

5 *DIB*, p. xix; I. d'Alton, 'Murdoch, Iris', *DIB*, vol. 6, pp 783–6.

6 Conradi, *IM*, p. 24.

7 D. Gerstenberger, *Iris Murdoch* (Lewisburg and London, 1975); Conradi, *IM*, esp. pp 3–33—'You ask how Irish she is'; '*Iris Murdoch: A Life* by P. Conradi', *The Guardian*, 8 September 2001.

8 Conradi, *IM*, p. 29.

9 F. White, '"I'm a kind of exile": the position of Iris Murdoch in the Irish diaspora', paper read at a conference, 'Neither Here nor There: Writing the Irish Diaspora', at the University of Limerick, 1 November 2008.

10 A. Norman Jeffares, *Anglo-Irish Literature* (New York, 1982), p. 248.

11 D. Kiberd, *Inventing Ireland: The Literature of the Modern Nation* (London, 1995), and *The Irish Writer and the World* (Cambridge, 2005).

12 I. Murdoch, *The Unicorn* [1963] (London, 2000) [hereafter *TU*], p. 21.

13 P. Conradi, *Iris Murdoch: A Writer at War* (London, 2010), p. 82.

14 S. Medcalf, 'Introduction', *TU*, p. xiii.

15 S. Osborn (ed.), *Elizabeth Bowen: New Critical Perspectives* (Cork, 2009); M. Ellmann, *Elizabeth Bowen: The Shadow across the Page* (Edinburgh, 2003), p. 162; N. Corcoran, *Elizabeth Bowen: The Enforced Return* (Oxford, 2004), pp 11–12, and esp. chapter 2 (pp 39–60).

16 Conradi, *IM*, pp 4–11.

17 R.B. McDowell, *Crisis and Decline: The Fate of the Southern Unionists* (Dublin, 1997), p. 4.

18 M. Maguire, 'The Dublin Protestant working class, 1870–1932: economy, society, politics' (unpublished MA thesis, University College Dublin, 1990); *idem*, 'The organisation and activism of Dublin's Protestant working class, 1883–1935', *IHS*, vol. 29 (113) (1994), pp 65–87; *idem*, 'The Church of Ireland and the problem of the Protestant working-class of Dublin, 1870s–1930s', in A. Ford, J. McGuire & K. Milne (eds), *As by Law Established: The Church of Ireland since the Reformation* (Dublin, 1995), p. 202; Saorstát Éireann, *Census of Population, 1926*, vol. 10, *General Report* (Dublin, 1931) (P.1242), p. 50.

19 McDowell, *Crisis and Decline*, p. 5; *Census of Population, 1926*, pp 46–7, 54–5; R.B. McDowell, *The Church of Ireland, 1869–1969* (London, 1975), pp 121–2.

20 *SW*, p. 48.

21 I. Murdoch, *The Red and the Green* [1965] (London, 2002) [hereafter *TRATG*], p. 310.

22 *SW*, p. 48. See also D. Akenson, *Small Differences: Irish Catholics and Irish Protestants, 1825–1922* (Quebec, 1988), p. 149.

23 *SW*, p. 17.

24 J.M. Hone, 'Five strains', *The Bell*, vol. 2 (6) (1941), p. 26.

25 *TRATG*, pp 9–10, 201–2.

26 R.F. Foster, 'Prints on the scene: Elizabeth Bowen and the landscape of childhood', in *The Irish Story: Telling Tales and Making It Up in Ireland* (London, 2001), pp 158–63.
27 E. Bowen, *A World of Love* [1955] (New York, 1978), p. 89 [hereafter *AWOL*].
28 Conradi, *IM*, pp 22–9.
29 E. Bowen, *The Last September* [1929] (London, 1998), p. 24 [hereafter *TLS*]; V. Glendinning, *Elizabeth Bowen—Portrait of a Writer* [1977] (London, 1993), p. 195.
30 C. Murray (ed.), *Selected Plays of Lennox Robinson* (Gerrards Cross, 1982), p. 184.
31 R.F. Foster, *Paddy & Mr Punch: Connections in Irish and English History* (London, 1993), p. 102.
32 G. Bachelard, *La Poétique de l'Espace* (Paris, 1957), p. 183.
33 S. Towheed, 'Territory, space, modernity: Elizabeth Bowen's *The Demon Lover and Other Stories* and wartime London', in S. Osborn (ed.), *Elizabeth Bowen: New Critical Perspectives* (Cork, 2009), pp 113–31.
34 *TLS*, p. 24.
35 *TU*, pp 18, 19.
36 *Ibid.* See also *AWOL*, p. 18.
37 *AWOL*, p. 26.
38 *TU*, p. 198.
39 I. Murdoch, *Nuns and Soldiers* [1980] (London, 2001), p. 200.
40 *TRATG*, p. 18.
41 *AWOL*, p. 112; *SW*, p. 48.
42 *TU*, p. 15.
43 *TU*, p. 162.
44 *TU*, pp 164–7.
45 *TU*, pp 7, 270.
46 *TU*, p. 164.
47 S. Day, *The Amazing Philanthropists* (London, 1916), p. 16.
48 E. Said, *Culture and Imperialism* (London, 1993), p. xiii.
49 *TU*, p. 29.
50 H. Lee, *Elizabeth Bowen* [1981] (London, 1999), p. 20.
51 J. Knightly, 'Visitors and visiting: a Kerry country house, 1912–39', in T. Dooley and C. Ridgway (eds), *Visitors to the Country House in Ireland and Britain, Welcome and Unwelcome* (Dublin, 2023), pp 220–46.
52 *TU*, pp 16–17.
53 *AWOL*, pp 66–7.
54 S. Deane, 'Irish national character, 1790–1900', in T. Dunne (ed.), *The Writer as Witness* (Cork, 1987), p. 101.
55 *BC*, p. 437.
56 *CoIG*, 21 July 1922.
57 B. Hayes & T. Fahey, 'Protestants and politics in the Republic of Ireland: is integration complete?', in M. Busteed, F. Neal & J. Tonge (eds), *Irish Protestant Identities* (Manchester, 2008), pp 70–83.
58 *TU*, p. 13.
59 *TRATG*, p. 185.
60 *TU*, p. 30.
61 *TU*, pp 16, 19.
62 *TRATG*, p. 171.
63 H. Lee (ed.), *The Mulberry Tree—Writings of Elizabeth Bowen* (New York, 1986), p. 125.
64 *AWOL*, pp 183, 112. In *AWOL*, the three women portrayed are perhaps the same woman at different ages. Likewise, in *TU*, Marian, Violet and Alice …
65 *TU*, pp 16, 29.

66 H. Crawford, *Outside the Glow: Protestants and Irishness in Independent Ireland* (Dublin, 2010), p. 180.
67 V. Glendinning with J. Robertson, *Love's Civil War: Elizabeth Bowen & Charles Ritchie: Letters and Diaries from the Love Affair of a Lifetime* (London, 2008), p. 244.
68 *TRATG*, p. 16.
69 Conradi, *IM*, pp 398, 415.

12. What makes Iris Murdoch's Irish short story *Something Special* special

1 A version was published as 'Iris Murdoch's Irish identity: the case of "Something Special"', *Iris Murdoch Review*, vol. 4 (2013), pp 23–30.
2 1952.
3 According to Peter Conradi, it was an insert in the first draft of *The Sandcastle*, a draft produced in the first two weeks of September 1955—P.J. Conradi, *Iris Murdoch: A Life* (London, 2001) [hereafter Conradi, *IM*], p. 646n—but this seems to have been a misunderstanding by Conradi, which he clarified in an email to Ian d'Alton (20 July 2012). Also Murdoch Papers, University of Iowa Special Collections, MSC 212, Box 33, holograph drafts 1 & 2.
4 London and New York, 1957, at pp 175–204.
5 I. Murdoch, *Something Special* (London, 1999), p. 41 [hereafter *SS*]
6 V. Valvano Lynch, '"Something Special": Iris Murdoch's Joycean odyssey' (unpublished paper read to the American Conference of Irish Studies, Marquette University, Milwaukee, 6 June 2002, copy in the possession of Ian d'Alton) [hereafter *Lynch*].
7 P. Martin & A. Rowe, *Iris Murdoch: A Literary Life* (Basingstoke, 2010), p. 61.
8 A. Gonzalez, 'The problem of gender in Iris Murdoch's "Something Special"', *Journal of the Short Story in English*, vol. 21 (1993), p. 19.
9 *New York Times*, 12 November 2000; *Lynch*, p. 2.
10 *Kirkus* review (1 October 2000), at https://www.kirkusreviews.com/book-reviews/iris-murdoch/something-special/#review (accessed 9 January 2024).
11 Martin & Rowe, *Literary Life*, p. 178, note 10.
12 These are reviews on http://www.goodreads.com/book/show/959772.Something_Special, dating from between 2007 and 2012 (accessed 9 January 2024); 505 ratings averaged 3 out of 5, incidentally—an endorsement of the Amidon view.
13 Conradi, *IM*, pp 437–42; also A.N. Wilson, *Iris Murdoch as I Knew Her* (London, 2004), pp 67, 75, 85, 88, 91, 97.
14 Despite this, though, we may note that neither writer figured on a 1976 list by Iris of works that influenced her: Conradi, *IM*, p. 524n.
15 Conradi, *IM*, pp 49n, 446–7.
16 H. Lee (ed.), *The Mulberry Tree—Writings of Elizabeth Bowen* (New York, 1986), p. 125.
17 Wilson, *Iris Murdoch*, p. 90.
18 P. Conradi, 'Holy fool and magus: the uses of discipleship in *Under the Net* and *The Flight from the Enchanter*', in J. Broackes (ed.), *Iris Murdoch, Philosopher: A Collection of Essays* (Oxford, 2012), p. 121n; Wilson, *Iris Murdoch*, p. 90.

19 'Mapping Samuel Beckett's *Murphy*', an online article on modernist and post-modern Anglophone literature by COMMA, the Center on Modern Culture, Materialism and Aesthetics at the University of California, Santa Barbara, at http://comma.english.ucsb.edu/node/22 (accessed 17 July 2012).
20 *Lynch*, p. 5; Conradi, *IM*, p. 446.
21 *SS*, pp 6, 16, 17.
22 See D. Foley, *The Bloomsday trams: Dublin's tramway fleet of James Joyce's* Ulysses (Dublin, 2009). There are over twenty individual references to trams in *Dubliners*.
23 *IT*, 1 August 2012.
24 *SS*, p. 17.
25 Murdoch Papers, University of Iowa, holograph drafts 1 & 2.
26 *Lynch*, p. 4.
27 I. d'Alton, '"A vestigial population"? Perspectives on southern Irish Protestants in the twentieth century', *Éire-Ireland*, vol. 44 (Winter 2009–10), pp 30–3.
28 See http://www.encyclopedia.com/topic/Samuel_Beckett.aspx (accessed 12 September 2012).
29 *SS*, pp 7, 8.
30 M. Levitt, '"The greatest Jew of all": James Joyce, Leopold Bloom and the modernist archetype', in *Spanish James Joyce Society, Papers on Joyce*, nos 10/11 (2004–5), p. 146.
31 *Ibid.*, p. 145.
32 Murdoch Papers, University of Iowa.
33 Ireland, *Census of Population, 1971*, 1, Table 1A.
34 Figures extrapolated from the 1946 and 1971 censuses.
35 *SS*, pp 3, 4, 10.
36 *SS*, p. 15. For a then-contemporary view of Jewishness by an Anglo-Irishman, see Arland Ussher, *The Magic People: An Irishman Appraises the Jews* (New York, 1951).
37 *SS*, p. 34.
38 *SS*, p. 36.
39 Murdoch was a philosemite: Conradi, *IM*, pp 100, 317–40.
40 See http://www.myjewishlearning.com/holidays/Jewish_Holidays/Tu_Bishvat/Ideas_and_Beliefs/Rabbinic.shtml (accessed 17 July 2012).

13. 'The unreasoning adventure': why the Irish gentry went to war

1 Read at Maynooth University, Ireland, 5 October 2018, to commemorate the centenary of the Armistice of 1918. An earlier version was published as 'Prisoners of war? Evoking an Anglo-Irish perception of the conflict of 1914–19', *Australasian Journal of Irish Studies*, vol. 17 (2017), pp 6–22. The quote is from T.R. Henn, *Five Arches: A Sketch for an Autobiography and 'Philoctetes' and Other Poems* (Gerrards Cross, 1980), p. 64.
2 I. d'Alton, '"Lay spring flowers on our boy's grave": Norman Leslie's short war', in T. Dooley & C. Ridgway (eds), *The Country House and the Great War—Irish and British Experiences* (Dublin, 2016), pp 76–86.
3 Norman Leslie to Leonie Leslie, 22 January 1909 (Leslie Papers, NLI MS 49,495/2/65). Norman's mother was Leonie Jerome, an American and sister of Jennie, Lord Randolph Churchill's wife, Winston's mother.
4 Leslie Papers, 'Introduction', PRONI, p. 74; NLI MS 49,495/2/65.

5 Norman Leslie to Leonie Leslie, n.d. but probably October 1914, with annotation 'his last to his mother?' (NLI MS 49,495/2/42).

6 T. Dooley, *The Decline of the Big House in Ireland: A Study of Irish Landed Families 1860–1960* (Dublin, 2001); P. Martin, '"Dulce et decorum": Irish nobles and the Great War, 1914–1919', and D.G. Boyce, '"That party politics should divide our tents": nationalism, unionism and the First World War', both in A. Gregory & S. Paseta (eds), *Ireland and the Great War: 'A War to Unite us All'?* (Manchester, 2002), pp 28–48 and 190–216 respectively; K. Jeffery, *Ireland and the Great War* (Cambridge, 2000), pp 69–71; R.B. McDowell, *Crisis and Decline: The Fate of the Southern Unionists* (Dublin, 1997).

7 For this essay I examined the families in *Burke's Peerage* and L.G. Pine (ed.), *Burke's Genealogical and Heraldic History of the Landed Gentry of Ireland* (London, 1958). My analysis corroborates the conclusions about participation in Dooley, *The Decline of the Big House*, p. 122; of P. Buckland thirty years earlier, using a different sampling technique, in his *Irish Unionism 1: The Anglo Irish and the New Ireland 1885–1922* (Dublin, 1972), p. 30; in Martin, "Dulce et decorum", pp 40–1; and in N. Perry, 'The Irish landed class and the British army, 1850–1950', *War in History*, vol. 18 (3) (2011), p. 328.

8 Lady Charles Beresford [the Beresfords were Marquesses of Waterford] to Leonie Leslie, n.d. (NLI MS 49,495/2/38).

9 J.J. Lee, *Ireland 1912–1985—Politics and Society* (Cambridge, 1989), p. 23. Less than a quarter of those in non-agricultural occupations joined up: D. Fitzpatrick, 'Home front and everyday life', in J. Horne (ed.), *Our War: Ireland and the Great War* (Dublin, 2008), p. 134; also N. Gallagher, *Ireland and the Great War: A Social and Political History* (London, 2019).

10 Dooley suggests that the farmers and townspeople of Monaghan—the Leslies' county—were relatively reluctant to join up: T. Dooley, *The Decline of Unionist Politics in Monaghan, 1911–23* (Maynooth, 1988), pp 8–9.

11 Perry, 'Irish landed class', p. 328; D. Fitzpatrick, 'The logic of collective sacrifice: Ireland and the British Army, 1914–1918', *Historical Journal*, vol. 38 (4) (1995), p. 1018.

12 J. Horne (ed.), *Our War: Ireland and the Great War* (Dublin, 2008), p. 6; http://www.irishtimes.com/culture/heritage/irish-soldiers-in-the-first-world-war-who-where-and-how-many-1.1884022 (accessed 14 October 2014).

13 Dooley, *Decline of the Big House*, p. 125. Dooley deals with the war in pages 122–7. See also J.M. Hone, *Ireland since 1902* (London, 1932), p. 28; M. Bence-Jones, 'The changing picture of the Irish landed gentry', in *Burke's Landed Gentry of Ireland* (London, 1978), pp xix, xx.

14 A. Grainger, 'Killed in War exemption', *Christie's Bulletin for Professional Advisers*, vol. 18 (1) (2014), pp 12–13.

15 Sir John [Jack] Leslie to Leonie Leslie, n.d. but probably around the second

week of October 1914 (NLI MS 49,495/2/41).

16 Dooley, *Decline of the Big House*, p. 122; L. Dooney, 'Trinity College and the War', in D. Fitzpatrick (ed.), *Ireland and the First World War* (Dublin, 1986), p. 46.

17 T. Brown, *The Literature of Ireland: Culture and Criticism* (Cambridge, 2010), pp 83–4; also D. Fitzpatrick, 'Militarism in Ireland', in T. Bartlett & K. Jeffery (eds), *A Military History of Ireland* (Cambridge, 1996), pp 381, 389–90.

18 See https://www.castleleslie.com/room/the-red-room/ (accessed 9 January 2024); NLI MS 49,495/2/66.

19 E. Somerville, *An Enthusiast* (London, 1921), p. 266; Fitzpatrick, 'The logic of collective sacrifice', pp 1017–18.

20 Henn, *Five Arches*, pp 64–70.

21 Letters from Jack Leslie to his wife (NLI MS 49,495/2/41), 1917–18, many from Finner Camp, Donegal.

22 Perry, 'Irish landed class', pp 309–10.

23 Somerville, *An Enthusiast*, preface, n.p.

24 J.W. Foster, *Irish Novels 1890–1940* (Oxford, 2007), p. 266.

25 Henn, *Five Arches*, p. 64.

26 Norman Leslie to Leonie Leslie, 28 September 1914 (PRONI, Leslie Papers, 'Introduction', p. 73).

27 Norman Leslie to Leonie Leslie, n.d. but probably late 1890s, account of such a match (NLI MS 49,495/2/42).

28 Brown, *The Literature of Ireland*, p. 84.

29 Fitzpatrick, 'Militarism in Ireland', pp 389–90.

30 The brothers Ross-Lewin, *In Britain's Need* (Dublin, 1917), p. 51; [R.S. Ross-Lewin], *Poems by a County of Clare West Briton* (Limerick, 1907), pp 7–9.

31 O. Rauchbauer, *Shane Leslie: Sublime Failure* (Dublin, 2009), p. 183.

32 Sometime wife of the conscientious objector Miles Malleson: C. Malleson, *After Ten Years: A Personal Record* (London, 1931), pp 79–80, 98–9, 111, 112–15.

33 C. Murray (ed.), *Selected Plays of Lennox Robinson* (Gerrards Cross, 1982), p. 141.

34 S.R. Lysaght, *My Tower in Desmond* (London, 1925), p. 417; Graves's poem is in D. Kastan (ed.), *The Oxford Encyclopaedia of British Literature* (Oxford, 2006), p. 340.

35 Quoting Simone Weil: M. Gibbon, *Inglorious Soldier* (London, 1968), p. 256.

36 See https://landedestates.ie/estate/50 (accessed 9 January 2024).

37 A. Jackson, 'Irish unionists and the Empire, 1880–1920: classes and masses', in K. Jeffery (ed.), *'An Irish Empire'? Aspects of Ireland and the British Empire* (Manchester, 1996), pp 132–3.

38 D. McCracken, 'MacBride's Brigade in the Anglo-Boer War', *History Ireland*, vol. 8 (1) (2000).

39 N. Robertson, *Crowned Harp: Memories of the Last Years of the Crown in Ireland* (Dublin, 1960), p. 55.

40 Letter from Brian Walker, *IT*, 25 February 2017.

41 J. Bruton, 'September 1914: John Redmond at Woodenbridge', *Studies: An Irish Quarterly Review*, vol. 101 (402) (2012), pp 237–41.

42 The Ross-Lewins, *In Britain's Need*, p. 7.

43 C. Reid, *The Lost Ireland of Stephen Gwynn* (Manchester, 2011), pp 140–3.
44 M. Headlam, *Irish Reminiscences* (London, 1947), p. 145.
45 Malleson, *After Ten Years*, p. 78.
46 Jennie Churchill to Leonie Leslie, 1 August 1914 (NLI MS 49,495/2/43).
47 Note from Norman Leslie, 'To be opened in the event of my death by my Mother' (NLI MS 49,495/2/65).
48 Bence-Jones, 'The changing picture of the Irish landed gentry', p. xxviii.
49 F. Moffett, *I Too Am of Ireland* (London, 1985); J. de Vere, *In Ruin Reconciled: A Memoir of Anglo-Ireland 1913–1959* (Dublin, 1990), pp 7, 39; P. Cockburn, *Figure of Eight* (London, 1985), p. 3.
50 L.A.G. Strong, *Green Memory* (London, 1961), p. 143.
51 Moffett, *I Too Am of Ireland*, p. 84.
52 *BC*, pp 434–5.
53 V. Glendinning, *Elizabeth Bowen—Portrait of a Writer* [1977] (London, 1993), p. 41.
54 Shane Leslie to Leonie Leslie, 22 December 1914 (NLI MS 49,495/2/42, folder 7).
55 *BC*, p. 436.
56 Foster, *Irish Novels*, p. 342.
57 W.B. Stanford, *Memoirs: Scholar, Senator, Churchman* (Dublin, 2001), pp 6–7, where he writes of what he sees as a rather bizarre 'death cult' promoted by Anglican clergy around the Remembrance ceremonies.
58 H. Jones, 'Church of Ireland Great War remembrance in the south of Ireland: a personal reflection', in J. Horne & E. Madigan, *Towards Commemoration: Ireland in War and Revolution 1912–1923* (Dublin, 2013), pp 74–81.
59 M.J. Farrell [Molly Keane], *The Rising Tide* [1937] (London, 1984), p. 103.
60 Mrs Victor Rickard, *The Fire of Green Boughs* (Toronto, 1919), p. 158.
61 E. Longley (ed.), *Culture and Diversity in Ireland: Proceedings of the Cultures of Ireland Group Conference* (Belfast, 1991), p. 10.
62 *BC*, p. 435.
63 Rickard, *Fire of Green Boughs*, pp 22, 26, 120–2.
64 M.J. Farrell [Molly Keane], *Mad Puppetstown* [1931] (London, 1985), p. 79.
65 Murray, *Selected Plays*, p. 155.
66 Lord Dunsany, *Tales of War* (Boston, 1918), pp 84–91.
67 Shane Leslie to Jack Leslie, 17 December 1914 (NLI MS 49,495/2/42).
68 R. Grayson, *Dublin's Great Wars: The First World War, the Easter Rising and the Irish Revolution* (Cambridge, 2018), pp 1–7.
70 E. [Daisy] Fingall, *Seventy Years Young: Memories of Elizabeth, Countess of Fingall* (London, 1937), p. 386 (ghost-written by Pamela Hinkson).
70 E. Grubgeld, *Anglo-Irish Autobiography: Class, Gender, and the Forms of Narrative* (Syracuse, 2004), p. 58.
71 B. Bond & S. Robbins, *Staff Officer: The Diaries of Walter Guinness (first Lord Moyne) 1914–18* (London, 1987), p. 7.
72 Lord Dunsany, *The Ghosts of the Heaviside Layer* [1955] (Philadelphia, *c.* 1980), p. 4, foreword by Darrell Schweitzer.
73 In 'Extra-mundane communications', *Stray-Aways* (London, 1920),

Somerville ascribes her new seriousness to the war: Foster, *Irish Novels 1890–1940*, p. 342.

74 Shane Leslie to John Leslie, 17 December 1914 (NLI MS 49,495/2/42).

75 *The Poems of Shane Leslie* (London, 1928), p. 96.

76 T. Smith-Laing, 'A lost cause', *Apollo* (March 2014), p. 101.

77 Sir John Leslie to 'Puss Cat' [Leonie Leslie], 11 November 1918 (NLI MS 49,495/2/41).

78 Shane Leslie to Leonie Leslie, 3 November 1914, in Rauchbauer, *Sublime Failure*, p. 247.

79 Foster, *Irish Novels 1890–1940*, pp 478–80.

80 Malleson, *After Ten Years*, p. 188.

81 Shane Leslie to Leonie Leslie, 3 November 1914, in Rauchbauer, *Sublime Failure*, p. 247.

82 *Lady*, 5 November 1914; *Northern Standard*, 7 November 1914.

83 Sir John Leslie to Leonie, n.d. but a few days after 11 November 1918 (NLI MS 49,495/2/41).

84 Dunsany, *Tales of War*, pp 48–52.

85 B. Blood, *Four Score Years and Ten* (London, 1933), p. xii.

86 Praise for these regiments is found in the Ross-Lewins' *In Britain's Need*, pp 15, 24, 41, 55.

87 *IT*, 11 April 1922.

88 *IT*, 13 June 1922.

89 J.H. Bernard to Cecil Harmsworth MP, 11 December 1921 (Bernard Papers, NLI MS 46,624/1).

90 Quoted in D. MacDonald, *The Sons of Levi* (Monaghan, 1998), p. 214.

91 E. Biagini, 'Minority studies and the making of an "alternative history" of twentieth century Ireland', paper delivered to the American Conference of Irish Studies, University College, Dublin, 13 June 2014 (copy in the possession of Ian d'Alton).

92 *BC*, pp 259, 436; M. Bence-Jones, *Twilight of the Ascendancy* (London, 1987); E. Bowen, 'The Big House', in *Collected Impressions* (London, 1950), p. 198.

93 Bence-Jones, 'The changing picture of the Irish landed gentry', pp xviii–xxi; Dooley, *Decline of the Big House*, pp 124–5.

94 *BC*, pp 435, 437.

14. A year of war: Cork Protestants in 1916

1 Read at a conference, 'Cork in 1916—A Revolutionary Society?', Cork Historical and Archaeological Society, 2 July 2016.

2 P. Hart, *The IRA and its Enemies: Violence and Community in Cork 1916–23* (Oxford, 1999); J. Borgonovo, *The Dynamics of War and Revolution: Cork City, 1916–18* (Cork, 2013), pp 15–16 [hereafter Borgonovo].

3 Listing of church services, *CC*, 1 and 8 January 1916.

4 Borgonovo, p. 15.

5 A.H. Exham: *Guy's Almanac, County and City Directory, 1916*, p. 122 [hereafter *GD*].

6 Borgonovo, p. 15, has the city treasurer as a Protestant. Thomas Ireton had a 'Protestant' name but is listed in the 1911 census as Catholic. Borgonovo also has the town clerk (Florence McCarthy) as a Protestant. He wasn't, and neither was Alderman Sir Edward Fitzgerald, Bt, chairman of the Fitzgerald Park and Museum Committee.

7 *GD*, pp 158–64.
8 For opposing views on the level of 'greening' see L. MacBride, *The Greening of Dublin Castle* (Washington, 1991), and F. Campbell, *The Irish Establishment 1878–1914* (Oxford, 2009).
9 *GD*, pp 151–8.
10 *GD*, p. 149.
11 B. O Donoghue, *Activities Wise and Otherwise: The Career of Sir Henry Augustus Robinson, 1898–1922* (Sallins, 2015), pp 74–5.
12 *GD*, p. 119.
13 *CC*, 8 January and 29 August 1916.
14 *GD*, p. 144.
15 *CC*, 17 January 1916.
16 *GD*, p. 60a.
17 *CC*, 2 March 1916.
18 *GD*, p. 111.
19 Borgonovo, p. 19.
20 *CC*, 11 February 1916.
21 *GD*, p. 81.
22 *GD*, pp 108–9.
23 *CC*, 13 January 1916.
24 *GD*, p. 109.
25 *CC*, 5 January 1916.
26 I. d'Alton, 'Cork unionism: its role in parliamentary and local elections, 1885–1914', *Studia Hibernica*, vol. 15 (1975), pp 143–61.
27 *GD*, p. 140.
28 I. d'Alton, 'Southern Irish unionism: a study of Cork city and county unionists, 1885–1914' (unpublished MA thesis, UCC, 1972), pp 236–52, and 'Southern Irish unionism: a study of Cork unionists, 1884–1914' (the Alexander Prize essay of the Royal Historical Society, 1972), *Transactions of the Royal Historical Society* (5th ser.), vol. 23 (3) (1973), pp 71–88.
29 Borgonovo, p. 15.
30 For Tivy, see A. McCarthy, *Newspapers and Journalism in Cork, 1910–23* (Dublin, 2020), pp 35–8, 101–2, 238–46.
31 Borgonovo, p. 16.
32 Borgonovo, p. 15.
33 The life of Arthur Hugh Smith Barry is dealt with in Chapter 4.
34 In 1899 eleven unionist councillors were elected in ten different towns in the county: *CE*, 18 January 1899 (towns) and 8, 9 and 10 April 1899 (county divisions); C. Shannon, 'Local government in Ireland, the politics and administration' (unpublished MA thesis, UCD, 1963); B. O Donoghue, 'From grand juries to county councils: the effects of the Local Government (Ireland) Act 1898', in F.M. Larkin (ed.), *Librarians, Poets and Scholars—A Festschrift for Dónall Ó Luanaigh* (Dublin, 2007), pp 188–91.
35 *CC*, 5 May 1916.
36 *CC*, 1 January 1916.
37 *CC*, 1 January 1916.
38 Borgonovo, p. 32.
39 *CC*, 15 January 1916, report of a recruiting meeting at Clonakilty.
40 *CC*, 8 January 1916.
41 Meeting at Bandon, chaired by Lord Bandon: *CC*, 18 January 1916; recruiting meetings at Lisgoold and Leamlara and at Courtmacsherry and Lasvolane: *CC*, 1 and 2 March 1916.
42 *CC*, 4 January 1916.
43 *CC*, 8 January 1916. One prominent Catholic donation was from the Convent of Mercy, Castletown Berehaven; also a notice for 'Bandon Gift Sale & Fete' in aid of the Red Cross and Wounded Soldiers' Fund

at Castle Bernard (home of Lord Bandon) on 22 June: *CC*, 21 June 1916.

44 *BC*, p. 436.

45 *CC*, 28 August 1916.

46 *CC*, 15 January and 3 October 1916.

47 *CC*, 21 January 1916.

48 *CC*, 1 January 1916, report of a 'War wedding' at Queenstown, and an article on [golf] 'amateurs and professionals and the War'; *CC*, 15 January and 16 May 1916, report of a wedding at St Multose Church, Kinsale.

49 *CC*, 5 July 1916.

50 *CC*, 28 August 1916.

51 *CC*, 2 October 1916.

52 *CC*, 4 January 1916.

53 *CGS Magazine*, the Grammar School, Cork (n.d. but 1916).

54 McCarthy, *Newspapers and Journalism in Cork, 1910–1923*, pp 88–9.

55 *CC*, 2 May 1916.

56 Borgonovo, p. 45.

57 Borgonovo, pp 44–5, for details of the reaction of public authorities in Cork to the aftermath of the Rising.

58 'Contemptuous', *CC*, 13 May 1916.

59 *CC*, 12 June 1916.

60 *CC*, 24 October 1916.

61 J.V. O'Brien, *William O'Brien and the Course of Irish Politics, 1881–1918* (Berkeley, 1976), p. 226.

62 *CC*, 19 and 21 June 1916; Borgonovo, p. 49.

63 Borgonovo, p. 51.

64 *CC*, 26 October 1916.

65 *CC*, 25 November 1916.

66 *CC*, 12 May 1916; Borgonovo, pp 55–6.

67 N. Perry, 'The Irish landed class and the British Army, 1850–1950', *War in History*, vol. 18 (3) (2011), p. 328.

68 *CC*, 30 December 1916.

15. 'A sinister and hateful memory': the 1916 Rebellion through the eyes of Protestants in Dublin

1 Read on 28 March 2016 at TCD to an RTÉ centenary event, 'Reflecting the Rising'; the quote is from *CoIG*, 5 May 1916.

2 Quoted in F.M. Larkin, 'From mythology to history: F.X. Martin and the historiography of the 1916 Rising', in M. Hay & D. Keogh (eds), *Rebellion and Revolution in Dublin: Voices from a Suburb, Rathfarnham, 1913–23* (Dublin, 2016), pp 195–217, at p. 204.

3 A population of about 50,000 within the city borough.

4 *Census of Ireland 1911, Province of Leinster, City of Dublin, Area, Houses and Population …* (Dublin, 1912), Cd. 6049-II, pp 16–28. See also 'Distinctively Irish, creatively modern: Roy Foster on Sarah Purser, the most successful portrait painter of her day', *IT*, 29 June 2024.

5 S. Ó Maitiú, *Dublin's Suburban Towns 1834–1930* (Dublin, 2003), pp 196–7.

6 *SW*, p. 48.

7 *SW*, p. 33.

8 *SW*, pp 36, 41.

9 S. Tucker, *Twenty-five Modern Plays* (New York, 1953), p. 753.

10 According to the 1911 census returns: https://tinyurl.com/yby8csg3 (accessed 1 September 2015); M. Maguire, 'A socio-economic analysis of the Dublin Protestant working class, 1870–1926', *Journal of the Irish Economic and Social History Society*, vol. 20 (1993), pp 35–61.

11 *CoIG*, 5 May 1916.

12 TCD's commemoration website, 'Changed utterly', at https://www.tcd.ie/Library/1916/; Rosamond Stephen's 'Record' for 1916: RCB Library, Dublin, MS 254.

13 C. Townshend, *Easter 1916: The Irish Rebellion* (London, 2006), pp 285–9.

14 R. Marshall, 'Lieutenant W.E. Wylie KC: the soldiering lawyer of 1916', in F.M. Larkin & N.M. Dawson (eds), *Lawyers, the Law and History: Irish Legal History Society Discourses and Other Papers, 2005–2011* (Dublin, 2013), pp 120–47, at p. 136.

15 M. Maguire, 'Protestant republicans in the revolution and after', in I. d'Alton & I. Milne (eds), *Protestant **and** Irish: The Minority's Search for Place in Independent Ireland* (Cork, 2019), pp 191–212; M. Maguire, 'Harry Nicholls and Kathleen Emerson: Protestant rebels', *Studia Hibernica*, vol. 35 (2008), pp 147–65. For George Irvine see J. Horgan, 'An Irishman's diary on a journalist's nightmare in 1916', *IT*, 16 September 2015; V. Jones, 'The case of the Norgroves: a Protestant family in the Irish Citizen Army', *Search—A Church of Ireland Journal*, vol. 39 (1) (2016), pp 15–23.

16 Mrs McDowell (Maeve Cavanagh), 53 Larkfield Grove, Kimmage: BMH WS 19. McDowell was a 'high church' Anglican, and this may have influenced his action: Maguire, 'Protestant republicans in the revolution and after', p. 200.

17 More soberly entitled 'A Night Ride to Belfast' by the *IT*, 9 May 1916.

18 See http://www.census.nationalarchives.ie/reels/nai000019577/.

19 Dublin *Daily Express* [hereafter *DDE*] and *IT*, 9 May 1916.

20 W. Irwin, *Betrayal in Ireland: An Eye-witness Record of the Tragic and Terrible Years of Revolution and Civil War in Ireland 1916–24* (Belfast, n.d. but probably 1968).

21 *DDE*, 15 May 1916.

22 *IT*, 5 May 1916. Such tickets, however, were not available in the more upper-class Rathmines district; Ó Maitiú, *Dublin's Suburban Towns 1834–1930*, p. 197.

23 Diary: Denis Johnston Papers (TCD MS 10066/192); Sir J. Ross, *The Years of my Pilgrimage—Random Reminiscences* (London, 1924), chapter 28, 'The Dublin Rebellion of 1916'.

24 The account of Eileen, Lady Chance, in M. O'Farrell, *1916: What the People Saw* (Cork, 2013), pp 152–3; Sir Henry Robinson's account: O'Farrell, *1916*, p. 197; F. McGarry, *The Rising: Ireland Easter 1916* (Oxford, 2011), pp 180–1, 183–4; *DDE*, 9 May 1916.

25 *CoIG*, 5 May 1916.

26 *DDE*, 6 May 1916.

27 *DDE*, 6 May 1916, eyewitness account by Revd G. Clements; 'A diary of Easter Week by Rev. Gordon Clements, ed. R Kain, "Diary of Easter Week: one Dubliner's Experience"', *Irish University Review*, vol. 10 (2) (1980), pp 206–7.

28 *DDE*, 6 May 1916.

29 L. Stokes, 'The personal experiences of Miss L. Stokes, 11 Raglan Road, Dublin, during the Sinn Féin Rebellion of 1916', *Nonplus*, vol. 4 (Winter 1960), pp 7–33.

30 *DDE*, 9 May 1916; A. Bonaparte-Wyse to N. Bonaparte-Wyse, 28 May 1916 (NLI MS 44,564).

31 *DDE*, 16 May 1916.

32 *DDE*, 8 May 1916.

33 *Sinn Féin Rebellion, 1916. A Souvenir of Presentations to the Officers' Training Corps Trinity College Dublin* (Dublin, n.d. but 1917), p. 58; B. O Donoghue, *Activities Wise and Otherwise: The Career of Sir Henry Augustus Robinson 1898–1922* (Dublin, 2015), pp 240–1.

34 O'Farrell, *1916*, p. 123.

35 R. McHugh (ed.), *Dublin 1916* (London, 1966), p. 66.

36 TCD MS 10,066/192; see also Isabel Fleming's 'diary' recollections of being caught up in the fighting on Northumberland Road, where her house acted as a station for wounded soldiers: O'Farrell, *1916*, pp 122–8.

37 *Sinn Féin Rebellion, 1916*.

38 *CoIG*, 5 May 1916.

39 McGarry, *The Rising*, p. 243, quoting a BMH witness statement by James Cullen (1343) (and a similar one by Martin Dunbar (988)). The Wexford raiding parties are confirmed in A. Shakespear Higginson [mother of the novelist Molly Keane], 'During the Rebellion in Wexford', *Blackwood's Magazine*, June 1916.

40 Minutes of the committee, 4 May 1916, Kildare Street Club minutes, 1909–29 (Kildare Street & University Club archives, 17 St Stephen's Green, Dublin 2).

41 *DDE*, 13 May 1916.

42 Frank Henderson, Capt. F Company 2nd Battalion Dublin Brigade, Irish Volunteers: BMH WS 821, pp 39–40.

43 R.B. MacCarthy, *John Henry Bernard 1860–1927: A Study of a Leader of the Southern Unionists* (Dublin, 2008), p. 24.

44 J.H. Bernard to Cecil Harmsworth MP, 9 May 1916 (NLI MS 46,624/1); MacCarthy, *Bernard*, p. 23.

45 RCB Library P46/8/17; *CoIG*, 5 May 1916; James Grace, BMH WS 310, p. 14.

46 *CoIG*, 5 May 1916.

47 Information from Dr Jason McElligott, Keeper (2018).

48 H. Pyle, *Cesca's Diary 1913–1916—Where Art and Nationalism meet* (Dublin, 2005), p. 219.

49 *CoIG*, 5 May 1916.

50 *IT*, 9 May 1916.

51 *DDE*, 10 May 1916.

52 *DDE*, 12 May 1916.

53 *DDE*, 13 May 1916.

54 *DDE*, 9 and 10 May 1916. The paper's sporting sub-editor was badly wounded, as was the Stock Exchange editor.

55 T. Brown, *The Irish Times: 150 Years of Influence* (London, 2015), pp 89–90; M. O'Brien, *The Irish Times: A History* (Dublin, 2008), pp 48–9.

56 *CoIG*, 5 May 1916.

57 *IT*, 3, 5 and 8 May 1916.

58 J. Luce, *Trinity College Dublin: The First 400 Years* (Dublin, 1992), p. 130; *Sinn Féin Rebellion, 1916*; *IT*, 8 May 1916; R. Sweetman, *Defending Trinity College Dublin, Easter 1916—Anzacs and the Rising* (Dublin, 2019).

59 G. Fitzpatrick, *Trinity College and Irish Society 1914–1922* (Dublin, 1992), p. 8.

60 TCD MS 2783/19, quoted in Fitzpatrick, *Trinity College*, p. 11.

61 Fitzpatrick, *Trinity College*, p. 10.

62 *CoIG*, 5 May 1916; report of Adjutant [of the OTC], Major G. Harris (TCD MS 2783/64).
63 *Sinn Féin Rebellion, 1916*, p. 3.
64 R. v. Governor of Lewes prison, *ex parte* Doyle *[1917] KB 254*.
65 *IT*, 10 May 1916.
66 *CoIG*, 5 May 1916; O'Farrell, *1916*, p. 122.
67 *DDE*, 10 May 1916.
68 *DDE*, 11 May 1916.
69 See *DDE*, 8 May 1916; 11 and 12 May 1916.
70 *DDE*, 13 May 1916.
71 *DDE*, 6 May 1916.
72 *IT*, 6 May 1916.
73 *DDE*, 11 May 2015.
74 Its two editorials in that edition were on 'The Rebellion and the Nationalist Party' and 'Compensation', with the latter taking up as much space as the former: *CoIG*, 19 May 1916.
75 *CoIG*, 5 May 1916.
76 *Freeman's Journal*, 5 May 1916.
77 *CoIG*, 5 May 1916.
78 C. Wills, *Dublin 1916: The Siege of the GPO* (London, 2009); R.F. Foster, *W.B. Yeats, A Life, II: The Arch-poet* (Oxford, 2003), pp 50–1.
79 A. Bonaparte-Wyse to N. Bonaparte-Wyse, 28 May 1916: 'The *sympathies* of the ordinary Irishman are with Sinn Féin—they want independence, & their only criticism of the rebellion is that it was *foolish* (not criminal or otherwise wrong)' (NLI MS 44,654).
80 *CoIG*, 5 May 1916.
81 *CoIG*, 26 May 1916; 'the Government have only themselves to thank for the whole trouble' (Shackleton Family, Private Collection, https://letters1916.ie/fullsearch/Shackleton; accessed 5 January 2024).
82 *IT*, 5 May 1916.
83 *CoIG*, 23 June 1916.
84 *DDE*, 15 May 1916, sermon by Very Revd T.L. Winder.
85 See https://www.bishopdavid.net/2016/06/being-here-before-pisky/ (accessed 5 January 2024).
86 *DDE*, 6 May 1916.
87 *IT*, 8 May 1916. The texts are from Psalm 10:1 and John 1:26.
88 *IT* and *DDE*, 8 May 1916.
89 For Methodist condemnation see *DDE*, 10 May 1916; for Presbyterian, see *DDE*, 16 May 1916, meeting of the Presbytery of Dublin, which 'recognises the necessity of just measures of repression' and advocated mercy, but only to the misguided.
90 *DDE*, 8 May 1916; *CoIG*, 12 May 1916.
91 Pyle, *Cesca's Diary*, pp 220–1.
92 *DDE*, 6 May 1916; J.H. Bernard to Cecil Harmsworth, 9 May 1916 (NLI MS 46,624/1).
93 Savage Armstrong Collection (PRONI MS D/618/166).
94 *IT*, 8 May 1916.
95 *DDE*, 9 May 2016.
96 *DDE*, 9 May 1916.
97 *DDE*, 9 May 1916.
98 *CoIG*, 5 May 1916.
99 *CoIG*, 23 June 1916; B. Hanley, 'Thoughts on the "Decade of Centenaries"', 8 September 2015 (at https://cedarlounge.wordpress.com/2015/09/08/brian-hanley-on-the-decade-of-centenaries/; accessed 5 January 2024).
100 J. Joly, *Reminiscences and Anticipations* (London, 1920), p. 235.

101 *Ibid.*, p. 236.
102 'Shebna the Scribe' [Revd W.S. Kerr, later dean of Belfast and bishop of Down and Dromore].
103 *CoIG*, 19 May 1916.
104 *CoIG*, 26 May 1916.
105 'Crocodile tears being wept over the poor traitors': 'Dot', Roebuck Hall, Dublin, to Cecil Harmsworth MP, 11 May 1916 (NLI MS 46,627).
106 M. Maguire, 'Harry Nicholls, Protestant republican and rebel', at the Christ Church 'Church of Ireland Rebels in 1916' lecture series, March 2006, p. 8 (MS in the possession of Ian d'Alton).
107 The Guild had a membership of 112 in 1916: *CoIG*, 23 and 30 June 1916.
108 Pyle, *Cesca's Diary*, pp 232–3.
109 *DDE*, 16 May 1916.
110 Townshend, *Easter 1916*, pp 309–10; McGarry, *Rising*, pp 282–3.

16. The birth of partition: the southern Protestant experience through the lens of the *Church of Ireland Gazette*

1 A version was the 'Archive of the Month', RCB Library (online), 6 May 2021.
2 *CoIG*, 25 February 1921.
3 D. Ó Corráin, *Rendering to God and Caesar: The Irish Churches and the Two States in Ireland, 1949–73* (Manchester, 2006), p. 2.
4 C. D'Arcy, *The Adventures of a Bishop—a Phase of Irish Life: A Personal and Historical Narrative* (London, 1934), p. 249.
5 G. Seaver, *John Allen Fitzgerald Gregg, Archbishop* (London and Dublin, 1963), pp 217–18.
6 *Ibid.*, p. 219.
7 *CoIG*, 31 December 1920.
8 'Belfast Notes' in *CoIG*, 24 December 1920.
9 R.B. MacCarthy, *John Henry Bernard, 1860–1927: A Study of a Leader of the Southern Unionists* (Dublin, 2008), p. 32.
10 P. Buckland, *Irish Unionism 1: The Anglo-Irish and the New Ireland, 1885 to 1922* (Dublin, 1972), pp 16–18.
11 R.B. McDowell, *The Irish Convention 1917–18* (London, Toronto, 1970).
12 Buckland, *Irish Unionism 1*, pp 83–185.
13 See Shane McElhatton's account for RTÉ's Decade of Commemorations at https://www.rte.ie/news/analysis-and-comment/2020/1218/1185261-partition-1920/ (accessed 5 January 2024).
14 Buckland, *Irish Unionism 1*, pp 18, 26.
15 In 1921, for instance, the primate at the General Synod referred to the secretary of the Representative Church Body as 'our Chancellor of the Exchequer': *Journal of the General Synod, 1921*, p. lvi.
16 D'Arcy, *Adventures of a Bishop*, pp 250–1.
17 *Ibid.*, pp 239, 245–9.
18 Seaver, *Gregg*, p. 246.
19 *CoIG*, 3, 10 and 17 December 1920.
20 *CoIG*, 27 May 1921.
21 *CoIG*, 3 and 10 December 1920.
22 *CoIG*, 24 December 1920.
23 *CoIG*, 17 December 1920.
24 *IT*, 18 February 1920.
25 *CoIG*, 24 December 1920.
26 *CoIG*, 31 December 1920.
27 *CoIG*, 26 March 1921.
28 J.A. Maconchy (ed.), *Journal of the Special Synod of the Church of Ireland ... 1920* (Dublin, 1921), p. v.

29 *CoIG*, 31 December 1920.
30 *CoIG*, 14 January 1921.
31 *CoIG*, 14 January 1921; Buckland, *Irish Unionism 1*, p. 198.
32 *CoIG*, 13 and 27 May 1921.
33 *CoIG*, 14 January 1921.
34 *CoIG*, 3 June 1921.
35 *CoIG*, 3 June 1921.
36 D'Arcy, *Adventures of a Bishop*, p. 245.
37 *CoIG*, 11 February 1921.
38 *CoIG*, 3 June 1921.
39 *CoIG*, 25 February 1921.
40 For instance, from Revd L. Handy, Skryne Rectory, Tara, Co. Meath, *CoIG*, 17 December 1920.
41 A map of the dioceses and their relation to the border is in Ó Corráin, *Rendering to God and Caesar*, p. 3.
42 *CoIG*, 6 May 1921.
43 *Journal of the General Synod, 1921*, pp lii–lix; comment on the synodical bill in *CoIG*, 20 May 1921.
44 *Journal of the General Synod, 1922*, p. liii. See also D'Arcy's letter to the clergy and laity of the Church of Ireland, reported in *CoIG*, 20 January 1922.
45 Ó Corráin, *Rendering to God and Caesar*, p. 243.
46 *CoIG*, 10 June 1921.

17. 'A tugging at the heartstrings': the place of the 1922 Dublin Castle hand-over in the southern loyalist narrative

1 Read to a centenary conference on the hand-over of Dublin Castle to the Provisional Government of the Irish Free State in 1922, TCD, 14–15 January 2022; the quote is in *IT*, 14 January 1922.
2 *IT*, 9 January 1922.
3 *The Guardian*, 23 April 1996.
4 *HL deb*, 30 January 1913, vol. 13, cc 770–3.
5 A. Bielenberg, 'Exodus: the emigration of southern Irish Protestants during the Irish War of Independence and the Civil War', *Past and Present*, vol. 218 (February 2013), p. 232; J. Coakley, 'Independence movements and national minorities: some parallels in the European experience', *European Journal of Political Research*, vol. 8 (2) (1980), pp 215–47; T. Wilson, 'Ghost provinces, mislaid minorities: the experience of southern Ireland and Prussian Poland compared, 1918–23', *Irish Studies in International Affairs*, vol. 13 (2002), pp 61–86, and *Frontiers of Violence: Conflict and Identity in Ulster and Upper Silesia, 1918–1922* (Oxford, 2010); R.B. McDowell, *Crisis and Decline: The Fate of the Southern Unionists* [1997] (Dublin, 2015), p. 119.
6 E. Rumpf & A. Hepburn, *Nationalism and socialism in twentieth-century Ireland* (New York, 1977), p. 62; M. Moffitt, 'Protestant tenant farmers and the Land League in north Connaught', in C. King & C. McNamara (eds), *The West of Ireland: New Perspectives on the Nineteenth Century* (Dublin, 2011), pp 93–116.
7 B. Walker, *Irish History Matters: Politics, Identities and Commemoration* (Stroud, 2019), pp 195–200.
8 A. Bielenberg & J.S. Donnelly Jr, 'Cork Fatality Register, 1919–1923', at https://www.ucc.ie/en/theirishrevolution/collections/cork-fatality-register/ (accessed 9 January 2024); B. Keane, *Cork's Revolutionary Dead, 1918–1923* (Cork, 2017); D. Wood, 'Protestant

population decline in southern Ireland 1911–26', in B. Hughes & C. Morrissey (eds), *Southern Irish Loyalism, 1912–1949* (Liverpool, 2020), pp 27–48.

9 *IT*, 6 September 2014, review of G. Clark, *Everyday Violence in the Irish Civil War* (2014).

10 McDowell, *Crisis and Decline*, p. 159; P. Hart, *The IRA at War, 1916–1923* (Oxford, 2003), p. 243; J.S. Donnelly Jr, 'Big House burnings in County Cork during the Irish Revolution, 1920–21', *Éire-Ireland*, vol. 47 (3–4) (2012), pp 141–97. For much more pessimistic views of the southern Protestant condition after 1922 see R. Bury, *Buried Lives: The Protestants of Southern Ireland* (Dublin, 2017), and D. Nuttall & T. Walsh, 'Affirmations of Irishness: assessing Irish Protestant identity', in B. McNamara and H. O'Brien (eds), *The Study of Religions in Ireland—Past, Present and Future* (London, 2022), pp 90–105.

11 P. Buckland, *Irish Unionism 1: The Anglo-Irish and the New Ireland 1885 to 1922* (Dublin, 1972); J.C. Beckett, *The Anglo-Irish Tradition* (London, 1976); T de V. White, *The Anglo-Irish* (London, 1972).

12 McDowell, *Crisis and Decline*, pp 196, 211.

13 *The Times*, 5 October 1921.

14 Buckland, *Irish Unionism 1*, p. 257; McDowell, *Crisis and Decline*, p. 109.

15 McDowell, *Crisis and Decline*, p. 109.

16 Buckland, *Irish Unionism 1*, p. 240.

17 *Sligo Independent*, 31 December 1921, H.R. Wood-Martin.

18 R.R. Hartford, *Godfrey Day—Missionary, Pastor and Primate* (Dublin and Cork, 1940), pp 112–13.

19 *Sligo Independent*, 7 January 1922.

20 *IT*, 10 January 1922.

21 *CoIG*, 13 January 1922.

22 *IT*, 12 January 1922.

23 *IT*, 20 January 1922.

24 *IT*, 20 January 1922; McDowell, *Crisis and Decline*, pp 111–12; Buckland, *Irish Unionism 1*, pp 274–5.

25 G. Seaver, *John Allen Fitzgerald Gregg, Archbishop* (Dublin, 1963), pp 116, 126; F.S.L. Lyons, 'The minority problem in the 26 counties', in F. MacManus (ed.), *The Years of the Great Test, 1926–1939* (Cork, 1967), p. 96.

26 The 1922 Minutes of the General Committee of the Presbyterian Association, 1918–1930: archives of the Abbey Presbyterian Church, Dublin (comment of the chairman, Very Revd H.P. Glenn); also reported in *IT*, 17 January 1922.

27 *CoIG*, 2 December 1921.

28 McDowell, *Crisis and Decline*, p. 110.

29 *CoIG*, 2 December 1921.

30 *IT*, 26 January 1922.

31 Buckland, *Irish Unionism 1*, pp 236–7.

32 *CoIG*, 30 December 1921; Buckland, *Irish Unionism 1*, pp 288–90.

33 *CoIG*, 6 January 1922.

34 *Dáil Éireann*, Treaty debates, 3 January 1922 (https://www.oireachtas.ie/en/debates/debate/dail/1922-01-03/2/; accessed 10 September 2021).

35 *IT*, 9 January 1922.

36 B. O Donoghue, *Activities Wise and Otherwise: The Career of Sir Henry Augustus Robinson, 1898–1922* (Sallins, 2015), p. 392.

37 *CoIG*, 20 January 1922.
38 *IT*, 14 January 1922.
39 *IT*, 17 January 1922.
40 R. Stephen to K.S., 10 January 1922, in her 'Record' (RCB Library MS 253). Her informant was a 'Miss Mitford'.
41 *Christian Advocate*, 20 January 1922.
42 *CoIG*, 20 January 1922.
43 *IT*, 17 January 1922.
44 *IT*, 17 January 1922.
45 R. Stephen to K.S., 18 January 1922, in her 'Record' (RCB Library MS 253).
46 S. Day, *The Amazing Philanthropists* (London, 1916), p. 16.
47 Quoted in D. MacDonald, *The Sons of Levi* (Manorhamilton, 1983), p. 214.
48 J.H. Bernard to Cecil Harmsworth MP, 11 December 1921 (NLI MS 46,624/1); McDowell, *Crisis and Decline*, pp 112–13.
49 McDowell, *Crisis and Decline*, p. 111.
50 N. Robertson, *Crowned Harp: Memories of the Last Years of the Crown in Ireland* (Dublin, 1960), p. 9.
51 *CoIG*, 9 December 1921; R.F.V. Heuston, 'British nationality and Irish citizenship', *International Affairs*, vol. 26 (1) (1950), pp 77–90.
52 *IT*, 13 May 1922.
53 *IT*, 10 December 1921.
54 J. Biggs-Davison & G. Chowdharay-Best, *The Cross of St Patrick: The Catholic Unionist Tradition in Ireland* (Oxford, 1984), shows a Catholic split loyalty, too.
55 *CoIG*, 16 December 1921.
56 *IT*, 12 January 1922.
57 *IT*, 13 January 1922.
58 *IT*, 17 January 1922.
59 *IT*, 17 January 1922.
60 *Freeman's Journal*, 17 January 1922.
61 *IT*, 17 January 1922.
62 *IT*, 9 December 1922.

18. Loose ends? The 1925 Boundary Commission and the Protestant border communities

1 A shorter, unreferenced version appeared in *Search—A Church of Ireland Journal*, vol. 45 (3) (2022), pp 215–23.
2 The Irish Free State submission to the Boundary Commission made references to the Versailles arrangements for plebiscites—e.g. see *Irish Boundary Commission Report, 1925* [hereafter *IBCR*], published in 1969, p. 62.
3 For a succinct account, see https://ipn.gov.pl/en/digital-resources/articles/9175,Plebiscites-in-post-Versailles-Europe.html (accessed 12 July 2022). The European context of the Boundary Commission is discussed at length in P. Murray, *The Irish Boundary Commission and its Origins, 1886–1925* (Dublin, 2011), pp 205, 240–63.
4 TNA, CAB 23/18, 17 December 1919, pp 247–8.
5 F. Packenham, *Peace by Ordeal: The Negotiation of the Anglo-Irish Treaty, 1921* (London, 1992), p. 167; but see a somewhat different interpretation in C. Kenny, *Midnight in London: The Anglo-Irish Treaty Crisis, 1921* (Dublin, 2021).
6 K.J. Rankin, 'The creation and consolidation of the Irish border', Working Paper 2 of the project *Mapping Frontiers, Plotting Pathways: Routes to North–South Cooperation in a Divided Island* (Institute for British–Irish Studies, QUB, 2005), p. 18.
7 Rankin, 'Creation and consolidation', p. 19.

8 *IBCR*, p. 3.

9 *IBCR*, p. 66.

10 Rankin, 'Creation and consolidation', p. 18; Kevin O'Higgins to W.T. Cosgrave, 10 May 1924 (NAI, NAD D/T, S 1801).

11 Murray, *Boundary Commission*, p. 152.

12 *CoIG*, 15 August 1924.

13 R. Lynch, 'The Boundary Commission', in J. Crowley, D. Ó Drisceoil & M. Murphy (eds), *Atlas of the Irish Revolution* (Cork, 2017), p. 829.

14 For a discussion of the Free State political manoeuvring over the Commission see M. O'Callaghan, '"Old parchment and water": the Boundary Commission of 1925 and the copperfastening of the Irish border', *Bullán: An Irish Studies Journal*, vol. 5 (2) (2000), pp 27–55.

15 Rankin, 'Creation and consolidation', p. 10.

16 K.J. Rankin, 'The provenance and dissolution of the Irish Boundary Commission' (Working Papers in British–Irish Studies No. 79, University College Dublin, 2006), p. 11; *Irish Independent*, 4 February 1922.

17 Murray, *Boundary Commission*, p. 154.

18 *CoIG*, 22 and 29 August 1924; Murray, *Boundary Commission*, pp 154–7.

19 *IBCR*, p. 71.

20 *IBCR*, p. 4.

21 Murray, *Boundary Commission*, pp 203, 306.

22 St J. Ervine, *Craigavon: Ulsterman* (London, 1949), p. 482.

23 *IBCR*, pp 6–7.

24 G. Hand, 'MacNeill and the Boundary Commission', in F.X. Martin & F.J. Byrne (eds), *The Scholar Revolutionary: Eoin Mac Neill 1867–1945 and the Making of the New Ireland* (Shannon, 1973), p. 234.

25 *IBCR*, p. 12.

26 Rankin, 'Provenance and dissolution', p. 17.

27 *IBCR*, pp 25–78.

28 *IBCR*, p. 59; see also C. Morrissey, 'Peace, Protestantism and the unity of Ireland: the career of Bolton C. Waller', in I. d'Alton and I. Milne (eds), *Protestant **and** Irish: The Minority's Search for Place in Independent Ireland* (Cork, 2019), p. 57.

29 Rankin, 'Provenance and dissolution', p. 19.

30 Hand, 'MacNeill and the Boundary Commission', p. 259.

31 *IBCR*, pp 79–88 (Londonderry/east Donegal) and pp 123–38 (Newry).

32 J. Swift, 'Review of *The Irish Boundary Commission and its Origins 1886–1925* by Paul Murray', *Studies: An Irish Quarterly Review*, vol. 101 (404) (Winter 2012), p. 459.

33 *IT*, 23 November 1925.

34 *CoIG*, 4 December 1925.

35 Murray, *Boundary Commission*, p. 193. There was a legal argument that, as an international treaty, it survived the 1937 constitution with its claim over the whole island—see E. Staunton, 'The Boundary Commission debacle 1925, aftermath and implications', *History Ireland*, vol. 2 (1996), at https://www.historyireland.com/the-boundary-commission-debacle-1925-aftermath-implications/ (accessed 18 July 2022).

36 Ireland (Confirmation of Agreement) Act, 1925, section 5 (5 & 6 Geo. V c. 77). The *Irish Times* (23 November 1925) was not alone in seeing the

Boundary Commission as just one of a suite of problems associated with the Treaty that needed urgent sorting-out.

37 Rankin, 'Creation and consolidation', pp 23–4.

38 *IBCR*, p. 72.

39 Evidence of Alexander Bryce, 26 May 1925, TNA, IBC, CAB 61/53, p. 187.

40 *IBCR*, pp 72, 85.

41 *IBCR*, p. 74.

42 Murray, *Boundary Commission*, pp 162–6.

43 *IBCR*, p. 87.

44 *IBCR*, p. 88.

45 Evidence of Revd B. Naylor, TNA, IBC, CAB 61/66, pp 247–50.

46 Murray, *Boundary Commission*, pp 169–70.

47 See D. Fitzpatrick. 'The Orange Order and the border', *Irish Historical Studies*, vol. 33 (129) (May 2002), pp 52–67.

48 Murray, *Boundary Commission*, p. 167.

49 *Ibid.*, p. 188.

50 Evidence of Revd R.W. Ross, Presbyterian minister, Burt, 26 May 1925, TNA, IBC, CAB 61/53, p. 177; evidence of Alexander Bryce, 26 May 1925, TNA, IBC, CAB 61/53, p. 187; evidence of Revd O'Donnell, Church of Ireland rector, Fahan, 26 May 1925, TNA, IBC, CAB 61/53, pp 200–1; evidence of Mrs Wilson, former teacher, Raphoe, 27 May 1925, TNA, IBC, CAB 61/53, pp 224–5. MacNeill (Minister of Education in the Free State) often questioned witnesses about these assertions.

51 Submission of Samuel Condell, farmer, Smithboro', n.d., TNA, IBC, CAB 61/39, p. 24.

52 Evidence of Capt. J. Scott, 25 May 1925, TNA, IBC, CAB 61/53, p. 58.

53 Letter of Revd John Gibson, rector of Clogh (Monaghan), 20 December 1924, TNA, IBC, CAB 61/39, p. 34.

54 D. Fitzpatrick, 'The Orange Order and the border', p. 62.

55 Myles served as a TD from 1923 to 1943. He played rugby for Ireland and won the MC in the Great War. See ElectionsIreland.org (https://electionsireland.org/; accessed 14 July 2022); evidence of Revd J. McClean, Presbyterian minister, Bogay, Co. Donegal, 25 May 2022, TNA, IBC, CAB 61.53, p. 104.

56 *CoIG*, 22 May 1925.

57 *CoIG*, 24 December 1925.

58 Submission by Bolton Waller, 30 December 1924, TNA, IBC, CAB 61/154, p. 14.

19. A vision of Church of Ireland disestablishment and where it might lead

1 Read at the Annual Conference of the Society for the Study of Nineteenth-Century Ireland, University of Leicester, 27 June 2019.

2 R. Chenevix Trench, *A Primary Charge Delivered to the Clergy of the United Dioceses of Dublin and Glandelagh, and Kildare: And, with some Alterations, to the Provinces of Dublin and Cashel, at the Triennial Visitation, September, 1868* (Dublin, 1868) (hereafter RCT, *Primary Charge, 1868*, and RCT, *Primary Charge, 1865* for the Charge given in that year).

3 [M. Trench], *Richard Chenevix Trench, Archbishop: Letters and Memorials* (2 vols) (London, 1888), II, pp 59–60.

4 K. Milne, *Richard Chenevix Trench 1807–1886* (Dublin, 2010), pp 5, 7, 9.

5 W.E. Gladstone, *A Chapter of Autobiography* (London, 1868), p. 13 *et seqq*.
6 Wilberforce, bishop of Oxford, quoted in R.B. McDowell, *The Church of Ireland 1869–1969* (London, 1975), p. 33.
7 H. Shearman, 'The economic results of the disestablishment of the Irish Church' (unpublished Ph.D thesis, TCD, 1944).
8 P. Bell, *Disestablishment in Ireland and Wales* (London, 1969), p. 36.
9 H. Shearman, *How the Church of Ireland was Disestablished* (Dublin, 1970), p. 20.
10 E.M. Crawford, *Counting the People: A Survey of the Irish Censuses, 1813–1911* (Dublin, 2003), pp 25–6. The 1861 Report had an introduction summarising attempts to collect religious statistics for Ireland since 1672.
11 McDowell, *Church of Ireland*, pp 32–3.
12 M. Moffitt, 'This "rotten little republic": Protestant identity and the "State Prayers" controversy, 1948–9', in I. d'Alton & I. Milne (eds), *Protestant* ***and*** *Irish: The Minority's Search for Place in Independent Ireland* (Cork, 2019), pp 66–81.
13 McDowell, *Church of Ireland*, p. 42.
14 Shearman, *Church of Ireland*, p. 20.
15 RCT, *Primary Charge, 1865*, p. 75.
16 RCT, *Primary Charge, 1868*, p. 20.
17 *Ibid*., p. 20.
18 *Ibid*., p. 20.
19 Milne, *Richard Chenevix Trench*, pp 5, 9.
20 C. D'Arcy, *The Adventures of a Bishop—A Phase of Irish Life: A Personal and Historical Narrative* (London, 1934), p. 37.
21 [Trench], *Richard Chenevix Trench*, II, pp 59–60.
22 Trench to his wife, n.d. but September 1868: [Trench], *Richard Chenevix Trench*, II, p. 60.
23 32 & 33 Vict. cap. 42 AD 1869.
24 As templates it had before it constitutions for the episcopal churches in Canada, New Zealand and the USA.
25 McDowell, *Church of Ireland*, p. 57; A. Ford, 'The cost of democracy: the Church of Ireland and its ritual canons, 1871–1974', *Church History*, vol. 91 (2022), pp 575–95.
26 McDowell, *Church of Ireland*, p. 50.
27 M. Elliott, *When God Took Sides: Religion and Identity in Ireland—Unfinished History* (Oxford, 2009), p. 112.
28 *Irish Ecclesiastical Gazette*, 1 January 1878.
29 Shearman, *Church of Ireland*, p. 63.
30 RCT, *Primary Charge, 1865*, p. 69.
31 *Irish Ecclesiastical Gazette*, 1 December 1879 and 3 January 1880; I. d'Alton, 'Case Study 12: *The Irish Ecclesiastical Gazette*', in D. Finkelstein (ed.), *The Edinburgh History of the British and Irish Press—Vol. 2, Expansion and Evolution, 1800–1990* (Edinburgh, 2020), pp 398–9; I. d'Alton, 'The *Church of Ireland Gazette* and the twentieth century: "a church paper for church people"?', in M. O'Brien and F.M. Larkin (eds), *Periodicals and Journalism in Twentieth-Century Ireland 2* (Dublin, 2021), pp 135–54.
32 C. Dowse, 'Preface', in C. Webster, *The Diocese of Cork* (Cork, 1920), pp ix–x.
33 For a further discussion of disestablishment, see a comprehensive series of

articles by R. Marshall in the *Church Review* (the diocesan magazine of the united dioceses of Dublin and Glendalough), running monthly from March 2019 to June 2022; also I. d'Alton, 'An unmitigated blessing: the disestablishment of the Church of Ireland', *Search – a Church of Ireland Journal*, vol. 42 (1) (2019), pp 5–15. Ireland recognised the 150th anniversary of disestablishment with the issue of a postage stamp in 2021.

20. Beneath the pulpit, above the parapet? The clerics in the Irish Convention, 1917–18

1 Read at 'The Irish Convention 1917–18: a centenary symposium', TCD, 25 July 2017.

2 S. Leslie, 'The make-up of the Convention', *Boston Herald*, 28 July 1917.

3 S. Hood, '"Good wishes for the great adventure": the Church of Ireland & the Irish Convention, 1917', RCB Library Archive of the Month, 25 July 2017, at https://www.ireland.anglican.org/news/7306/good-wishes-for-the-great (accessed 6 December 2022).

4 *CoIG*, 18 January 1918.

5 R.B. McDowell, *The Irish Convention 1917–18* (London and Toronto, 1970) [hereafter McDowell, *Convention*], pp 214, 217.

6 D. Meleady, pers. comm., 22 December 2016.

7 See McDowell, *Convention*, pp 43–69.

8 *The Times*, 21 March 1917.

9 D. Miller, *Church, State and Nation in Ireland* (Dublin, 1973), p. 360.

10 *Report of the Proceedings of the Irish Convention* [Cd 9019] (Dublin, 1918), pp 9, 50–1 [hereafter *Proceedings*]; McDowell, *Convention*, p. 77.

11 McDowell, *Convention*, p. 77.

12 Copy of telegram of 24 May 1917, T.P. O'Connor to Redmond, Dillon and Devlin (Joseph Brennan Papers, NLI MS 29,009/5).

13 *Proceedings*, p. 9.

14 P.J. Keohane to Revd J. O'Hagan, 20 July 1917 (O'Hagan Papers, HAG 1/1917/60, Archives Pontifical, Irish College, Rome).

15 R.B. MacCarthy, *John Henry Bernard, 1860–1927: A Study of a Leader of the Southern Unionists* (Dublin, 2008), p. 43.

16 L. Strachey, *Eminent Victorians* (London, 1971), p. 13.

17 W.B. Wells & N. Marlowe, *The Irish Convention and Sinn Féin* (Dublin, 1918), p. 91.

18 Plunkett to Redmond, 2 October 1917 (Redmond Papers, NLI MS 15,221).

19 I. d'Alton, 'Religion as identity: the Church of Ireland's 1932 Patrician celebrations', in J. Hill & M.A. Lyons (eds), *Representing Irish Religious Histories: Historiography, Ideology and Practice* (Cham, 2017), p. 200.

20 *The Irish Convention. Confidential Report by the Chairman* [Sir Horace Plunkett] *to His Majesty the King* (Dublin, 1917–18) [hereafter *Confidential Report*], para. 68; McDowell, *Convention*, p. 150.

21 B. Hourican, 'Harty, John', *DIB*, vol. 4, pp 506–7.

22 Shane Leslie, 'Make-up of the Convention'.

23 Wells & Marlowe, *Irish Convention*, p. 91.

24 Mulvagh, *Irish Parliamentary Party*, p. 146. See also C. Mulvagh, '"Rome Ruler?" John Redmond, a Catholic voice in a Liberal chamber, 1906–1918' (unpublished MPhil. thesis, TCD, 2008).

25 *CoIG*, 24 December 1920.

26 McDowell, *Convention*, p. 90; Leslie, 'Make-up of the Convention'.

27 Wells & Marlowe, *Irish Convention*, p. 91.

28 Also D. Kelly, *The War and Ireland's Food Supply: An Appeal to the Irish Farmer* (1914), and *Woman's Share in the Industrial Revival of Ireland* (1917).

29 P. Jalland, 'Irish Home-Rule finance: a neglected dimension of the Irish Question, 1910–14', in A. O'Day (ed.), *Reactions to Irish Nationalism, 1865–1914* (London, 1987), p. 299.

30 McDowell, *Convention*, p. 90.

31 *Report of the Committee on Irish Finance* [Cd. 6153], HC 1912–13, xxiv, 5–40; also minutes of evidence [Cd. 6799], HC 1913, xxx, 1–252; G. Daly, 'A divided hierarchy', *The Irish Catholic*, 15 December 2015.

32 W. Miller for the bishop of Kildare and Leighlin to Revd J. O'Hagan (O'Hagan Papers, HAG 1/1917/60, Archives Pontifical, Irish College, Rome).

33 S. Gwynn to Lady Parsons, 14 December 1917 (Robertson Papers, NLI MS 24,286).

34 Montgomery to Herdman, 16 June 1917, quoted in McDowell, *Convention*, p. 89.

35 *Notes from Ireland*, vol. 26 (1917), p. 54, quoted in Miller, *Church, State and Nation in Ireland*, p. 361.

36 Plunkett to Redmond, 2 October 1917 (Redmond Papers, NLI MS 15,221). Plunkett said that newspaper proprietor W.M. Murphy and MP Tim Healy (Healy was not a Convention member) were 'very angry' with the hierarchy for nominating O'Donnell and Kelly.

37 Wells & Marlowe, *Irish Convention*, p. 91.

38 *Confidential Report*, para. 38 (complete copy in the Redmond Papers, NLI MS 15,265/1/A).

39 *Confidential Report*, para. 69.

40 McDowell, *Convention*, p. 80, quoting Crozier to H. de F. Montgomery, 2 June 1917 (Montgomery Papers, PRONI MS D627/430).

41 Wells & Marlowe, *Irish Convention*, p. 87.

42 Miller, *Church, State and Nation in Ireland*, p. 363.

43 The primate reiterated his views on his abhorrence of partition in a press interview: *CoIG*, 10 May 1918; *Proceedings*, p. 35; McDowell, *Convention*, p. 183.

44 Plunkett to Redmond, 11 October 1917, quoting a 'Belfast source' (Redmond Papers, NLI MS 15,221).

45 McDowell, *Convention*, p. 90; Montgomery to Crozier, 6 September 1917 (Montgomery Papers, PRONI MS D627, 430).

46 *Proceedings*, p. 172.

47 *Confidential Report*, para. 107.

48 Copy in Redmond Papers (NLI MS 15,265/1/B); *Proceedings*, p. 54; *Confidential Report*, para. 19.

49 Wells & Marlowe, *Irish Convention*, p. 101.

50 Leslie, 'Make-up of the Convention'.

51 McDowell, *Convention*, pp 90–1.
52 P. Buckland, *Irish Unionism 1: The Anglo-Irish and the New Ireland 1885 to 1922* (Dublin, 1972), p. 137.
53 MacCarthy, *Bernard*, pp 37–9, 42.
54 Earl of Midleton, KP, *Records and Reactions, 1856–1939* (London, 1939), p. 236; McDowell, *Convention*, p. 101.
55 McDowell, *Convention*, p. 130.
56 MacCarthy, *Bernard*, p. 44.
57 *Census of Ireland, General Report* (1911), pp xlvii–xlviii.
58 Leslie, 'Make-up of the Convention'.
59 *Confidential Report*, para. 46, 28–30 August 1917.
60 Typescript note of Convention meeting, 14 March 1918 (Redmond Papers, NLI MS 15,265/1/B).
61 William Doran (d. 1941) was chairman of Louth County Council from 1913 to 1918. He was a Wesleyan Methodist and a Redmondite nationalist; McDowell, *Convention*, p. 220.
62 Census returns 1911, entries for William Alexander Doran, farmer, Clonkeen, Co. Louth, and William Whitla, Cromac, Belfast; *Confidential Report*, paras 57 (Whitla) and 73 (Doran); *Proceedings*, p. 53.
63 Plunkett to Redmond, 15 October 1917 (Redmond Papers, NLI MS 15,221); O'Donnell to Revd J. O'Hagan, 17 October 1917 (O'Hagan Papers, HAG 1/1917/84, Archives Pontifical, Irish College, Rome).
64 *Proceedings*, p. 173.
65 Miller, *Church, State and Nation*, p. 362; *Confidential Report*, para. 16.
66 *Chicago Tribune*, 23 April 1918.
67 Photograph by Lafayette, Dublin, at http://catalogue.nli.ie/Record/vtls000314093 (accessed 9 January 2024).
68 Plunkett to Redmond, 26 February 1918 (Redmond Papers, NLI MS 15,221); McDowell, *Convention*, p. 111.
69 *Confidential Report*, para. 44.
70 See *The Spectator*, 30 April 1911.
71 D. Fitzpatrick, *Descendancy: Irish Protestant Histories since 1795* (Cambridge, 2014), p. 43.
72 G. Lewis, *Carson: The Man who Divided Ireland* (London, 2006), p. 88; http://www.grandorangelodge.co.uk/history.aspx?id=99489#.WVSaBHjqCSo (accessed 9 January 2024); see also Education Committee of the Grand Orange Lodge of Ireland, *The Formation of the Orange Order 1795–1798: The Edited Papers of Colonel William Blacker and Colonel Robert H. Wallace* (Belfast, 1994), *passim*.
73 *Confidential Report*, paras 69–70; Wells & Marlowe, *Irish Convention*, pp 91–2.
74 *Confidential Report*, para. 57; Miller, *Church, State and Nation*, pp 364–5.
75 MacCarthy, *Bernard*, pp 39–41.
76 O'Donnell to Redmond, 3 October 1917—'my maxim is to refuse no service' (Redmond Papers, NLI MS 15,217/1); Plunkett to Redmond, 20 September 1917 and 2 October 1917 (Redmond Papers, NLI MS 15,221); *Confidential Report*, para. 83.
77 Plunkett to Redmond, 18 December 1917 (Redmond Papers, NLI MS 15,221).
78 O'Donnell to Redmond, 22 December 1917 (Redmond Papers, NLI MS 15,217/4).
79 McDowell, *Convention*, p. 139.
80 W.M. Murphy to W.L. Murphy, 22 December 1917, quoted in McDowell, *Convention*, p. 137.

81 McDowell, *Convention*, p. 135.
82 *Ibid.*, pp 148–9.
83 Confidential Report to the King—commentary by ?, pp 67, 75 (NLI MS 2,978); C. Reid, *The Lost Ireland of Stephen Gwynn: Irish Constitutional Nationalism and Cultural Politics, 1864–1950* (Manchester, 2011), p. 156; P. Maume, 'O'Donnell, Patrick', *DIB*, vol. 7, p. 398.
84 D. Meleady, *John Redmond: The National Leader* (Dublin, 2013), p. 451.
85 McDowell, *Convention*, pp 136–7.
86 *Confidential Report*, para. 54; Miller, *Church, State and Nation in Ireland*, p. 364.
87 P. Maume, 'Kelly, Denis', *DIB*, vol. 5, p. 69.
88 W.B. Wells, *The Life of John Redmond* (New York, 1919), pp 37, 273.
89 R.H. Murray, *Archbishop Bernard, Professor, Prelate and Provost* (London, 1931), p. 315.
90 *Confidential Report*, para. 106.
91 McDowell, *Convention*, p. 234 (index of Bernard's contacts); Buckland, *Irish Unionism 1*, p. 113 (Canterbury) and p. 121 (Curzon).
92 *Chicago Tribune*, 23 April 1918.
93 *Irish Independent*, 16 June 1917.
94 McDowell, *Convention*, pp 155–6.
95 *Confidential Report*, paras 46–8.
96 Copy of letter from Cardinal Logue to Dr Glennon, bishop of St Louis, 13 February 1918 (Joseph Brennan Papers, NLI MS 26,009).
97 P.J. Keohane to Revd J. O'Hagan, 20 July 1917 (O'Hagan Papers, HAG 1/1917/60, Archives Pontifical, Irish College, Rome).
98 Miller, *Church, State and Nation*, pp 361, 367.
99 McDowell, *Convention*, p. 165; Buckland, *Irish Unionism 1*, p. 183ff.
100 Reid, *Lost Ireland*, p. 153.
101 Miller, *Church, State and Nation*, p. 383.
102 McDowell, *Convention*, p. 170.
103 O'Donnell reported a meeting with Lloyd George on 14 February 1918—'I wish you had been present at our last meeting with the Prime Minister and the Chancellor. It was a real pleasure to discuss the principles involved': McDowell, *Convention*, p. 161.
104 Typescript of Plunkett's secret report, 17 October 1917–18 January 1918 (Horace Plunkett Papers, NLI MS 49,803/158/7).
105 Plunkett to Redmond, 26 February 1918 (Redmond Papers, NLI MS 15,221).
106 McDowell, *Convention*, p. 172.
107 *Ibid.*, pp 146–7.
108 T. O'Loughlin, 'A half-century after *Ecclesiam Suam* and "The 1964 Instruction": the practice of the historical disciplines within the practice of theology', *New Blackfriars*, vol. 98 (1076) (2017), pp 10–11.
109 *Ibid.*, p. 11.

21. A letter from the archbishops: the Church of Ireland and the dogma of the Assumption, 1950

1 A version of this essay appears in *Search – a Church of Ireland Journal*, vol. 32 (1) (2009), pp 39–52.
2 Pope Pius XII, *Munificentissimus Deus—Defining the Dogma of the Assumption*, para. 44.
3 A. Richardson (ed.), *A New Dictionary of Catholic Theology* (London, 1983), p. 48.
4 *Munificentissimus Deus*, para. 43.

5 *L'Osservatore Romano*, 14 August 1950.

6 J.M. Regan, *The Irish Counter-revolution 1921–1936* (Dublin, 1999), pp 279–304; F.S.L. Lyons, *Ireland since the Famine* (London, 1971), p. 520; J.J. Lee, *Ireland, 1912–1985* (Cambridge, 1989), p. 304; J. Cooney, *John Charles McQuaid, Archbishop of Dublin* (Dublin, 1999), pp 228–9; J.S. Donnelly Jr, 'Opposing the "modern world": the cult of the Virgin Mary in Ireland, 1965–85', *Éire-Ireland*, vol. 40 (1–2) (2005), pp 183–245.

7 J.S. Donnelly Jr, 'The peak of Marianism in Ireland, 1930–60', in S. Brown and D. Miller (eds), *Piety and Power in Ireland 1760–1960: Essays in Honour of Emmet Larkin* (Belfast and Notre Dame, 2000), pp 270–2; L. Fuller, *Irish Catholicism since 1950: The Undoing of a Culture* (Dublin, 2002), pp 10–23; E. Duffy, *Faith of our Fathers* (London and New York, 2004), pp 29–31, 34.

8 D. Ó Corráin, *Rendering to God and Caesar: The Irish Churches and the Two States in Ireland, 1949–73* (Manchester, 2006), pp 183–4.

9 R.F. Foster, *W.B. Yeats: A Life, I: The Apprentice Mage, 1865–1914* (Oxford, 1997), p. 1.

10 R.B. McDowell, *Crisis and Decline: The Fate of the Southern Unionists* (Dublin, 1997), p. 170; *IT*, 15 November 1950.

11 *CoIG*, 27 April 2007, letter from Revd A. Carter; K.T. Hoppen, *Ireland since 1800: Conflict and Conformity* (London, 1989), p. 249.

12 C. O'Halloran, *Partition and the Limits of Irish Nationalism* (Dublin, 1987), pp 79–85.

13 J. O'Neill, *Blood-dark Track: A Family History* (London, 2000), pp 326–7.

14 L. Pilkington, 'Religion and the Celtic Tiger: the cultural legacies of anti-Catholicism in Ireland', in P. Kirby, L. Gibbons & M. Cronin (eds), *Reinventing Ireland: Culture, Society and the Global Economy* (London, 2002), pp 125–33.

15 Maude material on the 'State Prayers' issue (RCB Library, MS 262).

16 Ó Corráin, *Rendering to God and Caesar*, pp 13–19; M. Moffitt, 'This "rotten little republic": Protestant identity and the State Prayers controversy, 1948–9', in I. d'Alton & I. Milne (eds), *Protestant **and** Irish: The Minority's Search for Place in Independent Ireland* (Cork, 2019), pp 66–81.

17 Cooney, *John Charles McQuaid*, pp 243–4.

18 D. Jameson, *The Tilson Case: Church and State in 1950s Ireland* (Cork, 2023); G. Hogan, 'A fresh look at "Tilson's" case', *Irish Jurist* (new ser.), vol. 33 (1998), pp 311–32; Lyons, *Ireland since the Famine*, p. 671, n. *; Cooney, *John Charles McQuaid*, pp 245–6; Seanad Éireann, reports of debates, vol. 57, 4 March 1964.

19 V. Bennett & R. Winch, *The Assumption of Our Lady and Catholic Theology* (London, 1950).

20 *CoIG*, 20 October 1950.

21 *CoIG*, 13 October 1950.

22 *CoIG*, 3 November 1950.

23 *CoIG*, 17 November 1950.

24 *CoIG*, 13 October, 10 November and 1 December 1950; 5 January and 16 February 1951.

25 *IT*, August–November 1950.

26 T. Gray, *Mr Smyllie, Sir* (Dublin, 1991), pp 199–200.
27 *IT*, 11 December 1950.
28 G. Seaver, *John Allen Fitzgerald Gregg, Archbishop* (Dublin, 1963), p. 117.
29 *Ibid.*, pp 54, 312.
30 Revd J.A.F. Gregg, *The Primitive Faith and Roman Catholic Developments* (3rd edn, Dublin, 1928); *Roman Claims; or, an Elementary Catechism on the Chief Points of the Roman Controversy Prepared by a Committee Appointed by the Board of Education of the United Dioceses of Dublin, Glendalough and Kildare* (Dublin, 1931 edn), pp 31–4.
31 Minutes of meetings of the House of Bishops, ii, meeting of 15 November 1950, p. 99 (RCB, Dublin). A copy of the letter was made available to each worshipper on 10 December 1950. The author's copy was found in the papers of his wife's aunt, Rose Peet, parishioner of St John's Church, Tralee, Co. Kerry. See also 'The Roman Catholic Dogma of the Assumption', 14 November 1950 (RCB Library, Simms Papers, MS 238/1/7).
32 *CoIG*, 10 November 1950.
33 *CoIG*, 22 December 1950.
34 Though not with Archbishop McQuaid: see Cooney, *John Charles McQuaid*; E. Duffy, *Saints and Sinners: A History of the Popes* (New Haven, London, 2001), p. 353; S. Shoemaker, *Ancient Traditions of the Virgin Mary's Dormition and Assumption* (Oxford, 2002 and 2006).
35 R. Knox, *The Belief of Catholics* (London, 1927), chapter headed 'Where Protestantism Goes Wrong'.
36 J.A. Gaughan, *Alfred O'Rahilly, III. Controversialist, Part 2: Catholic Apologist* (Dublin, 1993), pp 20–6.
37 *Ibid.*, p. 23.
38 *CoIG*, 3 November 1950.
39 *CoIG*, 9 February 1951.
40 Gaughan, *Alfred O'Rahilly*, p. 24.
41 R. Ryland (ed.), *Journal of Proceedings of the General Synod of the Church of Ireland* (Dublin, 1951), p. lxxxiv. The Standing Committee report for 1951 referred to the Tilson case but not to the Assumption: *ibid.*, p. 152.
42 Seaver, *Gregg*, p. 314.
43 *CoIG*, 20 October 1950. See also the comments of the Catholic priest Revd C.T. [later Cardinal] Heenan, quoted in *IT*, 16 October 1950, in which he suggested that the real problem for Anglicans was Church authority, not the dogma itself.
44 Gregg, *Primitive Faith*, p. 30.
45 *Letter*, p. 3.
46 Duffy, *Faith of our Fathers*, p. 172.
47 Bishop R. Warke, 'The character of Anglicanism', *Link* [the parish magazine of the Church of Ireland Naas Union], no. 190 (May 2007), p. 2.
48 G. Wilson [dean of Connor, later bishop of Kilmore], *A Critique of 'Authority in the Church'. Statement Agreed by the Anglican–Roman Catholic International Commission* (Belfast, 1977), pp 57–65, esp. 57–8.
49 Gaughan, *Alfred O'Rahilly*, p. 23, n.2; Seaver, *Gregg*, p. 314. A modern exposition of the Church of Ireland's attitude to the Assumption—much toned down from Gregg's rhetoric—can be found in V. Griffin, *Anglican and*

Irish Today (Dublin, 1976; revised and enlarged 2006), p. 50.

Afterword – *Alan Ford*

1 H. Temperley (ed.), *The Selected Essays of J.B. Bury* (Cambridge, 1930), p. 22.

2 C. Brady, '"Constructive and instrumental": the dilemma of Ireland's first "New Historians"', in C. Brady (ed.), *Interpreting Irish History* (Dublin, 1994), pp 3–5.

3 G. Huxley, 'The historical scholarship of John Begnell Bury', *Bulletin of British Byzantine Studies*, vol. 17 (1976), p. 81; see M. Moffit's revealing analysis of Edwards's first book, *Church and State*: 'History-writing, collective memory and identity in an Irish context: G.V. Jourdan and R.D. Edwards', in J.R. Hill and M.A. Lyons (eds), *Representing Irish Religious Histories: Historiography, Ideology and Practice* (Basingstoke, 2017), pp 101–19.

4 H. White, *Metahistory: the Historical Imagination in Nineteenth-Century Europe* (Baltimore, 1973).

5 R. Evans, *Lying about Hitler: History, Holocaust, and the David Irving Trial* (New York, 2001).

6 J. Young, 'Toward a received history of the Holocaust', *History and Theory*, vol. 36 (4) (1997), pp 21–43.

7 M. Bentley, *Modernising England's Past: English Historiography in the Age of Modernism* (Cambridge, 2005), p. 228.

8 L. Kennedy, *Unhappy the Land: The Most Oppressed People Ever, the Irish?* (Sallins, 2016).

9 Letter from H. de F. Montgomery in *The Irish Churchman*, 19 December 1918, pp 11–12.